# DARE YOUR SOUL

## A SOUL'S GUIDE FROM CONCEPTION TO DEATH

TOMMASO GRIECO

ISBN 978-1-64028-139-4 (Paperback)
ISBN 978-1-64028-140-0 (Digital)

Christian Faith Publishing, Inc.
296 Chestnut Street
Meadville, PA 16335
www.christianfaithpublishing.com

Printed in the United States of America

# Dare to Chart and Track Your Soul's 2ND Journey: A Soul's Guide from Conception to Death

Posted on *December 18, 2016 from ENAS Reviews*

Incomparable, highly imagined insight over his thoughts of wisdom, author has penned down artistically a thought provoking and simplified read that is based on 3 journeys- the 1st starts at conception and ends at our birth, the 2nd starts at our natural birth and ends at the death of our body or flesh and the 3rd is a journey after our death.

Truth and facts accumulated in the course of time through clairvoyant writing are worth respect and attention from a diverse range of readers irrespective of their religion and customs. For the sake of ones appetite of spiritual upliftment, 'Dare to Chart and Track Your Soul's 2nd Journey' is worth reading and passing on from one mind and heart to another. There is wealth of knowledge to be discovered between covers, highly attention worthy.

To read the full review, please visit :

*http://enasreviews.com/memoir/dare-to-chart-and-track-your-souls-2nd-journey-a-souls-guide-from-conception-to-death/*

Larry Gray of Outskirts Press had this to say about *Dare to Chart and Track Your Soul's 2ND Journey: A Soul's Guide from Conception to Death*:

You obviously have a great passion for what I may refer to as the science of the soul – you present your piece in a very well-researched, thorough manner. You really offer your readers a lot to consider and you present them with a wealth of information about the soul as humans progress through life, which I am certain others will enjoy reading about and learning from. I can tell that you have spent countless hours with your subject matter. You have presented your material in a way that just about anyone could understand and benefit from (thanks to the fact that you have really considered your readership, your audience). You included details that add to the credibility of your writing, and you really do come across as an expert, as well you should. Throughout your work, your narrative voice is great – very familiar and easy to follow. I have to say that you have put together an excellent piece here. It looks to me like you have meticulously gone through your document revising and smoothing things out. It flows nicely. It is one that should be well received by a wide audience.

write.publish.market

This book is dedicated to our Blessed Virgin Maria. I hope that her graces will be poured out to all that pray to her as she has for my family's second and third journeys.

# CONTENTS

# PREFACE

"The soul is willing, but the flesh is weak." What do these infamous words of Christ mean? That our soul can function apart from our body/flesh? That the two exist, although one can pull apart from the other? That our mind, free will, can operate in our brain or outside of our brain? This book will explore these mysteries and many more concerning our soul's heart and mind in our body/flesh.

We have learned in science that as human beings, our brain emits an estimated measurable energy to be able to light up a twenty-five-plus-watt bulb. Hmm, imagine that! Unknown to scientists is that the energy is of spiritual light and of the soul's mind working in the brain. Questions? What energy? From what light? From where? From whom? You see, the problem with us modern scientists and humanity as a whole is that we discover such phenomenon but cannot explain it. Our answer? We do not know!

Well, I believe that I have an answer. This energy is a spiritual light force, one that each of us is given at conception. I believe that what we are blessed/graced with is from ISL, Intellectual Spiritual Light. I believe that it is from this source that all light comes from, natural and spiritual. I believe that it is this light within us, which started as a spark, that ignited and got us started into our first journey. This magnificent light is spiritual and yet able to be detected through modern equipment in the body's brain and heart. This discovery is a wonderful accomplishment for humanity. The light energy is centered within our soul's heart and mind but not fully understood by scientists.

The Renaissance painters had it right all along five hundred-plus years ago in painting a halo around the heads of some of the figures they painted. Imagine that! Furthermore, I believe that this flame needs to grow within us. This occurs when our small flame receives oxygen from the Holy Spirit. How does this happen? Study the chart on this book cover. The second journey is a climb up to the summit of spiritual knowledge and wisdom. This climb includes all that any steep mountain climb would include. In being tested, at times even in misery, in charity, in love, we grow up into light as high as 9.99 on our summit platform.

# INTRODUCTION

D o we even have a soul? In these modern scientific times, we could be such skeptics. We are educated people, scientific people of theories and hypotheses that have to be proven. Without it, could this book have legs to stand on? So what proof? Are the images of human figures on negative films taken in a cemetery at night proof? Are people who have had out of body/flesh experience proof? Are witnesses who were in a physical coma observing what was occurring on themselves in the emergency room proof? Are the spiritual ghosts of departed ones returning to pay us a visit proof? Are witnesses that got a glimpse of all three third journeys proof? Are the living souls of living saints apparitions, at times in multiple places, proof? Are the apparitions of angels of light to a few of us proof? Are the appearances of satanic spirits, those of evil darkness, proof? Are the apparitions of our Blessed Virgin Mother Maria proof? Was the spirit/soul of Christ returning to be united to His body/flesh on the third day after being put to death proof?

We will explore these areas throughout this book. We will have examples that are proof for those of us that have faith. For those of us that are close-minded and close-hearted, perhaps we need our own experiences as proof. Let us keep in mind, though, that as a closed heart is not capable of receiving or giving love, so also a closed mind is not able to receive or share the light of spiritual knowledge. Hence, the dumbfounded that wander aimlessly in their second journey.

11

This whole book, as you will discover, has to do with light. Natural light, yes, but more importantly, the spiritual light of our souls. We will see that through our knowledge in Physics, all is made of light in our metaphysical world, even that of our flesh/body. This should help us open the door to spiritual light, the knowledge within that spiritual light for our soul's mind. Our soul is of light from the source of light that constantly needs the Holy Spirit to pull us through the first and second journey and into our third journey.

I write *we* because I am a small part of the equation, just a minor messenger that is attempting to do my best in writing this book. I have tried my best to put all that I have been given into words, into language, for all age groups to understand. It has not been easy, so this book is an invitation, a dare, a challenge, call it what you will. I think of it as a sharing of grace.

The planning of this book probably started with my conception. I am just a trivial messenger, a vehicle. At the same time, I could not have written it if I did not believe in the contents. Writing this book has helped me in my own journey, true, but the real reason is for the sake of those of us seeking answers to questions of our soul's mind. It is for all of us trying to understand the process in our soul's climb to the summit of our chart as is the one on the cover of this book. Reading this introduction, you are probably beginning to have questions. This is a good start. It is good for us to question ourselves now and then, such as: where have I been? Where am I? What do I have? What do I really want? Where do I want to be? Do I even know where I am going in my journey? Do I feel regrets in my life?

I will attempt to make this book as easy as possible to follow, especially for those in their early teens. I remember full well the difficulties of those years and how I had so many questions but no adequate answers. This is the reason for the dare in the title. As teens, we appreciate a challenging dare, so I dare anyone who has picked up this book to read through it. It does not matter if you are a practicing Hindu, Muslim, Buddhist, or Jew. It does not matter if you are Christian Roman Catholic, Christian Russian or Greek Orthodox, or Christian Protestant. It does not even matter if you are atheist or agnostic. Please just try to read it before slamming it down. Of course, you should not judge it until you are done with it. Afterward, you can critique it as you wish. This is my challenge to you, to challenge yourself.

Those of us that are older know that there are various stages in our life's journey that includes hardships and so many burdens. For the young, those of us still in middle school who are willing to read this book, it is harder, much harder, trying to understand stages that have not yet occurred. We need the experience. This is my greatest hope of all, that middle school children could be spared as teenagers some of the burdens and unnecessary hardships of life if possible. Life is full of trials. I have had my share for sure. Writing this book has been one of them.

The intention of this book is to simplify the various stages and why we have them. More importantly, how best are we to deal with them? After reading this book, the reader should be able to chart and track their own soul's journey and know where he or she is now. This requires a little self-quiz, but we will get to that later in this book.

In this twenty-first century, we know what is required of us to maintain a healthy body/flesh. We know that the right nutrition, sleep, and reduced stress helps our development. This is all good. The question is, what about the development of our soul? We will learn that the two, body/flesh and soul, are one and at the same time, also that the day will come when they will separate for a time.

This book will take you from conception to the death of the body/flesh and hopefully beyond. As you can see from the chart on the cover of this book, I believe that we all have at least three journeys. The first starts at conception and ends at our birth. The second starts at our natural birth and ends at the death of our body/flesh. This is the one that we will focus on the most. As the first determines the second, the second determines our third journey. We will go into all three. We will also learn that with all that we do in our lives, it all has to do with our eventual third journey, whether we like it or not, whether we accept it or not.

This book has been the most difficult and challenging part of my second journey. It has asked me to COMMIT, DEVOUT, SACRIFICE, and be RESPONSIBLE for the GRACES that I did not deserve yet received. I had forgotten about the important VIRTUES of my youth or, I should say, chose to put them aside. No, this book is not about feel-good-only experiences. It is so much more than that. On the contrary, this book is all about the graphs inside and on the front and back book cover. This book will try to explain what it takes to climb up to the summit of spiritual knowledge and beyond. It is about what is needed of us to be pulled up, Tira Mi Su, into #10, the heavens.

Most graphs speak for themselves, but when dumbfounded, as so many of us are, it needs to be explained. As an example, take the way that most of us have changed from our childhood due to the loss of innocence and spiritual light. Remember how as children we would hate for an intruder to come into our home and break up our family? Some of us as adults have become that intruder. From the summit, we see clearly each point where we lost spiritual light.

Yes, the summit in this book is comparable to a metaphysical summit on a high mountain. Only here it becomes our soul's summit. The #10 is heaven, one of three destinations for our soul's third journey after the death of our body/flesh. Position 6.0 to 9.99 in the degree of our soul's light is purgatory. Position .01 to 5.99 is hell. The time periods, the degrees of light, as we travel our second journey are started and better defined after we take our quiz in chapter 3. Our chart starts with our short first journey but will quickly shift us into our second journey. I will explain more about each journey in the chapters.

All that is in the following chapters of this book hopefully are within the standards, laws, and order of the Roman Catholic Church and the Gospels in the New Testament. If not, I stand to be corrected.

I sense that all that has been created has become polluted and defective to some extent, yet none more than humanity through which evil works. We cause all other forms of life to suffer in the process. How are we to change the current events that have caused so much harm to ourselves, to others, and to all forms of life on this wonderful earth? That is what we need to explore. I feel a sense of relief now that this book is done. From here, it is mostly out of my hands. How it will affect its readers is hard to ascertain. I have done my part. The rest is up to the readers and the Holy Spirit. We can only hope for the best, whatever that may be. Regardless, tomorrow holds promise of a better life ahead for those of us that live our second journey in faith, hope, and trust in the Holy Trinity. A third journey of heaven is one without pain and suffering, one without regrets of memorable sins, a relief—this is what I believe, this is what I live for.

I am wishing that this book may be of a little help to at least a few of the seven billion-plus people currently on this planet. This in itself will be compensation for all of the time and energy that went into the book. I am also planning on giving to Saint Don Bosco Charity, my choice, seventy-plus percent of all royalties present and in the future. All graces, as we will learn, need to be shared. I also hope that after reading the book, readers will pass it on to others rather than put it on a bookshelf collecting dust. I also believe that it could become a gift, especially for our youth to read.

CHAPTER *One*

The Beginning—Love—Marriage—
Seed—Egg—Conception—Mother—
Father—Our First Journey Starts

The beginning for all of us starts at our conception. For that, historically and traditionally, we needed a father and a mother. Today, much has changed, a little for the better, a lot for the worse. Man and woman, absolutely without any doubt whatsoever, are the highest forms of living art on earth. In all of creation, there are no masterpieces of life greater, the 3Ns—Nothing, Niente, Nada— in the entire cosmos is our equal.

Meditate and reflect on what we have done and continued to do with this art form. From ancient times to current times, study how often we have caused ruin and destruction of this art form. This is one of the greatest tragedies of tragedies. I will not get into who our first parents were or how they came to exist in creation, although we geneticists have traced humanity back to one person, one man— Adam. You could study Genesis if you wish to. I think that we have enough to deal with in ourselves in our modern age.

To start with, let us think of our beginning at conception as one in an incubator, that of our mother. Even here we start having issues of the beginning, our beginning. The beginning of our human anatomy, physical body/flesh, our soul and spirit, that sustains us is in constant debate, although it should not be. It is because we do not want to face the consequences of our choices. From here on out, when I write the 3Cs, it refers to the Choices, positive or negative, of our free will; the Consequences, positive or negative, in the tests that are the results for us; and Conditions that we have to endure in losing or gaining light in our souls. Again, to continue, we look for excuses for negative results, consequences, to try to justify our choices/actions. We even bring our issues into the US supreme court, although I don't see anything supreme about the nine members. These nine so-called supreme justices hide behind the Constitution of America but should not have any moral authority over us. They think and vote as if they do.

So often they are also playing politics with those that put them into their position. A vote to abolish them and let individual Republic states deal with their own moral issues could be best for all. Think about it—we liberal New Yorkers are not the same as those of us from moral-conscious Utah or conservative states. Each state should have the right to its own Constitutional State laws by the voters. I believe that a grassroots movement needs to be started to that effect.

I believe that as children, we start and consist of three parts: divine spirit, our soul, and our body/flesh. All three may very well come from the seed of man, having been instilled there since our omega man. All three originated in spiritual light with man, together with woman, entrusted to help reproduce new life. Notice that I wrote "help to," not make new life in babies as some of us think. The same holds true of making love. No, we do not make love like making wine. Rather, man gives his seed that contains life/light with love, also of light, if we have love, to woman. In return, men accept love/light, if we know how, from woman. We ourselves make nothing, again the 3Ns: Nothing, Niente, Nada. All is from grace/light. We are most often undeserving yet given a part in the process of procreation. Yet here also we find ways to make a mess. This seed of man is the most precious of seeds on earth, making the seed also holy. Even ancient civilizations believed in this. It should come as no surprise that when the seed of man is wasted, defiled as in the case of pop culture, mankind is degraded after losing grace/light. But the seed of man is of no value without the egg of a woman. Hence, the importance of marriage between a man and a woman, elevating the institution by Christ to the highest ever. The bond is holy. No, not man to man, not woman to woman, as in current corrupted pop culture.

As mentioned, I believe the human seed to contain spirit, that spark of light from our creator for our soul and our body/flesh. It is this spark within both mother and child that sustains them—both the metaphysical body/flesh and their souls. We are all children of spiritual light, and only spiritual light sustains us all.

From the start, our soul is perfect as light is perfect. The metaphysical, our body/flesh, being genetically inherited is imperfect, hence, the innocent soul of a child. But both need each other to develop and grow. Our character, our personality, is genetically inherited. In love, the seed of man and the egg of woman are united as was intended by ISD, Intellectual Spiritual Design. We have tried to change this with devastating results for all concerned. Note that the word *coupling* itself means male/female, as male threads into female threads and not two male or two female. We were created to be so. Our creator could have easily created us to be unisex, but we were NOT!

We already know that the seeds in nature could also be defective. Humanity is no different. Both work in similar ways: the seeds of nature needing all the natural elements to germinate and grow, we at conception needing all the elements of our natural mother in order to do the same. We will understand later how our free will distinguishes us from all other seeds. A good question to meditate on is this. Could life, spirit, be withdrawn from any forms? Think about this, think about all of the species that we, humanity, have caused to become extinct. Could the same happen to us? The answer, of course, is YES. All that has to occur is for that spark, that flame, within our soul to be disconnected from our source. We will also learn more on how this could come to be.

We are not only flesh and blood, not only physical heart and brain with all other body parts. No, we are so much more than that. We all also have from conception a moral imprint on our soul's heart as our ID and a moral voice instilled into our spark.

I think of our soul as having an imprint on it to be known and recognized at all times during our first and second journey. Note on the chart that I placed conception at 9.99 in degree of the soul's light. There is a reason for this. The reason being that I believe that a child during conception is borderline between heaven and earth. This has never changed in all of humanity's history. In the imprint are the mysteries to man and woman and the many mysteries to our future. The seed of man is not fully understood. The egg of woman is also not fully understood. But do we need to spend so much time, resources, and energy on what was designed to be simple? Apparently, we think so.

There are literally thousands of mysteries in the cosmos, but none raise our curiosity as that of human life and rightly so. I also believe that all forms of life—from plants to trees, sea life to all land life—all contain a degree and form of spiritual light. If only we were able to communicate with them all. There are so many mysteries— for example, is it understood that all seeds when suffocated die? An example of this is putting plant seeds into a sealed jar. In time, the seeds die. Seeds need to be planted in mother earth in order to reproduce. So also, the seed of man, when not cared for, not treated as was intended, becomes wasted. It should be noted that human seed disintegrates when used for the wrong reasons. The full mysteries of man's seed may remain a mystery to us until our third journey. Again, who as a whole has stressed out all forms of life on earth? Yes, humanity has and continues to do so. Not only that, we stress ourselves out even more so in the process. Study history to see what we have done to humanity. We have starved, imprisoned, enslaved, poisoned, executed, and even buried people alive. Are there bad seeds? Are we bad seeds?

One of the major responsibilities as parents starts way before conception. This as we will discover actually becomes a serious part of our second journey. This part of our second journey is what will affect our child in their first and second journey both. Sexual intercourse between a man and a woman is or should be much more than lust and physical pleasures of the body/flesh.

Before continuing to conception, have we ever stopped for a moment to meditate on this one most important aspect of conception, fertility? Few, so few of us, ever think about it until the time comes that we find out that as a married couple, one and sometimes both are infertile. For that 10 percent of married couples, this seems like the end of the world. Before we found out, we never really stopped to give this much thought. In other words, we never stopped to consider that maybe, just maybe, we are in that 10 percent bracket, which is, by the way, increasing due to our lifestyle. What was worse, we took conception for granted. The majority of us never even stopped for a few moments to pray for a healthy child. The Holy Spirit works in mysterious ways that have little to nothing (the 3Ns: Nothing, Niente, Nada) to do with our scientific or medical professionals. Those of us honest enough will attest to this fact.

At this point, I think that all of us should reflect back. Were we really ready to be a part of the creation process? Sad to say, and we should not be surprised, that a large percentage of us are not.

I recall a fictional story of the future where humanity was incapable of reproducing. Everything else was possible through modern technology except conception! Scary thought, is it not? Could this ever actually come to be? Just the thought of it is depressing. We take so much for granted. Few of us are sincerely grateful. We really believe that we deserve grace and that we are entitled to all gifts. Think again! We are owned, the 3Ns: Nothing, Niente, Nada. Seriously, for the most part, we are selfish, self-confident, self-centered, the 3Fs: Foolish, at Fault, Failures in regard to gratitude. Sadly, pop culture has never been worse that I could remember. Who among us is sincerely appreciative? Who among us practices the virtues anymore? Virtues? What were those again?

Is it possible that we are of bad seed? We have a way to test ourselves in this department as well. Isn't science amazing? Of course, I am being sarcastic. Besides, if our DNA were to be from bad genes, what do we do with this knowledge? Do we even want to go there? Do we want to feel handicapped or inferior? My whole point is that we are all born equal in soul, in spiritual light. We are all given that spark, that moral imprint for our soul with which to work. The imperfections of our genetic makeup could be dealt with. In the exercise of our free will and help from all associated with the Holy Trinity, our soul could also be helped.

We should begin to comprehend at this point the seriousness of our 3Cs: Choices, Consequences, and Conditions of conception. What conception is NOT: 1) it is not freezing your eggs until you are past the prime years of your fertile life to conceive; 2) it is not ever degradation of the seed of man; 3) it is not being irresponsible by trial and error; 4) it is not, considering abortion due to a mistake, an option; 5) it is not spermicides or other forms of seed extermination; 6) it is not about a perfect child; 7) it is not about planning to give up your child for adoption unless under extremely difficult situations; 8) it is not about, race, religion, or nationality; 9) it is not about simply a boy to carry the gene into the next generation. As we can or should see, it is more about eliminating the negatives and evils than anything else.

The seed of man and the egg of woman are already under severe stress. Both have suffered from pollution and toxins. Both are in need of a healthy lifestyle. From the summit, all of this is clearly visible. It is sickening to see and write about the abominations that are taking place in our so-called Christian community regarding sex, the seed and egg of man and woman. We need to remember that no, we are not so deserving. A little humility might do us some good. Above all else, we need to remind ourselves that conception is, after our own body/flesh and soul, the next biggest responsibility of all. We as parents take part in and help create the first journey for our children, one that will require a tremendous amount of work, time and money into their future. The job we do will help shape their second journey for better or worse.

What conception is about: 1) love that is within our soul's heart; love from love for the sake of love; 2) acceptance of all of the sacrifices associated with the responsibilities of taking part in the process of creating new life; 3) being sincerely grateful every day for all of the grace bestowed on our marriage; 4) having full respect for new life; 5) understanding that in this imperfect world we may have to deal with the imperfections; in other words, we may not receive what we desire; 6) accept the fact that we may not be able to conceive; 7) keep in mind that there are alternatives, adoption of kids needing loving parents; 8) pray to all associated with the graces of the Holy Spirit; 9) listen to your heart's voice as husband and wife.

For our child, for whom we gave so much of ourselves, he or she was not an orphan, not an outcast having to depend on the grace of others to develop and grow properly. No, he or she is a part of ourselves. Stop, take a good hard look at him or her before they grow out of their childhood and teens. How have we done as parents? Have we given them what they really need for the rest of their second journey? It is only a matter of time before our children are no longer children but adults. Have we prepared them well? As adults, we know what is out there away from home. We know of all the dangers, the pitfalls, and hopefully the unknown evil spirits of darkness. Are they ready to leave the safety of our nest? They were so dependent on us for sustenance and survival. If they leave the nest too early, they may not be able to take the hardships. If they stay in the nest too long, they will not fly.

When they were growing up, the years seemed to pass slowly. But here we are already with them in their late teens. Hopefully, we are grateful that they made it this far and in such good shape. We all know of families where this was not the case. We witnessed the tragic events.

They are anxious to leave: to college, to military school, just to work and be on their own. It is not really about an Ivy League college or any other university or job. No, it is about who they have grown up to be as persons. Did we help them with discipline to become self-disciplined? Did we help instill in them a true sense of right from wrong? Do they understand a good moral way of life? Did we help them be responsible citizens? Did we explain the importance of the virtues to live by? All these questions that we ask ourselves…did we, at least, do a decent job of parenting? If yes, we should not worry. If no, let us pray that the Holy Spirit of light may watch over them and protect them throughout their second journey.

Those of us that have climbed to the summit are fully aware that at times our study in and through college could hurt us more than help us. At times, it could easily become a false liberalization when it causes us to drift away from our core values if we ourselves had them.

It could actually become a trap into believing that academics and science are all that we really need in life. This is a false enlightenment. The majority of college students tend to track lower during their college years. I was no exception. A few of us spiral down with excessive blood alcohol, drugs, and sexual explorations. If we study the so-called party schools where students have funds to play with, we find that they are the worst.

We, of course, need to remember what insurance companies tell us, that our grown-up child will not really reach maturity until the age of twenty-four, if all goes well. Hmm, but they are only eighteen, what are we to do? Probably the worst thing that we do for them is to get them far away where in an emergency, it would take hours to reach them. Let us face it, our child, no matter what age, will always be our child. Others may help out, but when not their own child, can we rest assured?

Because of immaturity, before the age of twenty-four, risks are readily available and taken. We as adults recall those years and the stupid things that we did. Will our child be an exception? Maybe, but don't count on it.

Let us recall what we did during those years. And mind you, as grown-up adults, as parents, those years were conservative compared to the pop culture of today.

First, sex—I am not sure why, but it seems that as soon as our children leave home, they seem to think that now they no longer need to follow the moral standards that we gave them. Or is it that we failed to give them the right moral standards to begin with?

In America, the sexual revolution began toward the end of the last century and resulted (again, the 3Cs: Choices, Consequences, and Conditions) in a massive loss of soul light for most of the coming generations. Also, the current LGBT revolution and false liberalization of this century will turn out to be even worse. Again, the 3Cs for all involved. We will talk more about this in the following chapters. From the summit, we see that the revolution of the last century was a revolution against morality itself. It was a revolution that basically said and continues to say, "We do not want standards, we do not want to be decent human beings. We would rather be like basic animals that follow instincts. We were not created to become animals and follow basic body/flesh instincts. Hence, since that time period, human sexual activities without true moral standards have lost the light of love. All sexual activity between a husband and a wife was designed, ISD, to be the fulfillment of love.

It is important to note that the so-called sexual revolution in America took place in a supposedly Christian country. In Western traditional Christian Europe, this false liberalization did not take place as badly. It is also ironic that in atheist communist China, this sexual revolution did not occur at all. Only since opening its doors to the West and being influenced in negative ways toward sex has the marriage institution taken a hit there. So much for Western values and freedoms in these areas.

The 3Cs have been in play seriously since the sexual revolution in America. Remember that the 3Cs deal with the *choices* of our free will, the *consequences* of those choices, and finally the *conditions* that are the end result.

Take as an example a young girl that so easily gives up her virginity often to someone that is a minor acquaintance. I always wondered why. Why the giving up of the most precious part of womanhood often without love? Was it the upbringing? Was it the false revolution? Was it the friends? Was it the parents who themselves were promiscuous? Was it the environment, the atmosphere of being away from home? Or perhaps, this may have started much earlier, say, high school, even middle school?

As adults, as parents, we have witnessed the exploitation of our youth by advertising agencies, corporate America, clothing brands, lingerie companies, cosmetics companies, etc. Every decade, we have seen these advertisers push the envelope and lower the limits of what they are legally, even privileged, to get away with. What is worse is that we did not put a stop to it. Why? Because we were a part of the problem. We bought into pop culture. We did not want to be seen as out of fashion, out of style, and out of date, so we went along. This is actually guilt by omission, which we will get into more in later chapters.

Let us get back to why a young girl easily gives up her virginity to an insignificant other person.

The reasons are numerous: peer pressure, boyfriend pressure, insecurity, lack of self-respect, lack of self-discipline, lack of self-esteem, lack of intimacy, lack of values, lack of control, lack of light within her soul's heart and mind. It should be noted that the last reason, had it not happened, would have taken care of all the previous reasons and whatever else was added.

These are the pitfalls that teenagers have to face. They are enticed, persuaded, drugged, and under certain circumstances even raped. The scars on a young girl when these things happen go much deeper than her flesh and body; they scar her very soul. As parents, we never think that this will happen to our little girl; we are fooling ourselves. What is happening to our young girls in America is an assault from all sides from all sorts and none of them good, including the feminist front that has little to do with femininity. Only a solid foundation based on strong Christian moral values of light within them—within their soul—will suffice.

A young girl that is given this foundation is always aware that her body/flesh is a gift of grace that needs to be cherished, respected, and treated as a temple of her soul. The body should never be defiled or degraded by any means. Sex needs to be the fulfillment of love between herself and her husband, not just an act of lust and desire of the flesh/body. After all, her sacred womb is the womb for new life brought into the world. A man may have the seed, but what is the seed without the fertile healthy womb of his wife? A womb that has been polluted with STDs (sexually transmitted diseases), toxic viruses by a willingness (the 3Cs: choices, consequences, and conditions) of an ignorant young girl is sad enough. The willingness by an older, young woman, in her negative 3Cs due to her 3Ss: stubbornness, stupidity, sickness is far worse. A stupid pussy, as the Italian people reference her, for her degrading herself for M&M, money and material things. These are the tragedies of women who use their gifted bodies/flesh for the wrong reasons. The 3Cs are, at these times, devastating, often with results of abortion, infertility and, psychological damage. No woman should have to endure such burdens and yet, as we have discussed, so easily give in when tested to accept the temptations.

Young men are just as guilty, if not more so. A piece of advice that a wise older man gave me during my college years was that, "A stiff cock has no conscience," a great piece of advice for a young guy whose hormones were out of control. Problem was, it did not fully register. Recall that a young man does not really reach a degree of maturity until age twenty-four. Most young men are this way. Even if acting mature, it's just acting. Physically, mentally and emotionally, we are the 3Fs: *foolish*, at *fault* young guys who *fail* our good moral voice (conscience) and follow our bodies/flesh's sexual desires.

So from the summit, does a stiff cock have no conscience? Of course, a young man's cock has to do with his flesh/body that was by ISD, intellectual spiritual design, and ESD, emotional spiritual design, to procreate in marriage. There are the 3Ns: nothing, niente, nada wrong with this. It is, in fact, the positive process. The positive 3Cs of choice give positive consequences and contribute to the positive conditions in the miracle of new life. The problem is that outside the bond of marriage, his good conscience, that positive inner voice of his soul's heart spark, is hushed, even buried into his subconscious and kept silent. With the assistance of demons, the negative voices, man tempted without moral values easily becomes a victim. Women are no different when their body/flesh vaginal area is stimulated by various means or it is their time of the month when they are fertile. They also ignore their good conscience outside the bond of marriage. But men, especially young men, are more vulnerable. This is taking place in our teenagers at a younger and younger age. Hence, middle school children, little girls, are getting pregnant in their very early teens.

The whole educational system on sex in America is, for the most part, the 3Fs: foolish, at fault, failure. We are telling our children, "You are going to follow your basic negative animalistic instincts, so here is how you should go about it." Teenagers could prevent all the problems that they encounter with sexual abstinence until they are mature adults ready to get engaged for marriage. This worked well in the past thousands of years. The right standards should not have been thrown in the toilet.

And what have we adults, we parents, told our young girls and boys about dating? Play it safe. Hmm, remember what the insurance companies tell us? The reason that teenagers' insurance rates are astronomically high is that teenagers do not play it safe, not when driving. For example, I remember full well that time on a double date to my high school prom after-party. We decided to go to Niagara Falls from Youngstown, Ohio. We went in my Impala Chevy SS convertible car. Teenagers want to get everywhere fast, this time was no exception. I recall being pulled over by the NY Highway Patrol for not wearing seatbelts and clocking over 115 miles per hour. From the summit, I now see the madness in this and what might have happened that day with a tire blowout. Play it safe? This is the biggest joke of all. Excited teenagers most often do not play it safe, not when driving and not when having sex. The fad on certain college campuses now is group sexual activities, almost orgies. Alcohol flows until you pass out with the risk of high blood alcohol death. Depending on the college, drugs are readily available from weed, grass, to cocaine for anyone with the dare to try and not to be a boring wallflower. Is this what we want our child to experience? Do we seriously want to take these risks?

Again, the problem is that we as parents have forgotten what we were like at the same age.

Other phrases that we use: "Be responsible," "Be trustworthy," "Be sensible." I like this one, "Be sensible," not realizing that sensibility has to do with body/flesh senses and not-yet-discovered senses of our soul, which I will cover later in this book. People, listen to the insurance companies. They have the statistics, the facts. They basically have the 3Cs—choices, consequences, and conditions—for teenage drivers, and they are horrible.

I have given a glimpse of the worst-case scenario for a child, but this is something to meditate on. There are numerous party schools in America that pride themselves not in academics but in getting and being crazy. These are not creative or entrepreneurship schools that help bring out the best in students. With their low standards, they help bring out the worst.

Of course, there are also great colleges in America, many of which are the best rated in the world. To have some peace of mind and play it safe, I think that colleges with an affiliation to a Christian church could reduce the risks. For example, I spent some time on the campus of the University of Toronto, where the various colleges were directly affiliated with various Christian denominations. It was a wonderful campus and university, but I know that there are plenty in America as well as even Europe.

Finally, outside of the standards of true faith, sexual involvement is so often and becoming more often lawless, corrupt, and humiliating with what is happening over the Internet. This tends to be worse for young girls more than the boys, but both are affected by the 3Cs that have lasting effects long into the second journey. This is the sexuality of pop culture currently in our youth.

I could spend much more time on this most important chapter because I recall the turbulence in my own teens. I would have to say that this decade, which all of us need to pass through, could make or break our entire second journey.

When we do not grow into who we were created to be, it makes us want to put a sledge hammer to that image we see in the mirror in front of us. Part of this has to do with the expectations that others put on us—parents and others. Part of it has to do with peer pressure. Part of it may have to do with the American model of what is considered success. There are so many factors and outside variables. As an example, the suicide rate of teenagers in China is high in colleges, high schools, even middle schools. It is due to the extreme pressure and stress placed on the child early on, almost from the time that he or she, especially he, is born.

What are children to do until they reach maturity and are able to make adjustments in their lives? Make the best of "it"? I see that "it" does not matter whether "it" is in Asia, parts of Europe or America; the models of success are similar. They are based on M&M (money and material) things and power to attain M&M. This is perhaps the reason why only 25 percent of people are happy working in the field that they are in. Will our child be different? Maybe, maybe not, it depends on so many factors. The most important one is the progress of their climb up to their soul's summit. Have we helped with that? Have we helped ourselves?

Do we ever stop to wonder why we, humanity individually, have so many different talents, personalities, characteristics, values? For example, the arts: some of us were created to be artists in various mediums. What has happened to the arts in America? Funding cuts after funding cuts year after year. A few people have decided that the arts are not that essential to the success of our soul's second journey. Even sports has a higher priority. Yes, sports, where injuries are probable and a career is highly improbable. How much team spirit do we need? The arts and the artists are much more appreciated and respected in Europe than America. It has to do with the lifestyle in light and a good sense of what is important for the quality of life.

Without a reasonable foundation based on sound true moral values, our child is going to struggle regardless of the degrees, the job, the income, and the connections. If their soul is not tracking upward on the chart of their soul's second journey, they will encounter many difficulties.

Most often, our child will bring those difficulties back home to us. This is sad, but at least, at home we are still able to help them. In the hands of strangers, pimps, conmen/women and the endless users out there, they may end up in some rat-infested gutter. We hear of the abandoned child. We hear of horror stories of teenagers totally out of control. We hear of teenagers that turn physically violent on their elderly parents or, these days, on grandparents. We hear too often of these same parents and grandparents having to call professional people to come to the house in the middle of the night to take this troubled child off to some faraway place to discipline and make them come to their senses. Yes, these stories are becoming more and more frequent, and they are costing us dearly. They are taking their toll on our health and well-being. Again, this is a worst-case scenario. But meditate on this. Do not imagine that this happens only to others. We could easily become the others.

I know that this sounds so cliché, but it also holds true. Take the preventive measures when the child is young, the younger the better. The longer we wait, the harder it becomes on ourselves and our child to correct matters. Understanding the charts in and on this book cover about the child's and our second journey could be helpful. It all has to do with spiritual light, the light of our soul.

CHAPTER *Two*

Early Development—Childhood
Education and Formation—Our Second
Journey Starts—the Terrible Teens

So let us backtrack to the birth of our child. Now starts their second journey, as the first journey is over. Pregnancy was the easiest part. Here the real work begins. Let us see if we can get it right based on what we just learned could go terribly wrong from the previous chapter.

Yes, we read as many books as possible during pregnancy in order to keep healthy. We stopped smoking, stopped drinking excessive amounts of alcohol, we cut out this or that. Or did we? Let us hope so. It should be noted that when we care about ourselves in a healthy way, we will be capable of doing the same with our child.

There are numerous additional books out there to assist with teaching our newborn baby anything and everything imaginable. But I believe that what is most important is to try to remember what we ourselves thought and felt like in our early years. This is not easy; most of us are not able to recall. We do not remember our nine months of pregnancy after conception. Regarding the most beautiful years, birth through three years, we remember almost nothing. Hmm, so we have to observe our newborn child. Also, we need to actually learn to listen attentively. We could do that, right? We can differentiate a false cry compared to an authentic cry? Children have always amazed me how, when with certain people, they become afraid. At such a young age, what do they see that as adults we do not see? In their protected innocence, are they able to see the evils in others? I have read that as very young children we are able to see our guardian angel. If so, where is this all stored in us? Our subconscious? Does it make a difference? It does, but we will explore this later in this book.

As mentioned in the previous chapter, after our soul, the soul of our child becomes our next biggest responsibility. Recall the airline stewardess announcing, "In an emergency, help yourself first in order to be able to help your child." So very true when you think about it. And so true it is that as parents in our own second journey, who we are, everything that we say or do, affects the second journey of our child. This is an important part of this book. Where are we on our own chart? We need to ask ourselves, how could we be accountable for our child if we are not accountable for our own actions? Again, recall the 3Cs: choices, consequences, and conditions!

Today our youth have access to a tremendous amount of data, an overload if you ask me. But the question is, what data and from whom? Children naturally have endless questions yet so few honest, truthful answers. I remember as a child I thought that if it was in print, it was true. Imagine that! Social media, gossip magazines, songwriter lyrics that stir the imagination in this modern age of madness, how do we maintain a sense of control?

Giving our youth false hopes and dreams has to rate up there as the worst of sins. This is what is taking place today. Do we see this? Are we willing and able to see who we have become since our childhood with the bad choices, the wrong turns? Again the 3Cs! How could we if we do not make the time to reflect back to our past? Even if we do wrong or bad according to what standards? Whose standards? It should be noted that our 3Fs—foolishness, fault, and failures—most often could become the future 3Fs of our children.

The challenge, the changes, have to start with us, within our soul's heart and mind. Here all true change takes place.

We held our pediatrician accountable for monitoring our child's health, keeping track of the progress that full nine months. We did the best we knew how to care for ourselves and keep healthy. It really never ends, does it? It does not.

Seeing this, some couples decide not to have children. A few even dislike children, and a tiny percentage, thank goodness only a tiny percentage, even hate children.

We may ask ourselves why. Or why is it that some of us like pet animals more than children? They're complex questions that go deep into our subconscious. This also we will explore in a later chapter.

I believe that the absolute most difficult part of parenting starts when the child is around the age of three. Why? Because this is the age that a child begins to exercise his or her free will. Think back to see how this was the case for most of us. There is medical research going on as with the writing of this book on when a child starts to decide to accept evil choices. Save the taxpayer money. A child is tempted as early as three years of age.

I realize that it depends on the parents, the circumstances, the environment, etc. But still, here we are all equal. We are actually allowed to be tempted as early as three years of age. Notice the difficulty when you try to recall flashes of what you experienced between the ages of birth to three. Strange because these years witnessed in other children seem to be among the happiest. Yet they seem to get locked into our subconscious, why? To be rediscovered at a later time when we need to reach inside of ourselves? Again, people say that we are with our guardian angel in these years. These are the important formative years for our souls. Are we all given that help but not able to recall? In Italia, I have seen paintings of this. Is this to help us get started and stay on the right track for our soul's climb to the summit? Notice how we track high, 9.99 to 9.0 for our soul's degree of light on the book cover chart. This is because we have not begun to be tempted and tested. Our moral imprint on our soul's heart is formed here in these years. Here, after the months of pregnancy from conception, we are closest to the Holy Spirit. So as we can see, there is justice for all souls in getting started in our second journey.

The question we should be asking now is, why baptism? Baptism is a preparatory safeguard, if you will, for what we all have to face soon. Notice that the Roman Catholic Church always has Holy Water ready as a reminder of our baptism and for what our soul needs, the water of life, of Christ in our second journey. I think of baptism as the precautionary measure for a child against all of the evils of this world. We give our child the needed medical shots to fight off diseases of the flesh/body; more importantly, why not baptism for their soul?

As parents, our job is never done in regard to our child. There is always something that he or she needs. But that is what it is all about, is it not? I know that it gets tiring at times, but what do we have to do that is more important? Here we need to ask ourselves, am I a good parent? But what defines a good parent? Again, according to what standards? Whose standards? Starting at the age of three, not only is our wonderful and beautiful child tempted and tested, but as parents, so are we. In other words, this is where our second journeys can and do collide. Who is right? Who is wrong? When we as parents do not know ourselves, we have a problem that only gets worse and worse in the upcoming years.

When we do not have the right answers to the endless questions with which we are confronted early on, how is a child to trust our answers during the most difficult years ahead for them? This is the day of recognition. This is a test of ourselves. A few of us will accept this time to reflect on ourselves. Who are we? Who have we become? If we have our chart that we are tracking, it may help. If not, we continue on course, the same course of our own parents.

So again more questions, do we like our parents? Do we like and appreciate what they did for us, how they raised us? Are we grateful for the value system they gave us? Are we thankful for the virtues to live life by? If our answers are yes, we have not to worry. It is when the answers are no that a change is necessary. This is by no means an easy task. This self-confrontation, this having to face the truth is difficult, but the love for a child supersedes our own needs. This is a true love for a child. When we fail true love, we fail ourselves, our child, and everyone else as well. Perhaps, this is the reason that a few of us hate children. They remind us of who we once were, of what was lost. Perhaps, we hate who we have become.

This, as you see, takes introspection. It raises questions about where we are in our own second journey. We begin to, or I should say should begin to, search our own soul's heart and mind health. Were we brainwashed into believing this or that? What has worked for us? What was all a bunch of BS? Were we, are we a part of some gang that is a dead end? Were we the privileged spoiled ones that do not have any appreciation for anything? The vicious cycle of an immoral lifestyle is hard to break, but it is worth it for the love of our children and their future. We do not want them to deal with what we had to deal with the hard way.

This raises another question, does a child need to experience a loss of innocence? The answer is NO. By the way, for me, of all of the countless books that I have read, three sum up all that I needed for my second journey. They are the Bible, mainly the New Testament, and two books on the lives of the saints, as in Saint John Bosco of Italia who helped orphaned children and Saint Padre Pio also of Italia. As for the loss of innocence, Saint Padre Pio of the twentieth century was known to be like a naive innocent child, even in old age. Yet we need to be practical in this twenty-first century. Naiveté and innocence are being lost at an earlier and earlier age, so this would be wishful thinking, unless we start living the lifestyle of those smart Amish/Quakers. Few of us are willing to do that. So yes, we face a major daily battle trying to filter out the pollutants for our child. At least, until they are able to do so for themselves.

I remember as a child not liking when it was bedtime. It was because of the darkness, even though I had my whole family there in the same house. I remember that outside of the upstairs bedroom window, I could see a TV station light above the high tower. It would constantly blink off and on as if to say, "Although it is dark out here, I, Light, am always here. Do not worry, go to sleep." This naturally was a metaphysical sign. Yet a child needs that daily reinforcement directed to their soul to help them with their fears that, regardless of the darkness, the spark of the Holy Spirit is within them during their second journey, even after the parents pass away.

It takes so much energy to be a good parent. I wrote *good*, not *perfect*, as I do not think there is a perfect parent, only a parent that is willing to make the effort to become a better parent. As parents, we ourselves are constantly making mistakes and learning from our 3Cs. What is the right training method? So much is written about this way or that way as being successful. Successful how, in what way? A book from a PhD in this field or that field, but what guarantee does a parent have that a certain training method is the best method?

The second journey for a child is so complex, so much more involved than just the academics. It is so much more detailed than only a strong education, great career, and financial stability. It should be noted that the smartest children are also often the most challeng ing. They know and want much more in their second journey. They expect us to guide their way. If we are unstable, uncertain and inse- cure, what example are we for them?

A balanced mental, emotional, physical, and spiritual health is important and necessary. This is easily written but hard to accom- plish. Question is, if we do not experience this ourselves, what are we to say? In this century, we are putting less and less emphasis on the spiritual health, which affects the other aspects of health. We have come to think that science has all the proven answers. Science and scientists do not. Good health starts within our soul's heart and mind. In this, all other areas of health are possible. A child is being handicapped without the development of his/her soul's health and well-being. Also, only in this way are children able to help themselves when we have departed for our own third journey.

We should never deny a child this most important part of their lives. We could cut out certain classes, certain lessons, but never what their soul needs to grow and prosper. It should be comforting also that this gift that we give to them most often does not cost us any- thing but a little time. A child's second journey is not a game. It should not be conducted by trial and error. We should not leave it to chance, as there may not be a second chance to get it right.

The worst nightmare for a parent is a child that decided to leave home due to confusion, misunderstanding, miscommunication, and not being heard. This is how a child gets into trouble, being enticed by those that are out to exploit them. This is often how a child gets trapped into child trafficking, prostitution, drugs, suicide, etc. It takes more than only their moral imprint and inner voice. It requires more than primary school religious classes. It requires constant giving and caring to help build a solid true foundation in faith.

We have become a "pills" society. We think that the right doctor giving us the right prescriptions cures or can cure all of our ailments. They do not. Often, if our ailments do not kill us, the side effects of the medications might. And yes, our child picks up on all of this. There is no replacement for light in a sick soul. Only the grace of spiritual light heals a dark sick soul. Take as an example the power of love. Who does not agree that love heals? What is love? Love is light. The greater the love, the brighter the light. A child, even a disadvantaged child, knows this better than we adults. They will not be fooled. Animals are not fooled either. They understand when their owners care about them or not. A child that is loved in a genuine way does not want to leave home. On the contrary, a child eventually sees the importance of family and marriage. Notice how this has changed in the past forty to fifty years. Not only does a child want to escape home. At times, parents throw them out before they are adults.

Sad to say that although humanity benefits from new knowledge upon old knowledge, with our soul, it does not necessarily work the same way as, let's say, mathematics. In other words, even if we had grandparents, as an example, that were saint-like in every aspect of the word, we grandchildren may not be. Their saintly ways are not passed down and may not be learned. It has little to nothing to do with genetics or inheritance such as their wealth or property.

It is our systems of government, law and order, and enforcement of the laws that make us a civilized country. In our house, it's the rules, the regulations, the restrictions, and the standards of home that help our development. This is all important. But the education of the soul's mind in light of spirit of the Holy Trinity is far more important. This guides our choices, again the 3Cs, for right decisions in family issues and civil matters. Our child's soul is constantly faced with moral issues for himself/herself, moral issues for those around our child, moral challenges to their summit, and finally, moral issues for their third journey.

Note that even illiterate individuals who have very little as far as M&M (money and material) are concerned, when graced with light, are happier, have less stress and a better sense of what is important in their second journey. They have the right meaning of love and family. Regardless of their trials and hardships, they receive enough grace to help them through it all. In their faith, their priorities are in correct order, and they will not waver from the temptations. Money and power have not corrupted or taken control of their souls. Hence, they tend to have a degree of peace. True justice always takes place in our soul first and foremost before coming out into the body/flesh.

As a civilized country, we have the process to success very well wired. The right education in a demand field, in one of the top colleges, with the right connections, and we are set. It is a planned process that has proven to be successful.

Interesting enough, the education of our soul also involves a process. It should be planned out by parents. But these days, most often it is not. For parents, it becomes a choice of their free will to plan or neglect this for their child—again the 3Cs. Thank goodness that children are able to exercise their own free will as they are growing up. This saying, "Let a child decide for himself/herself when as an adult," is, of course, a cop-out. It is an omission of responsibility by parents needing help themselves with their own soul's second journey.

That is also the purpose of this book—to pick up where so many parents have failed in their responsibilities to their children as far as the education of their souls. Waiting for a child to reach adulthood is far too late, especially since the most turbulent years are coming their way into their teens.

This book hopefully will become reading material for middle school students, grades 6, 7, 8 and beyond. Study the charts. You will see that it covers all ages from birth to death. Children can, at least, begin to formulate what they are experiencing in middle school with their relationship between body and soul. In middle school, they are already able to meditate, reflect, and contemplate on all of the changes occurring within them. When parents and, at times, teachers fail to educate properly, a child needs to know that there is always hope from other sources.

I was blessed with the loving graces of Roman Catholic parents and Notre Dame nuns that instilled faith, hope, and trust in me. The nuns spent each morning of class nourishing my soul. At the time as a child, I questioned all of this. I was not able to distinguish between the metaphysical reality and the spiritual light of what was being taught in class. It was the light that these wonderful nuns knew of and understood to be necessary for my future, my soul's future for which they felt responsible. In hindsight, I know now that they also knew that their love for me would be rewarded many times over. Yes, they knew that the days of being tested for me would come and also the darkness when I failed. Yes, they knew that the foundation that they helped build in me would one day have to withstand a possible earthquake that only the Holy Spirit could help with. That foundation I know now was one of love, that is of light—light to help me through it all, anything and everything in my second journey. I know now that they had the grace of wisdom that has only one source, the Holy Trinity.

In the past forty to fifty years, our knowledge of the metaphysical flesh and world have grown dramatically. The opposite has occurred for the spiritual knowledge of our soul. In this, our soul has actually lost light. How could we say this? What proof do we have? How about our emotional and mental health? Both have deteriorated in all age groups. Yes, we live longer within this flesh of ours but in what condition? Again, it is the 3Cs!

Demand for psychiatric help has never been higher and is climbing. Psychological therapy has come down to the primary school level for children. The irony is that this is occurring in so-called advanced, industrialized, and developed countries. In poorer countries, they have different issues but not as many problems in the areas of mental and emotional health. So we have to ask ourselves, what is more important, especially for our children who are our future?

Notice the level of appreciation and gratitude of children in poor countries. Notice the levels of the same in that of children in advanced industrialized countries—a huge difference. A huge difference, but not in a good way, rather, in a negative way.

All too often, spoiled rotten children become the lazy leeches in society. They take everything for granted. They take high risks that, at times, endanger their lives. They are easily enticed to explore drugs and all forms of sexual activity. They run after anything that is exciting to try to fill that void within their soul. What void? The shallow emptiness, that darkness that replaced light.

This void begins to form from our childhood. It continues throughout our second journey for everyone with very few exceptions. How do we recognize this? Notice the changes that take place in personality, in character, in sense of humor and laughter. What has become of that loving child? It seems that there is a loss of identity. We cannot recognize the child any longer. This is that void where light was lost and darkness has taken its place. Some call it becoming street-smart. But at what cost? It is usually at the cost of kindness and caring. Is it street-smart or rather gutter stupid?

A child only has one childhood. The whole future hinges on getting it right, helping to make it a healthy, happy one. We have a lifetime to correct mistakes in other areas, but we should not rob children of the formative years that will shape their whole future.

Time and forgiveness have a way of healing much in a child's second journey. But a broken heart never heals 100 percent. The broken heart of a child that was once true, sincere, and honest will bleed throughout their lifetime. I feel sick in reading about children being abused in family, in school, and even in churches. These abuses could become deep-rooted problems that perhaps only the Holy Spirit could help to heal. Let us, at the very least, help them with this. The earlier we start, the better. Waiting should not be an option.

I am sitting here in Italy in Piazza Santa Maria Novella, in the heart of this marvelous ancient Renaissance city of Florence. I am writing, making notes for this book. I observe the young crowds, one with their guide or class teacher. They are so excited, thrilled to be here. Boys and girls mingling, all wearing blue jeans, all nonstop talking and playing, having fun as they should at their ages. They all seem to have smart phones and are taking photos of themselves, lots of photos of themselves with friends. Then I wonder, where are they in their second journey? Ever since starting this book, I catch myself wondering this with people. These young students do not seem to have a worry in the world. I want to talk to them and ask them what they are experiencing, what they are learning. What did they like the most within the church they just came out of? I now have a sense of where a person is at in their second journey by just talking to them for a few minutes. I study their facial expressions, their body language, but, most of all, their words. Are they followers, easily influenced by others? Do they have an open heart or a closed heart? Do their eyes shine? Are they filled with wonder? Are they opinionated? Are they still free-spirited?

I want to ask them what they think of the artists and their works in the church. I want to know if they know that all art, all creativity are gifts of grace. What do they understand of these great artists? What do they know of their sacrifices, their suffering for their art? Not just the painters and sculptors such as Leonardo da Vinci and Michelangelo and so many others here but also the artists of classical music from Haydn to Mozart, the artists of opera from Rossini to Verdi. They are all performed here in these churches, these works that were possible due to the gifts of grace.

So many questions that I would like to ask of them. Do they know also that they are gifted as we all are? Do they know that they need to make the most of these gifts, regardless of profession or vocation? Finally, are they grateful for all that they have? Perhaps, this is too much to ask of them. Let them just be happy for now. Are they talking about what to have for lunch, lasagna or spaghetti? This is how young children need to be!

Next, I observe people of all ages, with a tour guide carrying his little flag yelling 'this way, this way.' What country are they from? I do not understand the language. Continuous groups of people from all countries and of various languages, all races from all continents. I think to myself, is it not marvelous how art and culture brings people together? They are all here to discover art, discover history and the Renaissance.

Little do a few of them know that here in Florence as in Rome and in other churches in Italy, they will discover themselves. True, unexpectedly for a few, the Holy Spirit will move them to tears to let them know what is missing in their lives, in their souls. They will remember what they lost as children. Yes, here in Italia, a few of the visitors will be changed and changed forever for the better. They make new friends, and they finally have an appreciation for all that they have in their spouse and family. They now want to live their life to the fullest, sharing their experience of what transformed them. They will tell family and friends. They will get on the social network. Yes, here in Italia, the Holy Spirit is very active, even for those that have closed their soul's heart and mind. I see all of this and so much more because I see humanity in their weaknesses in their sorrow searching for pace/peace.

Yes, here in a city filled with grace, here I am. A joy is felt within that moves me to tears because I am here and a part of it all. Gratitude is not formal, it is not necessarily scheduled, and it is not always planned. Gratitude is spontaneous, instantly from within your soul toward the Holy Trinity when in union within your soul's heart tabernacle.

All in due course and time is what I believe. A child needs to learn this to be patient and to work for what they want. It should not just be handed out to them as if they are owed. This is some of today's pop culture youth. They think that everyone owes them—parents, social services, government, and employers. They are not willing to take available part-time jobs and would rather complain about their 3Cs—choices, consequences, and conditions—as well as their 3Ss—stubbornness, stupidity, and sickness.

There was a great gathering of world cardinals in Rome recently. They were all called in by Pope Francisco for brainstorming on the family that in some countries is in crisis. Pope Francisco to me exemplifies all that is beautiful in the Roman Catholic Church. He knows better than anyone else that when the family is hurting, all other hurts will follow for our soul, body/flesh, and society (again, the

3Cs). Yes, he knows that when law and order breaks down and is trampled on within the family, it all breaks down. He also knows that the Ten Commandments are the cornerstone of the family. People have just about thrown these out like ancient myth. This is one of the root causes of the illness entrenched in societies around the world.

Why are people doing this? They were probably never disciplined in their youth, so they lack self-discipline. Children do not like being disciplined, period. Yet this hard love is absolutely necessary. One of the greatest injustices to a child is to not discipline him or her. This lack of discipline will eventually hurt them in all aspects of their second journey. We should ask ourselves, do we love our child to a point of spoiling them? At what stage have they stopped listening to us? We can easily force our will on them when they are very young. Yet, those of us with children know full well that once children begin to exercise their free will in a negative way, they will lie, cheat, and steal to get their way. This, as we remember, starts as early as three years of age. When children, any children, get their way and they should not have, they are spoiled. Sounds familiar? This, as mentioned, occurs most in wealthy countries. In poorer countries, parents often do not have the means to spoil their child. What parents do not realize is that they are gambling and risking losing their children in the future by spoiling them.

When a grown-up child comes to grips that he or she lacks self-discipline to resist any bad temptation or doesn't have the tools in overcoming even the smallest obstacles to temptations, they know that they are in trouble. Here they could come to feel anger and resentment, almost as if betrayed. They may feel that they were not loved the right way. They were not!

Many of us have absolved ourselves of this responsibility. We simply turned it over to the teachers in the schools. We have used them as scapegoats, along with the entire school system, when our child gets into all sorts of trouble. We blame them for expelling our child. How dare they? "We will see you in court." Sounds familiar?

Let us be blunt here. Spare the rod, ruin the child. Where have we heard this? Have we heard it? Most of us have, at least, heard of this saying. It is not that antiquated. Notice that I wrote, "ruin the child." Look up the word. It means damage, almost beyond repair—almost.

The question we should be asking ourselves is: what will we do with the children when hate and darkness have entered their souls' heart and mind? Will we wait until we begin to feel vulnerable and incapacitated? At that point, all of the beautiful memories of the children will begin to fade away. Sounds scary, does it not? It should. I am trying to send out a warning before the SOS arrives. It does not have to come to that, although for parents this is becoming more and more frequent.

Not sparing the rod does not have to equate with physical abuse. Every child needs a slap over the head or a swift kick in the ass when necessary. Sorry to say this, but with physical punishment, you get their attention fast, on the spot, especially with boys. There is no need to figure out what their punishment will be. The child knows instantly that perhaps they are out of control. Psychological punishment may work to some degree until they outsmart and out-wit you. Psychiatrists and psychologists will have a field day with this but tough—I need to tell it the way I see it. This method has proven itself to work in beneficial ways for children for thousands of years. But perhaps, they—pop culture psychiatrists and physiologists—are afraid of losing patients and business rather if they admit what is right for human beings!

What were those doctors' Code of Moral Ethics again?

## The Terrible Teens

We gave our child everything. How could he/she do this to us? How did things turn out this way? What has gotten into her/him? Sounds familiar? Yes, perhaps, we did give him/her everything except what he/she needed the most—discipline.

Where does the countdown begin? Believe it or not, the count-down started when we helped conceive the child. Think back, were we disciplined, or was the child unplanned? Were we surprised to hear about the pregnancy? Very few children these days are planned out by both parents. So we need to ask ourselves, did we lack discipline in the first place? As you can see, undisciplined parents bring up undisciplined children. The problem actually started with us. It is hard to say when it will change. When love giving and receiving are limited to physical desire, lust, and things, we should not be surprised at the consequences and conditions of the 3Cs that unfold.

A child needs to be discussed, planned for, and prayed for by both mother and father. The Holy Spirit needs to be included from the very beginning. Each and every child is a gift of grace to begin with. If only we were able to communicate with each other and include the Holy Spirit, we would be amazed at how differently the 3Cs would turn out for us. For some of us, this may sound like nonsense, but for those of us looking back from the summit, it makes perfect sense. Including the Holy Spirit from the start makes raising a child less burdensome overall. This includes those terrible teen years. In this, our child may still have a difficult time changing into an adult, but we will experience a lot less hell from them.

When the consequences and conditions get totally out of control, we start into the denial mode, or we start blaming each other or others. We cannot, will not, accept that we failed our child by failing to bring in and include the light source of all new life.

If we could only get rid of the false notion that giving our child all the M&M (money and material) things will help them communicate better with us. We are fooling ourselves in a barter system of communication; the opposite occurs. We come to not like who the child has become, even though we helped in the process. Again, the 3Cs were in play—worse, we may not like ourselves for allowing it all to happen. The gap brings with it not only difficulties in communication but all sorts of other troubling issues.

A child loses a great deal of light in their terrible teens. They want to be adults yet may not really know how. The transition has its own set of rules and standards, requirements that need to be met. The problem is that they are most often those of peers from the wrong sources. They need to be the right standards for the soul for a healthy transition to occur.

If only both parents and teenagers knew how to chart and track themselves on their soul's second journey, these issues would become obvious.

As an example, a superintendent of city public school students recently announced that the students today simply do not know the difference between right and wrong. Hmm, imagine that, do we need to wonder why?

These students are to be our future world leaders, CEOs, and innovating entrepreneurs? Who will keep America a world superpower?

When we lose light for dumbfounded reasons, we as a country all lose. The comic book heroes are not going to come to our rescue. They are worse than the Greek mythological nonsense heroes believed in by ignorant people. The Hollywood heroes that never die against all odds give our youth a false sense of heroism and will not get the job done. We need to put an end to the garbage productions by refusing to pay for viewing such worthless material.

Notice how we have tied the hands of teachers in the past thirty years. We have misplaced faith, hope, and trust in a system that worked long ago into a physiologically pop culture failure. Many of us parents do not have a sense of morality ourselves. A sign of the times? A sign of darkness? A lost generation? Do we dare to help begin to make a difference? Do we dare to be a part of the solution instead of the cause of the problem? Again, it is the 3Cs, my friends. It is never too late and certainly not too early. Listen, listen to your inner voice within your soul's heart.

There was a time when children had real life role models and heroes, people that helped make a difference in our lives, heroes that strengthened America here at home and abroad.

Today we have let video games, fictional heroes, Hollywood reality shows that are not true reality and endless talk shows overtake the fundamental core values of our youth. This only worsens and compounds the issues that they already have to deal with in becoming adults.

Add to this the often negative influence by bad friends and adults, and we have the recipe for chaos. A child these days so often finds himself or herself not sure who or what to believe in. They may find themselves in a clique that at one time they despised. Yet after compromising their soul's correct values, they get caught up in that fast-moving current going toward the falls. Unanswered questions, unsatisfying answers, so much generalization only bring doubt and disrespect. Can we blame them?

As teens, our youth could be amazing and beautiful. The teen years do not necessarily have to be the worst years of our soul's 2nd journey. We simply need to take a few precautions that hopefully our parents/guardians can give us.

We are conceived and fully 100 percent dependent on our parents in our first journey. As young children, we are 90 to 99 percent dependent on them. Gradually in our teens, we are weaned off of them in our second journey. But our soul was, is, and always will be dependent on spiritual light. The sooner we see this, the sooner we can start to call and be in union with this source of power and light and prepare for our second and third journey. This power, this source of light within us, will require listening and strict attention. We may even find ourselves in turmoil in order to learn self-discipline. This is okay; what counts is that we are not forgotten.

I was gifted/graced with good, kindhearted parents that automatically had me baptized where I was born, in Bagnoli Irpino, Avellino, Italia. It is a small village in the Campania region with a ski resort known for their quality chestnuts and mushrooms. We were poor—almost everyone was after World War II. We were all suffering the same consequences and conditions. Again, the 3Cs were severe and were in effect at that time as well. It was what fascism and foolish war brought to the Italian people and the country. It was a time of massive immigration to faraway places. It was a time to say good-bye to grandparents and friends.

Our father, who preceded us by a few years to Ohio in America, was waiting in the NYC docks for our arrival. Again, my family and I were gifted/graced with a house to move into in Youngstown, Ohio. My father worked in the steel mill, earning a decent pay with benefits. We had the wonderful large Mill Creek Park with lakes and hiking trails, long winding roads to bike on, and picnic areas. Best of all, as in Italia, we also had a beautiful church, Our Lady of Mount

Carmel, across the street from our house on Summit Avenue. We were happy just to be together again as a family.

I often reflect on those years now. What was important during those years compared to what became important during my college years was like night and day. We change during our teens, and all too often for the worse. It is clearly visible on my own chart on this book cover.

I recall being an altar boy but did not like the discipline required for it. I was the youngest of three children and without any doubt the most spoiled. I recall being brought to St. Joseph Catholic Primary School, encouraged to do so by our parish priest. One block before the school, I recall my father looking at me as we were crossing the street of the intersection while holding my hand and saying, "I was asked to send you here to this school, but this Catholic training could have waited until an older age." Yes, I often reflect on those years. At the time, I did not like being disciplined, and Notre Dame nuns do just that. At first, I thought of the school as a prison.

But after a while, the loving light of those beautiful sisters changes all your negative thoughts and energy into positive thoughts and energy. My favorite was Sister Mary Rose. I remember that I just wanted to grow up and marry her. I close my eyes and still see her beautiful loving smile. I was such a naive foolish child.

I realize today that after my parents, these sisters were the most influential, the most inspiring, and the most important part of my youth in my second journey. I was too young at the time to appreciate that loving light that lightened up my soul. I am forever grateful to them and also grateful that this one time my father's thought about it was wrong.

High school and our teens tend to change us. The hormonal adjustments, a new environment, new friends, they all change us drastically at times. It is no wonder that parents go through hell during these years. As mentioned earlier, I do not think it has to be this way. As an example, I know for a fact that Asian students in their teens do not go through the wild swing changes as American teens. I observed this in teaching university students in Shanghai for about three years. For many reasons, the students are more naive, more innocent, shier, and much more close to their parents, even at the college age. As I mentioned, there are many reasons for this—a more sheltered lifestyle, more time spent on academic study, more restrictions on them, no mingling between boys and girls, etc. There are subtle changes but nothing like that of American teens.

I also know for a fact that these students, although growing up in an atheist communist country, also have the moral imprint and inner voice. They have a good sense of right from wrong and could be very kind and caring, especially toward teachers, parents, and grandparents. So no, American teens do not have to put their parents through hell during their teens.

I think that the biggest issue is the breakdown of sensible communication. Notice the word *sensible*, not just *communication*. Because even if communication does take place and neither side makes any sense, what is the use? If communication was open and trusting, with love as the fundamental reason for it during the first decade of a child's life, the second decade need not be that much different. It is usually the outside factors and outside world that tend to make matters harder and, yes, the 3Cs, negative choices that make life harder for everyone involved.

I remember a time when a teacher would ask in class, "What was the moral of this story?" In other words, what is to be learned from this story, or any story for that matter? What is the right or wrong in this story? With this being thrown out as if yesterday's outdated logic, how are students to learn? When students are at home, no one has the time to teach them. Parents are too busy working to have the money to buy all the latest material things. In modern education, morality has become irrelevant. As a result, again the 3Cs, students think, why follow rules and regulations? We students want to do as we feel right here right now, forget about right or wrong.

Every teacher needs to have a good collective moral base in students to work with. The students in a class, at least, the majority, need to have that good moral base as role models for the good of the whole class. Or else, a teacher wastes most of the time with disciplinary action, in which case, the whole class loses.

There was a time when a teacher was allowed to keep a large wooden paddle on the desktop. The purpose of its presence was understood. As soon as the class got out of control, all a teacher had to do was raise it and let it slam on the desktop. The result was instant silence in the classroom. There was no need to yell or give out detentions. For 95 percent of the time, there was no need to even use it. Very seldom was it used on a student's butt until after class. The teaching resumed, and the students learned. What became of this? This got thrown out the window as well.

A few parents thought that this was barbaric. How dare a teacher punish my child this way! For better words, if I cannot discipline my child, neither can you. Civil liberties, psychologists, psychiatrists, everyone pushed to do away with physical spanking that really never hurt any student that much but instead helped with discipline.

What are the consequences and conditions of it all after all these years? In many of our public schools today, the conditions are terrible. Some children hate to go to school because of their fears and being bullied. "No Child Left Behind" was a joke. Sad to say, some teachers go to work only because of the pay and benefits. Principals are focused on issues related to discipline and unrelated to teaching and learning. We keep throwing more and more tax dollars at the problems, but not much ever changes for the better. Discipline, my friends, without it, little good is accomplished.

The core of these issues start at home: broken homes with broken families—families where there is a fifty-fifty chance that both parents are there for a child. Families where moral consciousness has been lost or buried deep into their subconscious. Families where the moral voice and imprint have become unrecognizable. Yes, the choices, consequences, and conditions are definitely evident for those that have the eyes to see what has transpired.

A child has legitimate concerns about parents. Why are they not here for me? Do they care about me? Where is the love? It is sad, indeed, knowing how many children go to bed each night with this on their mind. What could be worse? The death of a parent? What we parents fail to recognize is that in a way, a separation, a divorce, is like a partial death of a parent for a child. But what does a child know? As parents, we are adults, we have our reasons, our excuses. We will justify our actions. We will get an attorney to clarify it all. No, do not blame me as a parent; others are to blame. Does it ever occur to us that if as a child we were not able to make sense of all this, we expect our child to make sense of it and accept it?

How do we explain to a child that the light of love did not grow in the marriage/family? Remember that an innocent child knows more about love than adults. The younger they are, the more they know of honest and sincere love. So who are we parents attempting to fool? It should be noted that when the love between parents is not true, not authentic, not of light, it could end at any given moment and for any reason, even trivial reasons.

In seeing all this, what is left for a child? How does a child make sense of the senseless? This throws a wrench into the child's development. Hence, a child needs to learn to climb to his/her own summit as early as possible, no later than the early teens. In this, there is hope that the child will understand the true meaning of love, marriage, and their own family in their second journey. In this, they may understand how spiritual light could be lost to them. Here, they may be able to grasp the meaning of the choices, consequences, and conditions of free will.

We need to stop throwing money away on psychiatric therapy as if it is going to cure the absence of spiritual light in us. It does NOT, especially by those who have no significant light within themselves. Our soul's mind needs to learn to understand the choices, consequences, and conditions of free will. Young adults need to learn to listen to their soul's good inner voice rather than talk to a person that is charging three hundred to five hundred dollars per session and counting the minutes to listen to a dark, troubled heart and mind for which they may not have any solutions.

True love is of true light, which is of Spirit that does not die. Ask a couple that has been married for fifty-plus years if you are able to still find one. Their longevity was not coincidental. It was due to the positive choices and consequences that gave them the conditions they experienced in their second journey.

Observe modern pop culture marriages. They are marriages that often have no solid foundation, marriages that have prenuptial agreements, marriages where bank accounts are separated, marriages that stay together because of financial resources, marriages that as soon as the hardships and burdens begin start to experience trouble, marriages that are scientific or academic, marriages that are only cosmopolitan in nature, marriages in which both partners are liberal and able to do as each pleases for pleasure. I could go on and on. You should get the picture. This is twenty-first century American marriage, like everything else—disposable.

Some of us have had chances, seven to eight times, to get it right, but right eluded us each time. The degree of success of any marriage is directly related to the degree of light that each spouse brings into the marriage and the degree in union which that light grows, period. I have examples of this in later chapters.

On a serious issue, the number of parents that have decided to walk away from their church in the past twenty-five years is very troubling. Adults have been dropping out of churches at an alarming rate. A child brought into the world in a Christian family was automatically baptized in the past, not anymore today. It appears that as we became more scientific, we became less Christian-oriented.

But science tells us that darkness, all dark matter, has to do with the absence of light. This is true also in the body/flesh and soul. They are one. A crippled body/flesh, we will leave behind, but our soul continues on. Where to is up to us. Destiny does play a part, but with our free will, we play the biggest part. Family and friends play a minor part. All other outside forces are also involved to a certain degree as allowed.

The seed, fertility, having or not having children, we already know affect the life span and health of both man and woman. Research has shown us what we were created, ISD and ESD, to be and do in our second journey. It appears that without this, we are of less value to humanity, although we do not necessarily have to be. It depends on what other value we add to humanity. Also, after our parents, it becomes our responsibility to keep educating our mind within this brain of ours.

How are we doing with this? Simply put, we are doing a lousy job. We just do not think this is that important anymore. But there is a much more serious issue here. We have been neglecting the spiritual needs of our child's soul. In the past twenty-five years, it has gotten worse, even critical, for some children.

Our child wants to know the mysteries of the universe and their own existence. This is what makes science fiction so popular. Yet what their soul is crying out for is the mystery of their being. This is not found in the science fiction of movie makers but in the church, Bible, and Holy Spirit within the Holy Trinity. They want to know the relationship of themselves with all of humanity, all of nature, and the universe itself. This curiosity is instilled in them. The problem is that we as adults have forgotten this ourselves. Their curiosities should not be denied, nor should their soul's heart and mind be denied the understanding of the importance of spiritual light.

Pain in the body/flesh is a sign that something is wrong. So we see a medical doctor, or should anyway. In other words, we help ourselves by letting others help us. Those with experience can and do help us most of the time. Sounds logical enough, right? A few of us have turned taking care of our body/flesh into an art form. We exercise, we eat healthy food, we get enough sleep, and we get regular physical checkups to catch any disease early. Preventive measures give us a good feeling about ourselves, our intelligence and wisdom. But, very few, a tiny percentage of all humanity, does this even now in the twenty-first century. Yes, even now that science and technology and the medical professionals have proven to us how to keep the body/flesh healthy, only a tiny percentage of all humanity does. The medical charts and graphs show this very clearly. Looking at ourselves naked in the mirror and seeing so many others like us, we begin to see what a piss poor job the majority of us really do.

Even here in Italia, I see, for example, people smoking tobacco cigarettes for fashionable fools the latest vapor gadgets—young and old, male and female, all smoking in a country that prides itself in living a healthy lifestyle. Yes, even developed countries have undeveloped minds. In China and undeveloped countries, I could understand, but in the major developed countries? Such is the fate of humanity that doesn't care in the way we harm our body/flesh. The question is: why?

Psychologists will have a lot to say about this, but when our child tells us, "I don't care," which is a common theme among our teenagers these days, we should see that the problem goes much deeper. Basically, this is saying, "I don't give a damn about myself or you as a parent and what you think." This is the warning sign that the soul is hurting. A healthy soul cares about the body/flesh it resides in. When our soul does not, it's a sign that the doors to that spark of light within our soul's heart tabernacle are closing. In better words, the soul is losing light and not being replenished. An unreplenished soul losing light could starve to death. This should be a red flag that our child is in danger. Unheeded, this sign could eventually become fatal in suicide that, although carried out in the body/flesh, is rooted in the soul. This is the reason to stop everything and focus on our child.

When a child is not given the foundation to support their soul with spiritual light in the most critical times of being tested, as we all are, the results could be disastrous. Is the moral voice and imprint enough during these times? Maybe, if they, at least, reach out to others. But what if no one is there? What if everyone is too busy with themselves? A child needs to be able to trust in that spark of light within their soul's heart tabernacle to help them through the worst and darkest times. This requires a degree of faith. There are times when only calling on Gesu Cristo will help us through. There are witnesses to this who have experienced hell itself. Do we care enough to read their stories? We should, if not for ourselves, at least, for our children.

How responsible have we been with this? Study the suicide rates of teenagers and early college ages in America in the past twenty-five years. We are currently in the most difficult times for teenagers. The influences on them could easily overwhelm them as many are negative, and even contain evil darkness. Notice that the wealthiest countries seem to also be the hardest hit and hurting. In poorer countries, teenagers are fighting for the basic necessities for their second journey.

In America, teenagers get easily bored with the same routine day after day. Same schedule, same monotonous everything is what they feel. Teenagers think, is this it? Is this all that life is about? So they explore alternative lifestyle trends, generally unhealthy pop culture youth trends that others have explored and gotten hooked on.

What is one of the trends? There are many, but by far the worst and deadliest is that of satanic cults. So what happens when a demon is allowed to enter a child's body? As mentioned, I believe that we are of three parts: 1) body/flesh; 2) soul with our moral voice and imprint or ID; and 3) spirit, that spark of light from the Holy Spirit that sustains us.

When a demon is allowed to enter a child, it enters the body/flesh. This is the reason that every child needs to be baptized. The original exorcist movie was a true story in which once the priests realized that the child was not baptized, they baptized the child in order to expel the demon.

The Roman Catholic Church has the experience in these matters and the knowledge that much more is needed to protect a child. A child needs the sacraments that the Roman Catholic Church has to offer as assistance for the child's second journey.

Note that during our first journey within our mother's womb, we are safe as long as our mother is not involved in any kind of witchcraft or demonic practices. People who are involved in such insane activities have no idea what they are dealing with. They are risking both their soul and that of their child.

Who can rescue a person who willingly accepts a demonic spirit into their body/flesh? Remember that evil spirits work through the body/flesh to reach the soul to help extinguish good spiritual light. Or better put, they help close the doors to the soul's heart tabernacle and spark of light that sustains our soul. Worst case, have the spark return to the original spiritual light source. The spark of light does not die; light travels and is forever. So what are we left with after this happens? A soul with very little light or worse, without light and with very little energy or without energy at all. We have a moral imprint/ID that has faded away, unrecognizable anymore or worst, vanished. We have an inner voice that is inaudible or worse, gone silent. We become basically a body/flesh, a corpse that is essentially dying or almost dead.

Remember that in our first journey, the responsibilities are on our parents to protect us from evils. In our second journey, they could still protect us with baptism and the sacraments until a certain age or certain point. Finally, as adults able to exercise our free will, we become responsible for ourselves, our second journey, and our soul. When an evil spirit is able to enter a child, the parents are to blame for not taking the necessary precautions. Hence, a priest who is trained by the Roman Catholic Church is needed for exorcism of the demon. Whereas adults, when we willingly accept demons into our body/flesh, we have ourselves to blame. But the question is, who will rescue us? We made our choice. Again, the 3Cs are in play. This is the reason why satanic cults are so dangerous and need to be recognized for what they are. Only the good spiritual light of our soul's mind can neutralize and stop their influence. Yet the ignorant, foolish, idiotic, stupid morons who have no clue of what they are getting involved in have to try to see for themselves. The negative 3Cs could be deadly killers for body/flesh and soul.

We should know by now in physics that light and darkness cannot and do not reside in the same space. So the question should be: what becomes of that spiritual spark, light, that sustains us when we allow darkness to enter our body/flesh? How does our soul survive? How do we continue? I believe that when this happens, our spark of light in the tabernacle of our soul's heart locks up for safety until the danger is over or our second journey is over. But the question is, aren't the body/flesh and soul one? Yes, but our soul is also able to separate from the body/flesh when necessary. I think that our soul's mind and Holy Spirit within our soul's tabernacle is capable of doing this. Could things change? They could; we should keep in mind that our choices, consequences, and conditions could change right up to the last split second before our death. It is always possible, especially with the intervention of other forces of good light.

We also need to keep in mind that what evil or Satan is really after is our soul. With that, the body/flesh follows, spiritual light leaves our soul, our moral good voice and imprint are gone. Hence, we no longer have a true ID. You think that this is a joke? Talk to parents that have been through an attempted suicide by their child or worse, a fatal suicide. You will see that this is NO joke. Talk to parents that have been through an exorcism and the hell that they went through for their child as the last resort, and you will not laugh about this any longer.

For those of us who have accepted a smaller degree of evil darkness, our soul's amber condition will require serious forgiveness, penance, and atonement. This has been a difficult section to write. I hope that I have been clear about it. I have done my best. Also, more will be discussed later in regard to the third journey of heaven, purgatory, and hell.

In ancient times, the metaphysical church was an actual sanctuary for people that were persecuted. So also, the Tabernacle of the Holy Eucharist of Gesu Cristo was and continues to be sanctuary for souls in distress.

There is so much talk these days over the Internet about mind over matter, mind to mind, intentions of mind, etc. But what is intention? What do we put our mind to do? Hmm, all of a sudden, our free will becomes "intention"? The question is, where does intention originate? In our mind? Yes, mind, not brain, as the brain is simply the vehicle, the metaphysical for mind to function. So where does mind come from? The soul, the soul's mind. Now where does soul come from? Did we create our own Soul? NO, we only helped in the process of creation with conception and childbirth. Is our soul a process of evolution? Spiritual light does not proceed from evolution of which is of ISD, Intellectual Spiritual Design, as the metaphysical body/flesh. Spiritual light always was, is, and will be perfect. There is no need to evolve what is already perfect. The metaphysical, body/flesh, is imperfect.

All souls are from one source, one light. What source, what light? The same light source that lights up all life forms, the light of the Holy Spirit. Where does the Holy Spirit dwell? Within the Holy Trinity of spiritual light.

We in ourselves were/are the 3Ns—Nothing, Niente, Nada—and will always be the same without the Holy Spirit of light. How do we comprehend this? By climbing to the summit of spiritual knowledge for our soul's mind to develop in light, that light of the Holy Spirit that is all good knowledge. Notice that I wrote "good knowledge" because there is the opposite knowledge of evil or darkness as well.

Again, what are our intentions of free will?

Some of us have intention to do evil and be evil. In this, we fall into the pits, the sewers of dark knowledge. Rather than grow in light in our climb up to the summit to the mysteries of light, we diminish the little light that we have in order to be in the darkness of evil.

You want proof of this? Test this out on yourself, test this out on people that commit hideous crimes against humanity. Now compare this to the saints whose intentions were, are, of kindness, caring, compassion, and healing.

We need to think of our life's force as coming out of a bonfire. That spark coming out is our soul's spirit that sustains us. This spark needs to catch fire, become a flame attached to and within our soul. Only in union with the bonfire are we able to achieve this. The Holy Spirit is the bonfire, of course, but unlike the metaphysical bonfire that burns off, the endless source of light and energy does not burn off. Not only our soul needs to be attached to this spark within our soul's tabernacle but, as our natural heart needs natural oxygen, so also our soul's heart needs the oxygen or breath of the Holy Spirit continuously, regardless of our power of intention of mind.

Our soul's mind is limited to the light it receives from the light of the Holy Spirit. Try it, try to have your intention of mind stop your nicotine, alcohol, heroine, and every other bad addiction. See the results that you get. Not convinced, try this: get the minds together of a dozen people in one room. Now have all of them set up their intentions on a child brought into the same room whose body has been invaded by a demonic spirit. Try performing with all combined intentions to expel that evil spirit. Try this by all means and see what the results will be.

Even good intentions of our soul's mind/free will come to the 3Ns—Nothing, Niente, Nada—without being in union with Gesu Cristo, who has been delegated authority over all humanity and evil spirits.

Notice that even evil intentions of free will/wills of our soul's mind may or may not produce the results what we want. Evil spirits are always waiting and ready to accommodate us with our negative dark intentions. Here also the Holy Spirit and archangels are in charge to allow or disallow the act/actions to take place. It depends upon the consequences and conditions, if needed, for the greater good.

Good fruitful intentions of our free will, although less restricted, still are accommodated or not depending on, again, the 3Cs—choices, consequences, and conditions. It depends on not only how they affect us but all those around us as well. Use your mind to meditate on this for a while. It is not that the Roman Catholic Church does not teach us this. It is that we refuse to accept parts of her teachings that we do not like.

From the moment that Gesu Cristo gave the apostle Peter the keys to his Church/bride, all mysteries of the first and second journeys of our soul have been gradually revealed through the Gospels, apostles and the Roman Catholic Church. We have been given a glimpse of heaven witnessed by a few. In faith, hope and trust, the promised mysteries of the third journey of heaven will be revealed. But this needs to be earned. In climbing our summit and being grateful for the opportunity and grace to do so, we begin to grow in light.

It is sad, but the majority of us do not get it even after a brush with death. We refuse to get it, refusing to accept it. Not only this, but we do not even believe in the intercession of good souls such as the faithful, the saints, and our Blessed Virgin Maria that try to help us. Our guardian angel, archangels can help us, but who are they again?

Notice the paintings, the sculptures within the Roman Catholic Churches, especially in older churches. Stop in, take a look, teenagers to adults, regardless of religion, denomination or whatever. Observe that Gesu Cristo is constantly shown holding and pointing to his heart. This is a sign, a guide that all answers to all mysteries of our soul are hidden there within his heart, his spiritual heart within the Holy Trinity. So also, our soul's mind needs to start within our soul's heart and tabernacle in order to begin to understand the mysteries of ourselves in relationship to Gesu Cristo, the Holy Trinity, humanity, and all life forms.

CHAPTER *Three*

A Self Analysis—Where Am I?—Quick Quiz—
3Cs: Choices, Consequences, and Conditions—
Charting and Tracking Our Soul's Light

In this chapter, we teenagers are entering into adulthood, eighteen to twenty-one. We are entering our third decade of life. How are we doing? We slowly begin to realize that our parents are becoming less and less restrictive of us, even less demanding. It appears that a load is being lifted off of their backs. It was hard at first, but now they seem relieved that we are becoming responsible for ourselves. But are we? This is more noticeable with us boys than girls. It reminds me of Verdi's opera, *Rigoletto*, where the father of a beautiful early twenties daughter tries so hard to shelter his daughter from the evils of the outside world and men. He, being a court jester for the duke, knew how to joke around with the men of the court and make fun of them. At the same time, he knew their wicked ways. It turned out that these wicked men, finding out about his daughter, kidnapped her to play a joke on the jester. Read the libretto to find out the consequences and conditions.

Yes, the years, seemingly slow at first, gradually seemed to have passed rather quickly. Some of us are not sure what to do next after college, trade school, apprenticeship, or military service. Do we need to start working? Do we want to travel while we can? Do we want to start to settle down, get married, and start our own family?

Some of us are sure of what we want to accomplish. Some of us are not sure. Some of us will take it one day, one month, one year at a time. After all, we are young, we have our whole life ahead of us. We are on fertile ground to try various things. We believe that we could take a few years of trial and error. The thought enters our mind, perhaps we should focus on fast money and retire young. Or maybe we could help change the world with a new idea, a new invention, a new technology. Silicon Valley, Wall Street? We have so many options, so many choices here in this great land of opportunity. America, America, America, land of freedom and capital, lots of capital!

Or do we? I recall a couple of boyhood friends that did not make it to their twenty-fifth birthdays. Yes, it sent shock waves through me. I never imagined these sort of things could happen at our young age. I had felt at this age almost invincible, able to do anything and everything that I set my Mind/intentions on doing. Great Expectations. I should have known better. In my early teens, I already had one brush with death, the 1st of three, when sled riding down a very steep hill and crashing into a pole. I rolled off the sled at the last second to avoid a head on collision. The impact to the right side of the sled still knocked the air out of me. Gasping for air, I was stunned, what was happening to me? I could not catch my breath, I could not breathe. Slowly, after what seemed forever, I was able to breathe again. Scary, yes, but was I grateful that day? NO, I did not think to even be grateful in my foolish youth. A head-on collision could have easily caused brain damage. Or as happened to General Patton in his automobile at the end of World War II, I could have become a quadriplegic, similar to his injuries, an accident, planned out or not.

Were these events coincidental? Only from the summit do I know better. This is how most of us in our youth are. Notice on this book cover where I was tracking at that age. I was losing spiritual light rapidly, spiraling downward, and continued to do so until the age of thirty.

In our early twenties, our life could go into our choice of direction. Yes, there are outside forces that will attempt to pull us this way or that way. There are people, family, friends, that boyhood friend, girlfriend that pull on us in their direction. There are events, circumstances, conditions that we cannot escape. But for the most part, our free will really kicks in now. Here the 3Cs, our choices give us our consequences that result in our conditions, which really begin to define us. For example, the expression, "boys will be boys," lets boys that are not really ready to be grownup play the field for a few more years—for some of us, many more years.

We think, why not? Especially with the wave of changes from young women that decided to join the sexual revolution, America became and is a playground. Young women overnight became promiscuous and wanted to just play, explore sex, and get crazy just like the boys.

It was a time for motorcycles and convertible sports cars and no worry about anything.

Yes, we had our pride, our ego, and were we not so smart? We had everything figured out, we had all of the answers. We were unfaltering, unfailingly so sure about everything. After all, we were the scientific generation, we had life wired. This was the late twentieth century. The twenty-first century, we have our high-tech smart phones that seem to have all the answers in the palm of our hands. They are called smart phones, but who is really smart? Notice that the makers of these phones are causing us to change from old models to new models often, too often. This is okay if we have stock in that company. But other than that, do we really need all the new data every six months? Do not get me wrong, I am amazed with my smart phone/mini-computer that has more data than was required to get us to the moon and back. I wrote most of this book with a smart phone, editing and all.

Ah, but at the summit, our current time makes me think of historic Babylon—yes, Babylon and the pride and ego of a generation who thought so highly of themselves. A generation of pop culture that thought nothing was sinful—not gluttony, not any sexual desires and with their pride and ego, and certainly not building their own tower of knowledge to prove their intelligence. Sounds familiar?

Never in the history of humanity have we been so connected with humanity, i.e., with IT, and at the same time also disconnected. With modern technology, we are so connected to seemingly endless data. But how much of it is really needed? Some of it is useless information about gossip and celebrities that only wastes our time and energy. Much of it is connected to advertising that just wants to sell us something, anything, whether we need it or not. We do not even realize it, but in the process, we are being manipulated and brainwashed into making decisions, not fully conscious of our choices. We think that we are in control, yet we are not. We become victims, unsuspecting customers of corporate advertisements.

IT could and has become a major addiction for millions of people around the world. People try to take control of it but are not able. Children, teenagers, adults, young and old, are addicted. I see people driving, walking across an intersection, and even going to bed all addicted. Probably 80 percent of what they think is important is mostly unimportant.

As an example, I recall in Shanghai children, teenagers, parents, grandparents getting together for the Chinese New Year dinners. Here was an important time to communicate with grandparents and learn from their wisdom. Yet what is everyone else doing? They are on their dumb phones and pads similar to the idiot TV tubes of the past. Yes, the sadness is evident on the faces of the grandparents, but no one notices. They are busy, dumbfounded with their phones, pads, and other high-tech gadgets.

Again, the 3Cs—choices, consequences, and conditions—are in play here. When the grandparents pass away, as they eventually will, we become filled with regrets. The choice was disconnection; the consequences, loss of communication and wisdom; and the conditions, loss of closeness and affection. This is becoming more and more frequent across the globe. Between supposed lovers, friends, and family members, we are disconnecting at a rapid pace. The losses keep mounting until we do not experience each other anymore. The eye to eye, the facial expressions, the body language, the voice and the touch are disappearing. The senses of the body/flesh are intended by ISD/ESD to gradually serve the senses of our soul. Without this, we do NOT develop properly.

From the summit, all of this is clearly visible, and we know why. When we disconnect from the light within our soul's tabernacle, we disconnect from our true ID and gradually from everyone that we love. In this, with our negative addiction to IT, we are not able to see it as such. Far worse, we are not able to control it. It controls us. Sounds familiar?

Thank goodness for allowing us to be tested in natural disasters, hurricanes, earthquakes, tornadoes, typhoons, and uncontrollable viruses with unknown cures. This is what brings us face-to-face with our reality, our foolish pride and ego, our fragility, and our 3Ss— stubbornness, stupidity, and sickness.

At this point, I need to write about a few of the choices that we make as young adults. I will write about sexuality, male and female sexual intentions, and lifestyles.

I want to make it clear that I am not anti-feminism, anti-LGBT, or anti-anyone. NO, but I am anti-evil and anti-darkness. I am anti-cold war that exists between man and woman. I am anti-hate and anti-revenge. Again, it's my hope that this book helps, someway, somehow to let us see how we lose spiritual light.

Imagine if you will our sun ceasing to give us light. All life forms on earth would gradually die, including ourselves. Forget about science fiction and going to a different planet. Well, the light of our soul and that source of light that sustains us all is far more important. I am basing this loss on my own experience and knowledge as well as that of friends, family, and relatives. This book is not intended to criticize, judge, or condemn anyone for their choices. It does hope to let us better understand the consequences and conditions of the choices that we make.

For our early twenties or younger, recall the insurance companies statistics about our abuse of just about anything. Yes, we are very vulnerable in this period because we are in between having left home or control and security by our parents and beginning on our own. Yet few of us are mature enough to do so, the perfect combination for being tempted by evils and a storm.

Let us explore a few of the choices that are more common in modern-day pop culture.

For me, who was constantly distracted at YSU by pretty women because it was/is one of my weaknesses, it is very tempting. It brings to mind the book by Oscar Wilde, *The Portrait of Dorian Gray*. The movie made a lasting impression on me. In the movie, Dorian makes a deal with the devil so that his sinful ways are shown or brought out on a canvas portrait of himself. While in flesh/body, he stays as young-looking as the original portrait. Finally, after such a sinful life, the portrait shows his very soul filled with evil. In a rage, Dorian destroys the portrait and, in doing so, himself.

At this point in our lives, we are all able and often do imitate Dorian Gray as Dorians and Dorianas. What's the problem? We do not see what our soul looks like, so the purpose of the chart in this book is to, at least, have us begin to see our soul's condition on our own chart. Recall that our overall health is dependent on the health of our soul's heart and mind. The best modern medicine, even with the knowledge of our genetic/DNA code of our physical body/flesh, is limited to the metaphysical by ISD, Intellectual Spiritual Design. It cannot compensate for our soul's sickness due to loss of light.

We can all be a little crazy when evils enter our soul's mind. Let us never forget, though, that the 3Cs are always in play, our choices of free will become our consequences, resulting in our conditions. From the summit, we learn that our choices are allowed to take place because they will become our tests. At times these tests come in gradually and at times like fast-moving storms. As an example, a young man or woman getting high on weed/grass. It seems harmless enough, even legally allowed for medical purposes, but when the high becomes an escape from reality, causing us to fail in our responsibilities to ourselves and others, it becomes a trap. Going further, when the weed high becomes not high enough, and we begin to use stronger drugs, it could lead to a fatal overdose. This is how evils work. If in the testing process we seek assistance with our bad addictions that we accepted to begin with, we can help change our ways. If not, because our pride and ego seems to interfere, it ruins us. It brings into our lives and the lives of family and friends suffering and devastating torment.

It doesn't matter what social class, status, race, nationality, or religion. At this age, we are all vulnerable, but most of all, those of us that have a weak soul's foundation of light or those of us that have turned off our soul's good inner voice. The strength and love of those who possess light in their souls can help us through the darkest and most difficult times. Will we listen? Most often, we will not!

Another choice that is common is continuing our education. Why not, especially with Mom and Dad paying for it all? I know that continued education could be very beneficial to help our development and career, but there are those of us that are afraid of the working world. We prefer to stay on campus another two, four, six-plus years; we like it here. I am being a little sarcastic, yet I have known people who want exactly that. It has to do with fear of change, fear of responsibilities, or fear of this or that. Yes, those childhood fears are back to haunt us. We think that we will have a hard time functioning. Yes, these fears should have been shed while we were growing up. They were not. Who do we blame? It's too late to blame anyone. We now have to help ourselves receive help from the fearless, those that only have one fear, the healthy fear of losing the light of the Holy Spirit by not doing what is pleasing in his/her eyes. All fears are mostly rooted in the ignorance of mind due to the absence of good knowledge that is rooted in spiritual light. The absence of light is rooted in the absence of faith, which is rooted in our 3Cs—choices of free will with the consequences, becoming an ignoramus, and conditions, all of the fears within our souls.

This is compounded with one fear ushering in more fears, hence, a possible nervous system breakdown of our body/flesh. Notice the chain of events—lack of energy due to lack of rest due to lack of sleep due to stressed conditions due to lack of peace due to a lack of light due to a lack of faith. Question? What is faith, hope, and trust? Faith, hope, and trust are the best parts of our soul's heart and mind that seek light.

The greatest of fears is that of the death of our body/flesh, which is foolish because sincere faith conquers even the death of the body/flesh. But this is for a later chapter.

Another not-so-common option for those of us that were poor in our education is Hollywood or Las Vegas or NYC. Each day there are countless young adults that head out from all across America to these three destinations. They want to make it big, fast, and have their fifteen minutes of fame. Upon getting to these destinations, they quickly find out how extremely difficult it is to make it there. So what are they to do? Go back home? The pride and the ego are against it. But what are pride and ego anyway? Pride and ego are those part of our mind, of our free will that say, "I can do it." When realistic, it is capable of amazing dedication in our professional and vocational accomplishments. But when looking realistically, we see that maybe, just maybe, we made a foolish mistake; pride and ego could hurt us and hurt us badly. Pride and ego attached to our soul's heart could produce miracles or could be dangerous, even fatal. We refuse to admit that perhaps we were wrong. Away from family and friends, our pride and ego could make us do things that before leaving home, we would never consider doing.

So we tough it out. We will get part-time odd jobs. We will pay for classes to improve our skills. When desperate, we will get facials, manicures, pedicures, vaginal and anal cosmetically improved looks. We will dye our hair any color for that second look from a director, producer, or anyone that could help us make it. Penis enhancement, breast implants? Can we afford it? If not, have someone else pay for it. A wealthy patron—how hard could it be to go to bed with someone that could help us? Morality? We left that behind a long time ago. This is Hollywood, baby, the selfish and self-centered capital of the world.

Having spent a little time in all three of these destinations, I have seen the faces, the signs of stress, anxiety, worries, expressions of uncertainty, gestures of uneasiness, body language that show signs of defensiveness. I have seen unimaginable tattoos on our young adults trying to say something, but what? They may not know themselves. It is as if these tattoos define who they are. These tattoos with ink, at times poisonous or causing skin infections after being put into their living, breathing skin, is popular culture.

Southern California is, without any doubt, a natural paradise on earth. The climate, sea, deserts, mountains, parks, natural beauty of the plants and floral are awesome. The aesthetically beautiful homes of Beverly Hills and Rodeo Drive boutiques are inspiring. But due to the accepted vices or evils of some of the people there, it's also a false paradise of lost souls having comprised the little light that they had. Behind the gates of some of those multimillion dollar mansions are chest drawers full of cocaine and paraphernalia, dirty money, jewelry, and, yes, guns should anyone try to expose us.

Yes, when the cameras stop rolling, what else is left? There is no more lighting, no more applause, nothing else to feed our pride and ego. We need to be a burning, shining, shooting star. But what is to become of us when the time comes that our fame is over, our body/flesh old and wrinkled? We get no calls to act, and our adrenaline doesn't work anymore. We have to meditate on it all. Was it worth it? Is it what our heart had hoped for?

There is probably a larger ratio of souls losing light in Hollywood than in any other city in the world. Las Vegas and New York City are not far behind.

Who encourages our pride and ego the most when we are definitely in the wrong regardless of the occasion? Lucifer, the fallen archangel, and his cohorts of angels that followed him. Think of this as mythology? Think of this as BS? Think again. A foolish person recently asked Pope Francisco if he believes in the devil, and his answer was a definitive YES. What all evil spirits want is to remain hidden. In this, our soul's mind and heart do not believe that anything is evil or wrong to do. Nothing is wrong, not pedophile acts, not polygamy, not incest, not forced slavery, not thefts, not prostitution, not criminal activity, not adultery, not abortion, not anything at all. Of course, this is their goal, to tempt us to do everything that will cause us to lose light. This is the reason for this book. When we figure out how we lose light, we figure out how to avoid losing light.

Outside of faith/light, we are all on the road of self-destruction. Through our body/flesh, this takes place. It may start off very subtle at an early age, like being on a calm river raft. But slowly, gradually, it gets worse and worse, we get caught in a moving current without a life vest, and the dangerous rapids unseen are ahead. We are not able to see ahead until there, unaware that there are the falls with a steep drop into the rocks below to self-destruction. We go along, all excited with others that help destroy us. This is the drop-down on our soul's chart. Instead of climbing, we fail and fall. We are so dumbfounded that we do not stop to consider going to the shoreline. Our con-science, the good inner voice, has been quieted. This procedure has never changed since the beginning of humanity. We think that we have everything under control yet are deceiving ourselves. First being deceived, next self-deception is how it works.

The saints of the Roman Catholic Church had this figured out a long, long, long time ago. Again, this is the reason that I have need of only three books for the guidance of my soul. First, the Holy Bible but mainly the New Testament; after all, why spend so much time on the Old Testament? Doing so is like spending a lot of time on a ceremony rather than getting to the reception or banquet. Second, a good book on the lives of saints in past centuries. They have been there, done the groundwork, done the research, and written about it for us. Third, a modern book on the lives of recently confirmed saints. What more do we want? Yes, their souls are alive and well. Their light continues to assist those of us that turn to them, pray to them. Their job is neverending in their third journey. Pray together, stay together—so true.

From the summit, all is seen for what it is. The sooner we get there, the better. It is only from there that we are able to see our soul's past 3Cs, from three years old and the silly little mistakes to sixteen with all the changes and turmoil to our early twenties, dumbfounded and ignorant. We see that the testing is getting harder as we grow older and the 3Cs are now for adults. Hard choices, difficult conse-quences resulting in, at times, unbearable conditions—this is how we are welcomed into adulthood.

No, as adults, we need not answer to our parents as before. Ah, but our conscience keeps trying to tell us that we need to answer to a much higher authority. Will we listen? A few of us will, most of us

will not. A few of us will even curse the consequences and conditions of our choices as I remember my own father doing often. But even this meant that the communication, the connection to his tabernacle's spark were still active. This is still better than a conscience buried so deep into our subconscious that it is beyond comprehension. If only we could listen to our soul's positive inner voice with our soul's mind ears, where our free will is present.

Our moral imprint is on our soul's heart that identifies who we are. But the positive inner voice is what guides us if we accept to listen. Yes, at times evil voices enter our minds, but our moral imprint of our soul's heart distinguishes the two. It reminds us that we were allowed to be conceived not just to survive and not to do evil but to do good, to grow, and to thrive in light.

Depression itself may be a sign, a warning to stop and listen, to meditate and reflect on where we are and what we are doing with our lives. It is like a rainy day in which sadness has us asking ourselves: am I wasting my life away? Hopefully, the quiz in this chapter and our personal chart could also assist each of us.

The majority of us attempt to get it right. We get married to the person who was not coincidentally there at the right time and place for us. Yet let us explore what has transpired in the past fifty years with the marriage institution in America.

To begin with, the divorce rate is now in the 50 percent range. Compare this to 5 percent in certain countries with planned marriages by family! This means that half of the marriages do not work out. Or, should I say, were easily given up on due to no fault divorce. This was a way by attorneys to a speedy end of a marriage, collecting their fees and moving on to the next couple. No waiting period for reconciliation, no counseling, no guilt, and no fault. A person could easily be able to repeat the process over and over a dozen times in their lifetime. Notice the wording, "no fault," as if to say no failure, no guilty feeling, no guilty conscience.

This was and is very acceptable to pop culture that wants everything today. The saying, "What do you have if 50 percent of all attorneys were to be dumped off in the middle of the ocean without life vests and drown?" The answer: "a beginning." Joking aside, the

American marriage institution is in shambles. This is the reason that the Roman Catholic Church has its own laws of marriage unlike some Christian churches that only want to accommodate people and keep them as contributing parishioners. It is a process, an education of understanding what a couple is getting into. The church realizes that, at times, a couple may marry for the wrong reasons. Since each person is only 50 percent of the equation, in all fairness, the Church has a process for an annulment. But this could take up to two years after a careful evaluation.

As for civil marriages, there are no rules and no standards. So after the 50 percent failure rate, figure out the percentage of the marriages that stay together only for various reasons, say, the children, finances, family, etc. I estimate that to be around 25 percent. So what are we left with? About 25 percent or one in four of marriages in which a man and woman are living according to their marriage vows to cherish and love each other through the good times and the bad hard times. Awful. This is the environment that children are growing up in. I recall the saying in my hometown, "Marry a person who is from Bagnoli Irpino, Avellino, and you also marry into your town, your roots, your faith, your culture, and your traditional way of marriage." Sounds antiquated? Remember the 5 percent divorce rate of certain areas of the world?

Do these percentages tell us something? Our chart will reflect the loss of light immediately during and after a divorce, and so will our mental and emotional health. Our chart reflects the various stages of grace/light and the losses of that grace/light. Grace is not permanent; we could easily lose it, as I did when I lost the love of my life in my late twenties. NO, I was not completely to blame, but my chart reflects my loss of light at that specific time. As our body/flesh bleeds and loses its lifeblood, so also our soul sheds light and loses energy and life. As mentioned before, when we lose light, we also begin to lose all else which is good in our lives. In marriage, when our soul's heart becomes cold, it becomes like the petrified tree in the desert of Arizona or as in the Old Testament, "a hardened heart in marriage as a reason for divorce."

Think about this for a moment. The greatest gift to man was/ is a body/flesh, a soul, and a spark of light with oxygen to start functioning. The next greatest gift was a free will for making choices. The next greatest gift was woman to share life with. The same holds true for a woman with man to share life with. Marriage was intended as the bond for the fulfillment of love between the two.

Now study the history of this relationship in the Old Testament. A divorce was allowed due to a hardened heart, adultery, or abandonment. In the New Testament, Christ elevated the marriage institution to the highest level in history. Now study what has happened to the marriage institution in America and other developed countries since that time. We are essentially going backward to before the Old Testament in regard to divorce with no laws, not even the Ten Commandments. This is pop culture marriage of the so-called civilized Christian West.

Failed relationships, marriages, son, daughter, parent gaps of communication are all signs of low tracking of our soul's second journey. A way to think of family is to think of it as a candle opera of lights. We start with one light, get married, and add a second light, have a child, and add a third light, add parents, add four more lights, add grandparents, add four more lights. This is family. Now notice what happens when one light, our light in the candle opera starts flickering. There could be such reasons as unhappiness, discontent, or any number of reasons. Notice how one light, our light, becomes very noticeable and distracting for everyone. It distorts the rest of the lights of the candle opera. Now think of what could happen if this light, our light, were to become extinguished and how it would affect the candle opera as a whole.

This is what happens also in divorce. One effects all in a negative way. Problem: as a selfish, self-centered person, we do not want to see it this way. Is all hope lost? Here again, the 3Cs kick in: choices, consequences, and conditions. Hope is not lost if we come to our senses of the soul. Remember that a candle, even when smoldering, can be relighted, even touching the smoldering smoke with light relights a wick. Could this happen? Yes. Does it? In pop culture, rarely. How do we correct what happened to us so that we do not repeat the same 3Cs in a second, third, fourth, fifth, sixth, seventh or eighth marriage? We have to meditate on our unhappiness, our discontent. Were we this way when we first got married? When did love go wrong and why? Was part of it our fault? Did we accept illusions from others of what happiness and contentment, love and marriage should be? This is complicated, I know.

What is happiness? What is contentment? Compared to whom, to what? Our parents, friends, siblings, celebrities? At times, we want it all but end up with nothing. A few of us think that we are content if we gain sixty pounds after getting married. A few of us think that we are content if we live up to someone else's standards. This could be one of the reasons that a very few of us take a swan dive off of the Golden Gate bridge. I hope that the quiz results and the position we are in will help with this complex issue. A level of contentment is measured not by how much we have in money and material things but by how much of it we are able to do without. Finally, it still has to do with Light, our loss of our soul's light, our spouse's loss perhaps, or both of us. When our light is diminished, a part of the collective whole of our family's light is also diminished. When we fail to get to the heart of the problem, everything goes to hell. Also, for a percentage of us, failing this test brings us an even harder test.

What is next for us? A few of us try to fill the emptiness with noise and artificial fillers with sleeping pills and antidepressants or alcohol or work or any number of escapes. But we cannot escape the 3Cs. They follow us wherever we go. We could go to the moon, and they come with us. They are within us, within our soul. In true reflection, we may realize that we disappointed ourselves. Without a change of our soul's heart, we only continue to disappoint ourselves and others because we will repeat the same mistakes.

In climbing to our summit, we learn that our marriage problems started before we got married. They started with our own soul's decline and loss of light. In marriage, we either in faith grow together, without faith stagnate or stop growing, or, worst case, lose what we had and go our separate ways. Since individually we are only 50 percent of the equation, we are dependent on the other 50 percent for success. Without this, our chances are fifty-fifty for success or failure. The key for success, of course, is faith.

What did we say faith was? It is belief in the light that sustains us, belief in the light of the Holy Spirit within the Holy Trinity. Belief in each other. Trust and put your hope in this; it works.

What happens when faith is absent in a marriage? A classic example of this is Verdi's opera in which Othello's enemies deceive him into thinking that his beloved and beautiful wife is having an affair with another man. All of it is a lie, a setup to enrage Othello, and it works. Anger fills his mind, and regardless of his wife denying it all, even expressing her love and faithfulness to him, he kills her. Upon realizing he was set up and deceived by his enemies, he kills himself. Sounds familiar?

In pop culture, murder, suicide are not that uncommon. Only faith removes the evils of suspicion, assumption, distrust, dishonesty, and jealousy. The light of love removes hate, rage, and murder. But in this day and age of wife swapping, multiple partners, swinging, etc., how is faith, hope, and trust in marriage able to survive? It usually does not.

Love/hate relationship in pop culture is common. We basically love or think that we love the good in a spouse and hate the evils in them. Question? Are we capable of loving and hating someone at the same time? Remember that light/love and darkness/hate cannot, do not, exist in the same space at the same time. So we seriously need to question ourselves.

One of the tragedies of our second journey is that we cannot begin to fully understand who we are until we have destroyed a relationship, a person, our spouse. We kill that person and their care and love for us. This is by far the hardest lesson in life. In America, this is causing us to lose the very meaning of marriage.

So who are we? What have we become? We can only begin to know ourselves, who we have become when we reflect back to our childhood. What has changed in us? For the better or worse? We have all this knowledge upon knowledge of everything, but what of ourselves? Listen to your soul's heart, take this quiz; it should give you an idea of who you were as a child and who you have become.

Make the comparison. Position yourself on your chart. When you start climbing, you may begin to understand not only yourself in relationship with light but also your relationship with the light in everyone else, especially your spouse. In this, hopefully, you can see the true beauty and advantages of marriage. When you do, you will be grateful throughout the day, every day.

There was a time when a marriage was considered a bond between a man and a woman. In pop culture, we have come to regard this as a curse because we don't want anything to stop us from whatever we feel like doing. We do not want a bond; we want to be carefree, to do as we please. So the question should be, why do we bother to get married? In pop culture, we do not want to miss out on anything. We think, "Let me get married and take the good that marriage has to offer and at the same time keep myself in a position to be able to do anything else that I want."

It doesn't work that way. This selfish mentality is what causes our soul's loss of light to start mounting. This is a good point at which to begin counting your losses. Sometimes we need to study this phenomenon. When we are not grateful for all that we have, study what we have lost. Make a list. A great example is those of us as young teenage girls that lost our virginity. The majority of times we will come to the conclusion that it was a waste and great loss to throw away a most precious part of ourselves.

I am sitting here in a coffee shop, having a cappuccino and a dolce in Signa, Florence, Italia. I cannot help but overhear a young couple arguing about this or that. Observing their position, I realize that they are probably lovers. They are getting into a heated discussion, cursing with a lot of emotion, hand gestures, rolling eyes, and other facial expressions. Each is attempting to win the argument. Neither one does, and they are both upset. I begin to think neither one is making any sense. Why? Neither one has a set of rules and standards to base their argument on. Outside of faith, communication does in a way become senseless. Only in light can true communication take place, never in darkness. As an example, the F word is used a lot by our youth. This is always a sure sign of where they are working or are going. It is visible in their irritability, frustrating impatience, and how easily they become annoyed. I see instantly their position in their soul's second journey. No, I am sorry, but I will not interfere. This is today's youth, tomorrow's married couple that will have children. A little sadness comes over me, but I know that the 3Cs will kick in soon, very soon.

I was always somewhat shocked to hear of a marriage coming to an end after so many years. To realize that twenty, twenty-five, thirty years of marriage, the sacrifices, the hardships, the sadness and sorrows are all becoming history. I could not understand why. It is as if a couple was waiting for the appropriate time to end the marriage. What were the reasons? Was it burnout, dissatisfaction, false expectations, what? "It was a mutual decision." That is often the reason for a legal separation. "We both respect each other's choice."

Sounds familiar? These are usually nothing but lame excuses, *rhetoric* might be a better word for it. I know that the odds in America are against a marriage till death do you part. I recall these words, having heard them perhaps a hundred times when serving as an altar boy at marriage ceremonies. I wonder how many of those marriages survived, "till death do you part"? I witnessed the blessings of so many couples in marriage, including my sister's at Our Lady of Mount Carmel Church. It was a time when "till death do you part" was the norm, not the exception. What have we done?

I assisted in many funerals as well—such a sharp contrast between the two. One moment great joy, another great sorrow. I thought this was life and everything in between. The problem is that everything in between has become a mess. There still are parts of the world, in much poorer countries, where "till death do you part" is believed in and lived out. Have prosperity and wealth ruined America? Has putting our faith into M&M (money and material) things been part of the collective problem? Have we been ungrateful? The Italian families of past generations honestly believed in "till death do you part." But this has all changed. Now it appears that everyone believes in pop culture marriage. Has a lifelong marriage itself become an unattainable illusion? NO, but seventy percent of couples entering marriage seem to think so.

Marriage is work, period. The sleepless nights with a sick child. The 24-7 thinking and planning of things out. At times, we burned our own candle from both ends. The doctor appointments, the dentist appointments, the private lessons for music, the pickup here and there. Stress about this, about that. Do people really have heart attacks in their thirties? YES. Mortgages, car payments, bills, bills, and more bills. Yes, parents are having health issues at an earlier age. We are essentially all in the fast lane of life in America, the fastest lane to our grave. These days as a single parent, the 3Cs have shown us what happens when we put our faith aside or behind us. We wanted to show that we were capable of being and doing everything on our own. Now we are exhausted, out of energy, and out of time.

We have medication for this ailment, pain reliever for that ache and pain. We lose count and control of the medications. If only we did not have to do everything on our own. If only we had someone to trust and depend on. Ah, but maybe we did at one time until we let our pride and ego interfere and ruin it all. Life could have been so much easier as husband and wife, as a family helping each other. We could have had much more time to enjoy the simple pleasures of living. Instead, all that is now past history that cannot be changed. Ah, but the present can be changed. The 3Cs, my friends, never forget about them—the positive ones, that is.

Of the 75 percent of marriages that end in divorce, legal separation, this is often their regret. So often this realization is not confronted until it is far too late. Sin today, confession later, maybe, if ever. That has become the belief of couples in modern-day marriage. After the sex toys, the pornographic, thongs and no underwear, no panties, what is left? The 3Ns—nothing, niente, nada.

Here we are fifteen, twenty, twenty-five years later, after a few of the major life choices in our second journey were made. Where are we? Those of us that decided to play the field for another ten to twenty years, now what? Those of us that became workaholic and only wanted to invest, now what? Those of us that decided to freeze our eggs, now what? Those of us that married and divorced or separated, now what? Those of us that choose an alternative lifestyle, now what? For all the rest of us that choose different avenues, where are we?

The two decades of the twenties and thirties are without any doubt the decades that if we made the right moral choices, we could be happy and content for the remainder of our soul's second journey. The same holds true that for the wrong, immoral choices, the rest of our soul's second journey could be difficult and unhappy.

Let us explore the consequences and conditions of our choices. Those of us that decided to play the field, play the game of being single and just have fun, how are we doing? This does depend on male or female. As male, we may still be okay with our consequences and conditions. After all, we are witty, geeky, charming, charismatic, even savvy investors. We are workaholic, but we have a lot to show for it. Are we happy? Are we content? Define happiness and contentment. It is a common goal for a male to try to get their happiness and contentment while still in the prime years of their lives, if all is going fairly smooth in their life. If there are no harsh consequences or conditions to have to deal with, things may seem normal. But are we wearing a mask? Masks are always a sure sign of unhappiness and discontent. The real danger is not so much that we fool others; it is that we fool ourselves. Those of us that are this way do not stop to smell the roses. We do not enjoy the simple things in life. We are not able to be like the child we once were, laughing the same way or singing. We are too busy acting, projecting an image to others of who we are not. We may say nice words, be kind, smile, and even fake a laugh now and then, but inside of us, inside of our souls, it may be a different story. We may be hiding our depression.

Chinese are fanatics about face, so they have many masks. A Chinese person may very well be known for being a lying, deceiving thief and yet put on a mask of being an honest, respectable person. Exposure, transparency of their true self, is protected at all costs. The Japanese, especially males, if dishonored, may take it to an extreme and kill themselves with a sword. They call it a form of art as to the correct way of using a sword to butcher and kill their flesh. The Italians call it *Faccia Rossa* or a red face of being humiliated and embarrassed and often figure out a way to get revenge.

Different nationalities have different customs for hiding the truth. It all boils down to the same consequences and conditions for the soul. There are signs, though, that masks cannot hide. Examples are sleeping more than necessary, being a clean freak, being super detailed about everything, trying to be a perfectionist, or being a slob, etc. These are all signs that reflect a soul's stress. These are signs that something is missing in our lives, and we may not even know what. Take as an example a home that appears to be clean when the windows and curtains are closed. Yet upon opening both and letting the sunlight come in, we see all the dust and every crumb on the floors. Unknown to us, these are outward signs that we are tracking low on our chart.

A few of us have a hint of something being wrong with us, so we try artificial fillers to fill in what we think may be missing. We may get into extreme bodybuilding, exercise, etc.—there are so many false fillers. The best way is to get up at 3:00 a.m. and take a long look at ourselves in the mirror. Ask yourself: what is missing? Is it love? What do we see in our face, especially the eyes? Do we like what we see? Do we see our true self? Do we respect who we see?

This forcing of ourselves to face ourselves in the mirror takes courage. If we have it, we may begin to see who and what we have become after all the past years. If not, perhaps a parent that knows us best or a childhood friend or teacher may help us. We need an honest opinion; only this will help us when we are not sure of ourselves.

For those of us who are female, the same questions apply. But for us, the twenties and thirties are critical, to say the least. This should be obvious, but these days, not much is obvious anymore. Unlike men, our body/flesh clock is different. The majority of us, 90 percent or so, are designed, again ISD, to conceive and help bring new life into this world. We are blessed, gifted, graced, whatever we want to call it. Yet, we are designed to be in our prime and to be a part of this grand design during certain years. The twenties appear to be the best. We are mature, the healthiest, and have the most energy in this time period.

The questions for us will be much more difficult and serious. Did we wait too long to marry? Should we have married when the opportunity came along? Were we too focused on our career? Should we not have frozen our eggs? After all, in our mid-thirties to mid-forties, our body has changed, and we are not as healthy as we were. Can we still conceive? Our employer helped out financially in freezing our eggs, but they also wanted the prime years of our life. Were we deceived? We wanted it all. What is wrong with that? This is America. I am woman. The problem was/is that this is a false liberation. It is an illusion because a true liberalization must occur within our soul from the evils of darkness. The same holds true for men.

The feminist movement encouraged us women with a deceptive self-determination and drive. Marriage could wait. I will to be "pro-choice." Or why even bother with it? As a single unmarried woman, what am I not able to do that a married woman to a man can? Hell, these days I can be with another woman, marry her, and still get what I want, right? It's the law of America, I have my rights. What do we need a chauvinistic man for anyway? Procreation? It is my body, I decide. Besides, today we can adopt children and raise them up with our own standards, our own church standards that are liberal and very accommodating. Question: what would have happened had our own mother in the last century been so liberated with "pro-choice"? There is a possibility that we so-called liberated women of today would not be here!

This brings to mind one of my all-time favorite operas by Puccini, *Madame Butterfly*. I cannot help but cry at the ending of this tragic opera. Madame Butterfly, a traditional young Japanese woman, marries a British naval officer and bears his child, a little boy. Her husband leaves for duty with the promise of returning. The time passes—one, two, maybe three years—with no sign of a returning husband. Madame Butterfly keeps up her hope that her husband will return as promised. Finally, the day comes when he does return, but he returns with a second wife, a British wife. Reality is confronted in Madame Butterfly's aria—all is lost, she was deceived. Her life is ruined, and her son needs to go with the father.

What is left for a scorned Japanese woman? So she does what Japanese people do—she kills herself. Such is the fate of lost love. But was it only one-sided? That of butterfly being true love and that of the naval officer a false love? I think so.

Does this sort of thing happen in modern-day America? It does, seldom, but yes, it does. Only the names and dates change. In fact, the nightly news and statistics tell us that it is far worse, involving murder and suicide.

Now think about the modern contrasting pop culture of Japan. This small country already has a problem with an aging population dying yet not being replenished with newborn babies. There are many factors, but the more serious ones are the attitude of the modern liberal, anti-men, anti-marriage, anti-traditional, anti-customs, and pro-choice women. Add to this the percentage of the lesbian and homosexual community. Add to this the infertility rate, roughly 10 percent. Add to this the children that do not survive to reach adulthood. Add to this natural disasters. Add to this countless other factors, and what do we have? What are the consequences and conditions? A dying nation that must import labor to run the economy. A nation losing identity, language, customs, traditions, etc. As we can or should see, the collective summation of evils/darkness does take its toll. This could happen to any people of any country, including America! Evil does not discriminate. It includes all of humanity. I have more to say about this in the last chapters.

The question is the same for women: am I happy and content with my life? If we are having regrets, we need to stop whatever it is that we are doing. If we are asking ourselves, "What if I had done this or that?" or if we dwell on this type of self-questioning, we have made mistakes in our choices. The self-doubts, the consequences, and the conditions are worse. To find out that we will have difficulties in conceiving because we waited too long will fill us with insecurities, self-blame, inadequacy, and guilty feelings. In not being able to conceive, we may always feel that yearning, that feeling of being unfulfilled as a woman. Motherhood is a life-changing experience.

This brings to mind my favorite opera soprano singer, Maria Callas. Callas had it all or, should I say, appeared to have it all. She most definitely had the voice. In Puccini's *Tosca*, no diva could match her. It is as if she was living the part. She changed how a soprano needs to sing opera, hence, before Callas or after Callas. But let me get back to the point of this little story. Callas also focused on her career in the prime years of her life. She married, never had children, and divorced after an affair with another man, which I am sure that she regretted. In the end, after retiring from the stage, she isolated herself from people in Paris. She passed away a lonely middle-aged woman, past her prime, in the city of lights in her darkness. She was a celebrity that made the news, as if it mattered to her after she died. But the point is that there are thousands of women like Maria that have and increasingly continue to have a similar lifestyle. People may ask, "How are you?" *Tutto bene?* And we generally lie, yes, "*Si, tutto bene.*" Why? Like men, and maybe even more so, our pride and ego prevent us from telling the truth. Or we could be in denial, ashamed to let the truth out. We may be afraid to face our soul's reality. Or are we blaming someone else, like the assholes that we dated? Blaming others is always an easy way out. Another escape is to load up on comfortable things for the body, material things that give us a temporary good feeling. Or as men, we get into extra physical fitness. Or as many women do, we get manicures, pedicures, facials, massages, etc. As the men, ultimately we need to come face-to-face with our reality of darkness that only light can cure.

This self-questioning isn't an easy process. Why? Whom do we compare ourselves to? What do we compare ourselves to? How do we know that the supposedly happy and content friend of ours is not faking it herself? Our own mother may not be of much help. These are tough, very tough choices. Who can we trust? Who has the right answers?

Like the men, we have to go back in time, back to our childhood when we were able to laugh wholeheartedly, innocently, and full of wonder. A time when we had no stress, no worries, and each day was a happy day. But question: how do we get back to those days? We have to unlock and unload. Unlock our soul's heart, where our positive moral voice has been silenced. Unload all of the toxins, the indecent nonsense, the garbage within our soul's mind. In doing this, we rid ourselves of the darkness and allow the light, that light of the

Holy Spirit, to shine into our souls. The moral imprint is there, still visible, still recognizable on our soul's heart. It is not too late.

The faces, images, voices of people continuously come to mind. Why? The what, when, where, and why need to be extracted from our soul's conscience. What is it that we need to meditate on and learn? The answers are in the climb to the summit.

Like men, ultimately, before that hour of desperation, we need to find the courage to look at ourselves in the mirror, face-to-face, at 3:00 a.m. We need to take a long look into our face, into our eyes. What do we see? How do we feel about ourselves? The eyes are the lenses to our soul. The Italians believe in "Malocchio" or evil eyes, meaning that the evils within our soul could be transmitted out through our eyes at people. Superstitious nonsense? Some people swear by it. What do they see?

We read all of the self-help books, self-improvement books, and psychology books, and here we are face-to-face with our reality of a darkness that does not leave us. Now what?

The process of unlocking and unloading starts, as with all else that we encounter, our free will of choice. The answer is and has been within our soul's mind and heart all along. This was always intended to be an easy process. Yet with the influence and help of outside evil spirits, it has become complicated. We have been persuaded to look for alternative solutions to our body/flesh, the metaphysical, the stars, the extraterrestrial for answers. Evil does not want us to figure the way to remove its darkness. In this, we fail to look into our soul's heart where the true answers and solutions are.

We get sidetracked, all of us have and do. This is human nature, this is one of our weaknesses. We need a quiet place to meditate, no distractions, no noise pollution, where we can listen to what our soul's heart has to say. It could be in a church, a forest, a mountain-top, or at sea. Anywhere free of all of the pollutants that prevent us from listening to our soul's heart.

One of my favorite places was and is the Anza Borrego Desert in southern California. Going there alone, sitting high on a huge rock boulder, having a clear view of the desert floor with only the sound of hawks above is awesome. I know that the root of all discontent and unhappiness is in our souls. Our body/flesh just needs basic food, water, and shelter. A little exercise and enough sleep and the body is ready to serve the soul's heart and mind. Our soul needs much more than the basics. Our soul hungers for light, that spiritual light of the Holy Spirit. Our soul knows that in this light is the good knowledge that is needed for sustenance, survival, and eternal life. Ah, this is true, but at the same time, this light informs our souls that we need to climb up to the summit in order to earn and gain this knowledge and wisdom. This climb also includes being tested all the way up. It requires a degree of blind faith, hope, and trust. It requires strength, of which we will be supplied within our soul's second journey. Contrary to this and refusing the challenge to climb, we think that we will have it easier, but we face a free fall on our chart.

This is the reason for the meditation. We need to see what hardships and burdens we have to deal within our climb in order to learn from them. This is the education our soul seeks. Here we rise above all of the physical handicaps of our body/flesh. There are three tools that could help us figure out where we are and where we are tracking on our chart.

The first one is the quick quiz in this book. The answers, when negative, result in the loss of points/light for our soul. These choices that we have been living by caused the drop on our chart. The second tool is the consequences of those choices that actually give us the testing that we mostly bring upon ourselves. As examples, these adjectives describe our consequences, adulterous, criminal, thief, deceitful, liar, cheater, pervert, unethical, prostitute, enslaver, animal abuser, environmental abuser, etc. There are literally thousands of tests. Make a list of the tests that you have. The list is yours to meditate and reflect on in order to contemplate how to handle them. The list is private but could be shared with a trusted friend. The third tool is the conditions of your being: body/flesh and soul's heart and mind. As examples, loneliness, jail time, isolation, symptoms of an incurable disease, distance from loved ones, symptoms of alcohol abuse, symptoms of drug abuse, etc. Here also the list is endless. Again, not to worry, we all suffer from the list of negative choices we make. Most often, they were of our free will and at times by events and circumstances beyond our control. At times, they were also from peer pressure or rotten friends. They could also be intentional and at other times unintentional. It may have been simply from omitting the right thing. We become like sailors that lost position in a storm at sea. Once we find our position, we can begin to get back on course. But let us not wait too long as another storm may be on its way.

Notice that I wrote previously contemplation after reflection and meditation. What does *contemplate* mean? How are we planning on going about to help change the negatives/darkness within our mind that allowed evil to enter as the intruder? Think about this for a moment. In Italian, when a person does not feel well or feels sick, he or she may say, "*Mi sento male.*" At the same time, *male* in Italian also means evils. People also believe that others could give them "Malocchio" or evil eyes. I recall my father using his fingers on the eyes of people while praying for them as if to extract the demons. He believed evils caused headaches and sickness of the body/flesh and of the Soul.

Note also, "see no evil" or avoid evil.

As a society, we collectively have a say in what is considered good or bad, decent or indecent. Examples are prostitution, enslavement, animal abuse, etc. So we pass laws for protection from those that make a choice to still commit these crimes. Seems practical, right? But how about when we get it wrong, like the prohibition of alcohol in the last century? This was an idiotic law.

Now let us consider what we have done with the marriage laws in the past fifteen years. I think that what is being considered as legal according to the high courts currently will come back to haunt us even more as a government, people, and country. After all, our Founding Fathers of the Constitution probably never imagined that the Constitution of America would be the tool used for marriages between the same sex. I believe that if they could look into the future, they would have amended it immediately. Yet collectively a majority of us Americans have accepted the immoral choices of a small percentage of Americans that have persuaded politicians (mainly for the votes) and nine justices to decide what is constitutionally right or wrong. I believe that this is a disgrace (meaning a loss of light) for all that support the ruling. Our fathers would probably turn over in their graves if they could see how the Constitution of America is being used and exploited by people for their own selfish immoral desires of the body/flesh.

Not only that, have we ever stopped to think that what we collectively accept as a society may actually be hurting those of us in question? Think of children that want all sorts of refined filled white sugar snacks, cereal, drinks, etc. Do we give them what they want to keep them happy? No, because we know that the damages (consequences) will ruin their teeth and health. The conditions of rotten teeth, white refined poison into their blood system will wreak havoc on their body/flesh.

What we collectively have accepted from the LGBT community as being sexual acceptable is causing more harm than good. The hijacked word *gay* and peace flag are bogus. Gay pride parades are a celebration of failure by all participants.

I believe that humanity is genetically imperfect, but genetic as in body/flesh includes the brain for the soul's mind to function in. The soul, being of light, is given to us perfect, as light is perfect from our source. The issues are in the body/flesh. It's similar to being born with the numerous diseases of the flesh passed down and inherited. All of the issues in reality become our tests to bear and overcome. Medically, psychologically, we work on the issues. We do not simply accept them for what they are. An example is physical blindness. We try to do everything possible to cure this disease or develop bionic eyes. Without a cure, this becomes the test of the blind. This test is what needs to be passed on the climb to their summit. We are all tested, each and every one of us. The 3Cs, they are always in play, till we die and leave this body/flesh of ours. Actually, the LGBT community has been crying and complaining about issues that are minor in nature and continues to do so. Good physical health is evident in the beginning of their second journey, the tests endured are not so hard. The 3Ss—stubbornness, stupidity, and sickness—develop starting with an immoral lifestyle currently condoned by society. Society is helping bring about the 3Ds—disgrace, despair, and death.

I believe that it all starts with our free will in our soul's mind. This is where evils are at times allowed to enter, even in our dreams. I believe that when the darkness of evil is accepted by us and kept by us, our spark of light that sustains us retreats into the tabernacle of our soul's heart. Here our positive inner voice is quieted. It is as if only our moral imprint is left to stand guard. I believe that darkness and light cannot, do not reside in the same space at the same time, hence, a soul's evil mind but not a soul's evil heart tabernacle. So what unlocks our tabernacle within our soul's heart? Our free will when we rid ourselves of the darkness of evil.

Contemplation, intentions of our mind's free will, is the key that unlocks our tabernacle. Let me also mention that the free will and light of love of other people can also help unlock our tabernacle. Notice that people in a coma respond to the prayers and light of love of those who care about them, whereas the medical professionals, limited to the body/flesh, could be clueless. I also believe that our soul is capable of exiting our body/flesh in extreme conditions when necessary.

How do we unload the darkness of our soul's mind? Start with the answers to the quiz. The negative answers that cause us to lose points and light need to be unloaded. As an example, an answer of falseness involving hate or revenge needs to be unloaded. The same with all the other false answers. This has little to do with our judicial court system. This is within us to deal with. It has to do with our choice of free will.

Take sunlight as a very good example of how important natural light is for us. Some of us get depressed in the winter months when getting the least amount of sunlight. Why? It's a reminder of what our soul needs in spiritual light.

To drown this message out with alcohol or drugs makes it worse, and the holidays can be the worst. After unloading the darkness and having it replaced with light, the problem vanishes with the darkness. Here also the 3Cs are involved—choices, consequences, and conditions. The 3Cs could be negative, causing us to lose light, but when positive and unloading darkness, light enters. Unbeknownst to us perhaps, but this test, to do so, has us reverse the choices, consequences, and conditions of our negative choices. Also interesting is that this is the process of returning our soul back to our childhood self when we were free of any kind of darkness of sin. Finally, this is climbing to our summit and learning, acquiring good spiritual knowledge.

Look at the chart on the cover of this book. See where our soul's light was at between the ages of birth to three. It was between 9 and 9.99. This should be our goal. It is not enough to be a BAC (Born Again Christian). Some of us will become a BAC a few times in our second journey. This only accomplishes an awareness of where we are after meditation and reflection. Contemplation of returning to who we were as children is what is needed. When we do not? For example, since people are involved in our civil judicial court system, what they bring into the court of themselves affects justice. I mean that their own position of their chart affects the outcome of every case. What is taking place in our American civil courts is a shame and at times criminal in itself. I believe that there is a degree of corruption in all civil matters, with attorneys and judges as well. We have found out about attorneys cutting deals, judges taking money under the table, etc. DNA results have set free prisoners serving life sentences, etc. Is this something to worry about? Yes and no.

Why? From the summit, we see that all true justice takes place in our souls. This happens 24-7, 365 days a year every year. This is pure justice, absolute and fair because it involves the gain or loss of light that our soul needs. In a way, we judge, sentence, and condemn ourselves.

Getting back to the children, is justice taking place for them in our civil courts? Absolutely not. We consider ourselves a Christian country and yet are no different than the pagans of Rome before Christianity that allowed abortion as a personal free choice under Roman Law. Thank goodness that we are not throwing the physically handicapped child into the gas chamber as in Nazi Germany, not yet anyway.

Only from the summit are we able to see that children, all children, are gifts of grace. Those not allowed to enter this world from conception because of our civil laws will need to be accounted for sooner or later. Those of us that are responsible for creating, carrying out, and enforcing these laws will need to answer to these crimes.

The children that come into this world who are severely handicapped physically are also gifts of light. My heart goes out to these children because I know that they did not make a choice to be in a body/flesh that at times their soul is not able to function in. These children suffer in silence with their pain. I admit that this bothered me for many years as I refused to accept the reasons. I see them now as the lambs suffering for our sake, the sinners of this world.

To hear those of us crying and complaining about trivial issues with our consequences and conditions of which we have due to our choices is pathetic. At times, we need to make a trip to the children's ward in a hospital to see what tough testing is out there. This might help us to be quiet, accept our minor tests, and start climbing to our summit. Let us think this over.

Notice that when our soul's heart and mind are void of spiritual light, it quickly affects our natural body/flesh. Our body's brain, heart, and entire physical condition deteriorate. Hence, the health of our soul needs to be our first priority at all times.

One of the great tragedies of life is a failure to love and be loved. This happens when light is lost, as light and love are one. Without light, we are not capable of loving or being loved.

## Self-quiz

This self-quiz could be taken at any time by anyone, although it is not for those of us that are convicted or unconvicted criminals, unless we are paying or have paid our dues and changed our ways of living. The quiz's answers are all either true or false. There are no right or wrong answers, just answers that position you on your soul's chart so that you may start to track yourself.

You start with 9.99 points, and you can only lose points, not gain points, on the same quiz. The quiz is not timed, and it has something to do with human decency and the standards of decent living. Remember that the final score represents the light of your soul: .01 to 9.99 on your chart. There is no pass or fail until the last split second of your life's second journey. The score could change a little bit or drastically at any moment for the rest of your life. The rules are: 1) Try to be honest with yourself. 2) Do not try to figure what answers will let you score high, or you will not get an accurate representation of your soul's light. 3) The answers should be spontaneous; no real need to have to think about it for a long time. 4) The quiz is for decent law-abiding citizens. Those who accept and live in evils, you already know where you are tracking, unless you are so dumbfounded and do not know. Then by all means, take it. 5) The answers are weighted, meaning that some are more important than others in the degree of light lost. 6) The answer sheet will have minus 0.1, 0.2 or 0.3 for each false answer. 7) After the quiz, do not panic. Only a tiny percentage of us score high. 8) We will cover the answers and the reasons for the loss of light in this chapter or later chapters. All of the reasons are covered throughout this book. 9) The quiz involves everyone regardless of race, religion, or beliefs. Let me give an example of why a false answer deducts points. Let us say that the question is, "I do not smoke tobacco." Had you been a smoker, you would answer false and lose points. Now you may ask why? It is because those of us accepting light know full well that tobacco smoking is harmful to our body/flesh and that our souls need a healthy body/flesh to function. After thirty to fifty years of research on the harmful effects of nicotine addiction and cancerous consequences, we should know better. Hence, we don't really care for whatever reasons.

New knowledge upon old knowledge for our own good or new stupidity upon old ignorance, what is our choice? I am surprised that Italians are just as guilty as Americans in this area compared to undeveloped countries. I see adults, teenagers, boys and girls, all smoking. The economy must not be that bad if these people can afford an expensive nicotine addiction that is harmful to their health and well-being. Notice how the 3Cs—choices, consequences, and conditions—are at work here. You may now start answering the quiz.

## Quiz Questions

1. I am always honest. T or F
2. I always forgive. T or F
3. I am charitable at heart. T or F
4. I believe in meditation. T or F
5. I am a modest person. T or F
6. Depend on others, okay. T or F
7. I respect all forms of life. T or F
8. I am grateful every day. T or F
9. Hate, revenge, NO. T or F
10. I believe in true justice. T or F
11. I believe in my free will. T or F
12. Life is a responsibility. T or F
13. I get emotional. T or F
14. I am at peace. T or F
15. I never despair. T or F
16. I have meaning. T or F
17. I am not suicidal. T or F
18. Glad to be born. T or F
19. Moral sex. T or F
20. I am not cold to anyone. T or F
21. I am opinionated. T or F
22. I try my best always. T or F
23. Life is NOT a joke. T or F
24. I am NOT wasteful. T or F
25. I am sympathetic. T or F
26. I am capable of loving. T or F
27. I Love children. T or F
28. I like pets. T or F
29. The future is important. T or F
30. I care. T or F
31. I believe in mysteries. T or F
32. I have weaknesses. T or F
33. I am trustworthy. T or F
34. I believe evils exist. T or F

35. Defensive war, okay. T or F
36. Science is minor. T or F
37. Money is basic. T or F
38. The past is important. T or F
39. I admit my mistakes. T or F
40. I say sorry when I'm wrong. T or F
41. Sacrifices are important. T or F
42. I respect law and order. T or F
43. I need to earn a living. T or F
44. Burdens are relevant. T or F
45. NO to bad addictions. T or F
46. I take care of my body. T or F
47. Life isn't coincidental. T or F
48. Inequalities exist. 1 or F
49. Be tested to learn. T or F
50. I am NOT an island. T or F

## Quiz Points

Deductions for False answers (0.1, 0.2, or 0.3):
1. 0.1
2. 0.1
3. 0.2
4. 0.1
5. 0.1
6. 0.1
7. 0.2
8. 0.1
9. 0.3
10. 0.1
11. 0.3
12. 0.1
13. 0.1
14. 0.1
15. 0.2
16. 0.1

17. 0.3
18. 0.2
19. 0.3
20. 0.2
21. 0.1
22. 0.1
23. 0.3
24. 0.1
25. 0.2
26. 0.3
27. 0.2
28. 0.1
29. 0.2
30. 0.1
31. 0.1
32. 0.1
33. 0.2
34. 0.2
35. 0.1
36. 0.2
37. 0.1
38. 0.1
39. 0.1
40. 0.1
41. 0.1
42. 0.2
43. 0.2
44. 0.2
45. 0.1
46. 0.2
47. 0.1
48. 0.1
49. 0.2
50. 0.1

GRIECO TOMMASO

# DARE TO CHART AND TRACK YOUR SOUL'S 2ND JOURNEY

ORB, NUCLEUS, FATHER , HOLYTRINITY

| | | | | |
|---|---|---|---|---|
| HOME | #10 HEAVEN, BRILLIANT WHITE | | | |
| | 9.9+ BRIGHT WHITE, TIRAMISU | | | |
| BIRTH | 9.0 +SUMMIT/PLATFORM + | | | |
| SOUL'S | 8.9 + SOFT | | | + |
| DEGREE | 8.0 + WHITE + + | | | + |
| OF | 7.0 + | + + | | + |
| LIGHT | 6.0 × | × | × | × |
| | **5.9** × | × | × | × |
| | 4.0 AMBER × × | | × | × |
| | 3.0 LIGHT × × | | × | × |
| | 2.0 × × | | × | × |
| | **1.0** × | | | |
| | .01 DARKNESS TO 0. NO LIGHT | | | |
| AGE | 3/4318 **212**730**404550556**063 | | | |

CHAPTER *Four*

Tools—Change Up—Free Will—Meditation—
Reflection—Perception—Contemplation
and Expectation for Our Third Journey

I n this chapter, we get more details of the tools to work for us. The quiz is a starter, but this is only a beginning. I have written about the 3Cs of our free will for us to become aware of our soul's mind and how it works. These 3Cs will be referred to throughout this book because they are constantly in play. Everything that we say or think, do or fail to do by omission in our second journey gives us our position on our chart and at the same time our soul's degree of light.

This book will not give you ten quick steps to a fast solution to start your climb. It will recommend tools that could help you to stop stagnating. This book will also give recommendation on drastic steps to take when with a sharp descent. For example, prayers bring up from your conscience the inner voice. Also, this book will not be a Bible-banging effort. The Bible is here as a tool for anyone who wants to start with it, especially the New Testament. The choice is always your own to decide. A reminder, there are plenty of people out there that are profiting from the name of Gesu, Jesus. There are also an obnoxious few that seem to go to extremely persuasive measures with their self-righteous behavior. There has been more harm than good done this way. It is a turnoff, and none of us need it.

Notice that in this book, I have been very mindful in using the name of God and Gesu. We know who they are with the Holy Spirit within the Holy Trinity.

Question: are the zodiac signs a tool? Yes, in a minor way, I think that everything in the entire universe is a tool to a degree. This is what brings us diversity. I believe our creator, our source of light, has put everything in the entire cosmos as tools at our disposal to benefit us. Earth is our nursery, playground, and school. Someone with a fatalistic view and without faith is not able to see any of this. Even those of us in the field of psychology and psychiatric therapy fail to understand this without some degree of light from faith. This could be the reason that those of us in these fields have one of the highest suicide rates of all therapists involving the human mind. If we fail to reach into our own subconscious, how are we to reach or help bring out what is in the subconsciousness of others? These fields, to be beneficial to anyone, require a degree of faith in a much higher supernatural spirit force.

Again, we are at most times ourselves the biggest obstacle with our denial and unwillingness to even consider the possibilities of the power of light from faith. This confines us and our very soul's mind. It is like a person who refuses to learn to read and write.

Compared to the age of the earth, we are here but a few minutes to discover the purpose and meaning of our lives. I think of myself as one of the billions of tiny twinkling lights on a lake or sea whose time life in this world is only going to last for a little bit, so we need to stop the procrastination, as we do not necessarily know our moment for exiting this world. I was shown my year of exiting this world and my second journey. Does it mean that it will be so? It may or it may not. It all depends on my 3Cs at that time.

This brings us to focus on predestination. Are parts of our second journey predestined? They are. As an example, our first journey, the nine-month journey from conception, is mostly predestined for us. But anyone who thinks that all is predestined is copping out. Our 3Cs shape everything to where we are. Those near us, with their 3Cs, and unseen forces. Good and evil are also at play at all times. I believe at times we are actually set up in order to make tough choices one way or another. From the summit, this all becomes evident. I am definitely sure about this in my own journey. I am able to see in almost every decade a major setup in which my choice, good or bad, gave me the consequences and conditions with which I had to live.

Two great examples in history of a setup are of Saint Paul and Emperor Constantino of fourth century Roma. Every Christian I think knows the story of Saint Paul. If not, Paul was hired by Israel's temple leaders after the death of Christ to hunt down and persecute the apostles of Christ. He was paid by the temple leaders and assisted by their guards to do this and relentlessly did so. Until one day, on the way to his destination, he was set up to be knocked off his horse. A bright light appeared to him that only he was able to see. We know, of course, that this was Christ appearing to him to put an end to what he was doing. This is about as close to an enforcement of the free will that occurs. Blinded by this experience, he still had to make a choice. Of course, he did with the help of the apostles that he was persecuting. Hence, he went on to become the great writer and witness to Christ. This goes to show us that a person who is possibly tracking near zero on their chart is able to correct it one hundred eighty degrees immediately if they put their heart, mind, and soul into it.

Another great example is Roman Emperor Constantino who, three hundred years after the death of Christ, was involved in another of the many civil wars that Rome endured. This one was different in that it would change the course of history. Constantino was shown the symbol of the cross to conquer and restore law and order. He did, and the rest is history. This was, of course, a major setup for a military leader to make a choice. The consequences and conditions of this choice effectively changed the course of history and the people living within the empire. It changed pagan Rome to Christian Rome and shifted the seat of the empire from Rome to Constantinople named after the emperor. This, in effect, put an end to the persecutions of

Christians within the empire. Yes, there is intervention in our second journey from sources over which we may not have any control. If you study history, you realize that we are not an island, unaffected and alone. Our entire second journey is exactly the opposite of this.

I give some credit to students who, although playing a game by breaking into a cemetery at night, are interested in the mysteries that exist there. This is more than a haunted house at an amusement park; this is death and corpses. What is there? This generally involved a dare of some kind, hence, the dare also in the title of this book. Dare to seek the mysteries of the unknown within our souls. A mystery solved by these students was the light of images on the negatives of the pictures taken with their cameras in the cemetery. A coincidence? Think again. These images may very well have been the images of souls left behind in the twilight zone or purgatory. Is this proof? We know that a camera lens is capable of capturing the faintest light—light that the naked eye is not able to see. A soul's amber light? Something to meditate on, for you to decide on.

We all need a healthy dare to change what we have seen in the mirror of ourselves. Is change possible? We all have doubts, and we have never changed before, how now? As our natural heart pumps blood to all parts of our body, especially our brain, so also our soul's heart becomes the tool that releases light to our soul's mind. Our free will is the tool that starts the process.

We were all destined to be children of light—we were at one time—but the image that we see in the mirror of ourselves is no longer an image of light. This is what needs to change. As mentioned earlier, evils work through the body/flesh to accomplish their deeds. At the same time, the Holy Spirit does as well, hence, the importance of being baptized, having the Holy Spirit upon us. Recall the true story of the exorcist. It is a hard process, and the Holy Spirit does help out in the process, but it starts within ourselves. The Holy Spirit does indeed help those that help themselves, so we have a supreme tool in the way, truth, and light in Christ.

Take as an example two twin boys, same parents, same inherited genetic makeup, same upbringing, same value system, both having the same spark and own moral imprint, etc. One boy makes the choice to accept and do evil, while the other makes the choice to do good. Who do you think has the greater chance to climb their summit fast? The boy accepting and doing good may not be tested as severely. The boy accepting evils will be tested the most and hardest. When hitting bottom, near zero on his own chart, he has the opportunity to turn his life around one hundred eighty degrees and climb up to the summit of spiritual knowledge. This, my friends, is the power of our tool, our free will.

There are books out there that claim we have in our minds the power to create our own grace, our own light. This is total crap. It is an illusion of mind that in time needs to be unloaded. True light has one source, and that is in the Holy Spirit within the Holy Trinity. When humanity creates its own light, it is an artificial light just as we can produce artificial light different from that of the sun. It is not the same. Even if we were able to produce enough artificial light to light up the whole world, without sunlight, all forms of life would still slowly die. This also holds true of the spiritual light that our soul needs.

Previously in this book I have mentioned the pitfalls of being selfish. There is one time in our life when being selfish may be necessary to help us change. That being the case, it is okay. When someone is near zero on their chart, it is an SOS moment. The catch, though, is that the opposite occurs on our climb up to the summit. I mean we turn out to become selfless instead. Meditate on this for a few minutes. We, unlike other forms of life, have a soul's mind operating in a brain capable of meditating on itself. This has always fascinated me to think about why we made the choices we made.

I wrote about the importance of meditation as a tool to help us reflect and contemplate on the changes that need to occur within us. I believe that we need to spend a little more time on the importance of this tool. There are all types of meditations out there—Transcending, Eastern, Western, Southern, Northern, etc. Some of the sages tell us that we need to empty ourselves, emptying our mind or unloading. The problem that I have with these sages is that once we have done this, what are we to replace the emptiness with? Outside of faith in the Holy Spirit, we may be fooled into replacing the emptiness with another evil or the illusion of light. These are the illusions of false ideologies and religions. They are man-made, fabricated mental and emotional hype. We know a tree by the fruit it bears. For example, there are almond trees that bear edible fruit, and there are wild almond trees that bear poisonous fruit as the ones that were used in the Nazi Germany gas chambers.

We all have a tremendous number of mysteries that we can meditate on. Most of us have not even scratched the surface. Like the metaphysical earth, we still have so much to learn. We have not discovered the depths of the oceans, the secrets of the deserts, or all that the mountains have to reveal to us. The mysteries of our soul's heart and mind are hardly understood as with our entire soul. We should meditate with anticipation on the revelation of the great mysteries of light. This is not fiction. For example, I meditate on my reunification of body/flesh with my soul. What will the transformation and transfiguration be like? What will the body flesh look like? In what condition? How will the body/flesh in reunion with the soul again function? All will be revealed in due time.

Meditation is like a computer server—we get out what we put in. Some of us do meditate, but too often we think only of our everyday grind, problems, how to get ahead, how to pay our bills, retirement, etc. Some of us meditate on sexual exploitation, hate, revenge, even criminal plans, so we could see that even in meditation, the 3Cs are at work. This is when our mind starts formulating a plan, good or evil, on that which we choose.

Now imagine, if you will, people all over the world beginning to meditate on peace and love. Contemplate what the outcome could be. Is this daydreaming? Perhaps. Why? Because we are collectively losing light in the world. With this, there is no PAX/Pace/Peace. Occurring events in Africa, the Middle East, and Asia confirm as much. What will change this direction? Most likely when we reach CMM, critical mass misery, of the choices, consequences, serious problems with war and the conditions, miseries.

Humanity has a herd mentality, and at this time, the herd is heading toward a steep cliff. There are signs, this book being one of them, that the course and the direction we are heading in are the wrong way. We should be climbing vertically to our summit, not following someone horizontally into a fall. Breaking away from the herd is not easy. We like going with the flow of things. This happened in Nazi Germany and Fascism in Italia not very long ago. The collective summation of the 3Cs ended in the terrible consequences of death and destruction, conditions that lasted for decades. So if we individually break away from the herd, we are, at least, helping ourselves. To hear someone say put your heart into it is basically saying put your soul into it. At the same time, doing it my way is often the wrong way when we think we can go it alone.

I recommend organizing a plan of action. A plan could also be a tool when positive and constructed according to the guidance of altruistic friends that are caring and loving in their charitable soul's heart. This is not perchance but a plan to meditate on and pray for. We should never forget that we hold the key to the tabernacle of our soul's heart. It is up to us in our free will to either keep unlocked or unlock and have the doors open.

Let me also add that prayer groups in retreats have been and will continue to be a strong tool for anyone. The climb up to the summit is indeed tough and even tougher climbing alone.

A quick recap: 1) Keep the 3Cs in mind at all times. 2) Know that our free will is a powerful tool that holds the key to all positive change. 3) Baptism protects our body/flesh from evils attempting to penetrate it.4) Have a face-to-face with yourself at 3:00 a.m. 5) Meditate on your consequences and conditions of soul. 6) Study the testing you are facing to see what you need to learn. 7) Realize that these tests are for the climb to our summit. 8) Know your weaknesses and ask for assistance. None of the above are easy, but then have we not learned that what is easy in life is usually not worth attaining? 9) Last of all, learn the meaning of gratitude. I know that it is difficult to be so when we do not feel grateful for anything. But comparing yourself with those who have far less is a good start. Keep in mind children who are poorest and most handicapped.

Question: how do we avoid repeating our mistakes in our second journey? The best and only way is to keep the light of the Holy Spirit upon you at all times. This requires faith in action throughout our soul's second journey. When we study history from the summit, we see that wars repeat around the world because of the collective accumulation of CMM, critical mass miseries, from the darkness of evil. But what is destroyed? Bodies and buildings and all that is near the destruction. This does not destroy the evil spirits that, accepted by humanity, are the root causes. They are still there to start the same process in the next generation of beings. This is why peace treaties do not last long. An example is the Palestine/Israel conflict peace treaties. They were/are just a pause from war, hence, the second coming of Christ to lock up the evils for a thousand years in the prophesied millennium.

The few that acknowledge the maddening herd retreat into the mountains as hermits to dwell with nature that could be trustworthy. Is this a solution? Maybe, if it does help us in our climb up to our summit, or it may not. Will this help us to help others? A hermit alone in the wilderness accomplishes little. Christian monasteries, on the other hand, offer up prayers for humanity and the world. Here the Gregorian chants echo the voices of the faithful throughout history.

Take as an example Saint Padre Pio of Italy in the last century. In reading about this saint, I was amazed that a man could remain innocent as a child. Here is a saint in modern times whose soul was not corrupted. Although evils tried in vain to tempt him, he always remained devoted to our Blessed Virgin Maria. Here was a monk that could read into the hearts of humanity. He heard the confession of another to be Saint John Paul II. What grace was this saint given to be able to look into the soul's heart of human kind? We know that he was given the stigmata of Christ. The last time that such a thing happened to a monk was with Italian saint, Saint Francis of Assisi, which was over eight hundred years ago. The stigmata in modern times? Here is a man with seemingly no darkness of soul. Is this possible? Here is a man living in prayer for his sake, yes, but also for others. Through his confessions, he was able to pull out of people their deepest sins of soul. How was this possible? We read from those who knew him that he did not eat much, constantly ran a high fever, and yet his body/flesh was not affected/damaged. Was this man human?

We know for instance that hypothermia could kill us within a few minutes. We also know that the human body can only tolerate a certain high temperature before the damage to various organs begin. We know that he was born of parents here in Italia. Yes, he was human, not an angel of light, but his very soul had the light energy of the Holy Spirit, a fire within his soul that was measurable. We also know that many witnessed whenever he left a room, he left behind a scent of flowers yet not using any cologne or scented soaps. A coincidence? Think again, this was a man known to be in more than one place at one time. I could only imagine where he was tracking on his soul's chart. It had to have been in the high nines, not an easy task. The most beautiful part of this man/living saint was that he did not consider himself to be such. On his deathbed, all he could say were two words, "Gesu, Maria." Yes, he is one of my favorite saints, along with Saint Francis of Assisi, patron saint of Italy, whose accomplishments reached the Holy Land. Another is Saint Don Bosco who helped orphaned children. There are many, of course—these men that lived their faith in charity, humility, and love of humanity. These were men that were selfless and with an understanding of the weaknesses of humanity. These men were admired and respected. These were men that gave out the gifts/graces with which they were blessed. No, these men did not hide themselves in a cave in the wilderness. Who can compare to these men today?

The above saints were in their called vocation. This is one reason that they performed well and without regrets. They were in that 25 percent bracket of humanity that enjoyed what they were doing. They loved their vocation. They had passion for helping humanity. It was not a job; they were not even paid. They were instead given the spiritual light of life, which is all they ever prayed for anyway.

At times, we need to just stop and ask ourselves: am I in a profession, a vocation, a service that I enjoy? Or am I in the 75 percent bracket that dreadfully goes to work?

Every profession, every vocation, every service, when done within the highest standards of faith, will be rewarded with respect and dignity. Notice what is taking place today in every sector of humanity. There is a degree of corruption/evil with theft, lying, cheating, and every vice imaginable, so these days we are constantly being compared to monkeys—monkeys that have sexual intercourse, incest, with any group member. We are also compared to dissected mice and rats. We do not need to be compared to animals. We are human beings for crying out loud. We were created to be the highest form of life.

Our instinct, which is, by the way, our moral imprint on our souls, tells us that we were created to accomplish good things. The catch is that this is only possible through charity and love of humanity. We were preprogrammed for this. It is our blueprint by design. It is when we get distracted and get off course that we experience trouble. Yes, our moral imprint is another tool if we are able to get a reading of it; in it is our true identity. The problem is that this also becomes blurred after losing light. In this failure, our moral imprint is left to fade away.

What about our senses, are they a tool? They most certainly are. Let us explore the five senses. We know what they are: 1) sight of our eyes; 2) touch of our flesh; 3) taste by our mouth; 4) smell by our nose; and 5) hearing from our ears. These are our natural body/flesh senses. There is no sixth sense as a few of us claim. What the majority of us fail to understand is that these five natural senses are given to us in order to develop our soul's five senses. This also cannot be understood until at the summit. Let us never forget that the body/flesh is for the development of our souls. Our entire human anatomy is for this purpose, especially the heart and brain. Our brains cannot function without our hearts. Our bodies cannot function without the brain. When there is a malfunction, we become incapacitated. Our soul's heart and mind function the same way for our soul. Both are critical, but the natural senses need to be transmitted and transformed into our soul's senses. This is what IT is not able to deliver on, as it is man-made fabricated information. We cannot stay in touch with this. We are not machines that after a crash results in chaos of not having the search engines available to us. We are flesh and blood, soul and spirit, with the Holy Spirit always there to help if we do crash. We need true communication, human expression of emotions, real body touch, smell, taste, eye searching, taking in lights, voice patterns, and listening to variations of sound of human beings on the same level. At the same time, our flesh needs to die. We should never think of our flesh as the ancient Egyptians did and try to preserve it.

Our five natural senses need to be elevated into our soul's senses. This only occurs in our climb up to our summit. It occurs when we are in communication with that spark within our soul's tabernacle within our soul's heart. Of our five natural senses, the eyes are what take in lights and give out light to others. As mentioned earlier, this is key to seeing ourselves face-to-face and seeing others eye to eye. The inner eye, centered between our natural eyes that some people reference, is our soul's eyes. When the spark of light that we started out with is allowed to turn into a flame, it radiates out of our eyes. When not, it is evident. Notice those of us that wear sunglasses inside or even at night. Hence, our eyes speak a thousand words. At times, words are not even necessary. In Asia, I learned that love could be expressed in three to eight seconds with the eyes alone.

The saints have this special characterization. We are all equally capable of emulating them.

Notice also that at night our eyes are impaired compared to the daytime; hence, darkness affects us. Too much sunlight, and we need a filter or sunglasses. So also our soul's eyes are less impaired in light yet need a filter from the full effects. There are filters of light also in the summit's climb of spiritual knowledge and light. This is true enlightenment, not like earthly data. Again, nine-plus should be our goal. Here we attain the eyes of an eagle that is capable of seeing all from the summit down to ground zero. At ten, we are absolutely in full light. Meditate on this for a while.

This brings to mind sitting in Piazza Santa Croce in Florence, Italia. I sat eating a tasty Napoli margarita pizza with chili oil and fresh oregano and a cold beer. Again, I was observing people in the large open piazza. I had next to me two children with their parents who all spoke English. I could not help but overhear a child asking the parents, "What are those symbols on the facade of the church?" They were pointing at the symbols of the alpha and omega. The parents were not able to give an accurate response. I looked at them, should I explain? It might embarrass them, so no. What they should have said is that the symbols of the alpha and omega mean the beginning and the end in our creator. The children will have to learn on their own. What really struck me as I was eating was the crowd of people in the piazza, the same people taking photos, talking, staring at the facade of the church. But how many people will actually go inside? I was here to pay my respects to Galileo Galilei, father of astronomy and physics, among other great Italians such as Michelangelo buried inside.

Another thing that I noticed was the large number of people taking photos of this huge marble statue of Dante Alighieri with the larger-than-life marble eagle at his feet looking up at Dante. I have to admit that a close-up of this statue is awesome. Dante, of course, was a giant of a writer in Renaissance Florence, having written "The Divine Comedy" about the inferno, hell. I was not sure why the artist chose to put the eagle in there, although the eagle is everywhere in the arts in Italy. I gave in to my imagination. I saw the eagle in eye-to-eye conversation with Dante. The conversation went like this:

> Eagle: Dante, do you see humanity's foolish condition? They see little to nothing. They do not have our eyes. Is there hope for them?

> Dante: Yes, Eagle, I can see it in their eyes. This is the majority of humanity. They were able to see more when they were children. I was like one of them until I climbed up here where you are.

When viewing this statue, you will see that the eyes are piercing eyes, both of the eagle and Dante. This is suggested by the artist that Dante had the eyes of the eagle. He had climbed to his summit. He was flying on eagle's wings. Only the wings of an angel fly higher. Yes, the eyes are the lenses to our soul's heart and mind.

The next important natural sense is hearing from our ears. There are those of us that think this sense is the most important. I suppose it depends on what we base it on. For a canvas painter, the eyes have it. We know that without light, colors cease to exist, hence, the saying, "Add color to your life." We also know that pure white is the foundation for all colors. We also know that without light, a rainbow cannot form. For us musicians, the ears have it. Regardless, they are the two most important of the five senses, even though all five senses navigate us through our second journey. The ears' hearing and the eyes' seeing are directed to our soul's mind, while smell, taste, and touch are directed more toward our soul's heart, hence the saying, "A way to a man's heart (or soul) is through his natural stomach." Of course, loving of our soul's heart involves all five senses, especially natural touch, constantly touching.

In hearing, we are able to detect fears, sadness and sorrows, pain and suffering, joys of happiness, and so much more. We can detect a pattern of sound in the high and low notes. The sense of hearing is indeed an important sense. As children, we knew all this; as adults, most of us have forgotten. This brings to mind a movie, *A Perfect Sense*. In this movie, people all around the world begin losing their natural senses, one by one. There is no cure and nothing to stop what is occurring. This is an excellent movie that I would highly recommend. By the end of the movie, desperation sets in to everyone. I will not give away the end. The end, though, is depressing. It was meant to be. Imagine this actually occurring. At the same time, this is what happens when our soul's senses are not communicating in the language of the Holy Spirit. We do not develop in the spiritual light of faith, hope, and trust. We do not grow in truths or wisdom. The natural senses die with the body/flesh. The soul's senses continue on into our third journey.

This is a problem with humanity. We do not really want to climb up to the summit for hundreds of reasons. We want the Holy Spirit to come down to our level at base level, even down into the gutter we have fallen into. There is a tremendous difference between the summit of spiritual knowledge and the gutters of rat-infested sewers. We do not want to compromise. This did happen once two thousand years ago. Yes, the prophesied Messiah, Christ Gesu, did just that. He came down to our level. We had Him condemned, persecuted, flogged, and crucified. He did not have to do this. He did not deserve it. He told us that He was the way, the truth, and the life to climb up to the summit and beyond. From the summit, we see that these three words summarize the entire Bible. We mocked Christ, and He still was forgiving. Do we deserve a second chance? He thinks so. A third chance? Are we taking Him all for granted?

We do not know our time. It could be tomorrow or next week or next month or next year when the angel of death comes calling to tell us our chances and time is up. When we fail to use our five natural senses to develop them into our five soul's senses, we have failed this tool as well. Our free will moves us—again the 3Cs—to read with our eyes the Gospels and to listen with our ears to what our inner voice is saying. In prayer, in charity, in love, this is possible. We have the absolute most complex body and soul of all creation. This body and soul needs nutrients to sustain itself. As natural foods sustain our body/flesh, the Holy Eucharist sustains our soul.

We do not know our time, but after the summit, we see that time itself is irrelevant because we see that our soul is timeless or without end.

Meditate on this for a while. With our five senses, we detect light or the absence of light, darkness. We detect warmth or the absence of it, coldness. We detect love or the absence of it, hate. We detect sounds of music or sounds of war. We detect the fragrance of flowers or the smoke of gunfire. We detect the spices of life or the arsenic of death. Now quiz yourself. Try to come up with others that involve the five senses, especially for light and love.

Another tool that works is the Ten Commandments of the Old Testament. Again, we have put these aside or behind us as being outdated and antiquated. These seemingly ten easy recommended laws to live by in the Old Testament were modified and simplified even more in the New Testament by Christ. He got ten down to one: "Love God with all of your strength, all of your heart, mind, and soul, and your neighbor as yourself." Easy enough, right? Now study history since the modification. We have had a difficult time of it, to say the least.

This tool in itself will take you straight up to the summit and #10 when observed. Only our Blessed Virgin Mother/Maria, the saints, and a tiny fraction of humanity have accomplished this. For the most part, my friends, the overwhelming majority of us are as pathetic as could be.

I could go on and on with the tools available for us. I do want to say that figures and formulas, muses, fortune-tellers, and palm readers do not fit into my description of positive tools. I need to wrap up this section with what I believe to be two more of the greatest tools of all. As I have written, the Holy Spirit within the Holy Trinity is the direct link to the highest summit of spiritual knowledge. After that, I believe that the next most important tool/ intercessor is our Blessed Virgin Mother/Maria. Her position has been confirmed and reaffirmed throughout history by the saints and those that she appeared to already and to this day continues to appear to. She is truly the queen of queens. If we study her apparitions, we see that she appears to the less fortunate, mostly the young and good-hearted. I do not know of her ever appearing to anyone evil-minded and dumbfounded. Even the illiterate are better qualified to receive her. This needs to be taken into consideration in prayer for her intercession. After her are the saints and angels of light. These souls continue to work with us in trying to help us with our climbing to where they are. Our knowledge and prayers to them only help us. This is their purpose of existence. Let me also add that the prayers of the faithful here in their second journey are also available to help and assist us in our climb up to the summit. As usual, if our soul is confidentially always in autumn and winter, we will not appreciate their spring and summer.

I recognize that most of us are afraid of what will be asked of us in turning to the Holy Spirit. We try to avoid this confrontation, we put it off, we delay it. But sooner or later, we all need to confront it. Again, the 3Cs need to be faced. From the summit, we see that the earliest is the best, as again we do not know the time left for us.

I will say that the benefits are without any doubt in our favor. That which is asked of us turns out to unburden us. That which is given up relieves us. We need as little as possible in our climb up to our summit; only the bare essentials suffice.

Seen from the summit, we would have prayed for a setup to help us with our choice of free will, but as I have written, this almost forcing of our free will seldom occurs. How we climb up to the summit and when we get there are all that is important. Question: how do we know when we are there? There are three very obvious conditions we experience. The first is that we wholeheartedly offer our free will up to the Holy Spirit within the Holy Trinity. Why? Because from the summit, we see that this is for our own good. We accept that our free will in union with the Holy Spirit will be accommodated and accomplish the greatest good. The second part is the need to be grateful throughout the day every day. We must let gratitude pour out of us because we are unable to hold it in. Ever bit your tongue without having said a word? Gratitude does not need to be formal, only sincere. It could take a few seconds each day. The third is an urgency to ask for forgiveness from all that we have offended, not with social media but face-to-face. There are few exceptions to these three conditions.

Being who we are, especially early on in our second journey, we will think of the above as mythology or theology for losers. This is understandable when we are on top of the world, a made man/woman. We have people by their balls, we're rising stars, have it made, have it all, we're set, etc. with all of the self-proclamations of success. We are only setting ourselves up for our fall.

An example is Julius Caesar, who had five triumphs in the Roman forum. This is like winning five Super Bowl rings as quarterback or five world cups in soccer in a century.

Regardless, Julius Caesar was murdered on the senate floor by the senators that proclaimed him to be all he wanted to be. Extreme, I know, but again study history, even recent history, and you will see a pattern of falling in all professionals, sports figures, political figures, celebrities, etc. The temporary elixirs slowly but surely fade away, and the harsh conditions of reality set in. This is when we see that we are not masters of our domain or any other domain in the universe.

At this point, we may only want to balance ourselves, to keep an equilibrium, with our feet on the ground. We may get back to nature, and even stop being arrogant and stupid. These are positive signs, but our soul is not quiet, as we have not started our climb. We are reminded when various illnesses attack our body/flesh. But as long as we are healed and survive, the majority of us continue our same course undeterred. The body/flesh is able to heal itself, but for how long? At times, we take it to electric shock treatment, but as long as we do not flatline, we still continue the same course. Yes, we are the 3Ss—stubborn, stupid, and sick—not to mention ignorant.

So before you put this book down, ponder the above before you forget about it. This is the time to make a conscious effort for your soul's sake. The time will come when our body/flesh is no longer capable of healing itself or being healed by anyone else. None of us really want to confront our death, but we must. Death will come calling. It is unpredictable, and we are very seldom prepared as we should be. The biggest problem in old age is that we may not have the courage or strength in a feeble body/flesh for our soul to operate.

From the summit, we are able to see the past, the present, and a part of the future. A past sinner sees present sin immediately. We see that in old age, we lose some of our abilities to perform or take the 3Cs as when we were younger. Visit an old-age-assisted care facility, and you may understand what I mean. You will see people with Parkinson's, Alzheimer's, and so many diseases that limit our soul's mind in a brain that is incapacitated. At this point, we are at the mercy of others to help us. We give our 3Cs to them. Is this what we want? If you are reading this and consciously aware that you have not climbed to the summit of your soul's second journey, there's time to do so. There is time to open the tabernacle doors of your soul's heart. There is time to unload all the demons of darkness. Even a rotten apple has the seeds within to begin life anew. We are a much higher form of life. If at the summit we give our free will up to the Holy Spirit within the Holy Trinity, we have nothing to worry about. Our soul will be taken care of.

Yes, a few of us do plan out our death. We figured out our will, who gets the M&M (money and material things). We purchase our plot, our casket, etc., right down to the details. Are we content with this? For the body/flesh, perhaps we are. Ah, but our soul is never content. Without having climbed to the summit, our soul is crying. Learn to listen to the anguish within. We want proof of this? Think while you can, what are you contemplating after the death of your body/flesh? Are you contemplative? Or have you already figured all is finished, *tutto e' finito*. Again, look into the mirror at 3:00 a.m. What do you see? Look into your eyes. Do you see fear of uncertainties? Is this enough proof for you? It is not too late to call on the Holy Spirit.

By no means is what I have written a complete list of the tools to help us. We need to understand that the Holy Spirit moves freely at will just as the wind in our natural world. Notice how the birds play with the natural wind. They delight in this. Those of us that have been selected and have been overcome by the Holy Spirit and changed within seconds also find delight within our souls. A few of us will start our climb only to stop when we reach a comfort zone. We become lazy and unwilling to make the hardest part up to the summit. Then there are those of us that it has taken a lifetime to reach the top of the summit of spiritual knowledge. As I mentioned before, our creator likes variations. What is important is that we are never discouraged, this is our birthright, our inheritance. Without this, we just grow old and senile till eventually we die and rot away into the earth. We should take note that even some pet animals remind us of the moral imprint that we have, as some of them may have one as well. Take notice of their instincts.

All of the knowledge upon knowledge of everything in the metaphysical does not make up for the spiritual knowledge of light. Only in light can we understand that our second journey needs to be a preparation for our third journey. The principles and laws of faith do not change with the times. It strikes me as strange now when I hear people use words such as *enlightened, brilliant, lighthearted, light-minded, illuminated*, etc. I think to myself, do they have any idea of the true meaning of the words being used?

As mentioned earlier, even if we curse Christ, we should not cut communications. After we are done cursing, of which we are cursing ourselves, let us bow our head in sorrow. Let us keep in mind not to make important decisions when our body/flesh is weak as at the end of a long day. We tend to be irrational at this time of the day. I find that the morning after a good restful sleep to be the best time to make choices. I believe that we need silence and solitude for communications to take place. There is no need for public display of our condition. Cover your face with your hands if needed and just listen in silence. Not ready for this?

Some of us will accept an alternative lifestyle, a pop culture form of spirituality of knowledge. These sorts of things are always in the news, especially with celebrities. But study their 3Cs, and in time the truth comes to the surface. In public, in front of the camera, an artificial image of goodness is displayed. In private, the story is different. This brings to mind the last emperor of China—a true story of an emperor that played his part as the last emperor of China. When nationalism took away everything, he was put into a nursery to work and live out the remainder of his life. Before his death, he claimed that these were the happiest days of his life. So much for prestigious power and a false image. Let us keep in mind that our soul does not want to be deceived. Take a look throughout history, the Napoleons, the Stalins, the Hitlers, the Maos, and countless others. They all portrayed an image of power and self-determination, self-destiny. I wonder what their souls experienced in the last few minutes of their lives. It appears that they took it to the edge of insanity and for what? These people suffered and suffocated in their senseless power games. A good stiff whiskey, a phone call, a pulling of strings—in the end, nothing worked anymore. Their gifts, their life wasted with the 3Cs that they chose for themselves. Grace misinterpreted? Maybe.

It is true that money and power can and do buy just about anything earthly in life for our body/flesh. Ah, but we are not talking about the body/flesh. We are talking about our soul's second and third journey. Here the money and power become charity, modesty, humility, and love.

For me, I wish that I had had a little of the information in this book when I was in my teens. I think that it would have saved me a lot of the troubles that I endured with my own 3Cs. Perhaps it was there all along, and I simply did not make the effort to recall it.

From the summit, I see that we are all prodigal sons and daughters to some extent. Until we return home, we are just wandering here and there but not really going anywhere worth going to. Yes, from the summit, we see what a waste of time it all was. At the summit, we see that this was the only place to be, so we had to return to faith first for guidance for the climb.

It appears that in order to appreciate light, we need to lose it. At times, even friends become obstacles when they pull us in their direction of going nowhere fast. The peer pressure does not really go away until we distance ourselves from those who like to be miserable and want us to join them. Why are we so connected, concentrated, and concerned with people who are obviously not climbing or remotely aware of the climb? Notice how plants, when growing in a shadow of light, will twist and turn into light. Are we dumber than plants? At times, it appears that we are. All of the tools help show the way, but do we stop to take notice? You decide.

I believe that one of the best motivating tools for the development and implementation of the climb is our parents. I was blessed with good-hearted parents. They were by no means perfect, yet they had a good sense of right from wrong. They knew the importance of working and saving. Most importantly, they were caring for their children as well as those of others. I am a fifty-fifty summation of the two of them. Yet in growing up, I took them for granted and did not fully appreciate them. From the summit, I saw the sacrifices associated with raising me. From the summit, we feel the pain and remorse of the lost years of closeness. I believe that this also contributed to my need to confront and climb up to the summit. I know that some children are not as blessed or happy with their parents. This is the time to pause and think and ask ourselves: why?

Remember that genetically we gradually become a reflection of both parents, so if we are not happy or content with them, now is the time for the adjustments. One of the worst feelings for a child is to feel unloved. At times, a mother or father or both may be incapable of love or demonstrate a wrong kind of love. It is one of the tragedies of life that makes a child wish he or she were never born. As children that do not understand the parents—3Cs of life—it almost becomes suicidal as a means to escape it all. It does not have to come to that. Recall that our soul's source is of spirit that starts us out equally regardless of genetics. In essence, we have two IDs—one genetic, one spiritual. The two need to merge in light. Study the greatest saints, and you see that this happened many times. So yes, if we do not like what we see, we can and should accept change. The free will is the tool for this. It determines the consequences and conditions that follow. The free will needs direction, though—not any direction but the right direction that is available in the light of the Holy Spirit. For example, only the spirit of Gesu is able to extract the demons that have entered our mind. From the summit, this is understandable.

But what of those that have not made the climb? A self-exam, an evaluation, an honest analysis, is needed. If our positive inner voice is silenced and an evil voice controls our mind, a diagnosis by someone of light is critical. Let us never forget that the evils of darkness have no power over light. Light needs to simply be accepted and to appear to have the darkness disappear. It is like entering a pitch-black room and turning on the light switch, and the room becomes filled with light instead. Here a good spiritual advisor is a necessity for our soul. The tragedy of tragedies is the failure of our free will to accept the graces that we need to make our climb in traveling our second journey.

At times, a good spirit of a loved one that passed into their third journey returns somehow, maybe in a dream to give us a sign as well. A dream could be a tool, but dreams are difficult at best to interpret. Evils can and do enter our dreams as well. Also, there are dreams where what is buried in our subconscious tries to surface, but we are not able to translate the meaning. At times, they could be our fears or desires of the body/flesh.

This takes us into our next chapter of who, what, and where to look for our guide to interpret that which we cannot acknowledge.

| | |
|---|---|
| HOME, HEAVEN. | #10 ORB,NUCLEUS,TRINITY |
| 1ST JOURNEY, SEED, | 9.9 3RD JOURNEY UP,3T'S |
| SPARK,CONCEPTION | 9.0 SUMMIT,WISDOM, |
| BIRTH,BODY&SOUL | POS. 3C'S, 3G'S, |
| 2ND JOURNEY | 8.9 CHILD 3L'S, CHARITY |
| MORAL IMPRINT, | 8.0 TAB. OXYGEN |
| FREE WILL,TESTS , | CONSCIOUSNESS |
| CONSCIENCE,3C'S, | 7.0 THE 7 VIRTUES, |
| 3S'S, 3F'S, | PRUDENCE, JUSTICE, |
| 3D'S, ACCEPT EVILS | TEMPERANCE, FAITH |
| FALSE WAY, TAB. | COURAGE , CHARITY |
| DOORS CLOSING | HOPE, DESERT, 3R'S |
| **MEDITATION** | **6.0 WAY ,TRUTH, LIGHT** |
| **SELF QUIZ** | **5.9 GRATITUDE, PRAYER** |
| AMBER LIGHT | 3.0 FREE WILL, ADVICE,TOOLS |
| DARKNESS, **DEEP** | 2.0 to 1.0 GOOD VOICES |
| **DARKNESS, DEATH** | **.01 to 0. GESU, BVMARIA , UP,** |

**A RIGHTSIDE PROCESS OF OUR SOUL'S RETURN HOME**

CHAPTER *Five*

---

Government? - Science? - Religion? -
Hinduism? -Buddhism? -Islam? Judaism?-
Christianity?- Teacher - Guide

In this chapter, we will explore the who, what, and where for our
3Cs to our soul's second journey. When is now, the present, but
also includes the past and, more importantly, the future.

Let us start with government, that is, bodies of people like ourselves, elected, unelected, also kings, queens, emperors, dictators,
tyrants, etc. Since the beginning of humanity, we have always relied
on others to lead us, guide us through life, hence our dependency on
the strongest, almost like the animal kingdom. But we are not the
animal kingdom unless we choose to be.

Since we are the Western civilizations, perhaps Greece and
Alexander the Great are a good starting point. No need to go further
into the past, although a key player, Troy, will figure in greatly after
Greece. Troy, out of present-day Turkey, will be transported to be
transplanted in Italia and become Roma, the cradle of all Western
civilizations. Greece was given the seeds of democracy, but let us

study what became of those seeds. Recall that all gifts of grace must be given to others in order to be replenished. Alexander the Great did take his 3Cs—choices, consequences, and conditions to the maximum. The title "Great" fits him. Here was a man that started in Greece with his army and conquered all opposing armies through the Middle East all the way to India. Yet he is remembered to this day as the conquering two-horned immoral devil by those that resisted him, not as a liberating hero.

The problem was that he died so young. The seeds of democracy were never really planted. Notice that upon his deathbed, his generals asked him who should take over his leadership after his death. His response was, "To the strongest." This was an open invitation to civil war. This is the animal kingdom mentality. But again, humans are not animals, so all of Alexander's conquests rapidly fell back to where they were before he arrived. All the spilled blood and deaths were a waste. There is that word, *waste*, as it has various types. We will see later in history two other greats, Julius Caesar's takeover of the senate after about five hundred years as a republic. Why? Power, yes, but also because the senators were taking care of themselves and the top 1 percent and not the rest of the citizens, including the legions. Sounds familiar? We will also see how Napoleon's 3Cs effectively changed Europe, eventually one by one getting rid of the monarchies and aristocratic bloodsuckers of humanity.

Greece, as we read in history, stagnated after Alexander the Great. All of her great philosophers, Aristotle to Zeno, would continue for a few more centuries, but they also would lose significance. Her man-made gods, Athena to Zeus, would follow into mythological nonsense. Her glory days were over. Her temples would crumble along with her power and influential dominance in the region. She would face the consequences of her immoral choices and very soul. Not as bad as Sodom and Gomorrah but still left to rot from her decadence.

It was time for a new power in the region. A power to control the people with civil law and order. A power to connect the region with the infrastructure it needed. A powerful force, an iron hand with trained legions to bring civility to the people. A force that chose as its symbol the eagle with sharp talons. A force to govern and help the region to prosper in trade and commerce. Yes, Troy would be reborn.

Those that escaped Troy would resettle in Italia and eventually on the Tiber river in a location of seven hills. This new city state would be called Roma, after Romulus as king. She would start small, taking a defensive posture, but slowly and patiently, she knew that she had to take over the entire peninsula of Italy. As a republic, her 3Cs would have her expand into Africa, the Middle East, Eastern Europe, and Northern Europe. She also started with kings but would become a republic with a governing body of senatorial voices for the people. She was harsh on the people who opposed her, at times, turning them into slaves. One had to be a Roman citizen to greatly benefit from her bread and wine. But still, there was freedom of religion, freedom to move about throughout the empire, freedom to make a living, freedom to take advantage of the public baths. Yes, the aqueducts were built to bring in fresh water, the roads were built for travel and for commercial activities. People did not have to go hungry. There was a sense of security, a feeling that you could make plans for tomorrow.

People were, for the most part, content. They were able to enjoy the fruits of international trade. They were able to prosper. Family was respected. The artists flourished in paintings and sculpture. Theaters were built throughout the empire for actors and actresses. Who was complaining? There were wars, yes, but not at home—they were at the frontiers defending the empire, annexing new lands, civilizing the barbaric tribes in the north. Even a civil war now and then did not disrupt the progress of civilization. The senators were organized, the treasury had taxes coming in. Money was not squandered on worthless wars.

A few centuries of this brought wealth to certain families and a lot of wealth to a percentage throughout the empire. Humanity was moving forward with time for leisure and recreational facilities and activities. Why would anyone want to disrupt the progress? Maybe someone who wanted too much, someone with an ego that wanted to be considered a god.

Enter Julius Caesar, a genius of war. Who will ever forget those infamous three words, "*Veni, vidi, vici.*" Who could stop a man that comes, sees, and wins battles? With Mark Anthony at his side, what would stop him? Caesar wanted power far more than the senators were willing to give him. He had his loyal legions that could force his will against anyone that stood in his way. Even Pompeii with far greater numbered strength in legions and another civil war could not stop him. He was determined and ambitious. He was proud and courageous. The warnings against his life went unheeded. He appeared invincible. Ah, he was being set up for his fall.

The senators were, of course, right. Caesar was a danger to the Republic of Rome. He needed to be stopped, but how? It turned out that the plan that they carried out on the senate floor to murder Caesar actually ushered in imperialism. Mark Anthony quickly and systematically had all associated with the conspiracy put to death. And yes, yet another civil war ensued between Mark Anthony and the legions of Agrippa at Actium. Yet with Octavian, Caesar's adopted son, being proclaimed Caesar Augustus, the Pax Romana ushered in pace/peace throughout the empire, even with the loss of the republic.

Caesar Augustus was one of the greatest of the seventy-plus Caesars that would rule the vast empire from Roma for roughly five hundred years. Another ninety-plus Caesars, starting with Caesar Constantino, would rule from the East until 1465 AC, the fifteenth century. Europe, Africa, and the Middle East were the known world. To the north were the barbaric tribes still being civilized. To the east, Asia was known, but the desert divide made it another world, so for the most part, Rome controlled the known Western world. A Roman emperor had immense power and wealth to force his will on anyone. We will see that after Constantinople, in 1492 AC, an Italian, Christopher Columbus, would begin the process to ultimately establish a new western Rome in America, in Washington, D.C. It should be noted that China sent ships out to discover new lands and did about fifty years earlier but abandoned the project. Coincidence? Think again. The Americas, named after Amerigo Vespucci, another Italian, were destined to become republics and not under imperialism or monarchies. As Constantinople was named after Constantino, the new Roman Republic would be named after Washington! Humanity, after 1,500 years, was dying to get back to a republic again. Notice how the inner voice of humanity begins within our soul's heart but comes out in civil matters as a voice of the people in a true republic! Hence, the critical need to learn to listen! When we are at fault, the 3Fs, fools at fault, we fail, in moral issues of our soul and civil matters as well!

The problem with imperialism is that the senators lose a great deal of influence in the control of an empire. Of all the Caesars, for every good one, there were two bad ones, and a few were lunatic. The great ones—Augustus, Claudius, Trajan, Hadrian, Marcus Aurelius, Constantino, Justinian, and a number more—did expand/improve the empire, but the bad ones ruined it. This was/is the problem with imperialism. The same with monarchies, there are a few good kings, but study history and find all the terrible ones. A government, country, people cannot be prosperous with right governance only one third of the time. If anything, this is one of the major reasons for the endless wars throughout history.

It should also be noted that starting with Caesar Augustus, Rome entered a golden age of prosperity. Augustus knew what had to be done for the good of the people and the empire. He quickly reduced the number of legions and the power of the generals to prevent another civil war and the expenses to maintain them. Roughly thirty legions were left intact to keep law and order. We need to remember that at this point in history, the population was far less than that of today in the region.

The result was forty years of prosperity throughout the empire without a major war. Augustus turned Rome's buildings from stone into marble buildings. Needless to say that word of the death of Caesar Augustus sent tremors throughout the empire. This was during the time of Christ, who entered into our world and had to go to Jerusalem with his parents for the census.

Now let us stop here for a moment. Think when was the last time America experienced forty years of prosperity without war? The whole purpose of the above lesson in history is to understand where we came from. There have been many comparisons of America to ancient Rome and rightly so. Notice all the similarities, us exiting from Europe for freedom and opportunities. The breakaway from kings and forming a republic with senators for the people. The defensive posture for stabilization and setting up a foundation. The expansion of territory was for security reasons, sea to shining sea, east to west. The eagle, as the symbol of strength, holds an olive branch in one hand but also arrows in the other. They have a trained army with engineering support and all of the logistics to support it through-out the world. A few great leaders include Washington, Jefferson, Lincoln, and Roosevelt—whose monuments stand to this day. There was a civil war to prevent a split up of the country. The assassina-tions of her leaders took place. Roman architecture and Roman laws were adopted by our founding fathers. America has become the new Western Rome on the great Potomac River.

World Wars I and II were the two Punic wars with Carthage that decided future events for Rome. Hannibal of Carthage was from across the Mediterranean Sea in Northern Africa. This was early Rome, a few centuries BC when the senators did what they had to do to conquer an adversary. The United States Congress was this way at one time, but not any longer. It has sold out to special interests. Hannibal was a genius of a general at war. He had the nerve to enter the north of the Italian Alps with a massive army, lose thousands of men, cross the mountains, and enter Italy. It was a totally unexpected surprise to Rome. Another genius, General Douglas MacArthur, would do the same in Korea two thousand years later except by sea.

The Roman senate did what was necessary to stop an adversary from taking control of the empire. Its decision was swift and unan-imous. It gave full support to the Roman generals and legions to put an end to the threat. The rest is history. Hannibal was stopped, Carthage was crushed and destroyed. This is the difference between the Roman Empire senators compared to the American empire sen-ators. Our senators squabble endlessly over the smallest, even trivial issues. We have wimps and, to be blunt, men without balls to do the right thing for our republic, our people, and our country.

Generals Patton and MacArthur, both great generals, knew at the end of World War II that the Soviet Union and Stalin would become a threat to America and her allies. They also knew that with our position in Europe, we could have put an end to the Soviet Union as we did with Japan. We had the advantages of atomic energy that no one else had. It could easily have been a defensive posture for liberty for every country. A few atomic bombs on strategic Russia/Soviet military or industrial complexes would have caused capitulation. We could have prevented anyone else from attaining atomic bombs and, thus, prevent all future wars. World War II could have been the war to end all wars. It could have been an evil to prevent future evils. It could have been a universal Pax Americana. It could have been but was not. For whatever reasons, dumbfounded Washington did not agree. They probably figured, what did these great generals know? They are not politicians. A true republic with a great general backed by a strong senate and the loyalty of his soldiers most likely would not have let an opportunity like this escape. This is the problem with America; we are not a true republic as was Roma in 450 BC. We need to rid ourselves of the executive branch, the lower federal house of representatives, and our not supreme court. Also, a true republic doesn't have individual state congresses, only a state governor and city mayor positions. It is a total waste of taxpayers' money to have more than this. Each state judicial system would be more effective and efficient. While we are at it, let us get rid of all the lobbyists that only work for special interests anyway.

After the two Punic wars with Carthage, Rome really never had another serious threat for several centuries. Now see what happened to America only five years following World War II. Even in the Korean War, General MacArthur was right in the surprise attack behind enemy lines. If the bridges had been blown up between Korea and Communist China, the war would have come to an early end. The split up of Korea may not have happened. This limited war strategy was decided by someone, President Truman, who did not know much about warfare. It was a failed policy that would haunt our armed forces for the next fifty years and counting. This policy of limited war only prolongs war at the expense of our boys' bodies. It benefits the war machine apparatus.

Great generals need to have the authority to do their job without having their hands tied by politicians. We have had nothing but problems with Russia, the Soviet Union, again Russia, North Korea, Vietnam, and the Middle East due to the incompetence of those in Washington, D.C.

Has America grown too prosperous and too powerful? If we study our current problematic choices in our body/flesh, just in food intake, we see the consequences and conditions of diabetes, heart disease, cancers, etc. This brings to mind a story that my father often told of Bartolo. Bartolo was a poor peasant in the dark ages of Europe that entertained the duke. The duke liked him so much that he invited Bartolo to live in his castle, which he did. After a few years of heavy alcohol consumption and dining on fatty foods, Bartolo lost his health, his wit, and his sense of humor. He passed away shortly after of heart disease. In history, we read of what happened to Rome at her height of prosperity and power in the fifth century AC. She was also physically unhealthy, and far worse, collectively her very soul was sick. The empire had split into two—the east and the west—in the fourth century AC due to various reasons but also due to moral issues. Now the American Roman Empire is having very similar issues with her soul's health.

A similar situation exists in her Northern and Southern states/ territories. Notice that there is, as of late, talk of States specifically in the southern part of the country wanting to break away from the union with the north. An example is Texas. It would be a large enough state to make it happen. The state/republic is large enough to be independent as a country. The southern states have always had their own philosophy of how a country should function and operate. Take as an example the southern border with Mexico. We are a superpower, and yet Washington cannot or just does not have the willingness to protect the border from illegal immigrants, drugs, and criminals. Bigger is not always better, similar to/in big business. At times, a breakup into smaller parts makes us more manageable and efficient. Are America, Brazil, Canada, Russia, India, and China too big for their own good?

It is always possible that the civil war did not lie to rest the differences between the North and the South. The bloodiest war in American history may turn out to have been a total waste. There is that word, *waste*, again. A civil war need not be a military war. As we witnessed with the Soviet Union, it could be a cold war that separates and divides. Sounds familiar? Who can argue with the Southern states? The very moral fabric of America is being shredded. These are the best and the worst of times that we are living in. The best in medicine, science, and technology but the worst in regard to morality.

Take as an example what is being allowed to happen in advertising from the agencies that are mostly in New York City. The false advertising by these agencies is ethically and morally wrong. Notice what was done with baby nutrition. Companies developed a formula substance as a substitute for a mother's milk. The advertising agencies promoted it with millions of dollars so that in a half century this substance was supposed to be better and more beneficial for a baby than the mother's natural milk. The American public bought it. We are not talking about a tiny percentage of mothers that have a difficult time producing their own milk. We are talking about a large percentage of parents spending a lot of money on a product that may not be necessary. We have proven what has been known for thousands of years, that a mother's natural milk is the best and safest defensive nutrition for a baby's development.

There are many, many issues to deal with. Another example is the constant lies about this shortage or that shortage. Take energy, there is no shortage of energy as a source of power. Why? Because all in the metaphysical earth and universe is made of light, and that is energy. The American public and all of humanity are confidentially constantly being lied to. The large oil companies selling us one of the worst polluting energies of all have been controlling the market for a century. With the technologies of today, we could turn our waste products that are filling up our landfills into reusable clean energy. How about clean drinking water that we pay taxes for? We are told to buy safe drinking bottled water without a monitoring of safety standards! A joke and ridiculous! This is the corruption and deception of advertising in the world.

Much of the lying is coming from American multinational companies and the advertising agencies. The whole world is buying into it because they themselves are dumbfounded from being in the dark. Whole countries are being influenced by unethical corrupt corporate Americanism. In the process, they are losing their identity, their special personality, and their character.

The formation of the United States of Europe needs to consider the issues that they will have to deal with in the process of what they are doing. I already see major problems with illegal immigrants, especially from Africa and the Middle East. These countries need assistance, I agree, but to have them bring their problems into Europe and not be accepted opens them up to prejudices, discrimination, and even hate crimes. As Europeans, it is better to help them help themselves in their own countries. Educate as many as possible in the freedoms under a democratic republic with congress/parliament and free elections. Add freedom of religion and speech to express a free healthy conscience. The formula has been proven to work. Forget about all the far right, left, center, etc. It is nothing but nonsense anyway. There is simply humanity needing civil rights, human rights, and rights for our souls. The problems are not in ideologies but in law and order of the soul.

Rome did have her headaches, especially from the Middle East, as is the case with America. It is a known fact that according to written accounts, Caesar could come down with an iron hand. Take as an example Israel, a pain in the neck for a few centuries, always causing trouble within that region. Here was a people that benefited immensely with the infrastructure, laws, commercial interests, and freedom of religion. We were not required to join the legions as other provincial regions. Yet we Jews were not content; we did not want to pay the taxes. We taught that due to our religion, we were privileged. After all, we were the chosen people. We were from the house of David and Solomon.

We were warned time and again, even by a few prophets. One, a Messiah by the name of Gesu told us to change our ways. "Give to Caesar what belongs to Caesar and Dio what belongs to Dio." Ah, but we are worse than mule heads; we had the Romans put Him to death as a pretense to appease Caesar. Also, we could not have anyone interfere with our Passover, could we? Of course not, everything was done before the Sabbath.

Herod, king of the Jewish community and Jerusalem, was held accountable first with his miserable demise and death after beheading Saint John the Baptist to appease a little harlot. Now seventy years after doing away with the Messiah, the Christ, our time had come. The day of justice was at our door. No, this had nothing to do with Passover. Titus and his legions were knocking on our door, all doors. We would have to pay dearly with our possessions, our properties, at times our lives, roughly 3,600. Our temple would be torn down, left only with a wall to weep on. Some of us who survived escaped into other regions of the empire. We went anywhere, even to live in caves. We could no longer be choosy. A few of us escaped to Herod's Masada. Ah, but the legions were even able to penetrate this stronghold. After all, it was Roman engineering that helped construct it.

We still did not learn our lesson. In 130 AC, we again started problems. This time, we would almost be wiped off the face of the earth. Emperor Hadrian would send his legions to massacre more than a half million of us. We turned to our wise elders, but they were not that wise after all, so we killed them. We as a people were separated, divided, and turned, and we started killing each other. Sounds familiar? Separate, divide, and subdivide. Have them turn on each other and kill each other. This was an end to Jerusalem, our home turned into Palestine, Arian with complete control from Roma. The few of us left had to scatter like rats into any region that would accept us. We stopped being fussy, we stopped being terrorists.

After nineteen centuries, a Christian president, Truman of new Western Christian Rome, gave us back our promised land. To think of the irony of all this, our 3Cs. We have been and are still crying on the same wall that was left standing nineteen centuries ago. It is good to be back home. A Palestinian state? No way, over our dead bodies! Peace? Give us time to land grab as much as possible. We will think about it. Fairness? Why? We should climb the wall and learn from it rather than cry on it! What for? We have a lot to cry about. Don't we? The greatest losers in life are those who fail to live up to their gifted potential. Even those of us who are physically handicapped yet try our best are far greater winners!

From the summit, we see that, at times, evil is allowed to and does take a certain course. It appears to be a part of the master plan. We may not have any appreciation of it when it is occurring. It may take centuries to see the results and understand what was transformed by certain events. Rome, my friends, was such a setup, a transformation, hence the Eternal City.

Rome was and is a part of the master plan. She is and will be a part of future prophecy. It is her destiny. So we can see that there was some justification for her 3Cs in the past 2,500 years.

We briefly discussed Constantino and his 3Cs to move the seat of the empire to Constantinople. This was back to modern-day Turkey, but this time it would be on the European continent across the Bosphorus Sea from the original Troy not far away. A similar event would take place across the Tiber away from the Roman Forum for the Vatican. A coincidence? Think again. Why this location for the seat of power and rule for the Eastern empire? We read from history of the importance of this location strategically, but why else?

Could it be that Caesar Constantino, now a Christian, wanted to no longer tolerate the pagans of Rome with the false man-made gods? He knew Rome's history better than anyone else, and he knew Greek history as well. Did he believe that the city should be abandoned to rot from her decadence? Was this his plan? There is that possibility.

We know that he built the Hagia Sophia in Constantinople right away. This was a marvel of its day, the largest Roman Catholic Christian Church within the empire. Yes, pagan Rome on the Tiber was no longer significant to Caesar. The transformation would take on a new face—no more gladiator killings in the Coliseum, no more horse racing in the greatest circus on earth. The empire was now Roman Catholic Christian. Caesar Constantino was the chosen one, the one that could help fulfill the master plan. Centuries later, it will be Washington, another chosen one.

Notice that there was no real attempt to stop the barbaric tribes from entering the empire from the north. In the current United

Kingdom, Londonarium/London never got reinforcements, and Hadrian's Wall was certainly not going to stop the invading savage tribes. There was no major defense on the northern frontiers, no real force of legions. Yet there were legions in the Eastern Empire where there were no real threats to that part of the empire.

The historians have come up with all sorts of theories and assumptions on the fall of the Roman Empire, from allowing the legion's men to marry to lead poisoning from the lead pots used to cook in, etc. They may have been all wrong. First of all, Rome as an empire never really fell. The eastern provinces were in control by Constantinople for many more centuries. Caesar Justinian, Constantino's heir, actually reclaimed Rome a century after the barbaric tribes invaded her only to let her go again within another century. Constantinople's fortifications withstood all invading armies from the south until the use of cannonballs in the fifteenth century by the Ottoman forces that penetrated her defensive walls. Taking Constantinople, what was the first thing that they did? Of all things, they changed the Christian Catholic Hagia Sophia church into a mosque. Yes, it was a time to start a new Rome in the Americas.

And what is it about a Byzantine Empire? What empire was that? Just because Greek was gradually spoken in Constantinople instead of Latin does not constitute a Byzantine Empire. In Constantinople, people considered themselves Romans. Again, I think that the historians got it wrong.

We see, of course, in hindsight that the barbaric tribes actually brought new blood into Rome. They were called barbaric but, in fact, overall were better people than the pagans that they infused themselves into in Rome. It should be noted that Caesar Caligula, centuries earlier, chose German guards instead of the traditional Praetorian guards that he did not trust. It was for good reason. They wanted to assassinate him. They eventually did anyway, as he was a madman, crazy with power and lust and not much else to help the empire. Also note that the guards of the future Vatican would be and continue to be Swiss guards.

Yes, *destino* was taking its course in ancient Rome. We will see how Pagan Rome became a renewed Rome but only after she suffers for her past sins. What sins? By whom? Sins toward the collective souls of people past with the inequalities, injustices, and injuries. All will be forgiven, but all also needs to be accounted for. The spilled blood of the saints in the Coliseum, the abused slaves' souls were crying for justice. Atonement was in order in a city that proudly powered her civil light of law and order into the world.

Now let us not think that this would happen overnight. The saying, "Rome was not built in a day," is accurate. In fact, we will see that it would take centuries, about as many centuries to come out of her darkness as the number of centuries of rule with an iron hand. This was roughly eight centuries in the West. We will see that it took the Renaissance for the rebirth to occur. This brought her into the thirteenth century

It is also interesting to note that the Eastern Empire and Constantinople did not enter the Dark Ages. On the contrary, she flourished in the arts, mathematics, and science. The 3Cs—choices, consequences, and conditions—of Caesar Constantino and following Caesars were evident everywhere in the region.

The Greek Christian Orthodox church would gradually evolve and be established to maintain and preserve Christian traditions. Later, the Russian Christian Orthodox church would continue to work into Northern/Eastern Europe.

Notice how all of this was unfolding for Christianity—from Israel to the center of pagan Rome to Constantinople and eventually to the Americas, mainly new Rome in Washington, D.C. Why would Peter the Apostle, having the keys to the Church and Paul, take Christianity into the center of pagan Rome? Why establish Christ's church there of all places? This, of course, was three hundred years before Caesar Constantino's move to Constantinople. This was a time when Christians were being sent to the lions in the Coliseum. Of course, Peter and Paul knew that to go into the very heart of civil power could and would eventually be the most beneficial. Yes, even if they did not think this way, they were certainly guided this way. We need to remember that there are always unseen forces at work that assist with *destino*. Again, at times, it may not be seen. It could take years and up to centuries to see the results. At the time, immediately after the death and resurrection of Christ, Rome was the most logical choice for the foundation of His church. All roads did lead to Rome. The roads, the infrastructure, the administrators in Milano, everything were already set up. No other places on earth had this. Jerusalem and her temple would be destroyed less than a century later. Saints Peter and Paul did do their part in bringing the Word into pagan Rome. This took courage, as we know the results of their 3Cs. Saint Peter was crucified upside down, and Saint Paul was beheaded, but their work was done. It would take again divine intervention to continue the process three hundred years later as mentioned earlier with Caesar Constantino.

Okay, this book is not intended to be a history lesson. We simply need to know a few of the events that took place in order to understand where we are at today in Christian America.

We read about the so-called Dark Ages of Europe while Rome herself was suffering from her own darkness. But the Dark Ages, roughly from the sixth century up to the fifteenth century, was a time of civil disorder due to not only the breakdown of Roman law and order but more importantly the breakdown of the soul's order. As mentioned, this did not occur in the Eastern Roman Catholic Christian Empire.

Through the centuries, even the new blood of the barbaric tribes became polluted in Rome. The Roman Catholic Church would endure like the empire's Caesars, some bad popes. I would say that of the two hundred-plus popes since Saint Peter, especially during this time period, two out of three were bad popes hiding behind a facade of infallibility. They were human with all the weaknesses of humanity. Yes, where humanity exists, evils also exist. I would estimate that there are more popes in hell today than popes in heaven, even if their bodies are buried in the Vatican.

Take as an example what occurred in the Inquisition in the nine hundreds. This was worse than the temple leaders of Jerusalem that persecuted the Christians. The church itself was persecuting people who did not obey her laws and authority. The popes and cardinals themselves had turned into the Pharisees and scribes of the past. Yes, history does repeat itself where humanity is involved. The church was now acquiring land, forming a papal army for power over her domain. This is what evil through humanity had turned the church into. Was this the intended effort of Saint Peter and Paul? Of course not, hence the Dark Ages would indeed last a long, long time. Rome was still destined to be the Eternal City, but she would also go through hell in the process. It would still be centuries before the Renaissance that would wake her up.

The Vatican itself would be turned into a whorehouse, a place for pleasure to wine and dine and cut deals with kings and the aristocratic users of humanity. I will not mention any names, but the history books in the Vatican library archives have all of the information.

Enter Martin Luther who had the audacity to post his comments and demands on the doors of the Catholic Church. It was a bold move by a decent human being that should have been considered a warning call. Was it? Of course not, hence the Christian divide, which is what evil wants. Separate, divide, and subdivide. Get them to hate and kill each other. Let them conquer themselves. The 3Cs were at work: the choice of the Vatican pope gave us the consequences of the separation, Inquisition, the Protestant churches, which gave us the conditions, divided up till now.

We will see that the Vatican herself took on a Machiavelli approach toward people. All of Europe did the same. It still would be centuries before the Vatican would truly change to the church of the twentieth century. It had to recognize that as Galileo Galilei saw the sun at the center of our galaxy, that the church and humanity were not the center but rather revolved around the light of the Holy Spirit. Ignorance takes time to overcome. Humanity had come a long way since the days of Egypt, pyramids, mummies, and Moses but still had a long way to go. We will see a big change during the Renaissance in Italy yet, as one of the great Florentine writers, Petrarca, would write the Dark Ages were far from over. The Church would not reach real maturity until the twentieth century. Why?

What is the Church/Vatican? What is her purpose?

She is supposed to be the guide, the interpreter of the Word of Christ. The pope and the college of cardinals themselves have to have the light of the Holy Spirit within them to be able to help us with our needs. In other words, the collective souls' light of their charts help us with our soul's needs. I personally have witnessed this in the past fifty years. Up until the last century, the collective light of the Holy Spirit within those in the Vatican was not truly evident.

We should note that the same collective light of people, the 3Cs, occurs in a community, city hall, a state capital, the federal government, any courthouse, or any body of people. The choices give us the consequences and conditions, good or bad. Light begets light. Evil begets evil. Immorality is like a silent plague that works from the inside out. This does not happen in other forms of life, only humanity.

What is civility? What makes us civilized?

Being civilized is being decent, being helpful toward others in need of help, the handicapped, the homeless, etc. It is avoiding the evils of discrimination, prejudice, hate, and violence toward others. Now notice that all of this and more are covered in the Ten Commandments. We are not able to be decent civilized citizens when our soul's light has been diminished. I regret to write that I see this more evident these days in America than in Europe. It was not this way in the last century.

Full faith and trust in the United States dollar, US Treasury? How? Put faith in Wall Street? How is this possible? Trust our banks? Trust our municipal bonds? A financial system rigged to benefit the top1 percent? A system from which politicians removed the safeguards with a liberalization of the rules to protect us from a disaster? Business ethics? Few, extremely few, companies have or believe in ethics anymore. We need to remember that some American companies did business somehow with Nazi Germany during World War II. So much for ethics. This is democracy corrupted. Is it any wonder that our foreign policy is hurting? It has been eroding since the Korean War.

Notice how in the past twenty-five years Congress has passed bills to help big businesses, corporate interests, special interests but not family interests. We have had a judicial, legislative, and, for the most part, an executive branch with puppet presidents that are influenced by the elite few who want their way. Sounds familiar? This was

Europe in past centuries with monarchies/imperialism from which we Americans escaped.

Notice how much was/is covered up or hidden from the American public. Sounds familiar? Evil hates transparency. There was this talk about the axis of evil not long ago. It is very possible that an axis of evil exists right in our own country between Washington, D.C., Wall Street, and the large corporation. Yes, my friends, America is rotting at the core, and we do not see it.

We are able to rely on the moral imprint of certain dogs more than some of the people in our current congress.

So NO, government is not a tool for our soul's second journey. For example, I remember a time when Sunday was a day of rest, to be with family, to be grateful in church, to reflect on the past week, and to simply enjoy the fruits of our labor. Large multinational corporations have changed the week to 24-7, 365 days a year with the threat of sending jobs overseas, which was done at the expense of the American working class. After that, they ship the production back to us to buy at inflated prices. American workers lost out and have been losing hard-fought union rights by those intent on busting unions. These are the 3Cs, my friends. The choices of a few give us the consequences and conditions of workers being exploited, under-paid, and treated like charcoal. Homemakers were pulled out of their homes to compensate for low or lost wages to the family breadwin-ner. Capitalism without controls, when corrupted/evil, becomes the most evil of all the ideologies. GM, losing money in 2008 and need-ing taxpayers' money while making a fortune in China? Not on the American books? Not part of the bottom line? By what accounting standards?

So let us study why America is in turmoil and incapable of help-ing us much in our second journey. Let us focus on the American empire. I have already written about the similarities of the two: Rome/America. But although America had started as Christian colonies, the people starting these colonies were mainly the same Europeans that escaped the turmoil of Europe. We study history to see what tough hardships they faced yet see what we Christian intruders did to the natives of the Americas, both North and South. We decimated

135

their population with the diseases we brought from Europe. Often, as Spain did, we killed them in South America in the name of Christ. Were we any different than the Crusaders that invaded the Holy Land?

I know that certain natives sacrificed humanity with blood running down their altars of sacrifice. At times, a lesser evil is allowed to occur to put an end to a much worse evil.

But if we study North America and see what happened to the natives there, we see a repeat of how the barbaric tribes of Europe were treated. A coincidence? I do not think so. It would take us Christian Americans nearly four hundred years to become somewhat Christian Americans. Now in the past fifty years, we are back stepping in many ways.

Rome conquered with the sword, European Americans used guns and rifles. Again, events are allowed to occur for a reason. The Native Americans, finally realizing it, simply gave up to settle on the worst land reservations possible for sustenance. For the past one hundred years, they were the poorest of the Americans until gambling casinos improved the conditions. They also had to face the 3Cs in their lives and learn from them. The American empire was and is most likely needed against the greater evils taking place in Europe in the twentieth century and around the world into the twenty-first century.

We as a country have been blessed with an abundance of grace. There is no doubt about it. Yet in the past fifty years, we have been losing light, that is, grace. I think that it started in the '60s with the assassinations of President Kennedy, Martin Luther King, and Bobby Kennedy.

We were the heroes of the free world after World War II. We were respected, honorable, charitable, and appreciated around the world. The assassinations and civil unrest due to the unequal civil rights began to expose our weaknesses. The worthless Vietnam War let us know that the lives of our boys' bodies were expendable when the profits of the war machinery warranted it. Our veterans, some mentally and emotionally sick and thrown out into the streets by a heartless Republican administration serving special interests, made matters worse. The two wars for oil interests proved that black gold was worth the cost of ruining our budget and giving us a deficit never imagined.

As Americans, we have done a great deal of good around the world. In education, the sciences, and charitable contributions, no one surpasses us. The majority of Americans are honest, decent law-abiding citizens that pay their taxes without complaining. We understand that we are blessed and are grateful. It should be noted that the degree of gratitude toward the Holy Spirit is always equal to or less than the degree of contentment.

It is the smallest 1 percent, the special interests, that ruins it for everyone. It is the untrustworthy attorneys turned politicians that work for their clients, not the people that elected them. It is the elected Hollywood actors that know how to act the part for the elite. It is the greedy Wall Street con artists that couldn't care less if their trading brings the entire financial system to the brink of collapse. It is the war mongers, the hawks that are vested in war machinery. It is the price-gouging pharmaceutical companies connected to congress through lobbyists. It is the atheists that believe only in evolution and science. It is the pro-choice that deny the unborn child a choice. It is the evil-minded white supremacists groups that hate other races. It is those of us that, with our free will of choice, cause the consequences and conditions of misery and suffering on humanity. I could go on and on, but we know the perpetrators.

When a government, any government, fails the interests of the people, it is time for an overhaul of that government. Currently, we have a divided and dysfunctional congress. It is time to take back our government, it is our constitutional right. Washington, D.C. is no longer run by Republicans or Democrats. It is run by the elite special interests at the expense of working Americans. It has been the largest buyout in US history. The family, the middle working class, has always been the foundation of America. It has been under attack from corporations and government for the past fifty-five years. When criminals think of other criminals as family, we know that we have a serious problem.

Let us never forget that where law and order end, tyranny begins. With the injustices, inequalities that have already occurred in America, we have taxation without representation. Sounds familiar? If I remember my history correctly, we fought a Revolutionary War due to this. The voices of the American people have been channeled into a soundproof vacuum and sealed. There is only a small amount of transparency.

Take as an example our prison system. The system with the death penalty is a definite failure in every sense of the word. First of all, who are we to condemn a man to death? We are now learning with DNA that there are innocent people serving prison time that were wrongly convicted. How many people were killed that were wrongfully convicted? This is—what are the words I'm looking for—ah, yes, collective unconsciousness of everyone involved in the process. These sorts of things happen understandably in an atheistic country, but in Christian America?

Our full-to-capacity prison system needs a complete overhaul. The death penalty needs to be eliminated. A person needs their chance to correct their wrong evil choices. The 3Cs need to be available to everyone until the destined time for their soul to leave their body/flesh. There is nothing wrong with hardships in prison. It should not be a resort to play ping-pong. We knew this at one time until a false civil liberalization ruined it all.

Crimes warrant the loss of certain civil liberties. I would recommend hard labor in three eight-hour shifts, seven days a week, as workers in a steel mill. This could easily take place on our remote farmlands and deserts. This would reduce by rotation the number of prisoners in a prison by one third overnight and the need for illegal immigrants now doing the work. The prisoners should work, get paid, and pay for their expenses of prison time and at the same time earn some money for themselves. These extremely high expenses should not be paid by the taxpayers for someone else's choice of crime.

If we want to put an end to illegal immigrants that fill the above jobs, this is a way of doing it. In the process, agricultural food prices would drop. The prisoners would regain their dignity and self-respect as being contributors to society. Prisoners are human beings, not animals like the ones at our zoo. No one has a right to deny them the basic freedoms as Americans.

Now as stated so many times, grace when squandered/wasted is not replaced. Why is state and Church not working together? I know that there needs to be different rules between Church and state, but the two could still work together for the good of humanity. If we have a tripod of state, church, and corporations working together with humanity at the top, the 3Cs could be truly amazing. This is not wishful thinking. If we look at Europe, in some countries, this is working for the benefit of all. The serene Republic of San Marino is a perfect example. I witnessed this myself in spending some time there.

Okay, as we can see, trying to get an institution such as the state government to help guide us in our effort to climb up to the summit is futile. Generally, the state or any other form of government has enough civil issues to deal with that it does not and cannot assist us—not in America, for sure.

So let us turn to education, science, and technology as institutions of knowledge. Perhaps these institutions offer some guidance. Let us try to decipher the Big Bang, cells, molecules, RNA, atoms, protein, nucleus, physics, nanotechnology, engineering genetics, evolutionary hypothesis, photons, etc. SD and ID, spiritual design and intellectual design, are not a part of most colleges except a Christian subcollege as in the University of Toronto.

There is a lot of excitement among academicians concerning the Big Bang. We think that all the answers to the meaning of life are to be found in the cosmos. It is somewhat like the people that thought all of the information and answers to life were in the Library of Alessandria until it burned down. The Big Bang that supposedly occurred around fourteen billion years ago does give some insight on light, though. Imagine that the light waves discovered by physicists from the Big Bang continue to appear and travel, also that the universe continues to grow and expand. Hmm, theoretical physicists are trying to study creation? The cosmos is but a reminder of the deepest mysteries of light.

I think that these are wonderful discoveries that help us understand the metaphysical universe. Humanity is great at this. The question is, where did the DNA, electrons, neutrons come from? Or better yet, how did they come to exist from nothingness to something? Genesis? Light and energy, nuclei and atoms? Hydrogen and helium equals nuclear fusion? Who created the formula? Around four to five billion years later, life forms on earth? The flow of photons captured by the lenses of a camera giving us images of figures on the negative film? Interestingly enough, these discoveries seem to confirm that all evolved from light. Light particle waves? Hypothesis theories, anti-theoretical, hmm. Evolution? $E=mc^2$?

So we are essentially proving that all matter has light, a traveling light or energy. Amazing, but who—what—is the common denominator? Notice that in mathematics, you must provide a common denominator for fractions to work. Math is true, honest. The laws of science, physics, biology, etc. work the same. But are the laws themselves metaphysical? No, they tell us how the metaphysical works. They were discovered by the mind of humanity that becomes knowledge. Knowledge generates more knowledge. Try E=ISD+ESD!

As an example, boiling water requires a certain fire or microwaves to boil, and here also light and energy are required. It always comes down to light and energy. Spark from flint, friction of rubbing two tree branches, the laws of fire. We are always dealing with the metaphysical, visible and invisible. Gravity and all in the universe work within defined laws. We discover the laws but refuse the creator that formulated the laws.

So what are we to learn from the laws? This is like humanity that up until Moses did not know/have the laws to live by. Humanity had to be given the laws first before being able to comprehend the invisible to our naked eye source. In better words, learning the benefits within the laws will help you learn to understand the light source. Notice how the Ten Commandments were rejected as laws by humanity. In doing so, their closed minds also rejected the source.♦ The original recipients of the laws always got in trouble for rejecting the laws. We have the same problems three thousand years later.

As scientists, we figure the causes of plagues, viruses, diseases, etc. What we are not good at is figuring how the causes came to exist. For example, natural light: we know what it is, we could explain it, but without an understanding of the source from which the light emerges, our understanding is limited, unless it is faith in the source.

Unlocking the genetic code of humanity is super as far as having the knowledge to be able to fight diseases and how the human body/flesh works, but it is still limited at best. For example, because of this knowledge, we know that we all came to exist because of one man. What does this tell us? We are all related, yes, but what else?

How about conscience and consciousness? We are now studying the consciousness of brain in our universities but in brain or in mind that functions in the brain? I think that a few of us have become Freudian fools of closed conscience. What are we attempting to do, clone the mind as we did with animals? What is next, downloading intelligence?

Before some of the mysteries of the metaphysical were discovered, did humanity think that it would be impossibly hard to prove and to be considered myth? In other words, if something is unseen, unproven, unscented, does this automatically make it myth? Were the deep sea monsters a myth at one time?

Enter Charles Darwin, who showed us that all life forms evolve continuously. But for what purpose? Take for instance a simple flower as the dandelion. It appears to be perfect already, even as a food source. Darwin, in a way, proves that the metaphysical on earth is similar to that of the galaxies, yet he did not get into what came first—the chicken or the egg. How did the chicken evolve and from what? In other words, how did the chicken begin and from what source? Another area that evolution does not cover is the male/female sex. How did they start and evolve? Notice also that Darwin did not get into natural light, which baffled him concerning the eyes of the creatures that he studied. We now know that in animals, there are a huge variety of eyes unlike humanity with only a few. The eyes of animals did evolve to fit their environment and help with their survival. But what of humanity? I do not see it (pardon the pun). We did not need to, but why? Because of our souls eyes? Because we are above the animal kingdom? Because of humanity's moral imprint? Because of humanity's superior soul? Without bringing the human soul into the picture, the entire evolutionary process explains evolving metaphysical forms that will simply die and rot away.

It is no different than in the field of medicine, biology, chemistry, physics, astronomy, anthropology and all sciences. They are limited at best. Let us remember that in the past century, it was science (the knowledge of mankind) having created the nuclear weapons of mass destruction that almost destroyed humanity, the animal kingdom, and the plant species. Yes, we could find cures, vaccines for the body/flesh. We can help prevent viruses from attacking the immune system. We can help alleviate the pain and suffering. All of this can only complement the discovery of the mind and heart within our soul where the real pain and suffering exist. This in itself could only be illuminated through faith in the Holy Trinity. This is not mythology; invisible spirituality needs discovering. For example, I recall seeing in the ruins of Pompeii frescos of sea creatures that looked like sea monsters. I thought this was mythological, as I never saw such creatures in modern times. Yet with the World Wide Web and photos by fishermen capturing the same creatures, I realized that they were not mythological. We, scientists and humanity, always want proof, but consciousness is invisible, and love is invisible until it is made visible in actions and experienced by the body/flesh.

Another example, three thousand years ago, two Egyptians were sitting on the desert pyramids gazing at the moon. One says, "Someday mankind will visit the moon on a chariot of fire." The other person says, "In your dreams." Why? At that moment, this was unfathomable. The human mind simply could not even imagine such a thing ever happening. Less than three thousand years later, it was a reality. The point is that humanity has to get there, reach a destination for the discovery as proof. But when we are close-minded, what could be discovered? Notice that when this is the case with the metaphysical world, it becomes more so in the soul's mind of the spiritual world. If humanity had a spacecraft that was self-powered by the light of the universe and could travel continually to the end of the universe, it would never reach that destination because there is no end. As astronomers, we know this, yet this also is unfathomable by our minds/brains. We are talking about the metaphysical, but this need not parallel the Holy Trinity.

Put all of the current so-called geniuses of the world into a conference hall to discuss the above issues, and collectively they are still only a tiny fraction of the knowledge of the Holy Spirit. Try this formula: S+HS=GK (Science plus Holy Spirit gives us Greater Knowledge). In this age of super computers and the World Wide Web, we no longer have an excuse or alibi for not knowing the Word and truth. Humanity is great with clones and drones, spaceships, electronics, and computers, but the *cuore* (heart) of the soul of humanity has become irrelevant in America, hence the degradation/evil invasion of our privacy that is invading our very souls. What of the civil liberties of the soul? Meditate on this for a while.

The Shroud of Turin continues to be another mysterious example. Is it real or man-made? We cannot find out about a mystery, any mystery, when no hope or faith exists. An atheist will ask, what is love? He or she may not have a concept of love. To them, it is a weak human emotion.

Also, the question of the dinosaurs still baffles us to this day. Why did they become extinct? Were they just an experiment of our creator to toy with?

We creationists do not have a problem with the evolutionary process. We just believe that there is much more to it. Without ISD, intellectual spiritual design, and ESD, emotional spiritual design, the evolutionary process is a dead end. For myself, I believe that if Saint Pope John Paul II had no problem with the evolutionary process; I certainly do not.

Now also notice how modern scientific society has ruined the rhythm of life. Study our lifestyle of scheduled appointments with stress, fast-paced living in our metropolitan areas. What does this do to our soul's second journey? It makes it much more complicated. This is the 3Cs—choices, consequences, and conditions—of the Industrial Revolution and the technological revolution. IT brings the world of information to our fingertips but nothing to our soul's heart. IT helps make our lives more manageable, easier to organize, but for what ultimate purpose? If we are so intelligent, why have we made our lives so much more difficult to enjoy? If IT is not a means to peace and tranquility, it is but another one of our toys. We need to ask ourselves why some of us—for example, we Amish and Quakers—have shunned automation. We believe that living within the confines of the past centuries is more beneficial for our soul's second journey. It is as if our soul's moral imprint, our DNA, is telling us to keep it simple. This also reminds me of ten simple basic commandments. Their simplicity originated in light three thousand years ago. Believe it or not, before these communications with humanity, there were no laws to live by. Men killed, raped women, stole, enslaved, lied, robbed, committed adultery, and did all other evil things imaginable. Humanity, you might say, was at a lower level than animals. They were not grateful to anyone. Sounds familiar? Christ, as mentioned, elevated humanity to an even higher level. The problem was the part that says, "Love your neighbor as yourself." It was a huge stumbling block that only a tiny fraction of humanity has managed to overcome. This is the difference between a theist and an atheist. An agnostic does not care one way or another.

Notice also the business ethicists in our highly advanced big pharmaceutical companies connected to lobbyists and congress. Not long ago, a new medication was introduced to fight Hepatitis C for people suffering from the disease. My mother was one of them. The cost? A thousand dollars per pill.

How did this come about? I remember a business class in college where the professor told us that on the final exam, we do whatever we have to in order to get a high grade. He left the room, and that is exactly what happened. Students used their notes, books, friends, anything and everything in order to get a high score. This is business ethics in America. It is only about the bottom line. Stay healthy, my friends, and learn about herbal remedies.

Do we as educated people know how to get and stay healthy? We have the knowledge. For example, I know that the studies done decades ago of the importance of eating five varieties of fruits and vegetables each day. This helps tremendously in enabling our body/flesh to ward off cancers. Do we heed this advice and warning? A small percentage of us do, but then you can see the long lines of people in our fast food drive-through each day ordering mainly fried, fatty, salty food. So NO, the majority of us do not.

The statistics on the physical health of the average American is now the worst in our history. Just about every part of the body/flesh is unhealthy from head to toe. From clogged arteries in our hearts to mental illness in our brains, we have become sickened. Our lifestyle, our priorities, and our sense of good health has been mostly lost. Is there a correlation between the health of the soul and that of the body/flesh? There absolutely is. Those few of us that place a priority to maintain a healthy soul automatically take care of our body/flesh. We realize the necessity of needing a healthy body to function in. Big Pharma only wants to sell us prescription drugs at whatever cost we can bare and keep us on them as long as possible. Trust Big Pharma? You decide.

In this highly educated century, for the first time in American history, we started having assisted suicide. This is by medical doctors that supposedly took an oath of helping to heal the human body. It appears that death of the body/flesh is the next uncontrollable, corrupt, capitalistic growth market. We have taken a leap back three thousand years. One of the Ten Commandments is "Do not kill," not only other human beings but also yourself. The 3Cs here—choices, individually and collectively by voters in certain states, will result in severe consequences and unbearable conditions for us highly educated Americans.

When I was growing up, I was taught that small sins were venial sins, but uncorrected, they lead to mortal sins or sins that could kill us. Think that this sounds silly? See what we are doing to the human body/flesh. Think that it is no big deal? Think again. To intentionally kill the body/flesh is one of the gravest of sins. There may not be forgiveness for it. The sin is mortal not only for the body/flesh but for the soul as well. Why is the US Supreme Court not doing anything to put a stop to this? This, of all things, is unconstitutional. This is an evil that needs to be confronted immediately. This is what we are teaching our children? The rotting unseen has already set in our highly educated minds/brains. Uncorrected, the very soul of America will descend into darkness. I cannot overstate the seriousness of this issue. This is a cancer and a plague combined. Our enemies do not have to start a war with us. Not corrected, we will self-destruct in time.

A parallel to pagan Rome? Atheism has taken a grip onto a small percentage of Americans, even if most fear claiming to be so. Are we becoming like the Japanese that think nothing about killing the body/flesh? This is something to meditate on. Again, it is also worth noting that America is not figured into prophecy of the future events that are to unfold. Why? At the rate we are going, we most likely will not be a major player in international affairs anymore, even if we do spend hundreds of billions of dollars on a bloated defense budget. Let us keep in mind that it took pagan Rome one thousand years for the 3Rs—repentance and reconciliation—to clear away the darkness of her soul. It took another five hundred years for her redemption and atonement. The Vatican as we know her today has finally taken on a positive, constructive role in the souls of humanity on a multi-national level. Thank goodness for the monasteries' preservationists, men and women, that kept the holy words safe. During the dark ages, the Roman Catholic Church was too much into politics and enriching herself. The choices of the American churches and government, new Rome (negative events) that we highly educated Americans have accepted in the past half century have to be accounted for. The consequences and conditions are clearly becoming visible.

To give us an idea of who we have become, let me give another example of the younger generation. While teaching in Shanghai, I asked my college students what was more important to them—IQ (intellectual quality/quantity) or EQ (emotional quality/quantity). The overwhelming answer was EQ. Remember that this is an atheist country with only their moral imprint. Ask the same question to American students, and their answer is often IQ. This should give us an idea of the direction we are heading in.

As we can see, the educational institutions are NOT much of a guide for us, especially when 50 percent of the scientists do not consider themselves theist. Notice that the more knowledge we attain of the metaphysical, the less knowledge we tend to accept of the spiritual. A true scientist would ask how it is that our earth tilts 23.5

degrees on her axis to give earth and her continents the different seasons every single year. Instead, half of scientists think of it as just another unexplained phenomenon. We do not stop to think that the seasons have to do with life and death as our own of body/flesh and, perhaps, soul. The winter, with the cold and longer darkness of night, should remind us of our own soul's coldness and darkness. It should be obvious, but with humanity, it is seldom the case. Spring should be a new beginning of light and growth. Summer should remind us of the fruits of our labor. Autumn should remind us that we are all here on this wonderful earth for a short time. What are we afraid of? To see ourselves for who we really are?

I always hear talk of the free spirited, yet I see people not interested or involved in the discovery of themselves. I hear the words *bright, brighter, brightest, brilliantly,* and *brightening* to describe people, yet I see people afraid of their own shadow. Without spirituality, we are but shallow illiterates. It is no wonder that a person who never learned to read or write could be tracking higher on their soul's chart than a scientifically accomplished scholar.

When a mystery of the metaphysical is scientifically proven, we are contentedly proud of our outstanding achievement. Ah, how small-minded we mortals can be. Make no mistake, without the light/mindfulness of intellectual spiritual design and emotional spiritual design, what we know is a drop in the bucket. I believe that we really need a healthy austerity program, a fasting of the metaphysical body/flesh now and then. Our dolce vita may be hurting us. The consequences and conditions of fasting might be of some guidance in themselves.

The majority of us need a guide that lets us understand the right choices for the development of our soul's second journey. There is an enormous amount of data to interpret dating back three thousand-plus years. Next, we will look into the five mainstream religions of our time. We have already been exposed to a part of the Roman Catholic Church, yet there are many Christian churches. We have pre-Christian, the Synagogue/Temple of Judaism. We have for the last 1,400 years the Mosque of the Islamic religion. From the eastern regions, we have Hinduism and Buddhism. We will explore all five.

Who among us has experienced Hinduism, Buddhism, Islam, Judaism, and Christianity all in a lifetime? Would it be a good idea to take the best of each of them? I mean do we need confession of our sins? Also, what about Satanism, communism, fascism, nationalism, socialism, imperialism, and Nazi law and order? Could these be considered religions, or are they only hallucinations for dying souls of dark ideologies? One of the problems that we encounter is that we are not asking the toughest questions. For example, what are the promises of a religion? A better example, does that religion spread love and peace or terrorism with hate, violence, and war? I understand that it is a tiny fraction of the whole, but what is the remaining majority fraction doing to stop it? Humanity, being the most sophisticated life form, can easily go from superior in light to inferior, to inferno with our 3Cs. Yes, even the dolphins laugh at us. The right religion is open to all questions, as there is a right answer to any and all questions. It is not a lottery or luck as with gambling and winning or losing it all. Certain religions are but philosophical pacifiers that only neutralize and incapacitate us from our climb up to the summit. We become victims of laziness, just mediocre citizens getting by.

I recall as a child walking past the courthouse in downtown Youngstown. The architectural design was Roman style and impressive, but what really made a big impression on me were the words high above the front facade. "Where law and order end tyranny begins." As a child, I know that these words had a significant amount of mystery and meaning. I never imagined that it would take my climbing the summit to fully integrate them into my soul. Law and order is essentially needed by our souls, not only from our moral imprint but also from our soul's tabernacle. As a youth, I had so many questions that would haunt me for many, many years. We now know that the mind is always at work within our brain, even as we are sleeping. It is working on our changing events of our 3Cs—choices, consequences, and conditions. The purpose is to get us on track on our soul's second journey. Maybe this is what some of our nightmares are about. NO, we need not go to the Himalayas to talk to some guru. The true Holy Spirit is within and without at all times; a quiet place will do just fine.

A religion is like a refrigerator full of food to eat, and yet we cannot decide because we don't have the appetite, or our soul's heart and mind don't recognize the food. With a closed mind, we cannot divide what is healthy from what is not.

This book is about Christianity, but what about those of us that were born into another religion?

Keep an open heart and open mind? Let our soul's conscience be our guide? What if we cannot even interpret our soul's conscience? Do we need a modern-day Daniel of the Old Testament? Who are the doctors of the Church for us? Are they the living saints? How does my free will work? How is it a key to the tabernacle of my soul's heart? This is seriously a time to be cautious. Who realistically looks forward to entering a desert, perhaps quicksand for their soul? Hence, a strong spiritual advisor is in high demand these days, as there is a shortage. Is this a mystery in itself? Not really, but as so often happens, we look into the wrong channel.

As with any subject, a well-rounded, educated, and mature teacher ultimately will benefit our soul's second journey. We are pop culture, we are easily influenced by any gimmickry. What do we compare heaven, hell, or purgatory to? Should we have a glimpse of each one of the three?

Most of us have a church, temple, synagogue, mosque, or whatever we choose to call our place of worship. The question is, are we being enlightened? Or can we not wait when we are there to leave? Is it all a monotonous, boring experience? Like food in a refrigerator that loses its nutritional value after a few days, is this what we experience in our place of worship? We have to ask ourselves, is it the food itself or the refrigerator or both? What is being offered to us for our second journey? What is being said of our third journey?

Notice that some religions have multiple gods as Hinduism, similar to the pagan Greeks and Romans. Notice that this is acceptable to communism along with Buddhism, as if not a threat to them. Why? How many gods do we need? A monotheist believes in one God as we in Judaism, Islam, and Christianity. Our light is from one source. A TE is a theistic evolutionist that believes in God and evolution as Saint Pope John Paul the II. It is a good synthesis and balance of science and God, with God as the creationist.

This should give us a better understanding of the spiritual and metaphysical working together from conception in the climb to the summit and ultimately our third journey. Of course, it's usually our parents that start us into whichever religion we had as beginners. As young adults, our own 3Cs are in action, and we have a level of comprehensive notions that run through our minds.

For myself, important events such as natural disasters, famines, plagues, and human calamities determine what *religion* and *religious* are truly about. The charity and love toward the suffering speaks a thousand words. The treatment of children particularly tells the whole world what a religion is all about. We will see that it comes down to a process of elimination. A religion that has the good fruits of the Holy Spirit or a religion of complacency or evil, bad fruit. A true religion will discuss the transformation, metamorphosis, a resurrection and transmigration with transfiguration of our soul from the death of our body/flesh to life into a third journey of heaven or that of purgatory or hell. A true religion acknowledges this process and has this as its theme.

The wrong choice with those who have alternating motives could be devastating, especially on the young. The right religion has an altruistic heart. In other words, she is helpful without asking anything in return and no strings attached. A true religion is concerned about you and your 3Cs, your climb, your hardships, and your suffering. It is, in essence, an adventure to travel for the soul. For the saints, three words summarize a religion—way, truth, and life.

If only we had some sort of test for a religion. These days, anyone anywhere is able to start up a religion. What assurance do we have as to the authenticity of a religion? Past tragedies of cult members ending in suicide from drinking cyanide in Jonestown, Guyana, was not that long ago. Another cult stayed with a fatalistic leader in Waco, Texas, perishing in flames that burned them alive also not so long ago.

It is worth noting here that recently studies have been done at Harvard University on the effects of prayer to our body/flesh. The findings to me were not a surprise, but for most people, they will be. The findings were that people who pray, for example, the Holy Rosary to the Blessed Virgin Maria experience a positive change that starts with the mind, free will to pray within the soul but manifests out into our biological body/flesh. This should not be surprising since the soul and flesh are one. I have tested it myself in a night when, having so much on my mind, I found it hard to get to sleep. By simply repeating the Hail Mary slowly over and over, the process reduces the stress, and sleep comes within a short time. It's interesting to note that an actual physical change occurs within the body/flesh. No, this is not counting sheep. This is a communication with spiritual light so that the communication could be with anyone of spiritual light—the Holy Spirit, our Blessed Virgin Maria, the confirmed saints and angels, etc.

Does this help us in our decision to the right choice? Is this any kind of proof? It's something to meditate on. It always comes down to the 3Cs, choices of our free will. It always comes down to a yes or no as with civil matters. Do I follow the civil laws or not? It's not a matter of maybe or "It depends on this or that." Our moral imprint is the same; it is either a yes or a no. Not maybe or it depends on what is involved. I know that it is hard to live the faith with all of the circumstances of the moment. Yet this is the purpose of the moral imprint as a tool. The right guide helps to interpret the laws and retain order in our souls. History tells us the civil laws that work for the benefit of humanity. For example, the percentage of alcohol in our blood allowed before driving a car saves lives. It took us almost a century to make it a law. The same holds true in the metaphysical laws of physics—for example, gravity. It took until a few centuries ago since the beginning of humanity for this law to be accepted and understood. The laws of the Holy Spirit have been presented to humanity for thousands of years, and yet few, just a tiny percentage of humanity, accept the common denominator for the laws of our soul.

There is always a degree of avoiding and rejection or wanting a modification of the laws. But why, for example, would the Roman Catholic Church want to modify Canon Laws that took centuries to develop? Another example for young children, although they may understand better than adults, is building a house. We know that it takes a foundation to support the house. It takes, for example, a lot of wood, two-by-fours, a saw, nails, lots of nails, and a good hammer. Now after the house is built, people say, "Nice sturdy house." But what is the common denominator? The carpenter that puts it all together and does all the work. Why we fail to acknowledge this in the Holy Spirit for our body/flesh and soul is a question to also meditate on. For the earth, cosmos, and entire universe, the same principles apply.

There are countless myths and superstitions out there due to ignorance rooted in false lights. Man/woman has inherited from past generations an enormous amount of false data. The result is the consequences and conditions, confounded and dumbfounded. For example, circumcision on baby boys is an ancient ritual that makes no sense. To torture a baby and risk infection is ridiculous. The human anatomy needs no modification unless deformed. It has no extra pieces or parts. The medical professionals say, "But it helps in the prevention of the spread of STDs (sexually transmitted diseases)." Yes, but the real question should be, where do sexual diseases such as AIDS come from? More importantly, what behavior causes the transmitting and spread of the diseases? Because a small percentage of people are causing the problem is justification for all children to suffer the Consequences and Conditions? This is unconstitutional and wrong.

I think that it is important, before we start into the five mainstream religions, to study the Renaissance in Italy. The giants of the Renaissance such as Michelangelo (whose name, by the way, is taken after the archangel Michel) and Leonardo da Vinci have a great deal to teach us. They helped bring us out of the medieval age of darkness. They helped restore faith and hope in a new age, a new beginning. Michelangelo left us his works such as his Pieta and the painting in Sistine Chapel, his children, to remind us not to fall back into the darkness. Leonardo da Vinci gave us the knowledge of the metaphysical body/flesh to dissect and study, combining the body/flesh to the figures in his paintings as if affirming that the body/flesh and spiritual soul are one. These artists and countless others reminded us of what it means to be created. They, being blessed with grace, are constantly reminding us that law and order are necessary not only for the body/flesh but for our soul as well. This is what it takes to remove the dumbfounded mentality and become enlightened, reborn into the Spirit again. These two men were not saints, but they possessed the tools that were put into their artwork to benefit future generations. Notice that in the major cities in Italia, Roma has the roads to law and order, Florence has the Renaissance/rebirth/renewal, Venice, the maritime routes to bring it out of Italy into the Eastern world. Napoli and Genova had/have the ports for the migration of Christian Italians to the Americas. Yes, Italia has been truly blessed with grace. During the Renaissance (the rebirth), grace was pouring into all the city states of the Italian peninsula. This blossoming of the arts was no coincidence. It is as if finally, after the darkness, the penance, the atonement, she was being rewarded. She would still have to wait three hundred more years for her reunification, uniting all the city states and forming the amazing country she is today.

So what are we looking for in our pilgrimage to faraway, distant holy places? We go to the Holy Land, the wall of sorrows and mourning, the places where apparitions occurred and are still occurring. We seek and want to touch the relics of the saints. What is it that we want? These all have to do mainly with the metaphysical. If this helps us to exercise our free will, wonderful, but we must recognize that within our soul's heart is all that we need. The means to climb up to the summit, our ascension to spiritual knowledge in light is within us. We do not need to make expensive and exhaustive trips around the world, and perhaps even be disappointed with the consequences. Again, study the lives of the saints. Many of them accomplished their own climb, their miracles, in a cloister of silence, prayer, and fasting.

Now let us start with Hinduism, which is mainly out of Asia and largely in India. Hinduism is not practiced much in the West and is a polytheism, meaning having many gods. As mentioned earlier, this is similar to the early pagan Greek and Roman civilizations. My question is: why are there so many gods? I recall visiting a few of these temples with multiple gods, and I must admit it didn't make much sense to me. We know that one of the apostles of Christ, Saint

Thomas, traveled all the way to India. His teachings did take root but not as strong, and neither did it grow as in other parts of the world. Hinduism would become more entrenched. It is hard to say why two thousand years after the fact. It would be interesting to know what miracles have occurred by their prophets within this religion, what apparitions by our Blessed Virgin Maria, if any, and what witnesses have to say. Are demons able to be expelled from a person? By which of their many gods? What is this religion actively doing for peace within the Asian region? Does this religion recognize everyone as being from the same family of families? I see more turbulence and chaos in this entire region than anything else.

For myself, this little known fact will summarize what I believe of Hinduism. The tiger exists in many parts of the world, but nowhere in the world does the tiger attack human beings as prey as the Bengal tiger in India. We are talking about twenty thousand-plus fatalities a year of adults and children. It should also be noted that the Bengal tiger is within the deities of this religion. In other words, a Bengal tiger that kills is not hunted and killed or moved into a sanctuary of some kind. What this does is elevate the Bengal tiger above humanity. Hence, the tiger hasn't any fear of humanity. I have a serious problem with this.

I cannot criticize this religion. Who am I to criticize or judge any religion? I believe that if a religion brings peace and harmony to people, then the Holy Spirit is at work in mysterious ways within that religion. That is the key: what peace, what harmony? Gandhi was one man; what has transpired since his death? At the same time, we Westerners think that we have all the answers for everyone; we do not.

Now let us turn to Buddhism. This religion is also mainly in Asia. Having spent a lot of time in Shanghai, I have had my share of Buddhism. I believe that those accepting Buddhism are interested in the M&M (money and material) things in their second journey. I remember people always talking about the good luck of a person comparable to the Buddha. This always dealt with the metaphysical body/flesh. For example, the size of the earlobes was to signify wealth—the larger, the wealthier. The same applies to certain facial features, belly size, etc. The golden Buddha reminds me of the golden calf made by the Hebrew people who fled into the desert from Egypt.

I did not see where Buddhism shows a way to the summit of spiritual knowledge for our soul or into the third journeys. Even the American natives, most likely descendants from Asia after crossing over from Asia into the Americas, believe in the spirits of their ancestors in a positive way. They call on them for assistance, not burning fake money to rise up to them, but for what? American natives believe in the same with the spirits of animals. Also, they believe in the light of the sun, metaphysical, yes, but also light from the same source of light. In Buddhism, I did not see anyone get involved in much of this.

Again, let me give examples of what some of the people of Buddhism are capable of doing. During the Cultural Revolution in China, millions of artifacts dating back many centuries were literally destroyed. Universities were closed. Professors were mocked and ridiculed. Western culture became illegal, etc. Sounds familiar? This is happening today in some parts of the world. So how could a people practicing Buddhism and following Confucius's philosophy allow this to take place? Another example, I recall giving my college students an assignment to look up a Chinese love poem to be translated in class. The poems brought to class were mainly about the love of nature and not humanity. Again, I had a serious problem with this. Love of nature is good, but what about the love of humanity?

I also do not want to criticize or judge Buddhism or the Confucian philosophy. Again though, I have to ask, what peace and harmony exists within this religion? What missionaries are spreading love and charitable contributions to humanity? What light and what way to the summit and #10 does this religion profess?

Our next religion is Judaism. Those of us that are Christians know a little bit of this religion. After all, it's the first half of the Christian religion or the Old Testament. Why the Hebrew people, of all people, to become the chosen people? We were and perhaps still are, to some degree, the most wretched of people of the past 3,500 years. Notice how Dio works in mysterious ways. From the Pharoahs of Egypt through Moses up to the Caesars, we have been and continue to be a difficult lot. We were promised a Messiah from the house of David through the prophets that came to be our King of Kings. We said, not from Nazareth, not from a poor family. We chose a common criminal to be freed by Pontius Pilate instead and had the Messiah condemned, beaten, mocked, ridiculed, and crucified. We got all this done in time so that it would not interfere with our Passover. On top of all of this, we made it seem like it was not our fault, that we were not to blame. It was the Romans, how could Pontius Pilate wash his own hands? We were there, we know what went down. Forget about Nicodemus, what does he know?

Ah, the Christians, what do they know? They are trying to twist things around. We are, after all, still the chosen people. We were decimated, our glorious temple destroyed by the legions of Titus, leaving us only a wall to cry on, and yet it doesn't change anything. Yes, we were thrown out of our beloved city of Jerusalem like rats to live in the slums and ghettos of whoever would accept us, but we are still the chosen people. We were almost exterminated by Hitler's SS, but we survived as a people. America, the new Rome, took us in with open arms. Her president even gave us our country to go back to. So we are back home where we started. No one in the region loves us, but that's okay as long as we are the chosen people loved by I AM.

I am sorry for the sarcastic paragraph above, but it's the way I see it through history. Being Italian and Roman Catholic, I am perhaps being a little biased, true. But how do we deny historical data? Is the German denial of the Holocaust due to the denial of us Jews' involvement in the killing of Christ? There is sin, darkness, penance, and atonement throughout our soul's second journey. It is the same, if not more so, for us chosen people of Israel. We have come home to a tombstone in the Wailing Wall to cry of our loss of our covenant with the Holy Spirit. Even the therapeutic discoveries of Sigmund Freud do not help us. Of course, we could always live in the past, in the days of David and Solomon when we were the recipients of graces. A new temple? A temple of Christ in the Holy Spirit of Christ? Please, we would rather hold on to the past. We have the Ten Commandments of Moses. We do not need a summit to climb up to; Moses did that for us. We are an intellectual people; look at our accomplishments in the metaphysical world. We have our Sabbath, our Passover, our new synagogues. What do we need for our soul? A soul's chart, a quick quiz and tracking of our soul's light? Why change? We like our rituals, our weekly routines. We like who we are as a chosen people.

Prophesied future events? Please, we have been studying Scriptures for thousands of years. We think that we know a thing or two of the Scriptures.

Enough said about Judaism.

The next religion we will explore is Islam.

I am writing this a day after Pope Francisco pleaded for the international community to help stop the savage attacks on men, women, and children in the Middle East. The minority Christian communities are being persecuted in Syria, Iraq, Iran, and other areas in this region of the world. I could see from the previous night at the Natale midnight mass the sadness and sorrow that this pope feels for what is happening in the Middle East and other parts of Africa and Asia. I saw no other religious leader of any religion come forward with the same plea.

This religion, Islam, is not old. It was started by Muhammad in the beginning of the seventh century AC, supposedly when one of the archangels communicated with him. In this part of the world, Iraq, Iran, and other desert countries, we were pleased to have our own religion, yet we in this region are all related in some way. The past prophets of the Old Testament in Judaism are also the prophets of Muslims, but that is where the similarities end. We Islamic people, although believing in the Quran and peace and love, are more of a warrior religion. We seem to be always at war among ourselves in our different sects of Islam against Judaism, Christianity, and every other religion no matter where we go. It's ironic because although we believe in the Blessed Virgin Maria as the Queen of Queens and acknowledge her supreme among all women, we think of her Son Christ as just another prophet.

These days, we do everything in the name of Allah, especially war, as if we know His will. Was it this way from the beginning with Muhammad in Mecca? Or was it some other influence, say,

Medina? Or perhaps are we trying to copy the Christian Crusaders that invaded the Holy Land many centuries ago? Perhaps do we want Mecca to be the Eternal City, the center of the world? Or do we want the entire region for ourselves and Allah, no one else?

This reminds me of us trouble-making Israeli people who tested Caesar's patience with Judaism. Only now we are testing the patience of the new Rome in Washington, D.C. and the reunited Rome of Europe. Notice how the 3Cs are at work here. We Muslims, like the Israeli people, have no idea of the ramifications that could result due to our choices of causing problems for everyone in the region. The consequences and conditions from an all-out war with a superpower and her allies could cause severe death and destruction in our region. The new weaponry of America is not science fiction or futuristic; it is now, today, constantly changing and being upgraded and modernized to cause mass destruction with the least amount of American and allied soldier casualties. The current drones being used are just a glimpse of what scientists have worked on. Recall Saddam Hussein, Osama bin Laden? Where are they today? New weaponry has people itching to see how it performs. As an example, one American general said, "An act of aggression by North Korea against South Korea would result in North Korea being leveled to the ground." Think that this is a bluff? Think about Japan at the end of World War II. This was seventy years ago. The weapons of today will be much more destructive.

Does it need to come to that? It does not. Although a few in America predict a World War III within fifty years, it does not have to occur. The 3Cs, especially the choices, are up to all of us of every religion. Remember that omission to do something about the current events taking place today is also a sin. We silent majority are almost as guilty as the perpetrators. We will all be held accountable within our souls. For the false martyrs, teenagers, and even children being encouraged by Muslim morons to throw away their lives and second journey is an evil in itself. We should not be shocked when the time comes that Allah will say, "I do not know you, A."

Ask any experienced army general about how to defeat the opponent, and he will tell you to separate, divide them, cut them off from their supply source, have them hate, fight and kill each other, and the rest is easy. Does this sound familiar? Recall also that evil begets evil. History shows how this happens over and over again. As mentioned, humanity, by accepting evil spirits, destroys humanity and all within reach (excluding the evil spirits that will continue to exist). When will we learn this?

I understand that the percentage of the Islamic religious in the world causing so much misery among people in all parts of the world with their radical terrorist attacks is a tiny percentage. But what are we, the rest of the Islamic community, doing to stop the beheading of the innocent, the forcing of people to convert to the Islam or die? We call ourselves civilized people? This is a disgrace (grace lost). People in the Stone Age did not commit such atrocities. I, a peaceful and loving Muslim, question all this. I understand full well that the West is sick with their immoral practices, especially regarding sexuality. But what are we to teach them? What example are we with our own weaknesses? We have our own evils to deal with. A true religion fears no questionable 3Cs directly to his/her name. Are we ourselves asking the toughest questions of our religion? It is hard for us to throw stones at others when we are guilty of so many sins.

There is an evil darkness within the terrorists causing so much suffering that is darker than the flag that they fly in the name of Allah. If peace and love are not given a chance, I am afraid that a heavy iron hand and the claws of the eagle will be used again. An evil to overcome a greater evil. In this, humanity loses, and evil wins out. Time to meditate?

As you may have figured out, I'm definitely not a fan of Islam. It is not about what most of the Quran has written in it or about mostly what Muhammad preached. It is about what I see on the daily evening news. It is about absent dialogue. It is about changing for the better. It is about peaceful resolutions. It is about Christ, Gandhi, and Mandela who have shown us an easier and better way. It is about the Ten Commandments that Islamic Muslim people are aware of, but a small percentage make a choice to ignore. It is about understanding that we are all related and that we are a tiny fraction of the whole. I am sorry to say that this religion has the "way, truth, and life" that is light all twisted up into a knot. Will things change? Probably not. Evil appears to have taken over the minds of Islamic Muslim terrorist groups. These groups are recruiting innocent youth for suicide missions that even their parents encourage such a thing happened with the kamikaze Japanese in World War II. Divine intervention? It is always possible but not probable, as this very seldom happens.

So let us move on to Christianity. Most of us in the West are or were familiar with Christianity. We know that the prophets of Judaism in the Old Testament wrote about the coming of the Messiah, the Christ. There are countless books and movies on the greatest story on earth. From the annunciation to our Blessed Virgin Maria by the Archangel Gabriel to the birth of Christ in a manger to Saint John the Baptist's announcement of preparing the way for the prophesied One to come to Herod the Horrible—we know much of the story. Who in the West does not know about the betrayed Christ by Judas and the condemnation by the temple leaders of Jerusalem to turn Christ over to the Romans to do their dirty work, as if the Romans would take the blame? The crucifixion, the resurrection, and the ascension of Christ are well known but very seldom understood in all of their mysteries. Yes, we know that Christ sent the Holy Spirit during Pentecost to assist humanity. He also gave the keys to His future Church to Peter and told his disciples to spread the Gospel to the ends of the earth. This all worked well for the most part except for a few of the Christians being persecuted for about three centuries in the Roman Empire. As mentioned, Roman Emperor Constantino changed everything for the better development of Christianity. This is a quick review of an often misunderstood Christianity. The mysteries would take many more centuries to be revealed.

This brings us to the divide. While Saint Peter and Paul went west into Rome, Emperor Constantino went east. The distance itself caused a separation as was the case with authority, law and order within the empire itself, hence the need for the Greek Orthodox Church and eventually the Russian Orthodox Church. All were Christian, all very similar in their teachings, yet not exactly.

Let us take a look at the Greek Orthodox Church as well as the Russian Orthodox Church. I have been to a Greek Orthodox Church Sunday service. I did not see much difference from the Roman Catholic service with the exception of Greek being used instead of Latin. The readings and, most importantly, the Holy Eucharist of wine and actual pieces of bread used are similar. The Russian Orthodox Church service I have not attended, but I imagine it is probably similar to the Greek Orthodox Church.

The point that I want to make is why the separation, why the divide even now in the twenty-first century? Remember, separate, divide, and subdivide. Having them hate and kill each other to ruin each other is a tool that evil uses throughout history. Also, we could see why there would be confusion on not only the interpretation of the Old Testament but also the interpretation of the holy Gospels of the New Testament. Who can clearly interpret Revelation? Prophecies require the help of the Holy Spirit found in the doctors of the Roman Catholic Church such as Saint Augustine, Saint Thomas Aquinas, and others. When there is a division and subdivision and more subdivisions, misinterpretation and confusion are bound to prevail. There should be one road map, one guide, one source for all Christianity. All roads did and should lead to one light as the Holy Spirit within the Holy Trinity. In this century of turmoil, isn't it about time to come together for the greater good of the souls of all?

We need to understand how evil works. Evil starts from the outside and works into the mind, penetrating through the weaknesses of humanity. For example, we know that a great many civil crimes are inside jobs. It works the same way with evil and any institution, including the Christian Church. Take, for example, the recent terrorist attacks in America; they were carried out by those living among us.

So what are we waiting for? Notice that the evils of terrorism are spreading from the Middle East to Western, Northern, and Southern countries and into Africa. We are all waiting for someone else to act, such as the new Rome, America. The radical religious Islamic groups are making it a holy war, which are the deadliest and worst kind of wars. It is no time for all other religions to do their own thing, which usually amounts to nothing. Remember that an omission to act is also a sin.

This brings us into the Protestant churches of Christianity. Again, separate, divide, subdivide, and keep subdividing. Sounds familiar? This is evil's trademark, to separate from the source. It reminds me of wild animal predators that try to separate the weakest from the strength of the center force that is united and as a unit is able to withstand a dangerous predator. This force, we Christians know, is Christ. The predator is Satan.

I realize that the Protestant Christian churches exist for good reasons. I have studied the reasons. Martin Luther was right, as I have mentioned, in wanting to correct the abuses of the Holy See, the cardinals, and those associated with Vatican City. This took place centuries ago. The question is, what are we protesting now, today? The statuary? The paintings? Baptism? The tabernacle of the Holy Eucharist of Christ? The laws of order in Canon Law? The confession of sins? Holy Communion? The mass? Now notice that none of these were issues before the inquisition and separation. Why should they be issues today? Martin Luther was a rebel with a cause. He was not a liberalization force to change what he loved in the Roman Catholic Church. If anything, he wanted to preserve the beauty of who she was/is. He never intended for a radical shifting to the extreme left. He knew that the Church was the dwelling place of Christ's body in the Eucharist and Holy Spirit. He understood the importance of the sacraments, the mass, the Holy Eucharist, Confession of sins, and communion. This is what he saw as being neglected and being exploited. He never intended for a split up and would be the first to accept reconciliation similar to Thomas Merton of the last century.

Merton saw that the Roman Catholic Church is not just bricks and mortar that could burn down or be wiped away from a natural disaster. He realized that the Roman Catholic Church is more than readings from Scriptures. More than anyone else, he saw from his own summit the wonders of the Holy Spirit within the Holy Trinity within the Roman Catholic Church. Merton was the prodigal son that came home. Now notice how this parallels with our own body/flesh and soul from the Roman Catholic Church. Martin Luther probably knew that this was not occurring in the Eastern Greek Orthodox Church. Here the traditional Christian Church was better preserved and maintained. Here she had not become corrupted as the Vatican.

Notice what has happened since the initial separation, division, and subdivisions that still continue to this day. We have startup Christian churches that anyone can start up. We have self-ordained ministers by their own authority. We have churches that have made up their own standards, whatever and whichever is pleasing to the congregation. Give them whatever they want, but let's not lose them as contributing parishioners. As Protestant churches, we are as unified as many of the unified public schools in America with the same standards and results. The cracks in our foundation, if we ever had a real one since our separation, are very evident today. We are becoming shattered and scattered in our disarray. We are not unified in moral issues and do not know which doctrines to follow. We allow pick-and-choose similar to a buffet. A parishioner has a right to ask, "What does your church have to offer me" The problem is that if we offer only what they want, like a child, what are we giving them? We have churches popping up all over the world like wild mushrooms. The hazards are that "some are edible, some will make you sick, and some are poisonous." Far too many people do not recognize the difference. We have one Church that claims to know where Christ went on the three days between His death and His resurrection. They have turned this into a religious Church in itself.

One is able to see clearly what has transpired in the Church of Christ from the summit. We see through the centuries, through the darkness, and through the evils of humanity even in the Roman Catholic Church. We need to ask ourselves: what has become of us as Christians? Are we not conscious of the damage done in separate channels trying to help ourselves and others? What is silenced in our conscience? Heaven, purgatory, and hell have not changed except in our mind's view of these places. It should not surprise us that people are becoming agnostic or atheist. They see how disoriented we Christians have become. We cannot find common ground on the basic freedoms of humanity. They see us divided on moral laws, so people turn to science and technology.

I think it is time to ask ourselves, who gives legitimacy to a Christian church? In Asia, for example, there are Christian churches that are run and controlled by Communist governments.

In parts of the world, even America, there are Christian churches that exploit their parishioners. Some of these churches have demons disguised as ministers. The times change, but certain things were designed to last an eternity. The Ten Commandments are a perfect example of this; they are timeless, yet there are those who try to amend and modify them. But who tells them that they are not allowed to do so? Cults, false religions appear to be able to do anything that they want to since there is no government or any other authority to stop them. How often do we see a so-called Christian church closed down after the people who ran it stole, took the money, and disappeared?

We need to meditate on the facts that there was and should be only one Messiah, one Christ, one Baptism, and one Holy Spirit within one Holy Trinity. Christ gave out one set of keys to Peter to build one universal church. He never said to divide and subdivide her into different sects. What is it with us geeky Greeks, reindeer Russians, preaching Protestants, and choosy Catholics that we cannot figure out? As there is one sun and one earth for all of humanity, so also there needs to be one spiritual light, one Holy Spirit in one Christian universal church.

The Church of Christ needs to be a church that in forgiving wants reconciliation and restoration of the souls of humanity. The Church of Christ is a Church that, in her charity, helps those who seek to climb to their summit of spiritual knowledge in light. This Church puts hope into the hearts of those who have fears. I believe with all my heart and soul that the Roman Empire was set up for a purpose. It was set up to evolve into the Roman Catholic Church. We need a series of meditations on this. Our free will is still our own to decide. The choice is always our own, yet the consequences and conditions have an effect on many. As Christ said, there is His "way, truth, and life" all in Him, His light within His one church.

This opens the doors to the Roman Catholic Church. We currently have in Pope Francisco a man for the times. Here is a man/pope that had his retirement paperwork in his hands as a cardinal until divine intervention set him up. Notice that this pope does not talk about conversion to those who believe in other religions. His focus, and rightly so, is on charity, inequalities, and injustices to humanity in certain people in the world.

His mission and his priority for the Roman Catholic Church and those in her service is the forgiving of sins through the 3Rs—repentance, reconciliation, and redemption. Here is a man/pope that has spent his lifetime teaching the value of penance and atonement throughout his own mission. Here is a man/pope that, known or unknown to him, is teaching us that we need to decide between light and darkness. Listening to what he has said about the terrorist activities recently around the world should cause us to pause and think about what is being said.

I think that the think tank that places this pope #4 in influence in world affairs after the leaders of the United States, Russia, and China is accurate. Based on the numbers, this pope yields a great deal of power. But notice that the other three leaders above him have to do with economic and military power, which we know is limited in making a difference in the lives of people. Whereas, this man/pope and those that serve the Church have to do with the hearts and minds of the souls of people. Again, study history to see that economic and military power changes from century to century in the world, but the power of the Holy Spirit within Christ within the Holy Trinity never changes, always being positive. This is true power of those who accept it and have the positive 3Cs: choices, consequences, and conditions that bear good fruit.

In America, we believe that we should give credit to where credit is due. This belief is based on the Bible of giving credit to Christ for what He gave of Himself for the sake of humanity. His name is above all names, and we respected and honored His name until recently. Notice that when we lost this, we also lost respect and honor for our body/flesh and Soul. We lost respect and honor of teachers, civil authority, and law and order. This is a disgrace (loss of grace/light) and un-American. Where did this start? Note that Lucifer, Satan, does not respect or honor his creator. In accepting this evil, we become the same. Hence, all the problems in America and the world are linked directly to this. All civil ills in America and the world are rooted in moral ills that manifest themselves out into society.

Our great Founding Fathers knew precisely what they were doing in our American Constitution, Bill of Rights, etc. They accepted Christ and the Holy Bible as the cornerstone to build up this great country, not any other religion. This was taken from the origins of a recognized official Christianity in Constantinople and the Eastern Roman Empire. In the new Rome of America, Christ was heightened to His rightful position. No other man made god/emperor, no king/queen, no one. After all, He is king of kings and rules all of humanity. He is also a jealous Dio and wants no other Dio before him. America adopted the perfect model for the souls of Americans. Another most important and critical key element was the adoption of what occurred in 450 BC Roma in the first true republic for the people as a model for civil law and order. This also eliminated kings and emperors in favor of the elected senators by citizens, which was/is key to success and prosperity. It should be noted that even the lower federal house of representatives is not really necessary in that it causes squabbling delay and duplication, wasting time, and taxpayer dollars. A full senate, full country representation is enough. A president and vice president? What for? To veto the voices of the people? A senate speaker is sufficient. Also, if we are going to be a unified country, a republic, why all of the individual state congresses? It needs to be one or the other, not both. It is a bloated bureaucratic waste of taxpayers' money. There are too many conflicting issues between federal government and state governments. Take the issue of medical marijuana, a major confusion between states and federal government. The judicial system is even a greater problem. As mentioned, what is the purpose of voting on the state level if the federal supreme court is going to overrule the state? More wasted money, time, and energy. There is that word *waste* again! The EU is having similar, if not worse, headaches with the same issues. In the Roman Empire,

Roman law was the same in Rome, Britain, Germany, Egypt, Spain, and the rest of the provinces. This was uniformity that eliminated any confusion of law. The EU is having similar problems, perhaps even worse being different countries.

In Italia, the situation is similar to America, a bloated, wasteful bureaucracy, but there is still a good connection of government officials with our Blessed Virgin Maria and Holy Spirit of Christ within His Roman Catholic Church. Hence, the respect and honor of family is well rooted. But here also, a shift is occurring with more detachment from the Roman Catholic Church. This is very noticeable in the apathy of a percentage of the youth and adults. One only has to travel throughout Italy to see the graffiti and garbage everywhere. Disrespect and dishonor start with our relationship with our creator and manifest outward from within us.

So the youth in the world everywhere are causing a shifting away from the Church, away from family, and away from the good of humanity. I recall my mother speaking in tongues before she passed away. This is communication with the spiritual souls of others. She had a strong devotion to our Blessed Virgin Maria. Who among us in our generation will be able to do this? I do not want to be negative, but the disconnect and disloyalty to the Church of Christ that I am witnessing are obviously influencing my writing.

The good news is that the past few popes, Saint Pope John, Pope Paul, Saint Pope John Paul the II, and our current pope, Pope Francisco, are doing their best to bring us all home together within one Church as a unified strong body against the evils of darkness. We should not be separated and divided. In this way, we grow weaker. We should be helping each other climb up to our soul's summit, assisting each other. Just imagine attempting to climb Mt. Everest alone or independent of others. This is where we Christians are in these most difficult of times.

It is difficult but not impossible to change the current events of disunity among us Christian Americans and Christians around the world. Again, it comes down to the 3Cs of all Christian leaders in wanting to become one force of influence in world affairs. We need to be number one in influence for real changes to occur. As humans, as men and women, we find it most difficult to be like Christ or like Blessed Virgin Maria. But we could, at least, take our cue from the lives of the saints to be our guide.

After all is said and done, it is our moral imprint, our soul's light, that determines our fate and the fate of others. It is not ancient philosophy or pop culture that brings about love and peace.

In Christianity, all of the positive pieces have to come together in the Holy Spirit. Faith in the Holy Spirit is the only way to bring all Christians, continents, governments, and people together for pax, pace, peace. All roads need to lead to one light that could become a beacon for all. Only this removes the evils of tyranny, hate, revenge, wars, death, and destruction in people around the world. When light is restored, law and order is restored as well. This should not be a mystery, as history tells us in our second journey. The mother lode of all mysteries is in the third journey of heaven, but we must get through the second journey first.

We Americans have started to take our freedoms and graces for granted. This is a huge mistake. It is due to this that we have many of the negative issues with continuing racism, prejudice, discrimination, and inequality in the twenty-first century.

In Italia, it is no different, perhaps to a lesser degree, yet the writing is on the walls with the graffiti on our public civil monuments of those who made this country wonderful. We are ruining our heritage and cultural identity. The artists flourished with divine grace, and we take it all for granted. Do we even deserve what we have?

What is it that we need? An epiphany to see who we have become? Our confirmation of faith was moved into our teens from childhood for a reason. We needed to be reminded of our youth as children of our devotion and beliefs. In mass, even when distracted, our mind stores all of the readings and helps us to listen to our soul's conscience and recognize our moral imprint. But we need to be present for this to take place. The acceptance of the holy of holiest from the tabernacle, the Eucharist, nourishes us to give us strength to carry on. It reminds us of our own soul's tabernacle, and we accept the oxygen of life.

In the mystery of our soul's subconscious, most sicknesses are cured with a sincere and honest confession and communion. This is available to all. A peaceful heart and mind will help us get the sleep we all need to confront the hardships and burdens of our soul's second journey. Take as an example celebrity Michael Jackson, a super popstar that could not even get a good night's sleep without being put under anesthesia, a somewhat suicide/murdered body/flesh. What was it all for?

We need a leap of faith but how? When we do not have the foundation or the cornerstone to build upon, what leap can we take? We hear voices coming at us from every direction: here this way, no, the other way, no, this religion, no, another religion. We hear voices telling us to forget about all religions and concentrate on the metaphysical, on science, on the stars, on the ancient prophets, on philosophy, etc. We simply need a little time to listen to our soul's heart and mind in silence and prayer. The answers are weighted according to our soul's spiritual knowledge. Yes, we need to return to that stage. We need to be conscious of who we are not and who we pretend to be. The findings in the tabernacle of our soul's heart will astonish us.

We are all tested from the prophets of the Old Testament to our Blessed Virgin Maria to Christ to the saints, all tested along with the Roman Catholic Church herself. Pope Francisco is right to say that the Roman Catholic Church has become a bloated institution in need of a strict diet like any corporation.

I am working on this page of my book from Rapallo, Genova, Italia. A most wonderful experience I had here was the blessing of the animals at Saint Francisco church. It is only fitting that at this church, which was named after the saint who befriended animals, a day is set aside to bless these beautiful creatures. Cats, dogs, pets of all kinds—but mostly dogs—were blessed with holy water. We all felt like children at play, all were happy, along with the animals. All of this due to one man called upon at the age of twenty-one. In accepting his calling, this one man would become the founder of the Franciscan Order, receive the stigmata, become the patron Saint of Italy, and become the intercessor of the poor. This one man born into a privileged family chose to give it all up for the development of his soul's second journey, to climb up to the summit of spiritual knowledge, and to be pulled up, Tira Mi Su into #10, the brilliant light of the Holy Trinity. That one man/saint who could achieve all this is awesome.

Again, we are all called to be achievers of good deeds. It is up to us in our 3Cs. I was blessed with several wonderful spiritual guides to assist me. Father Susko and the Notre Dame nuns in Youngstown, Ohio. Father Gallagher in San Diego, California, was an amazing influence on me. In Lastra Signa, Ponte Signa, Signa Firenze, Tuscany, Italia has raised my level of awareness and insight. In Rapallo, Italia, the older priests are overflowing with the grace of wisdom that they are happy to share.

There is no shortcut, no cramming, no cheating to spiritual knowledge in the climb to the summit. Hence, we could be gifted in so many ways and yet still be dumb souls. We talk of soul food, soul mate, soul this or that; most often we have no idea of what we are talking about. Putting our faith and trust in the latest fads and deceptive people wastes precious time and energy. Think about this. What has stood the test of time? Two thousand-plus years and counting, the Roman Catholic Church has survived the worst of times along with the best of times, being now at this very moment. If we take the time to read, listen to the witnesses that give testimony of their faith and trust and hope, we may ourselves become enlightened.

Notice that the word *testimony* itself contains the word *test*. Those who are tested and pass and learn in their testing climb up to the summit. This is what we need to learn, all of us, rich or poor. Individually, we are just one person, yet we can make a difference. Collectively, we have strength in numbers. We Christians need to stop being separated, stop being disconnected from each other, and start to become a unified force that can and should make a difference in world affairs in matters of the soul and civil issues of humanity.

What are we waiting for? Do we see what is happening in the Middle East, Africa, and other parts of the world? None of us are fully independent and self-sufficient, and thinking so only proves our ignorance. We are always dependent. From our parents to our teachers, to family and friends, we are always in need of others to help us in our second journey and into our third journey where we need light to sustain us. Only this way gives us peace and happiness. Only in Christianity are the words "way, truth and light/life" used to reach the third journey of #10. These three words should never be modified or distorted. In doing so, we dilute their purity and meaning. These three words are at the heart of our second journey. The 3Cs, in acceptance of these three words to live by, determine our entire future. Yes, there are alternatives, other options, as we have studied. But study the history of humanity. Cults are everywhere waiting with open arms, giving us false promises. Do we want to risk it? We are talking about our soul's life, not a wager of monetary goods and services. Do we want to gamble our soul's future? Do we know an illusion put before our eyes? Do we see the conflicting hypocrisy of fashionable religions? Life should be an adventure, an adventure in truth and light, not adventures in dead ends. I, for one, am playing it safe in the right "way."

With three words, Christ fully summarized the entire Holy Bible. Study other Religions. Are these words written in Buddhism, Hinduism, Islam, or Judaism to guide us? Even if they are, without Christ, they are shallow words. Two thousand years ago, they became known. So what do these three words really mean?

The "way," of course, is Gesu. There is NO other way.

Truth, for those of us too ignorant to know, is the opposite of a lie or falsehood. But in what? The words themselves. We know, of course, that some of us are chronic liars in the spoken or written word. How do we trust anyone like this? We do not. Now study pop culture, advertising, and promotional messages from marketing agencies and the rhetoric of political figures. The "truth" has, for the most part, become lost. It is mind-boggling trying to decipher what to believe and what to reject. Christ, aware of this, simply said, "I am the truth." In other words, my words you can believe and trust. In this is the beginning of understanding "life."

What is "life"? At this point, we should know this. But what is important here is that Christ said, "I am the life." In other words, stop wasting your time and energy on false lights or illusions of light. Notice that only in understanding "truth" are we able to understand light. By now, we should also know that all of us need Light to sustain us. We began with a spark from light and were conceived in light in our mother's womb in our first journey. This continues throughout our soul's second journey, yet the light of our parents and family is not enough. What do we do when our parents depart into their third journey? What will we have to sustain us? Enter the light of Christ in the Holy Spirit within the Holy Trinity. In all that I have read and studied, especially from the saints, I see no other better "way."

Christ does not mince words: "I am the way." His words are direct, precise, and for all to follow. Again, why experiment with any other way? Christ is basically saying, "You want spiritual knowledge? You want to climb up to the summit? You want to reach number nine-plus on your soul's chart? You want to be pulled up to number ten? Accept what I am saying to you today, now, this moment.

The quiz in this book helps to give us an idea of where we are in our own soul's second journey. The 3Cs—choice, consequences, and conditions—are what we have to deal with in our second journey. The true measurement of who we are is within our soul's heart. In union with the Holy Spirit within the Holy Trinity, we will never go wrong.

Observe the Roman Catholic Church mass. It is a confession, confirmation, and communion in Christ. Faith, hope, and trust in the Holy Eucharist are what bring about the transfusion and transformation. This transcends and transfigures us into our third journey. Rise on top of the clouds, the platform, to see the sun always shining.

Our soul's ID, moral imprint, is recorded in the Book of Life, along with our baptism and name. We are never forgotten unless we elect with our free will to erase ourselves from it. Some of us will be given a second chance in the twilight zone or purgatory, not that we deserve it. But many of us, I believe roughly 40 percent, will go there for a period of time. We should never think that this is a nice haven. As Dante, accompanied by the Roman writer, Virgilio, his guide, wrote in the *Divina Commedia*, he found himself lost in a dark forest, a metaphor of his time of lawlessness within the Roman Catholic Church and society. This was also the darkness and fear in his own body/flesh and soul's middle age. In trying to reach light, three beasts—lust, pride, and avarice—impede him. Sounds familiar? Seven hundred years later, what has changed?

We still have the same demons that offer us lust, pride, and avarice. We still accept them. The metaphysical world has changed drastically since Dante in the 1330s in Florence, but notice that the soul's second journey has not. Light and darkness do not change. As mentioned, the twilight zone or purgatory is not a nice haven. There we are totally dependent on the mercy and grace of others, notably our Blessed Virgin Maria. There is no assurance that we will be pulled up out of there and when it may or may not happen. What if no one prays for us? What if it takes another one thousand years? There are far too many unknowns. We read where Christ visited these areas in the time following his crucifixion, but this is a gray area. Is this what we want for ourselves? Dante in his dream navigated through hell on a boat; will we need to do the same? A few of us will visit purgatory and hell within our soul's second journey. Is this what it is going to take for us?

Old age of the body/flesh does not bring with it wisdom and spiritual knowledge. The Roman Catholic Church, being brick and mortar, is part of the metaphysical body of Christ. Within her is the natural holy water that in baptism cleanses our body/flesh of sins. Within her is also the metaphysical tabernacle that contains the natural Eucharist of Christ. Always, the two—natural and spiritual—are one.

This is what is missing in Protestant Christian churches and what makes them feel cold and empty. Also, a once-a-week sermon is limited in every aspect of the word. Some of us need two, three times per week. Notice that people are most interested in visiting churches when visiting Italy and for good reasons. One can sit in a church for long periods of time and be amazed at the beautiful paintings, sculptures, and architecture. To have an opportunity to attend a high mass in Latin or Italian adds greatly to the overall experience. One should not leave Italy without participation or, at least, observation of the holy mass.

The Renaissance in Italy did not occur in most other European countries with the exception of Spain. The question is, why? The answer is perhaps because the legions of Rome that once went out with swords would soon go out with the Bible and holy rosary. Their efforts in charity would focus on the souls of humanity more so than building roads, bridges, aqueducts, theaters, temples, and sports facilities. We have a great deal to learn from the Renaissance spiritual awakening but even more so on the missionaries that Rome sends out to all parts of the world. Let us learn to listen to Pope Francisco. His words are more important than the words of the US Federal Reserve chief that we analyze word for word. One deals with money and economy, but the soul of humanity is far more important in the words and works of the Roman Catholic Church.

We Roman Catholics do not have a monopoly on Christianity. We do take charity and love seriously and want more than anything else to bring it out to the world. We need help from all Christians, not complacency, division, and indecisiveness. The evils of darkness are getting an upper hand as the writing of this book. The current events in Europe are frightening. It is up to all Christian leaders to take charge with a clear voice and action. We have become too comfortable within our little niche while Christians and other innocent people, even children, are being exploited and executed in the name of Allah.

I have witnessed in the past fifty years Christianity becoming a mythological nonsense of antiquity for some in America. This in a time when radical extremism is spreading like a plague in all parts of the world. What are we waiting for, an act of God? As mentioned earlier, we all have a free will that very seldom is interfered with. The real bells of Italian churches call the faithful to prayer and mass. What is calling us to action in America? There appears to be far too much silence and little dialogue regarding what to do.

Where is the dialogue, real communication, with the terrorists? Why are all religious leaders not involved in finding out the reasons for what the terrorists do? I see no effort being made from anyone to reach a compromise or common ground. Terrorists do not just wake up one day and decide to become a jihad and throw away his/her life for nothing. The issues are complex and deeply rooted. They did not occur overnight. We in America and Europe are not so innocent. We have in the past sixty-five years exploited and killed with our drones many people for the sake of oil interests and other special interest groups at the expense of our boys' bodies and the lives of innocent people as well. With the wars, intrusions, and occupations, the only winner here is evil itself. In a way, we are all guilty either by action or inaction, omission. We are all from the same source of light.

Prophesied events may very well materialize in the Middle East without the positive 3Cs. Is this what we want? We help fulfill prophecy, each and every one of us.

A big failure of humanity is not thinking about the other side. It seems to be always about me, myself, and I. With this mentality, how could we not have the conflicting issues we have in the twenty-first century?

Take as an example Saint John the Baptist compared to Herod two thousand years ago. One cared only for himself being allowed to remain in power as a puppet lavished with money and material things. The other, Saint John the Baptist, lived in animal skins and was concerned about the preparation of the coming Messiah, the Christ. One lived a full life in his earthly riches, the other was beheaded to please a young bitch. These are sharp contrasting figures two thousand years ago. Now look at the newspapers/Internet of what is taking place around the world. Only the dates and names change. The evils are the same.

Hence, the reason for little peace in the world. How could there be more? Peace in our soul and body/flesh is only possible in light. When our mind's consciousness and our soul's conscience are not at peace, we will not be at peace with ourselves or with others regardless of the exercises, yoga, tai chi, etc. Save your money; going to India or anywhere else will not help either.

The willingness to exercise our free will, the 3Cs in a positive constructive way, does make a difference. It is simply a matter of doing what is morally right, if we even know or remember what it is. We knew as children—innocent children caring for one another. This is what we need to regain. The enemy is not humanity or religion; it is the evils that are all around us like hungry wolves. What is it about us joking Jews, moronic Muslims, and contesting Christians that we refuse to get it together? One Dio, one light, one Allah, One I AM, one Father, one Holy Spirit, one orb as monotheism is not complicated. Children understand this better than we educated adults!

If only we could see each other as members of one family, from one source of light, perhaps we could begin to benefit from this. There is a beauty about all the different races, nationalities, and their personalities and characters. The world is not about tofu and vanilla ice cream. It is about people who are far more important than we could begin to know. When we do, we will have a deep appreciation for diversity. From the summit, all of this becomes visible, as we have the light to see. We need to become like the Red Cross that, regardless of race, nationality, or religion, comes to aid humanity. It doesn't matter if we came out of Africa, Europe, or Asia forty thousand years ago or four hundred thousand years ago. We are all one family.

Recall that the failed former Soviet Union Communist Party leaders were quoted as saying to America, "We will win without firing one shot." Is it not ironic that it was America that did not need to fire one shot in the implosion of a foolish adversary? Also, although it is not fully understood, was it a possible communist conspiracy, the attempted assassination of Saint Pope John Paul the II by two or three bullets? It was not luck that the bullets did not strike the major arteries. It was simply not his time. He had much more work to get done.

Currently, Russia and her citizens are going backward to the last century with cold war tactics. This is what happens when humanity allows one tyrant, president, prime minister, etc. to take control of a government. Sounds familiar? A free democratic system with the collective voices of a people with a healthy conscience and moral imprint under freedom of religion and speech with civil law and order of a true republic works. Even united, as supposedly the BRICS (Brazil, Russia, India, China, South Africa) countries are, with corruption/evils at every level of each country, they will fail and fall united. It is only a matter of time.

Study history, the ideal model, a true republic, was formulated in 450 BC in Roma, but paganism hurt overall success and prosperity. Between 300 AC and 1300 AC in Constantinople, the Eastern

Roman Empire, the second main element/ingredient was added, Christianity. This was actually the height of the Eastern Roman Catholic Empire. The only missing piece was a true senate having an emperor in charge. Still, study the prosperity in the region during the time period. With an uncorrupted senate/republic, the missing piece, the Ottoman forces may never have taken control. Was it due to becoming uncharitable to her citizens? I think so! The Ottoman dominance basically took control of the same model of success and prosperity and added charitable contributions for humanity. This was their success until the genocide of Christian people. Again, it was only a matter of time for justice to take its course as it did through World War I. This is a lesson for all governments, including America and Europe, regardless of ideologies.

# THE COLLECTIVE SUMMATION OF LIGHT AND RATIOS FOR 7 BILLION PLUS PEOPLE WORLD WIDE .

1/10000-.0001-.01% #10 HEAVEN, BRILLIANT

9.9 TIRAMISU  ISD/ESD

1/1000-.001-.10%     9:0 SUMMIT,PLATFORM

A%OF WORLDWIDE 8.9 BRIGHT LIGHT

POPULATION         8.0 SOUL'S LIGHT

BETWEEN            7.0 DEGREE FROM FREE

6.0 AND 8.99=40%   6.0 WILL POSITIVE 3C'S

**A% OF WORLDWIDE 5.9 3G'S, 3L'S, 3T'S UP**

POPULATION         4.0 OR NEGATIVE 3C'S

BETWEEN            3.0 DOWN , 3S 'S 3F's

.01AND5.99=59.99% 2.0 3D'S NEEDING 3R'S

1.0-.01 DARKNESS TO

**0.  NO LIGHT**

**THE FIGURES ARE CONSERVATIVE ESTIMABLE  DATA**

**OF OVERALL WORLD POPULATION, AS I SEE THEM !!!**

178

# CHAPTER *Six*

Faith—Hope—Trust in the Holy Spirit within
the Holy Trinity—Baptism—Communion—
Holy Eucharist—Confirmation

I n this chapter, we will explore faith, hope, and trust in the Holy Spirit. I will try to break it down to three sections. The first is the level of light on the chart from .01 to 5.99. The second is 6.00 to 8.99 and the 3rd 9.00 to 9.99. The reason for this is that we are throughout our soul's second journey in faith somewhere in these three ranges as the charts on and in this book show. We could fluctuate in all of the three ranges from time to time depending on our 3Cs.

So the first question for ourselves is: what is *faith*?

We hear this word tossed around like a relic that few people care or dare to hold onto. Faith also defines who we are, as in whether we are faithful, faithless, and unfaithful. So to be faithful means to believe, in this context, in Gesu. Notice the positive connotation here. A person who is considered faithful is also thought of as a good respectable person, the opposite of unfaithful. So with faith, hope and trust follow. In other words, a faithful person living in faith also has hope and trust in their minds. In return, that same person has the hope and trust from others. As an example, I recall my Zio Raphael being that person. I was only a child, yet around him, I sensed a warmth and light that has always stayed with me long after his death. An atheist that does not have faith or beliefs at all usually is not considered one that others can put their hope and trust in.

So let us start from the bottom .01 to 5.99. We will see that the degree of faith correlates with the degree of light. We were not born equal genetically or given the same opportunities in life. Some of us were given no chance at faith and are not even aware of our moral imprint. Notice that most animals, even the domesticated ones, do not trust us until they get to know us better. Children could be the same way when first meeting us. They seem to sense or be on guard of who we might be. We cannot blame them in light of the number of animal and child abuse cases. Are they able to see into our eyes the degree of light that we emit or fail to emit? A pedophile can easily rob a child of faith, hope, and trust in humanity. When we accept that outside intruder of evil, it is sensed by the innocent.

AA (Alcoholic Anonymous) is another great example of faith in which the 3Cs are profound. In AA, we faithless and hopeless are able to reach out to others of faith for helping ourselves.

It all begins with a choice of our free will to seek help in those that have the same issues and demons to deal with but not alone, never alone. No one knows better the trap of believing only in ourselves due to pride and ego, the dangers of falling off the wagon and into the gutter over and over again. It is at times such as these that the moral imprint of a dog is stronger than that of a human being. Our eyes, having received light on the wagon and then falling off into darkness, again are blinded. We wonder, was this our destination, the insanity of alcohol abuse?

It becomes very apparent when our faith is in M&M (money and material) things. Our ingratitude and ungraciousness surface through our eyes, whereas when our faith is based on our sufferings, hardships, and burdens, this shows as well but in a positive way. This faith need not prove itself to anyone. It is honest, sincere, and deeply rooted in our soul's heart.

Many of us will remain in the low to very low ranges of our chart because we refuse to listen. We become those class students who are distracted by so many things when our professor mentions what will be on the final exam. We fail to listen, failing the exam and ourselves in the process. The same process occurs within our inner voice. Our inner voice does not need to prove anything to us. The days of parables and metaphors came, do we need more?

How about this one: notice how, when sitting near the edge of a lake on a sunny day, we observe not only the sun's rays but also the reflection of the sun sparkles off the lake. On a cold winter day when the daylight is brief and the nights long, this makes a huge difference in warming us up. Now compare this to the light of the Holy Spirit available to us directly and through the faithful very near to us. This light not only warms us but also helps with purification when we are in the abyss of our soul's second journey.

In the lowest range of our chart, when apathy, self-pity, and self-neglect imprison our soul, it is time to re-energize. The biggest problem? We are not able to trust ourselves to be competent enough to reach out to others for help. At times, our high IQ but low EQ prevents our association with the faithful. Instead, we want a sign, a miracle of some sort. Our mind has become foggy from being dumbfounded for so many years. Two thousand years ago, our excuses were misunderstanding and ignorance. What are they today?

We need to come face-to-face, again probably best at 3:00 a.m., to realize our stupidity and wasteful past thoughts and actions. Only the supernatural light could show us who and what we have become. There are few absolutes in our soul's second journey, but the ones that are all have to do with light. This is what makes hell miserable—it is absolutely without light. Hell on earth works in a similar way. It is people killing people in darkness. It need not be this way. We could easily be angels of light and be instruments of positive change if only we could get out of the gutters. In other words, we are all able to be protagonists, instruments of positive change instead of antagonists stuck in our negative darkness. We have one of the best tools as a gift to us in order for this to take place. Remember the tools we covered previously? The free will is within us. This is where Christianity rises above all religions. For example, Islam believes that all is predestined for us, as if humanity has no say. This is absurd. In fact, just the opposite is true. Our free will in union with the will of the Holy Spirit can produce miracles—miracles in which humanity plays a key role.

We are all equally invited to the beggars' banquet to re-energize our souls. This banquet begins with the breaking of bread accompanied with wine and water. This is how the saints traveled their own second journey. There is no other better way known to humanity. Light travels at what speed? The Holy Spirit does not need to travel; the entire cosmos is filled with the Holy Spirit at all times.

Searching, searching, searching when all along the answers were, are in the tabernacle of our soul's heart. If we were to stop and observe the paintings and sculptures of Christ and our Blessed Virgin Maria, we would see that they are often pointing to the heart. These are metaphysical artist signs of where we should be looking, but these artists were gifted with knowledge, whereas Hollywood and her writers could let their imagination run wild with fabricated special effects, often giving us illusions of reality or fiction. Christianity is not that complex until we, or rather the evil through us, will complicate everything. Their illusions need to be burned out.

We are those tiny sparkles on water. Each one of us represents one of the billions of sparkles. Each sparkle is a tiny image of the source of light, and so are we. Notice that even when we rotate away from the light source, the source is always there, always present. At times, the moon is used to reflect the light onto the water, and at times, light is hidden from us but still always there, always present.

Faith can go against all human odds and win. A great example is George Washington against the British in our Revolutionary War. Why? As mentioned earlier, when light enters, darkness vanishes. This is how the light of the Holy Spirit works within us. Our spark alone is not enough to overcome all darkness, but in union with the Holy Spirit, it is. Hence, even if tracking at .01 on our chart, we are able with our free will to climb up to the summit and to 9.99 of spiritual knowledge.

The demons know and understand this better than we do and try everything possible to prevent this from occurring. They are constantly busy with their lies and deceptive means through various channels to have us become victims, hence the saying, "All show, no substance." In being fooled, this is what we become—shallow and eventually empty of meaningful substance. What substance? Good values, principles, and standards to live by. These are all in our soul's heart that manifest themselves outward in charity. This should not be confused with the pretense of fake substance that plenty of us have. All true substance is of grace and not man-made. It takes wisdom to see the difference, which is available in the climb to the summit.

Take as an example the teenage gangs in America. This is an excellent example of youth tracking low on their charts. Why? Because as long as the gang members are involved in criminal activities, they, knowingly or unknowingly, have accepted darkness into themselves. All of the nonsense of comradeship and family is an illusion, a lie, and the opposite of faithfulness in light. Hence, truth and trust are nonexistent; they only have empty words and pledges that will soon evaporate. All corruption works this way. Teenage gang members grow up into organized mob members. Those of us involved in these activities just don't see it because from the gutters and sewers of life, we are looking down and not up.

Enter the testing that we will have to endure. It should not surprise us; this process has been taking place since the beginning of humanity. It continues to take place throughout our soul's second journey. It may be juvenile hall, a serious knife wound, a lost loved one, loss of a close parent, illiteracy, etc. The list, as mentioned, is endless, getting harder and harder until we either get it or die. Figure .01 is not 0 or a soul without any light at all on the chart. Yet this, my friends, is a living hell but still within our soul's second journey. Be grateful, as there is still time left to change. The question is, how much time? Each is an individual story of tests, setups, and the 3Cs, chances of climbing up for our souls. Each is personalized— what works for one may not work for another. Now multiply this by roughly seven billion people, and you begin to see how mind-boggling the job is. Each person has to be integrated into those around them, their environment, and all other life forms. Only supernatural spiritual light could manage this. Look at the little quiz for geeky people in the back of this book. Who, what could possibly handle solving such a quiz?

We may think that teenagers growing up in street gangs in America are tough, yet as of this writing, I am seeing on the late news little children being trained to kill and use guns on people. The insanity of the adults involved in this madness must be stopped. They are ruining our lives, our childhood, and our future, if we even have one left. I have stated that evil itself is the perpetrator of what is occurring in the minds of Islamic fanatics and other terrorist groups. The problem is, when all else fails to change or deter the inhuman stress and destruction by those that elected to spread evil, the vehicles themselves need to be brought to justice or put to sleep. It becomes a case similar but much more complex than putting a loved dog to sleep once they become mad. If anything, it may be a merciful defensive position to take.

We are taught in Christianity to forgive and love our enemies. This is correct, as forgiveness and love change the worst of us. Yet at the same time, we should not become pacifists as the lives of innocent children are being ruined. Pacifism works when we as protagonists defend our humanity against the antagonists that are, at least, half-civilized. Gandhi, Nelson Mandela, and Martin Luther King showed us how this works, but when people themselves accept being transformed into the very instruments of evil, it changes the rules. This requires a strong well-coordinated and united international front to show the world that all other options were tried and exhausted.

When we as human beings give up our free will to evil demons themselves, our very tabernacle doors have been closed. We have lost control of our moral imprint, our soul's hearts and minds. Our inner voice becomes the voice of evil itself. This is as close to zero on our chart that is possible before death itself. At this stage, perhaps only divine intervention could help us, as our very tabernacle needs to be unlocked in order to survive. Remember that light and darkness cannot dwell in the same space.

We may or may not have those three minutes right before the second journey ends and the third journey begins. The three minutes is the amount of time that our brain has after blood oxygen from our natural heart ends. This may be symbolic allegory of the soul's heart but is not a theoretical hypothesis of a soul's death. This is the reality of body/flesh and our soul's second journey coming to an end.

Notice that when people kill and destroy in the name of Allah, their Allah is not our Allah. So how many Allahs are there? There are only two invisible spiritual forces in our world: one of light and goodness, the other one of evil and darkness. Each is known for the fruit borne through humanity. Study the 3Cs of the terrorists of humanity in what is occurring in the world today. What do we see? We do not need to be at the summit to recognize the obvious. At times, a spirited sword of light is called upon through defensive humanity to stop evil that is totally out of control. History tells us what will happen without the prevention taking place. Remember Hitler and the SS? The concentration camps?

There are terrorist cells everywhere around the world. It could be our next-door neighbor. It could be a coworker. Evil penetrates all circles and spheres in disguise, so we need to be on guard. Like any contagious disease, evil needs to be isolated and contained. Containment in the Middle East? Why not? Remember that evil begets evil. Perhaps we need to let hatred deal with hatred. The Iran, Iraq War was not that long ago, Muslims killing Muslims, years of killings, a decade or so, thousands of deaths simply due to their sects and civil war. Sounds familiar? Study the civil wars currently taking place in Syria, the Ukraine, and other hot spots.

Notice how evil works in all circles: separate, divide, and subdivide, even though supposedly the different sects believe in one Allah. The Middle East is like a hornet's nest; it's been this way for centuries. Fanaticism is turning parts of the Middle East into poisonous snake pits, worse yet, hell islands in the desert. The minority Christian and Judaism communities feel the heat and smell the smoke of these infernos. Our Blessed Virgin Maria warns humanity of the evils of war often in her apparitions. The people in this region believe in our Blessed Virgin Maria but not in what she has to say? A contradiction?

Notice also that the overwhelming majority of the region does not believe in Christ. Neither Judaism nor Islam believe that Christ was and is the Messiah, the chosen one, the Son of God. Could this be the root of all their problems? All is predestined? We have no free will? Humanity is irrelevant? Created for no reason? The book of Revelation, the last Book allowed at the end of the Bible, is not important? Additions and amendments to the Holy Bible?

The Roman Catholic Church and the Constitution of America, along with the Bill of Rights, have always been firm on the defense of liberty, life, and freedoms of humanity. We are not talking here of minor offenses against humanity that are forgivable. We are talking about serious evil transgressions against the very souls of humanity, perhaps only forgivable by divine intervention.

Notice how amendments work. They are the ways that humanity deals with what they cannot abide by; from the Bible to the Constitution of America, people want it their way, even when it's not right. Sounds familiar? I am surprised that the Ten Commandments have not been amended. NO, they are simply ignored. Note that the word ignore makes up the words *ignorant* and *ignoramus*. Hmm! There is not much substance in any word or set of words that modifications dilute and contaminate.

For every positive, there is the opposite—negative—as is with light and darkness, good and evil. This is set up for humanity and their free will. If we are tracking low or near zero on our chart, we someway, somehow, somewhere made the 3Cs, choices to have the consequences and conditions that we bear. This, my friends, is no mystery—just reality. No matter what race, nationality, ethnic group, sect, etc., the rules are the same for all. This includes whatever sexual orientation, philosophy, revolutionary ideologies identify us. We may all be individuals that are genetically different, but generally our composition is similar. Our body/flesh is similar, and most importantly, our souls are similar. We are truly all brothers and sisters, my dear friends, whether we like it or not.

There are few guaranties in our second journey, and the warranties are limited at best and always changing. This may be a cliché, but there are always two sides of a coin, and the sword is indeed double-edged. What we choose or choose not to do and be is mostly our choice. We could choose love and peace that result in joy and happiness, or we can choose hate and war that result in tearful regrets and miseries.

We seem to all want to become celebrities but celebrating what? Pop star, porno star, mafia star? We tend to follow illusionary ways and have false celebrations of life. These are all man-made in pride and ego of darkness that will end when our body/flesh dies. Only a soul at the summit is worth any celebration.

All of us enjoy one of those rare days when no evils are allowed to bother us. This gives us a glimpse of what is inherent in peace and light that is available for us in our second and third journeys. There is protection from the evils of darkness only in light. Take as an example an urban city block in a crime-infested area. Notice the positive changes when lighting is added, video cameras, an honest cop actually walking the block and getting to know everyone. Notice what happens when the people within that same city block all get involved for positive change.

This is the combined light of free will at work.

This must occur within our soul's heart and mind first. There are always three plus wills at work, ours, that of light, and that of evil. The plus is everyone else involved, so positive change in light is always possible. Those who think otherwise are lacking in faith. Take the Christian missionaries around the world as other examples, the three plus is always at work. When we observe the first commandment, we will observe all of the other nine. It is much like loving good parents first and foremost and doing what they ask of us. In doing so, we help ourselves and are helped by the graces of our good parents. Take as an example those of us that ignored our parents during the hippies' crazed sexual revolution in America. We doped out of reality. What became of us? Some of us, due to our 3Cs, are still suffering from the consequences and conditions of that time period with our own children.

If we do not live in faith with reflection on our past, we will or should always see our stupidity, ignorance, and missing love/*charita*. This is why we never feel content, satisfied, or fulfilled and are always wanting. Our soul cannot really be fooled, only hushed. For example, women in the past lived their faith much better than men. Perhaps this was due to the birth and raising of a child. A mother's role in assisting in creation and nurturing in love is undeniably beneficial to the giver and the recipient. Notice how this is changing in the past fifty years. Women are growing on par with men in faith.

We blame family members, religions, the economy, our bosses, our jobs, other races, other nationalities. We blame events, circumstances, and conditions. We very seldom take a look at ourselves, our hearts, to see who we have become, who we really are compared to who we were when young and innocent. Without faith, little is possible; with faith, all becomes possible. What will we choose? Our soul's health and well-being that affect physical health and well-being, or the opposite, no faith, that affects us in a negative way throughout our soul's second journey? I choose my faith and my soul's health as my first priority.

It all begins with a yes, in which we stop blaming anyone or anything in the past or present. We stop with the excuses. In this, the doors to the spark within the tabernacle of our soul's heart stops closing and rather starts opening. Through charity, we receive oxygen and grow in light. Here the evils of darkness fall off to the curbside. In this, we are renewed, regaining our lost laughter, singing, and being joyful for life. Here we develop a no-nonsense attitude, a need to play, explore, and discover the true mysteries of our lives, our calling, and our meaning. All in all, our purpose for being in this flesh of ours recognizes the need to achieve and accomplish good deeds. In this, we begin our ascension to the summit. Along the way, we see that the metaphysical world is intended for the climb.

Will we continue to have our fears, phobias, insecurities, uncertainties? Yes, who is voided of these things overnight? Yet the higher we climb, the more these things fall off to unload our soul's burdens. Are we 100 percent free of these things at the summit? No, far from it; we have to continue to be tested to achieve wisdom. I personally had a dream telling me not to fear anything at all. Our undoubted trust in faith gradually gives us the freedom from all fears. This is not easy in any way. Faced with everyday physical and social realities, it is difficult at times. Yet when we consider where we are, climbing the summit, we are reminded by the voice in the wind of how we got to that point. We will think of when our fears began as early as the age of three. Baptism, communion, and confirmation are keys to faith, hope, and trust in a higher source, a spiritual force. At the offset, our understanding is fuzzy, hazy, or simply unclear, but in our climb this all burns off. Recall that *The Exorcist* movie was based on a true story of a child not being baptized. This is a crucial first step in the climb to the summit.

The summit and ultimately #10 should be our destinations. This is accomplished as, for example, an object is put under a magnifying glass that is between the sun rays and the object in which the object receives magnified light enough to set it on fire. For our soul, the magnifying glass is an undoubting faith.

Dropped off in purgatory as a dim-faded soul does us little good. Here we have lost the use of our free will to do anything, like a totally handicapped child. Having our soul extinguished into darkness is the worst. Yet look at the chart. I believe that those of us tracking between .01 and 5.99 at the death of our body/flesh will undoubtedly end down in Dante's inferno. Those of us who are tracking between 6.00 and 8.99 at the death of our body/flesh will most certainly be deposited into the twilight zone or purgatory. Even 9.0 to 9.99, without Tira Mi Su into #10, we probably need a stopover in purgatory.

I have mentioned all along the power of the free will and the 3Cs of our souls' second journey. Without faith, nothing happens—nothing positive, that is. In essence, without faith, we stagnate and unknowingly are still losing light. What is crazy about this is that we are not forced to exercise our free will or to have faith. This is our option. Just as an example, no one can force us to vote in a civil election, yet in not voting, we lose our voice or vote.

For us Roman Catholics, a way for us to show our gratitude is in attending mass. Here we make the time to express our gratitude in silence. But the mass is far more important than that. The mass is an affirmation of our faith. We do not go to mass only to listen to the words of the Bible interpreted for us. No, we are there mainly to receive the Holy Eucharist. When receiving this Eucharist, we are in communion by faith in Christ. This is what is pleasing to our creator. But notice that in this, we are given the grace to help us in our climb, and we never lose; we only gain. Those of us that just go to church once a week, if that, and daydream while we are there may be better off trying to read the Word at a park or in the beach.

Our moral imprint began with our creation and evolves more clearly, more recognizably in faith. Even the cavemen had this. Some animals may have this as well, especially the wolf/dog species.

The story, "Romulus and Remus," of ancient Rome tells of a she wolf nursing them as infants. This may or may not be mythological nonsense, but the caring of dogs for humanity and from possibly their moral imprint is to this day a reality. Think about the ways that dogs help humanity in helping the blind, in rescue missions, in companionship, in security, etc. Yes, dogs could be humanity's most faithful friend. This honor should and, at times does, go to a spouse, but here also that percentage has dropped along with our dropping on our chart.

Now take faithfulness between humanity overall. Are we truly above dogs? It depends upon where we are on our chart. The lower we are, the less faith that people are able to have in us. Some of us are really below the level of man's best friend, the dog. Take as an example modern-day feminism that many of us women have put our faith in, as if we could find completeness of ourselves in this modern movement. The attitude of being better than males, being independent of males, not needing males for friendship, companionship, or marriage has gotten us where?

How could this mentality not result in anything but disappointment? Oh, excuse me, should I have taken the word *men* out of the word *women*? Do we see the stupidity of it all? This division, cutting off, almost war with men within our soul's second journey is a reflection of our faith within ourselves. I know that men could be stupid assholes at times, but men, after our free will, are an important part of our soul's second journey. Their role as father figure is irreplaceable, even though some of us foolish women believe otherwise—such as two women raising a child and one playing the father figure. Men could be just as ridiculous with two men raising a child. What is more pathetic is that we expect the child to understand and accept all this. Yes, there is a high demand for child physiological therapy these days. It is a field in demand.

Again, faith in our creator, in the Ten Commandments, in the Gospels of the Bible, and the Sacrament of marriage and family eliminates all of the interference and confusion. As mentioned, this started in the Old Testament and was elevated in the New Testament. But without faith in the Sacraments themselves, what do we have? Faithlessness, loneliness in a second journey that could be hard and arduous. Unless we have a devotion to a vocation that marriage is not necessary, we only frustrate ourselves and those around us with the 3Ss—stubbornness, stupidity, and sickness—in futile attempts to happiness.

At eighteen to twenty-one years of age, when our hormones are actively trying to tell us that we need to have a soul mate and get ready to get married, we need to listen to our body/flesh and quit putting off the calling if it is our calling. Our sexual activities outside of marriage only cause disruptive growth swings like a roller coaster that becomes evident on our chart. The STDs, AIDS, emotional and mental stress only make our soul's second journey harder and harder because we give ourselves the tests to overcome. Again, it is about the 3Cs of our mind, in choices that give us the consequences and conditions.

What has not already been said about the benefits of the family institution? Yet in pop culture, we are losing faith even in this. We are experiencing different lifestyle cohabitations, wasteful diversions from what was created by ISD and ESD given to us in fulfilling our lives. With faith in that which does not bear good fruit, we cannot escape losing light and our soul's descent.

The tabloids make a ton of money on the false freedoms and absurdities of humanity in pop culture experimental independent lifestyles. It only makes matters worse when people are suffering from depression, isolation, and a false sense of freedom outside of true faith. The result is a false sense of liberalization that actually plunges our soul into darkness. Notice that children here know better. We adults become victims of our own illusions offered readily by evil spirits.

Notice how those of us criminal-minded find it so hard to change even after doing time in prison. The wrong upbringing, wrong schools, wrong neighborhood, wrong friends, wrong everything, wrong parents, wrong environment, wrong philosophy of life, what are we to do? All of us are tested with one or more of the above circumstances. Is this reason for us not to change and make our life better without the criminal activity? If we ourselves are not willing to change who and what we are, who will? If we put our faith into evil deeds, we will become evil. What makes us different than the terrorists living with fatalistic ideologies? Murder is murder; whether we are trained hired assassins in it for the money or assassins for some mob, the results for our souls are the same, a drop to near zero on our chart. There is no justification for our choices, but there is in the consequences and conditions of our soul.

Only faith in a higher source of light and those who have this light could help bring about a true change even when we ourselves are smoldering. We may be brainwashed victims of despair, but when there is even the tiniest degree of hope, faith is possible. We should never listen to the faithless, who may be atheistic dying souls, hating even the mention of Father, Son and Holy Spirit. These people have made their choice, but it does not have to be our choice. We may be afraid of the unknown, the unnatural, seeing only the metaphysical ironies of our existence, but if we stop to listen and rise above the maddening herd, there are answers in the wind.

A stifling humidity, a warm front, a cold front, lightning and thunder, dark clouds, darkness and finally we get rain. This rain cleanses the filth of humanity, cleansing our earth, supporting new life and all life forms. So as with nature, the metaphysical, natural water in union with the Holy Spirit in baptism cleanses our souls. In faith, the Holy Spirit becomes the living water that cleanses our hearts and minds that we may be renewed for a life in Spirit, in light.

192

This is what we are promised and were all destined for until our free will makes the choice to do otherwise. There is hope for humanity, even those of us in our smoldering moments at .01 on our chart. Even in the worst and darkest times, a tiny fraction of faith is able to turn our lives around, heading us into a vertical movement up for our soul.

In a study of all the self-improvement books available out there, the motivational speakers, the philosophical manipulative practices by others, they are limited at best. Some will do more harm than good. Without a degree of faith in Gesu within the Holy Trinity, we will forever be waiting and wanting throughout our soul's second journey.

Without the intercession of our Blessed Virgin Maria, the apostles, the angels, the saints and the faithful in our everyday life, it is tough, very tough, and could be the toughest travel into the unknown.

Having and keeping faith is not easy in this scientific, high-tech life. Grace and love at times do not seem to exist, much less any renewal, transformation and transfiguration of ourselves in the third journey of #10 on our chart. But looking at the innocent children at play should remind us that in the grace of love that is of light, there is hope eternal. Faith and trust go hand in hand. How much faith and trust in the Holy Spirit is in the world today? A precious little amount. I believe that this is what keeps the earth within our galaxy and the sun always shining. Without faith in the life and light of the supernatural, spiritual, what have we? Nothing! Without hope and trust, where are we? Nowhere! We become victims of con artists for our souls. So often this is not visible to us due to our soul's ignorance and darkness. In faith, our soul becomes flooded like the flooding of the Nile River that overflows into the desert, giving nutrients to all she covers. This is the power of grace, my friends; we should never underestimate the potential of the Holy Spirit.

Notice how we try in vain to cheat death. We have been trying for thousands of years. We foolish Egyptians tried to preserve the body/flesh with earthly ingredients entombed into colossal pyramids as if we could go on living the afterlife as we did in our earthly second journey. What became of us? The very builders of our tombs, the slaves, those that suffered from our injustices came back to rob our tombs. Ramses, Ramses II reaching the age of ninety accomplished what? He spent most of his life planning and spending the treasury fortune on preservation of the body/flesh of his entire family. He made the choice that resulted in the consequences and conditions of an entire nation. Where are we Egyptian people today, 3,500-plus years later? We are in chaos. What is more pathetic is how we modern scientific French accepted the same corpse of Ramses II in the twentieth century to further preserve a mummy. We even gave this same mummy a presidential welcome at the airport as if he were still alive. Are the words *stupidity*, *wasteful*, and *dumbfounded* appropriate?

There are many wasteful monuments to the dead in the world, Caesar's, Hadrian's tomb in Rome, now transformed into Castel Saint Angelo, etc. But look at our cemeteries around the world that take up some of the most fertile lands on earth to see how everyday people do the same. We, to this day, continue to build elaborate mausoleums for the body/flesh of humanity. Knowledge upon knowledge or stupidity upon stupidity? At times, we need an outsider to show us who we have become. We do not see it ourselves. We are in a stupefied state of mind, ignorant of the darkness that we are in.

Only the light of someone else may be of help.

This is reflected on our chart. Notice that those of us that are between .1 and 5.9 in the degree of light of our soul are in darkness. This should be a cause for serious concern. These figures are my estimations from what I see in people around the world. We are fooling ourselves if we do not consider the eye of the needle that our soul's light needs to pass through to reach#10, heaven. I estimate that 59.90 percent of us will end down in the inferno for our soul's third journey. This estimation is not about only the Christian countries; it includes all of the estimated seven billion-plus people currently on the face of the earth. I think that .001, which is 1 in 1000 or .10 percent of the seven billion of us are prepared to reach the summit. Also, I believe that .0001, which is 1 in 10,000 or .01 percent could be pulled up into #10, heaven. This section of this book is precisely about that. Is it fate? It is not; it is as I have mentioned all along in our 3Cs—choices, consequences, and conditions. We murderers, rapists, terrorists, atheists, etc., without a positive change could expect our third journey to be down into the bowels of the earth. We need a drastic change from who we have become.

Enter purgatory, where I estimate 40.09 percent of us will most likely be deposited into our third journey. Why? In all fairness, it cannot be only about heaven and hell regardless of what some of us Christian Protestants think. Purgatory is the twilight zone for repentance, atonement, and purification through the intercession of others. This zone is for the lukewarm souls, the part-time faithful, and the mediocre of us so-called Christians that avoided our climb up to the summit. It is a zone for us not willing to be generous with the graces we were given; rather, we gave to charity our extra petty change.

This zone is reserved for those of us who were loved but failed to love. Our light degree on our chart is between 6.0 and 9.99. Notice that even at the summit, 9.0 to 9.99 degree of light, it is no assurance that we will be pulled up to #10, heaven. As I have mentioned, it is not easy.

The summit is for spiritual knowledge. What we do with it will decide whether we will be pulled up or have to spend a little time in purgatory. Notice also that often our sufferings start before the death of our bodies/flesh here in our second journey. Take notice that the lower we are tracking, the higher the amount of penance we need to endure. A serious problem is that the lower we are on our chart, the dumber and stupider we are to make the changes to climb up. Again, I believe that one out of ten thousand of us are able to be pulled up immediately after our passing away out of our bodies/flesh.

This is for us adults, and even teenagers, that have knowledge of good versus evil. It is not about the unborn child who will return to #10 instantly. It is not about the innocent children killed, murdered by us adults and teenagers. It is not about those of us handicapped lambs that I referred to. No, this is about us adults and teenagers who knew better but ignored our full responsibilities. It's for those of us that closed our eyes to the needy, the hungry, and the persecuted. As I have mentioned, omission to do right for others is almost as bad as the bad deed itself. Also, as mentioned, this book is not about feel-good-only Christianity; it is absolutely about our soul's second journey and what it entails.

Now let us explore those of us who are currently the estimated 40 percent of the population of seven billion whose soul's light is between 6.0 and 8.99 on our chart. We are not bad people; we may even try to better ourselves in the Christian way of living. Yet we tend to contradict ourselves. We object to certain commandments. We bend the rules a little. We treat our faith like a buffet to pick and choose only what we like. We do not really believe every word of the Gospels. We do not fully accept the Holy Trinity. We are grateful part of the time. We fail the Apostles' Creed. We do not take our calling seriously. We act ignorant to the parables of Christ. We refuse to give oxygen to our spark. We refuse to seek the mysteries of Light. We keep most Grace. We have addictions of our flesh that we prefer to keep. We think we are better than most human beings. We do not care enough. We do not accept the opportunities to receive more light. Sounds familiar?

What many of us in this category do not think is that all within the entire universe of any goodness is of divine grace. We see the corrupt body/flesh, sicknesses and dying, not as a test of our free will to climb but rather as a misfortune. In old age, we see ourselves as pitiful old creatures racked with pain, unable to see ourselves in our creator's image. We understand the hypotheses and theories of science but are not so sure of light within the tabernacle of our soul's heart. Evolution of humanity has bogged us down. It has wounded our faith. Does our soul evolve? Does the spirit of all life forms evolve? Does the Blessed Virgin Maria truly intercede on the souls in purgatory? Do the angels of light, the apostles, the saints and the earthly faithful actually help us in our climb up to the summit and the third journey? There is a purgatory, really? So prison is for the body/flesh what purgatory is for our soul? Turn over our free will to divine providence? What assurance do we have that we will be taken care of? That spark, that moral imprint, is within us from conception? ID, intellectual design, how? Wind travels wherever, whenever, same as the Holy Spirit? Can the Holy Grail benefit us? The chalice is just as important as the wine and water within the chalice? Why such a huge variety of races and nationalities in Christianity? Is the wine and water in mass only a symbolic gesture? Who exactly is the protagonist and antagonist in Christianity? So since the source of light was, is, and always will be, should not that same light within all created forms be similar? As a trusted theist, I need not prove anything to anyone? *Hidalgo* was a true story of a horse and the spirits of tribal ancestors? How could the five senses be transmitted to be the five senses of the soul?

These kinds of doubtful thoughts are constantly nagging those of us within the above category. We are in the middle upper range of light on the chart. Our second journey tends to be like a roller coaster that fails to reach the top summit. We may be decent law-abiding citizens that pay our taxes, vote, try to be honest, give a little bit to the poor over the holidays, and even say a prayer before dinner. We do not miss going to church once a week and actually listen to the sermon. Ah, but when the testing gets tough, we take a break, we put our faith aside, we become preoccupied with our education, occupation, and all forms of preoccupations. In hindsight, from the summit, I saw very clearly the exact moment that this happened to me. If you look at my chart on the front of this book cover, a second major dive or descent occurs. I'll explain why it occurred.

At the age of forty-three, all was going well in my life, and I could not complain. I had a job that I actually enjoyed, along with perks. I had a house with a low mortgage, investments, and a couple of cars. I lived in an earthly paradise in San Diego, California. I was somewhat happy. Yet I felt the need to achieve and accomplish much, much more. I should have been grateful, but my gratitude was more of a self-gratitude in being able to stay focused, working, saving, investments, and security. Anything wrong with this? I was caring for myself and my future. This was the American way, the Christian way, right?

Here was the problem. I thought that I alone was making everything happen. I believed that I, through my free will and hard work, was the reason for success. I got caught up in that river, riding a fast-moving current that was heading for the falls without a life jacket. I was taking more than a little risk; I was taking large risks that involved large sums of money when things went my way. There was a lot of money to be had. M&M (money and material) things were no problem. Cruises, vacations, wine and dine year after year became the norm for about a decade. What I had not figured into the equation was a financial crisis beyond my control.

Now granted, I was not the only person that was blindsided by this event, and a lot of it was out my control, or was it? At this time, I had put my faith aside, but gradually, slowly, aside became behind. In essence, I stopped climbing, and foolishness caused me to become desensitized to light. I was unknowingly losing light. The first dive, also seen on my chart, had to do with stupidity, playing, diversions, experimental youth. After that, all had to be explored and exploited, endless dead-end adventures without substance of reasonable choices.

Tragedies could cause us to wake up, as was the case with the bottom of my first dive or descent and loss of light. A loss of a true love easily could cause this, as was my case. A loss of love is a loss of light since the two are one and the same. Notice that this happened at age thirty. It was only when reality, or I should say the light within reality struck me like a lightning bolt that I saw the 3Cs—choices, consequences, and conditions—in my life for the first time. We all could be the prodigal son or daughter more than once. Sounds familiar? This time I was helped by the grace of the Holy Spirit, especially through our Blessed Virgin Maria, to stop the descent and start a sharp ascension.

For the second descent, I should have known better. There was no excuse. It had everything to do with my pride, ego, arrogance, and a false sense of self-worth. Yes, we are all forgiven, my friends, but not without a bruising atonement, penance, and a charitable Heart to make up for our wrongful choices. How else are we to learn? Do not be fooled by anyone into believing otherwise. As I have mentioned, true justice takes place in our souls, but as soul and body/flesh are one, one is accountable for our 3Cs. I testify to this. I only pray that I will not have to experience a third dive or descent because from the summit, it will be painful, awfully painful. A Richter scale type graph with sharp descents could and may kill us.

There are different linear movements of our soul's graph similar to business charts and graphs. For example, the W is a linear movement of sharp ups and downs in, let us say, a stock price. We have the same for our souls' degree, loss, or gain of light. The W, as explained, are sharp ups and downs for adults. A top line at birth from conception is a straight horizontal line from 9.99 for children less than three years old that did not survive long in their second journey and returned to their origins #10 where they came from. It is also for the severely handicapped children, the lambs, as I have mentioned, that survive but need us healthy ones to care for them. Unborn children due to natural or forced abortion remain at 9.99 and return to #10, so no chart or graph is needed. The vertical descent I is, of course, none other than the archangel Lucifer, Satan, with his comrade angels that fell from grace straight to hell. The L is the sharp descent that remains at .01 or near 0 until death. These are extremely evil people who refuse to change—for example, current terrorists and satanic cult members. The U is a sharp descent with a slow turnaround until the sharp ascension—for example, born again Christians that truly are turned around through charitable works. The V is a gradual descent and gradual ascension as, for example, Saint Paul.

I hope that this helps, as we are not equal in body/flesh, even if our souls are in our second journey. As we can see, there are various ways to climb up to the summit and be pulled up to #10, heaven, or descend into hell. Those of us stationary, stagnated in 6.0 to 8.99, are neither of them but rather like a wave just moving horizontally to our death. We are the unsure and not fully decided. Which one you are is for you to figure out. When we accept bits and pieces of grace, that is all that we benefit from, like crumbs from the dining table rather than the full banquet itself.

Note also that two people, soul mates, share light—for example, a husband and wife. Let us say that the husband has a soul light of 8.0 and his wife has a light of 9.0. Their average is 8.5, which means that they could help each other to 9.99. A couple, 6.0 and 7.0, average 6.5, which means that it is possible yet harder to help each other. A couple 3.0 and 4.0, average 3.5, is going to have a tough time simply staying a couple. It all has to do with their morality and degree of light, not man- made BS or nonsense such as ten steps to better sex and intimacy. Bet against morality and light, and you will lose every time—for example, people who marry up to eight times but never figure out why their marriage does not work. Hence, a low light person of, let us say, 2.0 with a high light person of say 8.6 equals, average 5.3 but, what could happen here? 1) The first person of 2.0 could be raised up, as we know does happen; 2) The second person of 8.6 could be brought down to a lower level as we well know also happens; 3) Both live with their average of 5.3. We see that happen as well. The point is, who helps whom? Who hurts whom? There are so many variations of what is possible in faith. There are just as many variations of what is possible without faith, hence the utmost importance of accepting the right person in marriage. We at times think that we can change someone through sheer will, even love. It may happen, but when there is no willingness on the part of the other person, the odds are against us. Take for example a person who is involved in criminal activity, say, illegal drug selling. That person making large sums of money with ease is going to be super difficult to change. Another example is two people living together outside of moral law. Their combined average of light will determine how long the relationship is going to last. Notice how some of us go from relationship to relationship to endless relationships but never are happy or content. Take note that the degree of contentment/hap-piness is equal to the degree of gratitude to the Holy Spirit within the Holy Trinity! How is this accomplished? By charity toward human-ity! The greater the charity, the greater the gratitude, the greater the contentment/happiness!

The problem with humanity is that in a way we all have our rebel-without-a-cause moments within that effect who we are with-out amongst others. It always comes down to faith, moral laws, and the graces in light. We could only take credit for our good works, deeds of our free will, and be rewarded with grace/light. For example, the saints, Mother Teresa, Warren Buffet, Bill Gates, etc. Let us also keep in mind that, for example, we help bring clean drinking water to those who have none. In this deed, we ourselves receive the grace of living water in Spirit with our tabernacle doors open, shedding light into our souls.

We could also, by our own free will, do works of evil or bad deeds and bring in darkness that replaces light. Examples are Hitler, Mussolini, Stalin, the current and past two tyrants of North Korea, etc. This brings to mind Poland in Europe. Here was a country whose people, largely Roman Catholics, went through hell to get rid of the tyrants that subjected them to their false ideologies to live by. How did they overcome such overwhelming odds and keep the faith? With their free will and the intercession of others. For example, at the time, Pope John Paul II and our Blessed Virgin Maria helped out. It has worked and continues to work. I am sure that there were days when it seemed hopeless and days when people just wanted to shout out to their faith in anger. It is hard to live the faith 100 percent of the time when events seem to drag on for years. Indeed, there were many who lost their faith altogether. But for those persecuted that persevered, their children and grandchildren should be grateful, very grateful.

We are never alone. For instance, notice that there are representations of the spiritual in the metaphysical—the light of the Holy Spirit in the sunshine, our Blessed Virgin Maria that reflects grace as the moon reflects sunlight, the lights of angels as guides as the lights of stars are guides. Actually, there is no north, south, east, or west for earth. There is simply a magnificent sphere of creation filled with a variety of life forms of every kind. There is no longitude or latitude without the stars, sun, and moon. These are all reminders for us that we are not and never will be alone. If we are, we chose to be. If we feel lost without a compass, it's because we chose to be so. Meditate on this for a while.

Remember that there are at least three journeys, if not more. If we are lost in our second, what becomes of our third? If we refuse to understand the mysteries of light in our second, how are we to understand the mysteries of light in our third? What are we to pass on to our children and grandchildren? Again, it comes down to faith and our 3Cs. It always has.

We all have our weaknesses, but do we recognize them? Pride, ego, arrogance, self—everything, M&M, celebrity, vanity, etc. These all interfere with our climbing to our summit. There are three accomplishments that all of us need to have, and none of them are doable on our own. They all require grace directly or indirectly through others. First, know yourself in relationship to light, our Holy Spirit. Second, be willing to be tested and climb up to the summit, a mystery that reveals other mysteries. Third, pray for the strength, courage, and intercession of our Blessed Virgin Maria, the angels, the saints, and the faithful to help you reach not only the summit of spiritual knowledge but to be pulled up to #10, heaven.

"The soul is willing, but the flesh is weak." These words of Christ are the explanation of this book. They prove to me that although our body/flesh and soul is one, they also are distinguished and may be operating apart from each other at times. We know that this does happen mainly during the night hours of natural darkness when our body/flesh is weakest. I recall my father saying a bed's name is Rosa, as if to imply that our body/flesh at night needs to be in a clean, naturally scented, comfortable place for lying down to rest and sleep. From the summit, one can understand this wisdom. Think of all the problems that people get into during the night's darkness. Evils are indeed most active at night when our body/flesh is at our weakest. How many of us wake up on a morning, think of the night before, and have huge regrets for our choices? It is as if we brought into our body/flesh a tapeworm that is consuming us. But you see, my friends, the tapeworm for our soul is evil itself that we accepted into our souls. This ruins our rhythm of life of ISD, intellectual spiritual design! It is bad enough that we have allowed corporations to put us on a stressful 24-7 schedule outside of emergencies, which wreaks havoc on our body/flesh. The bigger problem is how we do this to ourselves with our lifestyle. It is literally killing us.

The mysteries of Easter give us the whole purpose of the first and second journeys. In honest and sincere faith, hope, and trust in the resurrection of Christ, the summit becomes just a stepping stone, a platform to be pulled up to #10. There are different paths to the spiritual knowledge up to the summit. For example, we could easily take a helicopter to the summit of Mt. Everest, but that would defeat the whole purpose, would it not? The learning process is in the climb itself, in being tested to our full endurance. In hindsight, we see that this is the case for the climb to the summit of spiritual knowledge as well.

Some of us think of ourselves as tough guys and gals. We know how to beat up an opponent with our hands, causing harmful injuries, brain damage, and even death. We think that we are tough, yet we are without a clue on the toughest conquest of all. The climb to the summit of spiritual knowledge is absolutely, without any doubt, the toughest conquest of all. All others pale in comparison. This is also my dare to all of the so-called tough guys and gals out there: attempt the climb.

Again, we could learn from the saints. They learned that through an altruistic charitable path, climbing to the summit was like taking an escalator up. Also, the forgiveness of our sins from Christ does not mean avoiding accountability. It is contingent on us doing the same to others. Let us be honest with ourselves, how many of us live this?

Purgatory glimpses are not that common; in fact, they are rare. Purgatory is not hell but a continuation of soul into a zombie state of being. Visitors to hell are infrequent as well, although to scare the hell out of us literally is not a bad idea. Heaven, #10, seems to be the most visited by humanity of all ages, from children to the elderly. The Holy Spirit seems to like to put a positive spin on our second journey. Living in the metaphysical, the comparison is indeed surreal or dreamlike. After all, the visitation is generally not that long.

I believe, though, that seeing family members in heaven, especially parents and grandparents, is a powerful message to want to join them someday somehow. This is what we Roman Catholics believe in, family, not only in our second journey but more importantly the third journey. Only faith brings us there for that reunification of hearts and minds. This is the reason that we do not mind the hardships, burdens, sacrifices, trials and errors, feast or famine, even death itself. I find it ironic, though, that the Apostles, the popes, the priests were and are all men, and yet at daily mass women outnumber men, nine to one. Hence, of the estimated 40 percent, I think nine to one are probably men to women in the low range. Women have the mind's eye or the eye of the soul, whereas men have more the eyes of the metaphysical. Women are more sensitive to the beautiful rhythm of life in association with our creator. They, in faith, understand the mysteries better than men.

I returned to Italia in the spring, Easter of 2014, to put all of my notes together to write this book. I was reminded that with spring, with the blossoming of all plant life forms, our earth is in love with the cosmos. It should remind us that our seed, our spark, is also connected to the cosmos in spirit. The wheel of life is predestined by ISD, intellectual spiritual design, for us mortals to pass through death into new life. The education of the Holy Spirit is given to us in small doses for us to interpret, just as with children. We are not able to handle large quantities of spiritual knowledge at once, hence the slow, time-consuming climb. Learn, digest, and rest day after day, monthly, yearly to the summit.

Think: no Christmas, no Easter, no third journey of heaven, no more light or love, no alpha or omega, no more anything—just nothingness. As in the opera *Pagliacci* by Leoncavallo, in the end, he sings "La commedia è finita," the comedy is finished. To think of life as an ending comedy, we become tragic actors.

How does the Holy Spirit know us at all times? The Holy Spirit is within that spark in our soul's heart, in our tabernacle from conception, throughout our soul's first and second journeys, knowing all that we do and all that we are. This seems profound but is the only reason why we live and have life.

I think that because of childbirth, women sense that we are all in transit in our second journey. "Ave Maria *pieni di Graci*" or "full of grace" is in a woman, not a man. Yes, our Blessed Virgin Maria is everywhere in Italia. Her statutes and portraits are in the millions throughout Italy, even the smallest villages. She is in churches, homes, piazzas, the exterior facade of buildings, and the bridges. She is supreme, above all saints and angels. She is truly the queen, the very essence of womanhood and motherhood. We Italians call on her because she knows us. Grace overflows from her to us. She is well connected to Christ in the Holy Trinity and has knowledge of the spark within our soul that needs oxygen. Again, as our physical heart sends blood and oxygen to our brain and body, so does our heart's spark send light to our soul's mind to be enlightened. Call on her, she is truly helpful in our second journey, but even more so in our Passover into our third journey. From the moment of conception, we are in need of protection due to our innocence. At the time of starting to exercise our free will, we are still in need of protection from the evils that can overwhelm us. Hence, the protection of our Blessed Virgin Maria is important to us.

I recall turning away from my faith when I was not able to understand the suffering of some of the innocent children in the world. It didn't make sense to me. I have since learned from the summit that the children are at times the innocent lambs that suffer for our sake to help us change. In faith, hope, and trust in the Holy Spirit and intercession of our Blessed Virgin Maria, this is possible. Without this, we are fragile, limited creatures without a real future.

As mentioned, that spark, a gift for us from Dio/Father/orb/ supernatural spiritual light lives within the tabernacle of our soul's heart. At our passing away, one of three destinations will be ours to take. The first is #10, heaven, in which that spark travels with our soul. The second is hell, in which that spark returns to #10, the original source, without us. The third is purgatory, in which that spark is outside of our soul and put on hold for safety. This is where our Blessed Virgin Maria is able to continuously help us, to pull us out of the twilight zone to reunite with our spark in light.

We have no choices, only consequences and conditions at our Passover after our death; our time is up. As an example, for a pedophile priest that abused children without confession, penance, and atonement before his death, the third journey is no longer his choice. Regardless of priesthood, the angels of death will accompany him to his third journey. As I have mentioned many times, all are held accountable in our second journey.

In order to understand the climb to the summit of spiritual knowledge, we need to understand the depths of the oceans or the subconscious of our soul's heart. Know that the depths of the oceans are as deep as the heights of the highest mountains. How are we to do this? The depths of the ocean floor brings us fears of going there and seeing what is there. As the ocean's deep waters become dark, so also our soul's consciousness may be the same from evils that we accept. At times, we need to shut down so much worthless knowledge, harmful artificial intelligence, and give time and light to our conscious mind. Let light clear the way to our heart's tabernacle. In this and in faith, we are able to see into the spark of our soul's heart and subconscious.

As mentioned, the metaphysical earth was created to serve all forms of life but specifically humanity. The tallest mountains should remind us of our climb up to the summit of spiritual knowledge and the ocean depths of our soul's heart and subconscious. All of the various viruses, diseases, and evils in between should remind us not to get trapped in between the two.

Again, our spark is a gift to us to grow in union with our soul into light. If we never grow from the metaphysical alone, how are we to grow that spark into our soul, climb to the summit, or be pulled up to #10? It is not possible. The body/flesh is only a corpse that could become comatose. In union with our soul, we have consciousness. In union with the spark of the Holy Spirit within us, we have the spirit of conscience and the mysteries of ourselves and light.

For example, we scientists know that it is not just the sun that makes life possible on earth but even more so the lava river that flows within the earth. Without this, we would all freeze to death, so it is with our body/flesh and soul needing the light of the Holy Spirit to fuel the spark within us to sustain us.

It is not easy. In fact, it was probably easier three thousand years ago than it is today. We have made our second journey like walking a tight rope often without any safety net. We are always trying to balance things in our lives, but we have made it so complicated, and the complexities drive us crazy. This is the reason that a few of us join monasteries, just so we can get away from the maddening herd and stressful lifestyle without peace.

The true answer is simplicity in our everyday life. We talk about it but don't know how to live it. The solution is and always has been within our soul's heart. The tabernacle needs to be opened with our free will to let the oxygen in. Any degree of faith allows this to happen. In this, we are given the grace/energy to make our climb to our summit. In this, we simplify our life. We unload all of the monkeys on our shoulders that are bogging us down. Hence, we are able to gain a degree of peace of mind and some sleep for this body/ flesh of ours.

Our 3Cs, choices of our free will to accept the evils into ourselves, result in the consequences of sin that let darkness into our soul's mind and closes our tabernacle doors. This suffocation of the spark within our soul's tabernacle gives us the conditions that cause us sufferings. You see, we gradually, slowly close the doors ourselves and in the process lose light. A sincere confession, repentance, atonement, acts of charitable deeds, and gratitude cause the doors to gradually, slowly reopen. The intercession of our Blessed Virgin Maria, the angels, and saints is crucial in how quickly the process takes. It also depends on our learning so as not to repeat our mistakes.

Also keep in mind that our tabernacle doors are self-locking from the inside. This is for our safety. In other words, when we are totally out of control, the doors close and lock up until we or the intercession of others that have the faith, hope, and trust unlock them again. This is the case in self-induced or force-induced comatose victims. Notice how the prayers of others cause this to take place—family for family for the good of the family of humanity. Notice also how the older churches of Renaissance Italy were designed. They were designed in the shape of the cross, yes, but more importantly the shape of man/woman with outstretched arms and the tabernacle of the Holy Eucharist at the heart of the Church. Mankind is the same. Coincidence? Think again.

What came first, the hen or the egg? Neither. The rooster was created first with the seed. The hen was created next to deliver the egg. So also, humanity was created with body/flesh, seed, and soul. What was important here is that man, given the spark, needed the breath of spiritual oxygen to begin life. Woman was next with body/ flesh, egg, soul, and spark with the spiritual oxygen to sustain her. The beginning of humanity and of all other forms of life—animal, plant, and all other species—occurred during the same week as described in Genesis.

What came first, rabies or microorganisms? Microorganisms, yes, but how did microorganisms come to exist? Evolution? Yes, but evolving from what, when, where, and why? All viruses, good or bad, have a purpose. Only in light can we attempt to have an understanding of their purpose. The good viruses are easy to deal with. It is the bad ones that hurt humanity and are difficult to comprehend. Were they given to us in order to unite us to one cause? To help each other collectively?

One man, Louis Pasteur of France, was one of those rare men caring for children and humanity. He was not a medical doctor, yet his charitable heart brought medicine into the twentieth century. His interest in the microscope and microorganisms helped with the vaccine against rabies. He was outside of the medical school but was more open-minded than those who, although medical doctors, were close-minded to new research. At times, an outsider is needed to bring in new ideas, much like in business in which minds can become stagnant.

Think of all the lives saved since 1865 due to one man and his assistants. Think of the focus on parasites, new laboratories, pasteurization, antiseptic, sterilization of equipment. Think on an international scale regarding the suffering and lives saved! This was faith, my friends. This was/is the meaning of a charitable heart for children and humanity. These are the positive 3Cs of one man who, with his associates, collectively and effectively helped bring consequences and conditions to alleviate intolerable diseases.

The similarities should be obvious for our souls. At times, it takes an outsider with an altruistic charitable heart to make the difference between a descent to a climb up to the summit of spiritual knowledge.

In avoiding the Scriptures, we bring onto ourselves the worst fears and problems. Fear is the absence of faith, hope, and trust. In what? The Holy Trinity. This is what interferes and causes disruption in our lives and our climb up to the summit. We Roman Catholics believe in the Apostles Creed. This is our faith. Read the words. In living these words, we are able to climb up to our summit.

How did Saint John the Baptist understand what he was doing in the baptismal acts that he carried out for people? He had faith in the words given to him. Even Christ, who did not need to be baptized, was baptized as an act of faith for others to follow.

The last supper of Christ, why did it take place? Again, Christ did not need it but did it for the sake of humanity. In faith, the apostles knew this and incorporated the bread and wine into the Church and the mass. This is where we Protestant Christians are losing out and losing the most important piece of Christianity. In Holy Communion, we are confirming our faith and communication in Christ within the Holy Trinity. In this, our spark receives the oxygen and nutritional strength we need to survive. This becomes evident in our soul's heart and mind. It all begins with our free will to make the choice.

There was a time when people fasted, did not eat meat on Friday, etc. This helped with self-discipline. Have we lost their meaning? Has the Roman Catholic Church become too lax, making us lazy and undisciplined? Some of us in public make the sign of the cross, especially in front of large audiences or the camera. What are we truly trying to prove? That this is our faith? It appears more like a celebrity's moment. Some of us want the Holy Spirit to do our will on our terms. We want to enter into an agreement as in business. We want certain consequences so that we have the desired conditions. New dumbfounded upon old dumbfounded is what we deserve and have in our scientific generation. Of course, when disappointed, we turn to Satan, whom we can will and deal with. Unknowingly, we automatically lose the deal, grace, and light. Here our 3Cs backfire, not into our face/flesh but into our soul.

Dogs and dolphins, birds and butterflies, raw untamed nature at times make more sense than humanity. They are honest and true to their created limitations of imprint. Whereas in humanity, we could be sinners or saints, but the majority (90 percent of us) are sinners for the most part. What do we want? There are only two choices of our free will: in union with the will of light or the darkness of evil.

Take as an example the war in Sarajevo-Bosnia between Christian and Muslim. People in Europe after World War II were quoted as saying, "Never again, never again, never again." But this was a different generation. The new generation of the 1990s had not experienced the same hell fifty years earlier. As mentioned, we destroy bodies of people, but the evils are still there for the next generation. Who were the antagonists of this conflict? The younger generation. Why? Why the hatred between so-called theistic people? Here was a conflict in our backyard as Europeans, and what did we "never again" people do as protagonists? We let Americans and NATO deal with it! Sounds familiar? Physiologists have yet to figure out how this could happen. A New Jerusalem? An incompetent EU? Joan Baez singing about peace and love? From the summit, as discussed, the reasons are very obvious.

The Japanese were quoted as saying, "Never again." As of this writing, issues are brewing again in Asia, and Japan is rearming. America is trying to resolve the issues. Are the documentaries of the suffering, death, and destruction of World War II going to help? I doubt it. Does history repeat itself with the negative 3Cs? It does. Chart the collective summation of light of a people of any government and country, and you can get a glimpse of future events.

It is the same in Israel. President Truman failed to set up the boundaries of the region between two stubborn people, again supposedly both theistic. What has been the outcome of the past sixty-five years? We Jews and Palestinians have a lot to meditate and reflect back on.

Notice how some of us invoke the "gospel truth" with others as if to prove that we are truthful. Why do we do this? For example, listen to the three words, "honest to God," said quite often by many of us. Why? Now listen to the terrorists and how often they invoke the name of Allah, almost every day as if Allah is on their side. Is this blasphemy? Are we being blasphemous in bringing Allah into the arena of killings, death, and destruction? Holy, holy, holy, but what is holy in our activities against innocent humanity? Now listen to these words, "Say the word, and I will be healed." These are the words of faith in prayer and in our mass before receiving the Eucharist."*Abitate di noi*" (Live within us). This is our faith. Have faith in the words! This reminds me of Verdi's opera, *Nabucco*. The opera chorus of *Va*

*Pensiero* always brings tears to my eyes. I know of the blood spilled by those who helped unify Italy. Although the words were written for the Hebrews in exile in thinking about their homeland, Verdi knew what he was doing by putting these words to music in the opera. The words were more instrumental than the notes for the people, pardon the pun. The Italians needed words of encouragement against the Austrian occupation and revolutionary war. The words of *Va Pensiero* worked (go thoughts) in a unified movement to drive the Austrians out of Italy for good. Such are the power of words in faith.

I know full well that it is very hard for some of us to have faith in anything or anyone, much less in words that do not seem to relate, at times, to our hungry, homeless, cold, penniless reality. But there is no better alternative. We all have a mission, a calling to accept or reject with our own free will. In acceptance, it may not make us saints, but it will give us light, purpose, and meaning to enrich our lives. A Nobel Peace Prize is never out of the question. Study the people who have been honored to receive it. For example, a mother living in faith could raise a child to be the next world leader to usher in improved equality, justice, and peace into a region. In rejecting our calling, our mission, what do we have? The fruition in our second journey is no accident or coincidence. We are all created for good works; we decide.

The light and Spirit of Christ in the Holy Trinity need no introduction. Our Blessed Virgin Maria, I have written about. The saints, I have also made reference to. But the angels, not as much. I also believe in angels, archangels for sure, such as Michael, Gabriel, and Raphael. But guardian Angels? I do, I believe that our guardian angel tracks and has full knowledge of where we are on our chart. He/she has access to our graph, a report card if you will. There are no secrets, nothing is hidden. All is revealed and simultaneously transmitted to our source, our creator. Our guardian angel is a shield of light but does not decide our 3Cs. He/she is always there, trying to persuade us to do right based on the highest standards and not wrong or evil. It is a daily battle for guardian angels, but it is their job. Law and order for our souls, this is their mission, what they were created for. and gratefully they accept for our sake. Think that this is all fairytales?

Think again, some of us see our guardian angel as they are crying due to our stupidity. They are crying because they are losing most of their battles in this twenty-first century of pop culture and evils.

Even with the advantages of living in faith, we will have days that we experience isolation, desolation, coldness, and emptiness to remind us of what we have without light, spiritual knowledge, and wisdom. This reminds us of the climb that we all need to make. During these times, we need to meditate in silence and prayer and figure out what we are not doing rather than what we are doing. Think of our natural sun dying and not doing what it was created to do. Think about the 3Cs as if the sun were a person. Think about the effects the dying sun would have on all life forms on earth. All would die. Now try to understand what our soul needs to do but don't in our 3Cs. Think about the effects on family. Finally, think about the light of the Holy Spirit and the 3Cs. Think about the effects on all creation if the Holy Trinity did not do what has been done since the beginning of time. All would cease to exist. It is incomprehensible.

If evil were allowed to penetrate the tabernacle of our soul, we would be dead already. Again, light and darkness cannot, do not, dwell in the same space. Evils can and do penetrate our minds, causing us to do evil deeds through our body/flesh. This does darken and harden our hearts, but our soul's spark is safeguarded in our tabernacle until our death.

In the twenty-first century, we are multitasking. Look at ourselves, it seems that everyone is multitasking in stress and maddening consequences and conditions. It is like an employer trying to squeeze every ounce of intelligence out of us at the least amount of cost. We are trained to do this at work and ultimately bring it home. We multitask when driving, eating, and even attempting to give love (TV, cell phone) in bed to our spouse. For example, another one of my near-death experiences occurred while I was biking and a car driver was checking her text messages or whatever on her cell phone at an intersection. I had the right of way, and she just happened to look up in time to hit the brakes. Our priorities are out of whack. Another example, think about how many of us die from choking to death each year because we are multitasking—trying to talk and eat at the same time. What we are doing with our body/flesh in a negative way affects our soul as well since the two are one. We do not need to multitask; we need to focus on the one most important need for our soul, which is love in light. Everything else can follow, as there is a right time for everyone and everything.

Take a look at the charts again. Notice that the 59.9 percent of us tracking between .1 and 5.9 in light think that in time we just die and all ends. So we multitask as if trying to get everything out of life before we die. Those of us 40 percent who are tracking between 6.00 and 8.9 simply want to live a decent life with little stress and enjoy the fruits of our labor in hope that we have earned a right to the after-life of heaven. Those of us .001, .10 percent or 1 in 1000 tracking between 9.00 and 9.9 in light at the summit, want to work at reaching #10, heaven, but we are not willing to give up our free will to do so. Finally, the .0001, .01 percent of us, which is 1 out of 10,000, will turn over our entire being of body/flesh, mind, heart, and soul to the Holy Spirit in order to be in union—in perpetual light.

Difficult to comprehend? For the sake of young readers that I hope are reading this, let us simplify it. Think of a tree, an apple fruit tree, for example. Let us say that this tree is healthy and bears delicious apples each year as long as it is maintained and gets the water and nutrients it needs. Now this tree will age, get old, and eventually die. Those of us 59.9 percent will say, "Okay, let it die. We got the most out of it," the end. Those of us 40 percent may say, "Let us try to prolong the tree's life. Let us prune the tree, give it additional nutrients, and try to preserve the tree as long as possible to get the most apples out of it as possible before it dies." Those of us, 10 percent may say, "Let us take the seeds of the apple tree and plant the seeds in order to try to get more of the same apple trees." But we know from genetics that this chance does not always work. Finally, those of us 01 percent say, "Let us graft the apple tree while still healthy into an apple tree even healthier so that in union we will continue to have delicious apples." Meditate on this for a while. Ask yourself, in what percentage group am I in? Who determines my climb? Who is able and willing to assist me?

We need to ask ourselves what prevents us from having faith in order to get to that elite .01 percent. It is the same as three thousand years ago—evil spirits that persuade our free will in choice. It is our pride and ego. What is the cure? Grace, love in charity from light. Try this: help anyone who has far harder consequences and conditions than your own. Put your free will to work and see what happens. Evil does not know what to do with love and charity. It is like darkness does not know what to do with light. Light simply appears, and darkness vanishes.

We cannot see spiritual grace, love, or light with our naked eye as something concrete, but neither can we see the wind with our naked eyes, yet we know the effects. Natural wind cools us like a sea breeze; it moves out stagnant bad air, it is a toy for birds to play with, it moves our sails to travel, it carries seeds all over the world, it moves rain to reach covered areas, etc. So it is with the Holy Spirit. We cannot see our free will, but we have it. We cannot see faith, but we can see the consequences and conditions in ourselves and humanity when we put it to work. In fact, what we do see in the metaphysical is what passes away, but the spiritual does not.

We cannot see our soul's mind, only our brain, but what is our brain without our mind? So also we cannot see the spark within our soul's tabernacle, but what is our soul without it?

Yes, having faith can be confusing. It is like a boy/girl meeting for the first time. We tell ourselves that the physical attraction, the chemistry, is either there or not, either we feel it or we do not. Again, this is the metaphysical, which especially these days, can be very deceptive. Notice that when we think we are not attracted to someone at first, after getting to know them and their inner beauty, we might change our minds. Whereas that person that we thought we were physically attracted to, finding out how cold and hard-hearted they are kills the relationship. Again, what is important is what is in the person's tabernacle, that spark within their soul's heart, in relationship to their entire being.

This brings to mind Enrico Caruso, one of the all-time greatest tenors that ever sang opera. He was a celebrity of his time throughout the world. He had it all—or he thought he had it all. You see, the woman whom he thought loved him deceived him in running off with their driver. Yes, even love (or should I say a false love?) can be very deceptive.

We mortals have this thing for physical beauty—I am no exception, but when it comes to putting faith in someone, what should we look for? Notice that if this person is consumed in their physical body/flesh and not their soul's spiritual health and wellness, there is a malfunction. We can clearly see this in their unhealthy choices—for example, tobacco and drug use, alcohol abuse, eating habits, etc. In other words, they make unhealthy conscious choices for their body/flesh. This is one of the warning signs. I know that none of us are perfect, far from it, but where is the willingness to change for the better?

This is a far more important issue and warning sign. There is no faith when there is no willingness to accept change in light.

Some of us just want to age gracefully. What does this mean? Notice the word *grace* within the full word? We put the word *grace* into many of our words—graceful, gracefully, gracious, graciously, graced, graciousness, etc. But what makes us gracious people? Is it our lifestyle, our professionalism, our attitude, our character? Now notice that the word *grateful* goes hand in hand with grace. So it is the application of grace into ourselves and sharing of this grace that make us grow gracefully old. For example, I am so grateful for receiving the words and having the opportunity to write this book to share with you. In my appreciation, I have decided that 70 percent-plus of all proceeds will go to the charity of Saint Don Bosco that helps poor and disadvantaged children around the world. Their needs are huge, but only few offer to help. In this, I hope to grow graciously old. This, my friends, is an example of a conscious choice that stems from the conscious soul's mind.

A disgrace is the opposite; it is a dis-light or, in other words, a loss of light. We use this word a lot—or used to use it a lot. Today, though, what is considered a disgrace? As long as something, anything, is in our self-interest, nothing is disgraceful—or at least, that is what we think. Remember, all in life has to be integrated and is held accountable. This starts and takes place in our souls and comes out into our bodies/flesh since the two are one.

Our second journey is about faith in elevation. Look at the charts again. Notice that all that is near zero on the charts is low elevation or ground level, street level, water level, river level, sewer level. Now study the eagles. Their level is high elevation, yet they could see all at the lowest level. This should be our goal as well. In faith, in the climb itself, we see what the eagles see. Notice also that most diseases of humanity have their origins at the lowest levels of earth, similar to the charts, near zero.

Science, the knowledge upon knowledge of humanity, has taken us to the moon and is planning on taking us to Mars, yes, star-trekking. This is okay, especially in dealing with the metaphysical aspects of our lives. But my question is, what about the consciousness of our conscience? We scientists say that we have no scientific model, equation, or proof that our soul even exists. Hmm, no exploration into the core of our soul's tabernacle, much less even into the outer core of our souls. Is it a lack of faith, being away from the mathematical formulations? Yet these are the greatest mysteries of all. No faith, no elevation, no revelation, as in the Book of Revelation.

Those of us in physics who have discovered the metaphysical mysteries of the universe in relationship to light are actually closer than we dare to believe in discovering the mysteries of spiritual light. The two are one; just that one natural light is in a different form but still from the same source. Again, an unwillingness in any degree of faith prevents discovery. Our minds are elevated into the metaphysical universe but not the spiritual. If we physicists study our own chart, we are probably tracking in the middle range of light in our soul. In better words, we are not climbing to our summit. We need to meditate on this and change our discussion among ourselves in union with those who have climbed to the summit of spiritual knowledge.

I suppose that the best example that I could possibly give on faith is my own experience in a near-death accident, or I should say a setup that easily could have been fatal. I was on my way home after work on freeway 163 southbound in San Diego, California, going about sixty to sixty-five miles per hour. I was cruising, minding my own business, and taking my time. At this point in my life, in hindsight, from the summit, I think that I was tracking between 8.00

and 8.9, a wannabe summit achiever but with too many other things on my mind. Anyway, when almost at my exit, I felt a blast from behind. I quickly realized that I had been rear-ended. My head hit the car ceiling, causing a three-inch gash in my skull and bleeding. These things happened in split seconds. I was in the number 3 lane, which is the third from the center divide, a three-feet-high cement wall. The rear impact caused my foot to press down on the accelerator, causing the car to speed up. The rear impact also caused the car to turn into the direction of the center divide. I traveled from the number 3 lane heading into the cement wall without anyone being in the number 2 or 1 lanes. The car was out of control, and I had no time to hit the brakes or maneuver it at all. As I said, these events happen in split seconds. I quickly realized that upon impact, I could die. In that moment, all I could think were these seven words, "No God, not now—not this way." After impact against the center divide, my car turned and headed the opposite direction across the freeway toward the shoulder, crossing all four lanes. All traffic behind me had stopped, even the perpetrator, a young teenager that was speeding and snaking through the lanes. When finally my car came to a stop, I was facing traffic, bleeding and almost unconscious. All I can remember were people yelling, "Don't move him; it could cause more injuries." Also, I heard the perpetrator yelling that it was his fault and saying how sorry he was. The event took place across from Sharp Hospital, so once the paramedics came, I was five minutes away from the emergency room. I recall them asking me all these questions such as my birth date and telling me not to close my eyes. Next thing I recall was a CHP officer asking me questions about the event that took place and stating that the eyewitnesses confirmed what I had said. I was released after that, hurting badly and given a prescription for pain killers. I had stitches in my head but was alive to go home, needing a ride since my car was demolished.

Was this an act of faith? Were those seven words what saved my life that day? As I said, at the time, I thought that I was fortunate or lucky to survive the accident. From the summit, twenty years later, I believe otherwise. I know that it was no accident but instead, a major setup for me to start my ascension to the summit rather than staying stuck in a cozy high range. No, my survival was not luck and had nothing to do with fortune. It did have to do with the seven words that I called out to the Holy Spirit. A split second, how is this possible?

I realize now that my voice did not have to travel far. That spark within the tabernacle of my soul's heart is within me. My calling was instantly and simultaneously heard. I was given more time in my second journey. I was not thankful or grateful that day so long ago. Today, after the summit climb, as I have stated, I let no day pass without expressing my gratitude not only for that day so long ago but also for all with which I have been graced. At times, it takes tragedies, severe testing, near-death experiences, a visit to purgatory or hell to move our free will. Be grateful that you are not forgotten. How could you be? The spark is within your soul's tabernacle, at least, until the death of your body/flesh.

Now the .001, .10 percent or 1 in 1000, of us do reach the summit. These odds are amazing. Even more awesome will be the odds of .0001, .01 percent or 1 in 10,000, that are able to reach 9.9 on the chart of our soul's light. When you think of the "eye of the needle" in relationship to light, you can appreciate these figures. We need to look at our chart and ask ourselves, why am I charting less than 9.9? The answer always has to do with the fruits that we bear, good or bad. It has to do with faith, love, and charity.

Open your eyes. One of the greatest means of relief for sore eyes is seeing someone living their faith in action, in love, and in passion for charity. The saints are examples, but everyone could be included, such as our ex-President Jimmy Carter and what he accomplished for those needing a home/shelter or the missionaries, all of whom volunteer their time, energy, and resources to help the poor and disadvantaged in the world. Now learn from them.

There is such a thing as blind faith. There is faith that wants to climb the summit and wants the grace to do so. Remember that works or actions in charity fan oxygen to the spark within our souls' tabernacle. This inflames our spark to grow and glow, bringing out grace upon grace into our soul. This grace is also spiritual knowledge and wisdom. This is what we unfaithful fail to understand, hence being dumbfounded. We cannot be too hard on ourselves, though, since all of us have a starting point. Remember that our free will and a yes open the doors to our heart's tabernacle. We have a key.

Think of the keys given to Saint Peter. If you study the statue of the apostle, he is holding two keys and one isn't a copy of the other. One key is for the church doors. The other key is for the tabernacle. Now think of the metaphysical Saint Peter's Cathedral. The Renaissance artists, as I have mentioned, were graced with knowledge in building the church. Notice the entrance in front of the church. The pillars are symbolic of open arms for everyone. They open across from the Tiber river, as if to say, "Come over to this side, away from paganism into Christianity." The marble, bricks and mortar of the church are the metaphysical, like our metaphysical body/flesh. Inside the church, the artists poured their hearts out of the graces given to them in the paintings and sculptures. This is the metaphysical that is symbolic of the soul of the church, as is our soul within our own body/flesh. The metaphysical sacristy is the brain, symbolic for the soul's mind, as is our mind within our brain. Now the most important part of the church is the metaphysical tabernacle that is the heart of the church, as is our natural heart as well. But most importantly, the metaphysical host/bread within the tabernacle in faith becomes the Spirit of Christ, like the nucleus of an atom. So it is with the spark within the tabernacle of our soul's heart. The pope has the keys to the church and tabernacle; we have the key to our free will and to our tabernacle. Notice also that above the dome of the church is also a summit, similar to the mountain top summit where the city can be seen below. Here the dove of the Holy Spirit replaces the eagle.

The Holy Spirit of Christ is never far from us. Recall my own experience and the split second to communicate. Even our thoughts are communicated. Multiple this times billions to begin to understand how awesome it is. As Saint Augustine wrote almost two thousand years ago, "What I have written is like straw." Mind you, this is from one of the greatest writers of the Roman Catholic Church. Yet his knowledge was like a twinkle in the full knowledge of light. Saint Augustine received a tiny percentage of knowledge of what to write by grace. We also need the same to reach the top of the summit and

#9.9. Keep in mind that we need a plus to get from 9.0 to 9.9, hence 9.0 plus 1/9 increments to 9.9. From 9.9 plus to 10—this is the most difficult part yet. This is the difference between the saints as Saints Padre Pio and Don Bosco over mere mortals. It is pure intercession. So it is that St. John Paul II is buried in St. Peter's Roman Catholic Church.

The Roman Catholic Church is unique. Pagan Rome was not built overnight, so also the Roman Catholic Church took centuries. She is a work of art to be appreciated and admired for her beauty. She is open to all races and nationalities, all social levels, and all ethnic groups. She is the metaphysical, yes, but also the mystical and spiritual. No Christian church is her equal, especially the Protestant churches. Is it any wonder that children find empty churches without artwork and stained glass windows that relate stories so boring, boring, boring? Our churches should be temples of metaphysical beautiful works of humanity, as the metaphysical body/flesh of humanity is also a temple of beauty. Our churches should stand for procreation as humanity is designed for procreation. Notice the connections. Notice also that children like storytelling and that children have a wonderful curiosity of how they came to be, to exist. What are we telling them?

What will we tell our children and grandchildren and great-grandchildren about our environment and how we as adults—parents, grandparents, and great-grandparents—ignored all of the warning signs of hurting our environment due to our carbon dioxins and footprint? Maybe we are not so worried because we think that we as scientists have fixed it all. Maybe we think we will self-destruct anyway. What faith, hope, and trust are we instilling in children? In whom?

Our eyelids are the veils that we are able to close and through which we can look at the sun and still be protected. We still see the blood within our eyelids in doing so, but how long before our eyelids cannot protect us due to the destruction of the ozone layer? We seem to move so slowly at preventative measures, the same as we do with our own health and care of body/flesh. We wait and wait until the damage is done. We tend to do the same with our souls. The mysteries of the soul are revealed to the faithful but very seldom to the faithless, to the poor but very seldom to the rich, the innocent but very seldom to the guilty, to the simple-minded but very seldom to the complex-minded, to those without doubt in the Word but very seldom to those that doubt any word. An atheist will question the Word, truth, light, love, and soul, and so why have faith? A Christian will answer for #10, dummy. An atheist will not understand this.

Notice that as we have separated ourselves from our church and her words, so also we have separated our body/flesh from our soul. In doing so, we have separated our hearts from love and minds from spiritual knowledge. How could we possibly understand the alpha and omega when we do not understand our own connection, body/flesh to soul? Our moral imprint is not encrypted for those who want to read it. The only password is faith. Even Christ was given a moral imprint, and we are, indeed, in His image. Father into Son, into Holy Spirit, into humanity.

From my hometown of Bagnoli Irpino up on top of Lake Laceno to the very top of the mountain summit, on a clear day you can see the Sea of Salerno. But it is hard to see the seafloor, which is two to three miles in depth. This is often the case with humanity, which can see the body/flesh but has a hard time seeing into the soul and into the tabernacle of their soul's heart. If we were to extract the DNA from the saints, would this help us? Could it help us? When there is no faith, what could possibly help us? Only the Holy Spirit knows. Learn to listen.

What will we do when our brain grows old and is not able to respond to our mind? Our soul will become tormented for having wasted time and opportunities. It will blame itself. This, my friends, is hopelessness, depending on others for help. But what, who will liberate us? This is a stage of tragedies. This is worse than those who wanted Napoleon Bonaparte to liberate them from the aristocracy of Europe. Everyone was so disappointed when his army raped, plundered, murdered, and destroyed their livelihood. Beethoven even wanted to dedicate a piece to him but changed his mind. Napoleon turned out to be another tyrant, a self-proclaimed emperor.

Was he a man-made god? His defeat and time to meditate on his 3Cs on the island of Elbe was justification. Had he taken as a role model George Washington, he may have turned out to be one of the greatest generals in human history. Note how all this changed after his imperialistic ambitions. His success ceased as he transformed into another mad militaristic failure. Or take Hitler and Mussolini, who promised to liberate the people from past injustices but only fooled the masses with their physiologically disturbed, dark souls. Human tragedies go back to past centuries—for example, Herod whose soul was lost to darkness and whose body/flesh was eaten up by worms. How could entire nations be fooled?

Humanity, although the most magnificent creatures on the face of the earth, could be the most imperfectly stupid, much more so than other life forms. The only perfect part is the spark within our soul's tabernacle. Our body/flesh is definitely imperfect. Our soul starts out perfect but in time loses light's sense of perfection with few, very few, exceptions, hence the need to go backward to our childhood. The climb through love and charity helps get us there to #9.9 in light. With the disconnect from our spark, it is not possible. Humanity tries to figure different formulations and pathways, but they are only man-made, fabricated mental nonsense. We become those fools following false leaders as those mentioned above.

We even have messengers come back from their third journeys to warn us to have faith and stay the course of climbing, but we do not listen. We have become deaf. Our Blessed Virgin Maria has, through her apparitions, warned humanity how many times of the dangers of war and how to prevent them.

Notice that our Blessed Virgin Maria's paintings and sculptures have her with her feet over a serpent/Satan as well as the moon. This represents her power over evils as well as how she reflects grace onto others, similar to the metaphysical moon. A coincidence? Think again. The artists knew what they were doing. Our Blessed Virgin Maria does not generate light/grace but receives an abundance to give out. Hence, we pray for a sharing of her grace. It is not about the metaphysical locations or paintings or sculptures but her soul and spirit. This is what makes her a wonderful motherly guide.

No one can force our free will. It could well be that we simply do not understand our own free will. What is a free will? Our free will is that part of our soul's mind that makes choices, which gives us the consequences and conditions of our choices. Also, our free will is only free in light, not darkness. It is like trying to make conscious choices for directions in pitch darkness of night without the moon, stars, or a compass. It does not work.

The biggest problem that I see in humanity today in America, Italia, and most so-called Christian countries is that we are taking our freedoms for granted. We easily forget those who suffered persecutions, inequalities, injustices, injuries, and spilled blood for the freedoms that we have. This, my friends, occurs first within our soul's mind and free will. There is no doubt about this. When this occurs, we do not feel the need to be grateful. In fact, we become apathetic. We say, "Whom should we thank and why?" The highest form of art is art that praises the Light of the Holy Spirit; the highest level humanity could ever reach works the same way.

Notice how some of us feel no remorse after being found guilty of murder. Why? For us, the doors to that spark within our tabernacle are almost locked. Our soul's light is near zero, so we think nothing of another person's spark or light. This works the same in all crimes against humanity, be it abortion, slavery, child labor, forced prostitution, etc. This is how evil works, without remorse, and evil likes company. At times, evil will work through false kindness to entrap innocent victims and at times, through comedians making fun of everything. I have witnessed so much. From the summit, all becomes visible—for example, pimps that entice young girls with kindnesses for the purpose of making them become dependent. In time, they force them to sell themselves, their bodies for money, and take the highest percentage. Organized criminals work in similar fashion, just more direct, as if it is an honor to be a part of a certain family that commits crimes against humanity and cities and states. These people are most definitely tracking near zero. They pride themselves in the jobs that they do in their 3Cs. I found it surprising that here in Italy that captured mafia, Camorra, etc. criminals were, until recently, not stripped of all their assets within their entire clan.

The reason that people are involved in most criminal activities is for the M&M (money and material) things. They obviously don't mind spending time in prison as long as their assets are in the hands of family members. Think of the effects that freezing all assets would have on them and their families. Not only that, where is the compensation for the victims? For example, how were the slain officers' wives with children compensated for protecting Falcone years ago? When the laws work in favor of the criminals, it is time to change the laws, and perhaps even the people that make them, if necessary. The same holds true for corporate crimes, political crimes, etc. Hit their pocketbook, bank accounts, and bottom line we get positive results. Remember that our 3Cs need to be put into action to correct all forms of criminal offenses. Those stand-ins occupying this or that in America have accomplished what? They remind me of a different version of Woodstock more than anything else.

Yes, there will be good days as well as bad days in fighting against the evils of darkness, but this is how we learn defensive tactics. In faith, we grow in strength and unity. This replaces apathy and ignorance. Think of no one caring about our oceans and how criminals try to dump everything imaginable into them such as chemical toxins, garbage, etc. How long before all life forms in our oceans would die? How long could humanity survive with dead oceans? We did not create the oceans, and neither can we replace them if they were to die.

It is a tough second journey for most of us—for some, extremely tough. As mentioned, we are never alone unless we choose to be alone. A percentage of us are good, kindhearted, and caring people that will help each other in need. But the daily battles require much more than this. Enter prayer for our next chapter.

# CHAPTER *Seven*

Prayer—Desires—Wants—Needs—The Lord's
Prayer Updated—Ave Maria—Apostles' Creed

Where should I begin with the subject of prayer? Again, in modern-day pop culture, prayer has become an almost obsolete word. Prayer? Who prays anymore? For what? To whom? So let us find another word for prayer, say, dialogue. What is the meaning of prayer/dialogue anyway? Prayer/dialogue is communication. Yes, but with what visible person, object, or entity? Prayer/ dialogue with the spiritual. What spiritual? This is modern-day humanity. We do not believe that which is not visible to the naked eye. As mentioned, we cannot see wind, sound, or our soul with our naked eye, yet we know by now that they exist. So as the saying goes, when all else fails, pray or engage in dialogue. Think about this, in an emergency, say, a car has dropped onto a mechanic. He is trapped and being crushed to death. A fellow mechanic lifts the car up to help save the person's life. In normal circumstances, this is not possible. Yet where does the strength, energy come from to save a human life? There is no time for prayer, but there is a belief in the power of prayer in faith and free will.

Silence is practiced in monasteries for a good reason. How can anyone pray with noise pollution? At the same time, prayer without a degree of faith is almost worthless. It is like having hopes or dreams that we do not believe will ever happen. This type of prayer is just about wasted. Yet with the right selfless intentions, grace could also be unlimited from prayer. The Holy Spirit does delegate at times, through others, graces to those who have earned it. For example, our Blessed Virgin Maria who is the recipient of great amounts of grace is able to distribute graces. Notice that even Christ turned to prayer in communication with His Father before becoming a part of the Holy Trinity. He, of course, was given in prayer, through faith, unlimited grace.

There is a saying that says, "When you have your body/flesh health, you have everything." So why is it that we people that do don't feel it? It is because our soul is telling us otherwise. Perhaps we are not developing as we should. Perhaps we want to be much more than what we merit. There are different reasons; we may have taken the wrong path. We may be in need of a life change. Testing is being done now to study the effects of ten to thirty minutes of prayer on the body/flesh. The findings are encouraging as far as the changes that take place in our physical bodies and reduction in stress levels. Prayer to the Holy Spirit is the highest level of meditation when done in silence and sincerity. It also opens the door to reflection and con-templation. But notice how prayer usually becomes our last option. Who turns to prayer as a first option? We seem to turn to prayer when desperate with no option left or forget it because we never did. Yet prayer affects not only our soul's heart and mind but our entire being since the two are one.

Prayer also is a process of will, in which answers to our prayers involve a process that takes time to unfold, so we should not feel inadequate or unworthy when we get no immediate response. For example, is our prayer/will for our sake or the sake of others? As discussed, there is more than our own free will at work at all times. There are prayers and the free will of others. Most importantly, there is the will of the Holy Spirit that sees all, past and present. That which is pleasing in the eyes of the Holy Spirit is what is most important. This is for the good of all concerned, not just ourselves. Only from the summit is this understood. Another example is, as men, our virility. Yes, much of this has to do with the genetics of our body/flesh, but without prayer, how are we to know if our virility is our potential best?

This brings me to the 3Ls—light, love, and life. The three are one, but notice that without the first, light, love, true love do not occur. Neither does true life. How do we acquire light? Review the past chapters and meditate on this.

At the summit, for myself, I like one-on-one prayer. For me, it is more personal and, with humility, a constant confession. The first one, The Lord's Prayer/Padre Nostro is the most important. I have learned from the summit that this prayer that was given to humanity two thousand years ago needed to be updated in order to give credit to Christ. Let me explain by breaking down The Lord's Prayer as we have known it since childhood. I updated it for myself this way. It was "Our Father/Padre Nostro, who art in heaven, hallowed be thy name." I update this part to include, through Christ and the Holy Spirit, confirmation of belief in the Holy Trinity: "Thy kingdom come, Thy will be done on earth as it is in heaven." Update: "Thank you for your kingdom come since Christ and His kingdom did come to be amongst humanity." Update: "Thank you for Thy will since this was done in and through Christ." For myself, "Thy will be done" becomes "in me, for me, and through me for the sake of others." "Give us this day our daily bread." Update: "Thank you for yourself in your Holy Eucharist every day, our daily bread, and forgive us our trespasses/debts/sins as we forgive those who trespass/debt/sin against us." Update: "Thank you for the reminder that our sins are forgiven us as we forgive the sins of others against us, and lead us not into temptations/tests, but deliver us from evils/the evil one." The word *but* is the key word here. For myself, this *but* means "although I do not like or want to be tempted/tested, it will all to be done to me that I may climb to the summit platform of 9.9. Here, I have no regrets on what was needed of me—to reach the platform and be "delivered from evil." I learn in the process to finally call out, tiramisu (pull me up) to #10.

Notice also how we in the world use Arabic numbers one through nine. This should remind us that the classic Greek/Roman culture did not enter into the Dark Ages in the Eastern Roman Catholic Empire region as in the West. Their prosperity continued for another five hundred-plus years until the Crusaders ruined it in the Holy Land. Still, it would continue up till the fifteenth century in Constantinople. The countries changed politically and from the rule of Constantinople but continued to prosper. The first Renaissance/rebirth started in Spain, Europe with the Muslim entering the region. Rebirth, renew, and relive in prayer. Spain was the first Northern European country to make an early exit out of the darkness. The seven virtues—prudence, justice, temperance, faith, courage, charity, and hope—of Islam, knowingly or unknowingly, ushered in prosperity.

I know that many of you readers are wondering who I am to update The Lord's Prayer/*Padre Nostro* and rightly so. Yet consider that The Lord's Prayer/*Padre Nostro* was given to humanity before the crucifixion, death, resurrection, and ascension of Christ—in better words, before Christ became a part of the Holy Trinity for humanity. Notice also that the link between the Father, the Holy Spirit, and humanity is Christ. The Holy Spirit continuously is the oxygen for humanity that shapes and forms us into herself. It makes sense to give Christ credit, recognition, and gratitude for what He gave of Himself to humanity. "*Io sono la via, la verita, e la vita, nessuno viene al Padre se non per mezzo di me*" ("I am the way, the truth and the life/light, no one comes to the Father if not through me"). Notice the 3Ls—light, love, and life as the fulfillment for humanity. Our Holy See and the Vatican College of Cardinals should take updating The Lord's Prayer/*Padre Nostro* into consideration.

Notice how the updated Lord's Prayer sums up our entire second journey with our conscious positive or negative 3Cs—choices, consequences, and conditions. It also sums up the 3Gs—grace, gratitude, and graciousness. Furthermore, it sums up the 3Ls—light, love, and life. This gets rid of the 3Fs—foolishness, fault, and failure—

that could result in the 3Ds—disgrace, despair, and death. Examples are the negative 3Cs, suicides, or doctors giving assistance in suicide. Other examples are our negative 3Cs with mortal addictions as a heroin overdose. This is the collapse of prayer. We simply do not stop to think that it is okay to pray for death when in unbearable pain and suffering. There is nothing, *niente, nada*—the 3Ns—wrong with this. With the 3Rs—repentance, reconciliation, and redemption—we give the responsibility to our higher source.

This brings to mind people whom I witnessed to in prayer in Shanghai in a nearby park. I would go to this park for a little quiet time to get away from the air and noise pollution. In this park was the largest Italian maple tree that I have ever seen. It was a gift from Italy to the Chinese people. Anyway, I noticed a few of the older people touching, even hugging the tree and seemingly praying at the same time. Again, this is in a supposedly atheist country, and yet people still prayed to the Spirit within the tree. This had nothing to do with Christianity, other religions, race, nationality, etc. It had nothing to do with good karma or bad karma but faith in prayer. In a way, reverence in creation, even in a tree, is reverence to Dio as all true nature lovers will attest to. We all have a moral imprint, moral inner voice, and tabernacle. We should never let anyone or anything deter us from prayer. If with our eyelids closed we look up into the sun in prayer, we see the red lifeblood within us. If we look down without prayer, we only see gray.

Tears should be in gratitude, not despair. For example, when our free will is given up to good parents or family, we are blessed. Now multiply the 3Gs—grace, gratitude, and graciousness—two, three, four, five, six, seven, eight-plus times and see the consequences and conditions that are the result. We knew this at one time in America/Europe, but we are losing it. In fact, we seldom eat, have activities, talk, or pray together after distancing ourselves from Church/Holy Spirit. In Italia, it is not as bad, but we have gotten lazy. For example, we do not accept the thousands of jobs that are available throughout Italia, letting illegal immigrants supply the demand. A lazy soul cannot be creative without grace from prayer. Is it any wonder that we, even as a family, do not get what we pray for but rather what we deserve? We are in need of relearning the meaning of sacrifices, work, and humility in prayer. We should count our blessings that are modified to our needs. We need to start our climb up to the summit, or we may never understand. We Roman Catholics have Ash Wednesday for a good reason. It reminds us of what we need to pray for in our souls before the needs of our body/flesh that will die and become ashes.

Prayer doesn't go unanswered when for good intentions that benefit more than ourselves. If we sincerely, in an altruistic manner and in charity, are determined by a strong will, miracles can and do happen. Our vocation is an excellent example of this. When we are uncomfortable with uncertainty in our calling, prayer is the solution. We all need direction and guidance when having doubts. At the same time, we must make time for listening and see the signs. We are each a part of the master plan of ISD (intellectual spiritual design) in our second journey.

Prayer could also help us with understanding our hardships, burdens, sacrifices, trials, and errors. In better words, pray for the 3Ls—light, love, and life—for enlightenment and understanding.

My second most important prayer is the Hail Mary. I say this without reservation. Notice that I have dedicated this book to our Blessed Virgin Maria. She is responsible for helping my entire family throughout our second journeys. I have mentioned that she was and continues to be full of grace that she distributes to those who merit it. I have not yet mentioned that she is also associated with surging natural water where she appears or is prayed to. This, like natural water, tells us that graces pour out of her. An example is Istanbul (Constantinople), where some historical evidence tells us that she resided for a part of her second journey. There is a location of surging water related to her. The Turks know of the location and also venerate her there. The Hail Mary prayer needs no introduction. We Roman Catholics know it by heart. For others, look it up. For me, the most important part is the ending "now and at the hour of our death. Her protection is unequivocally necessary against the evils of darkness in our 2second journey. Recall the final repetitive words of Saint Padre Pio on his deathbed as he was calling on our Blessed Virgin Maria until he passed into his third journey. From 9.99 on our chart, the platform to #10, we only have one ending prayer, *tiramisu* (pull me up). In fasting and prayer, this is possible.

Next in importance are the prayers to the angels and saints, especially those martyred for their faith. Think that this is ridiculous? Think again. Here in Italia, we have many, many saints. I think that every provincial territory has at least one saint, if not more. These saints have been responsible for miracles for those who turn to them in prayer and a degree of faith in Christ. Think about this for a moment. What is a saint to do in their third journey? They do not sit on their laurels and twiddle their thumbs. Remember that the Holy Spirit enjoys delegating responsibilities of governing the cosmos for the Souls of humanity and the metaphysical. The Angels and Saints have their work cut out for humanity still on earth. We should be keeping them busy in our prayers to them. Our inner voice from the tabernacle of our soul's heart reminds us of the need to pray to our Blessed Virgin Maria, the angels and saints for their assistance. Notice that the opposite occurs within our soul's conscious mind in the voices of evil trying to persuade us to not pray at all or to pray to evils such as witchcraft or satanic cults. For example, a serial killer only listens to the evil voices of evil angels, whereas we could instead turn to Archangel Michael against evil spirits.

Grace cannot be bought, although it can be with prayer traded in acts of charity. I mean when we give to charity our M&M (money and material things), we help open the doors to our tabernacle. This in itself lets out the light of grace into our soul. Hence, in our second journey, we may need to give up or lose everything (M&M) in order to gain everything (graces). This is a reasonable trade-up for us. Prayer helps us with the options.

Notice these phrases, "Be true to yourself," "Keep your promise," "Have self-esteem," "Have self-respect," "Be self-sufficient," "Trust your instincts," etc. These phrases all have to do with prayer in oneself. This is a joke. We cannot pray to ourselves for grace that we can't produce. All prayer needs to be directed to those who have earned grace. Our five natural senses need to be elevated into our soul's senses so that our prayers could be soul to soul or soul to spiritual in the Blesses Virgin Maria, the saints and angels.

A few of us pray for a fortune. There is nothing, *niente, nada*—the 3Ns—wrong with this as long as it is earned. Regardless of certain ideologies, monies invested in uncorrupted entities are healthy when worked for and earned. What we do with it afterward is another story. Charity definitely needs consideration. For example, I could probably make a fortune right now investing in foreign currencies. How? Putting economic models aside, I would simply study the level of corruption/evil for a currency in the injustices and inequalities of its federal government, judicial system, and law enforcement. Why? The value of a currency, including the American dollar, is based on the faith and trust that citizens or foreigners place in the institutions. As the corruption/evil increases, the value of the currency drops regardless of the interventions. The greater the corrections to change and end the corruption/evil, the more the currency value rises. Want proof of this? Study the Mexican peso. Study the level of corruption/evil in their government, judicial system, and law enforcement. Study their losing war against the drug cartels for the past fifty years. The consequences and conditions? A peso is currently sixteen to one against the US dollar. I recall it being eight to one years ago. Study the ruble of the Soviet Union and Russia. A coincidence? Think again. The American US bonds, AAA rated as far back as I could remember, were downgraded a few years ago. Why?

Study the corruption/evil that took place in Washington, D.C., Wall Street, and financial institutions, mainly investment brokerage companies and banks. A coincidence? Think again. There was a correction, but was it enough? Time will tell. I did not see many people go to prison. I did not see heavy, heavy fines against companies that perpetrated the criminal activities. Take the current BRICS (Brazil, Russia, India, China, South Africa) countries—note the massive corruption/evils at all levels. Put your Ph.D. in Economics aside, you are on average only right 50 percent of the time. I could toss a coin and get the same results. Study their collective summation of light chart? What works in our souls chart, my friends, works in other aspects of humanity, governments and their ideologies.

How many angels and saints do we really need? How many Christs do we need? How many Holy Spirits do we need? How many Blessed Virgin Marias do we need? How many confessions do we need? Now think, how many tests do we have? How many climbs are there? How many deaths do we have? How many prayers and to whom? Notice that faith in prayer deals with all of our needs. When we venerate our Blessed Virgin Maria, the angels, and saints, we give thanks to the Holy Trinity that is their source. After all, how many of us are worthy and in a position to approach the Holy Spirit one on one? Although when the Holy Spirit initiates the conversation, it may well be one on one as was the case with Abraham and Moses in the Old Testament. Notice how Christ took over the responsibility in the New Testament as with Saint Paul and continues to work with others to this day as well.

Notice also how our Blessed Virgin Maria took over the responsibilities of those in purgatory. As mentioned earlier, in purgatory, we lose the communication of prayer and need the prayers of others to help us. Our Blessed Virgin Maria is that channel for loved ones that may be in purgatory. Only from the summit is this realized. It has taken me a lifetime to see this. It is the thoughts of loved ones that could be there that lead me to pray for them. Those of us thinking that everyone goes to #10, merited or not, are being deceived. Remember the 3Ss, 3Fs, and 3Ds? Go back a little and review them.

In my three years of being an altar boy, I had three *nonnas* or grandmothers. They were at every daily morning mass. One was Angelical with a charitable heart and a large family that loved her immensely. Another was saint-like, whose life was much harder in the sacrifices she had to endure. Her husband had passed away, leaving her with one unmarried daughter. The third, although attending mass daily, was wealthy in real life but not charitable, lonely, without husband or children, and very money-conscious all of the time, even in old age. At the time, I did not see the difference between each one. From the summit, they become very clear. I wonder who will pray for the one that most likely is in purgatory.

An essential part of prayer is listening to the Gospels in order to know what to pray for. Notice that we Roman Catholics make a small sign of the cross on three locations when listening to the readings of the Gospels by a priest. One is on our forehead because our mind functions in our brain. I think of this as a blessing to consider what to think, guided by the Holy Spirit. The second small sign of the cross is made on our lips. I think of this as a guidance in knowing what to say before speaking, as in speaking goodness and not evil. The Chinese have a saying for this, "A sweet mouth." The third small sign of the cross is on our body/flesh heart. This is by far the most important one because, although it is our physical body heart, our soul's heart functions within this chamber. This is important in that, recall throughout this book, our soul's heart contains the spark within our tabernacle. Think of all this as silly symbolic gestures? Think again. Some of the saints' physical hearts had actual various imprints on them that were discovered after their souls left behind their bodies/flesh.

Now observe all of the curse words that come out of our mouths. It all starts within our ignoramus minds. Also, observe the lack of caring on our part regarding even the minor things in our everyday lives such as being polite and kind. Does the above paragraph make sense? Now observe how some of the 3Fs and 3Ds have occurred in teenagers who are joining the terrorist groups in the Middle East. Again, go back a little for review. Some of us are being brainwashed with propaganda from evil into throwing away our lives for an evil cause. Is prayer too little too late? It may well be. What have we been doing all of this time? When people choose evil, evil will consume them, and they will go to their choice destination. Never forget about the 3Cs in life.

Now study how certain movie directors take a script and put it into their own philosophy, ideology, of how they interpret the world and humanity. For the young minds, this is powerful information through our natural senses. Often, it has a great number of subliminal messages that our mind does pick up on, even if we are not conscious of it. Evils are always wanting ignorant minds to play with, especially minds that never pray or have broken off communication with the Holy Spirit.

Pray for what ails our body/flesh? Hmm, let me see, what ails the soul ails the body/flesh since the two are one. This makes sense, but how are we to help our ignorance? Pray for enlightenment? Can we do that? So let us recall the past chapters. An ignorant Mind lacks Spiritual Light when that Light is lost to the acceptance of darkness and vice versa. But notice that we could have a healthy Soul even if we have a handicapped body / flesh. But now consider a sick Soul within a sick body / flesh. This is the worst since this is a living hell. Only a degree of faith in prayer could cure us of this. Yes, prayer is essential from us and for us by others. Again, study the lives of the saints. They were in prayer throughout the day every day. Their prayers continue to help humanity in everyday life. They are aware of the obstacles, pitfalls, temptations, and weaknesses of humanity. They were and are here among us as their souls endure the third journey.

The education of our souls is a long, slow process. It's like learning mathematical formulations one at a time from basic arithmetic to calculus. Prayer has others help us to let others assist us as in a mathematician—daily, weekly, and monthly. It requires patience, and so do the answers to our prayers. It is like attempting to understand our first journey when our mind cannot handle it at as a child. Prayer keeps our doors open, though, so that when we are ready, we may receive the knowledge. The answers to our prayers are individually suited to our needs with consideration to those around us.

Thoughtful consideration has been the case with humanity since the beginning of time. Not much has changed through the thousands of years. Ever since Dio began to communicate with humanity, we were recipients of His words. In mental prayer, our thoughts were sent back. Christ demonstrated how we are able to communicate with the Holy Spirit. No, high tech will not help us with prayer. The Holy Trinity does not use a smart phone or laptop. Notice how flowers begin to wilt as soon as they are cut from their nutritional source. So it is with us when we forget about prayer in communication with the Holy Spirit. We begin to lose our fragrance, our color, and slowly die. No one cuts us off; we cut ourselves off.

Some of us will ask, where are the prophets, the apostles, the angels, the Blessed Virgin Maria? We get frustrated, confused, discouraged, and disheartened so quickly and easily stop prayer. We are used to getting our way quickly today, no later than tomorrow. But this is not how the Holy Spirit works (or I should say very seldom works) unless it is an emergency. What is our emergency? Also, the Holy Spirit does, indeed, delegate to all of the above that we question. At times, it is in dreams, at times in visions, at times through total strangers, a child, an animal. The ways of the Holy Spirit are like the stars in the universe—too many to list or count. Most often the answers are in the testing that we are given.

Many of the answers to our prayers are within the Holy Eucharist for our soul. Yes, we can pray from anywhere, even from the moon, but the Holy Eucharist of Christ is only in one place—the tabernacle of the Roman Catholic, Greek and Russian Orthodox churches. We need to go there unless we are incapacitated or dying. Are we? This is usually reserved for the last rites in our second journey.

Ah, we are youth, we only know love. That will suffice. Notice in music lyrics how so many artists write about love but very seldom sing about how to bring forth love through prayer? This is like expecting love without faith in the light of love. No belief in prayer, no light, no love. Why are we dissatisfied and disappointed? In 100 percent faith and in prayer, the full force of light in love would kill us. Consider the full force of the sun. Now multiply that times ten. Blinded and consumed yet?

What humanity, we so-called Christians, tend to forget is that we are all debtors for what we are already blessed with, especially in America and Europe. We pray for this or that as if we are owed what we want. We just do not stop to pray in gratitude for what we have been given and yet keep asking for more. Then we wonder why we do not receive the answers to what we think we have a right to. During the mass, together we pray for our intentions but notice that in the end of the mass, the priest will say, "Peace be with you," which is not what you may want in your prayers. This is as if to say peace is of the utmost importance to your soul, not necessarily what you pray for. In peace and love, what else do we need? Peace and love on earth encompasses all that is good for those of good will, "*Pace in terra agli uomini di buona volonta*." Also, for those that are grateful in prayer, "*Ti rendiamo grazia*," much more is given to the good-hearted. When this is the case, most often we have no need to ask for anything else. Our needs are already known. Notice that the graces are gifts, blessings to the soul, and not necessarily for the body/flesh or of the metaphysical world. We need to get our prayers in order.

Take as an example a happy family. When there is prayer as in "pray together, stay together," and there is peace and love within the family, what more could we possibly ask for? In this, there is strengthening grace to overcome all hardships as a unit. Each member of the family knows the weaknesses of the other, and each helps the other. Now take a look around into families that do not pray at all and are not grateful for anything. Notice the difference in all aspects of the family. Yes, my friends, prayer does, indeed, make a huge difference. We see families break apart for trivial reasons. Shattered and scattered, sounds familiar? This is the reason that evil uses sexuality to tempt humanity. In helping to destroy moral sex between a man and a woman, it destroys marriage and positive procreation. After this, what is left? The 3Ns—nothing, *niente*, nada!

We got to the twenty-first century with the prayers of the apostles, saints, and the faithful. Without this, where would we be? Better yet, where are we individually, as a family, as a community, and as a country? Take a hard good look around you, who prays anymore? Where is the Church without prayer? We cannot claim ignorance anymore. So many of our failures are present due to a lack of belief in prayer.

Some of us do not pray, but in living our faith, we inspire others to prayer. People like George Washington, Jefferson, Roosevelt in America, Garibaldi, Moro, Pertini in Italy, perhaps they did not pray, but they inspired the young to have faith, hope, and trust in the good within humanity.

Today, political figures have figured out that we ourselves do not know our real needs. They promise us what we tell them we need, even if they know that the needs are not practical or deliverable needs. Assassinated by evil in humanity, President J. F. Kennedy said,

"Ask not what your country could do for you, but what you can do for your country." In better words, we Americans have already been blessed with enormous graces. What are we giving back to nature, our rivers, and our lands? What are we doing to end discrimination, racism, and inequalities? It always starts within ourselves. We, in essence, turn politicians into liars in order to get our votes. Pertini, former president of Italy, said that a political figure needs to have two qualities, "honesty and courage," with clean hands to do what is right for the people and the country. Do we, in fact, corrupt these figures with unreasonable demands and false expectations? Or is it that we have all become corrupted in civil rights and economic issues? For example, Northern Italians complain of the Southern Italians bringing corruption/evil into the North, but who forces official leaders in the North to accept bribery, dirty money, etc.? Let me see, what were the words, "When moral Law and order break down, civil law and order follow." It doesn't matter whether it's north or south, east or west. Yes, so often we elect political figures who mirror ourselves. We need to pray for ourselves before we can pray for anyone else.

How we perceive certain events should be a sign of who we have become. For example, honest people being killed for their honesty. Good examples of this are those who are not afraid to speak out for the injured who suffer inequalities and injustices in the world. How do we react? What goes through our minds? Do we pray for an end to these events? Do we close our eyes? Do we do nothing? Notice that this also positions us on our chart of our soul's light. It doesn't take much to offer up a quick prayer for those in need. Listen to Pope Francisco; he knows the power of prayer as did all of the saints.

Prayer is becoming a rare commodity, somewhat like rare earth minerals. Yet like reaching rare earth minerals, prayer brings up from our conscience what we need to know in order to make the toughest choices. At times, with certain events, M&M, machinery, technology, and science are not the solution to the needy. At times, it is love and compassion, which are becoming even rarer than rare earth minerals.

Notice that the mind at various levels could function without the brain, but the brain is useless without the soul's mind. Again, recall a comatose victim. Is this what we need, an out-of-body experience? Or will we let prayer help awaken our inner voice? Try to recall and reclaim childhood when life was so much easier. We perhaps did not pray then, but we did not have to deal with the evils that we have as teenagers and adults. Some of us are, indeed, on life support not for the body/flesh but for our soul. If we are tracking low on our chart, if we are just getting by, prayer could change our condition. How long could we endure until the plugs are pulled?

We with our free will can pray for the intercession of others. In this, we help ourselves with our insecurities, anxieties, depression, and grinding of our teeth. We need a good night's sleep, a healthy body/flesh. Prayer is an expression of hope, even with the slightest amount of faith. What we also need is a tiny bit of trust in the Holy Spirit. Those of us that have been through it all in hell, in the desert, and in our climb remember what it took. Hence, we have empathy for those who are stuck anywhere between .1 and 8.9 on their chart. It is always up to the 3Cs, my friends.

Some of us are like dark closets/corpses without light. We bring food, drinks, vitamins, etc. into our dark closets, but it does not change anything. We are still dark closets/corpses. We are void of light. It is up to us how long we want to remain this way. Prayer could begin the process of bringing light in. The sources of light we have discussed. You should know whom to pray to. This is not 72 AC ultra-decadent Pompeii or Herculaneum when people perhaps did or did not know how or whom to pray to. No, this is the twenty-first century, and we are not excusable any longer. Volcanoes usually give warnings, and so also we get warnings. By estimates, the eruption of Mt. Vesuvius was comparable to fifty atomic bombs being detonated. Must it come to that, a third world war? When will we learn individually, consciously, to put an end to the war within ourselves with prayer? Collectively, consciously, prayer would make this world a better place for all of us.

Could prayer work in the Middle East, in Israel, Jerusalem, Palestine? It would depend on what is being prayed for! For example, we Hebrew, Jewish people prayed to return to Israel as our state and Jerusalem as the timeless city; our prayers were answered. Now we

Palestinians want a State of Palestine, but we Hebrew, Jewish people say, "No way." Even though statehood is already recognized by the United Nations and the Vatican, I am still trying to figure out why our American government is holding out. Where is our Pax Americana? Manipulation in congress? Next, we Hebrews/Jewish people pray for peace, but true peace eludes us. For better words, our prayers seemingly go unheard. Need we ask ourselves why? We need to study our own history. When we rejected the messiah of peace, we suffered the consequences and conditions. When we accepted a false messiah, the consequences and conditions were devastating. The irony is that the Gentiles' acceptance of Christ in prayer helped us. So what is it that we pray for again? When government/state, judicial/law, science/education, religion/religious are not working in Union with the Holy Spirit, expect what you do not pray for.

CHAPTER *Eight*

Realization—Repentance—Reconciliation
and Redemption—Forgiveness—Detox—
Atonement—Penance—Tests—Sufferings—
Climbing—Learning—Growing in Light

Next, we will explain the forgiveness, penance, and atonement for our souls. We are forgiven for our aggressions, criminal activities, harmful acts, damaging events against humanity and ourselves. Yet all of our actions are accountable, good or evil. The good needs no brainstorming, as in these deeds we are given additional light, which is grace. The bad, evil deeds, which by now we should be aware of, are the ones that most of us are confused about. I am not sure where some of us have gotten the notion that once forgiven, there is no need for accountability. Let me be very blunt—all are held accountable. For example, a child that does something wrong gets caught, confesses, says, "I'm sorry," and shows remorse is usually forgiven by the majority of parents. Soon after, without some form of punishment, that same child is going to repeat the same wrong over and over again. It's one of our weaknesses. What child these days can resist the games offered by high tech? A child could and does become addicted without strong measures to stop the process. Once they figure out that they will be forgiven without punishment, they are not able to stop themselves. We covered some of the same issues in earlier chapters in regards to discipline, self-discipline. As adults, we are no different. In fact, being undisciplined as a child leads us to a lack of self-discipline as an adult. Take for example a husband at work having adulterous affairs after work. Even should the same adult go to confession on Saturday, be forgiven, receive communion on Sunday, he could be back into adulterous affairs on Monday. So what is the purpose? That same man having to pay a heavy price for adultery may change. What would be a heavy price? I think that most women know by now. The same holds true for women who these days are just as guilty.

Notice that a priest will say after confession, "Now say your act of contrition." An act of contrition is admitting fault for your wrongdoing and involves a promise not to repeat the same sin. Also, after that, the priest will say, "For your penance, say so many Hail Marys." This is to say, "I know your weaknesses. Do penance and learn about your weaknesses." Also, ask for intercession to help you. So what do we have here, admission of guilt from sin, remorse in heart and mind, a promise not to repeat, penance or accountability, intercession, as in our Blessed Virgin Maria, for assistance. A priest does not say, "Try to not be adulterous." He does not say, "Same time next Saturday." Now read where Christ said the same, "You are forgiven of your sins," and bluntly he added, "Sin no more." At the same time, everyone went through a period of penance and atonement for their sins. A good example of this is Mary Magdalena, who endured her own penance and atonement and sinned no more.

I know that these days, pop culture does not regard anything as sinful, and hence the ignorance of not knowing why their loss of soul's light. Notice that one of the quiz questions has to do with saying sorry when at fault. This is also another issue in Christian Protestant churches. When there is no confession, there is no remorse, no accountability, no penance, and no atonement. There is no need to get into the other religions; they are even worse.

When we are bitten by a poisonous snake, we need to get the poison out of our body/flesh as soon as possible or risk the consequences. The longer we wait, the worse our condition could become to a point of dying. There is a process of getting the poison out of the body/flesh, and it is not a pleasant one. There are also the aftereffects to our body/flesh to remind us of the ordeal. The same applies for our soul from evil/sin/darkness. Talk about stress; this is stressful.

We discussed what brings stress into our lives. Firsthand stress within ourselves due to our 3Cs and secondhand stress from the 3Cs of others—for example, our children—if uncorrected, these can bring on madness. So at times, we need to take ourselves out of a certain environment, circumstances, and conditions. We need to just get away from certain people that are wrecking our lives. At times, nature, the desert, a mountain, the beach could be very helpful as a place for penance and atonement. Notice that at times, for a criminal, prison could be that place. For a child, their room without any toys could be the place. The place is not as important as the overall results. Take for example the concentration camps of Germany for the Jewish people. It is difficult to write about this, but were these events for penance and atonement? Only we Jews know for sure. As I have mentioned, the Holy Spirit works in mysterious ways as far as allowing or disallowing certain events to take place. Manifestation into transformation is, indeed, a hard road to travel.

The same holds true for natural disasters. We are constantly being reminded that our second journey is limited to a certain period of time. There are 3Ns—nothing, *niente*, nada—that we are able to do about it. They should be reminders of repentance, reconciliation, and redemption to turn in the right direction up to our summit, so a large part of our penance and atonement should start in our second journey. Be grateful; at least, here you have some conscious control of it. Think of what you have to face and deal with it, learn from it. Think of all your past trials and turbulence through which you had to learn and grow.

When we reach the point of almost wishing to go back in time to correct our wrongful ways for ourselves and toward others, we have made progress and are climbing up our summit. Here our conscience is reaching our consciousness. For example, a lover who forces himself on his girlfriend, forcing sexual intercourse, and getting his girlfriend pregnant may wish to go back in time to change the event. Of course, he is not able to go back in time, but at least now he is aware of his 3Cs and able to change his ways. With a sincere, humble change of heart, will he be forgiven? It would depend on what? Remorse, penance, and atonement—we are all sinners, my friends. Believe in the process, it works. Although Christ suffered for our sake, it does not exempt us totally.

It is always the sins of evil/darkness that ruin relationships and marriages. Even when we are forgiven, we do not forget. It is better this way, or how are we to remember not to repeat the same wrongful acts? We have to keep in mind, though, that we are mere mortals. We, those of us sinned against, are only able to take so much. When we reach critical mass, we may forgive but also wish to be apart. Note that the higher the climb to our summit, the greater the amount of tolerance for forgiving others. But we do not forget until #10. This, of course, is not entirely up to us. Our timing will have to do with our mission in life and the conclusion of that mission. At times, we actually feel the evils grabbing our ankles to try to stop our ascension to the top of our summit, especially past 9.0, the platform. Again, I am sorry to say that at times, in order to understand light, we need to experience and understand darkness first and then remorse, penance, and atonement.

For example, a woman who is choosing to be a bitch like a female dog in heat will have the consequences and conditions of her choice. For a dog bitch, it is one thing, but for a human bitch, she loses light with each male suitor. A woman bitch sleeping around with anyone can never experience love since love flows out of light. In fact, she diminishes both light and love in her soul. The darkness of sin affects not only ourselves but also those near us, as in family.

Other examples were the evils that took place with the assassinations of some of our loved public officials such as Falcone and his bodyguards in Italia. There is no escape for the criminals of such evils. Their punishment needs to be prison time, yes, but also stripping them of all of their assets and possessions to compensate the families of the victims. The penance and atonement for their souls, if not starting in their second journey, may see time run out for them, and they will be sent to the destination of their choice, hell. It should be noted that although we criminals are forgiven by those that we offended, if we ourselves do not do the same toward others, we are not fully forgiven. This is something for us to meditate on. It's not a simple process, my fellow criminals, but be grateful for the process itself. At least, it gives us a chance, not that we deserve it. We have until that split second that our time is up. After that, it is a done deal.

Repentance, reconciliation, and redemption for atonement are in themselves a gift. They give us a second chance, even with the worst hideous sins and crimes against humanity. The problem is that we do not see them that way. For example, even Judas that betrayed Christ did not have to make the choice to kill himself. The Apostle Peter also betrayed Christ but with a different choice after doing so. Again, what is important is what we decide to do once we have fallen into the gutter. What the sunlight does to germs in gutters, the Holy Spirit can do to our soul's darkness. This reminds me of how my father each year had to clean out the old house furnace in Youngstown because it had gotten built up with soot. This soot would affect the pilot light and gas flame itself if not cleaned out. The same happens to us, slowly, a little each day, and after many years, we have pounds of soot that need to be removed out of us. If not, it also affects our soul's light. It's no wonder that we become lethargic and cannot think straight; we have poisonous soot running in our veins. Without removing it, it eventually could kill us. When we do, it becomes one of the very few things that we can be proud of in our second journey. It starts with admission, my friends, not denial. Even if we were never true to anyone else, we must be true to ourselves at least one time. It only requires a tiny bit of faith at 3:00 a.m. facing ourselves in the mirror.

Again, Saint Paul did not have to make the choice to accept the process of repentance, reconciliation, and redemption, but in doing so, study what he did with his talent for writing. Read what he went on to accomplish with his credentials and Roman citizenship. The same is true with most of us. We are gifted with so many talents and credentials that often are wasted or not fully utilized toward good deeds. We need to ask ourselves: what became of those precious dreams of our childhood when we wanted to rise above everyone else? What became of wanting to be honorable and respected?

The long climb up to the summit is much harder if we are attempting to climb burdened with guilt and regrets of our past. Remember, unlock and unload from the previous chapters. In doing so, you will feel relieved. In this, we regain the vigor and vitality of our youth. Others may help us, but ultimately it is our climb.

Take note of the self-redemption books in the bookstores. We can do that? Redeem ourselves? Hmm, by whose authority, an atheist? How could we possibly be self-redeeming? Evil does not redeem. It would be as if darkness removes darkness. It doesn't. It only adds to more darkness. It is true that the Holy Spirit helps those who help themselves, but imagining that we are able to replace our darkness within on our own is self-psychological nonsense. Only the light of the Holy Spirit in the spark within our tabernacle and the souls of others can accomplish this. We are being as idiotic as those who practiced self-flagellation on their flesh as if they controlled the redemption process. Or take the example of the bloodlettings in order to rid the body of viruses/sicknesses when in fact this made the flesh weaker. Would this have helped the victims of the Bubonic plague?

Evil tracks us more than the NSA in America. It keeps a copy of our 3Ss—stubbornness, stupidity, and sickness—on our chart. It knows our weaknesses and how to trip us up. A mistake we make is from the misconception that what works for the body/flesh will work for the soul. Take for example the rigorous workout that we put our body/flesh through. This may work for the body/flesh in order to rid us of our excessive fat but does very little to get rid of the darkness in our souls. A physically healthy body/flesh is good for us, yet there are millions of people worldwide physically strong that have darkened souls. This reminds me of the millions of people worldwide that practice yoga every day. Yoga is wonderful and is very helpful in so many areas of our body's health, I agree, but there are yoga instructors who know how to exploit beginning students for their self-interest. The point is, yoga in itself is a tool for meditation, reflection, and contemplation. It is a means to reach light and doesn't contain light in itself.

This is why a good confessor such as Saint Padre Pio is necessary. A good confessor is able to detect our darkness quickly, even when we don't recognize it ourselves. The reasons are that they know how evils penetrate our souls. There are countless ways, as mentioned, but here are a few of the major ones again: 1) pride; 2) ego; 3) sex/lust; 4) gluttony; 5) power; 6) M&M. These are the ones that usually trip us up. These are the major ones that try to separate, break us apart, and cut our lifeline from the covenant of our soul's heart. When this happens, we become the serial killer, the child molester, the executioner, the cult leader that puts cyanide in the drink of followers and every other despicable act. Civil crimes are also spiritual crimes since the body/flesh and soul are one.

My motto and prayer are simple: "Let all be done to me accordingly, through hell, the desert and all penance, just get me to #10." This book in itself has been like a test, a penance, a hardship, a grace/blessing, and a learning experience. It is my hope that it will be the same for a few readers as well.

Remember that purgatory is like a missed connecting flight to our destination, but hell is like the Apollo spacecraft that disintegrated without ever being able to reconnect. Yes, there is sadness in this second journey, but how we handle sadness determines how long its grip lasts. Yes, there are good people as well as bad people in our lives. How else are we to learn? It's by the light of the good and the evils accepted by the bad that we learn how to differentiate between the two. Evil begets evil. Better yet, love begets love.

This brings to mind Luciano Pavarotti, my all-time favorite tenor. I have not read his biography, but I know enough about what he did in his late second journey. A mega-superstar tends to lose their personal privileged privacy quickly. This is the price they pay for being a celebrity. Anyway, I recall an interview done with Pavarotti in which one question stayed in my mind. The question to him was, "Are you grateful to Dio every day?" His answer was no. Notice that this is one of the quiz questions. The answer to this question carries a great deal of weight, much more than the points deductible with a no/false answer. It positions us quickly on our chart. Why? Because as I have stated all along, those who are at the top tier on their chart are grateful every day throughout the day. Contentment is equal to gratitude. For instance, we eat food and drink each day, so we give thanks each time. The weaknesses of any superstar or celebrity is that he/she thinks that they are above it all. They think that they are totally responsible for their success in fortune and fame. This is what trips them up every time. They may be given a chance to redeem themselves, but there is no guarantee. As for Pavarotti, I saw his final days as a chance for the 3Rs—repentance, the process of penance from remorse; reconciliation between himself and the Holy Spirit; and redemption, a process to be redeemed for atonement. Yes, he made amazing charitable contributions, especially for children, but he also did what his parents would be ashamed of had they been alive to witness his late life. Did Pavarotti accept the 3Rs process of repentance, reconciliation, and redemption? Only he and the Holy Spirit know. Again, everyone is held accountable for everything in their second journey. Other celebrities such as Elvis Presley, John Lennon, and countless others fall into the same category.

The 3Rs is not an easy process by any means. It is like a person coming out of a hospital after having caught a life-threatening disease in time and being operated on. The operation may or may not be successful. Even when successful, it is not the end of the threat. There is a long recuperating process in which we are in need of others to help us. We need to heal, to regain our energy and stamina. It is, at times, such a slow process. Where would we be without faithful, trustworthy family members and friends? They are there for us, and we are not deserted. So it is with the Holy Trinity for our soul. You have just been given an example of the body/flesh 3Cs that parallel the soul's 3R process in relationship to light. The two are part of one, body, and soul. Include the third part, our spark, and we are complete in one unified light.

We have so many superstitious fears and worthless data from the time that we enter this world. As stated, we need to have only one healthy fear, that of losing light. In this, in our climb, in our 3Rs of repentance, reconciliation, and redemption, we dump all superstitions. This brings moral law and order into our souls. For example, I have stated in past chapters the harmful ways that attorneys hurt people. Now I realize that this is in civil matters, but recall that civil issues affect moral issues. So when no ethical standards are observed, what happens? The 3Cs impact clients in a civil and moral way. For example, the unfairness in a divorce that doesn't allow the process of reconciliation between a married couple another chance to work things out. Most attorneys worry about their success track record of winning cases for clients and not what is fair. Hence, many become despised by humanity.

Now notice what happens when we turn to people who have no authority to listen to our confession, like a priest who offers penance for remorse as a means for Atonement. The whole process falls apart, and there is no reconciliation. How many false confessions does it take? In such false confessions with the Holy Spirit, we do this with family, friends, and people overall. Some of us are sly. We do not want the 3Rs to occur. We are more concerned about our selfish interests and look for excuses not to let the atonement process take place. Ah, it only takes a tiny fish bone caught in our throat to close the passageway to our lungs and cause suffocation. True love is forgiving but needs to be accepted as forgiveness for the 3Rs to take place.

Now study the cumulative effects of the above in humanity since the very start of humanity to modern times. Study the collective 3Rs of a city such as Babylon, Cairo, Peking/Xian, Athens, Roma, Moscow, Tokyo, Berlin, Washington, D.C., etc. The cumulative negative 3Cs affects the cumulative negative 3Rs that bring on wars after wars after wars. But notice what happens after the war of death and destruction when people are no longer able or willing to go on with the hell they helped create. There is somewhat of an austerity program in government that takes hold in order to get rid of the evils of war and start to rebuild bricks with mortar, bodies with souls, and law and order or civility. Notice how the process repeats itself over and over again. It's as if we are given the 3Cs of free will, yes, but then also the 3Rs, whether we like it or not. For lack of better words, we are forced to fast in an austerity program in order to get back to health. The lost victims are the ones that did not make it through the war. They are the ones that were killed, gassed or starved to death. For them, we build monuments and place wreaths in front of them as if this is compensation.

The mysteries of evil are not always that obvious, as, at times, they hide themselves. For example, comedians can turn anything into comedy and, at times, use the sickest comedy. At times, evils are concealed. In fact, most times evil wants it this way. In darkness, only light reveals evil's intentions. Discovered mysteries of nature, the metaphysical, could help us discover the mysteries of light and evil/darkness. Get close to raw nature; she has words of wisdom. When we see how wildlife is tested, we can begin to see how we are tested. Yes, raw nature is true to her creation. She could help us do the same.

Most of us are ignorant of our soul's needs just as we are ignorant of the financial needs of our second journey. We get lazy and do not want to be bothered with the study of investing in stocks, bonds, real estate, etc. We, at times, just put on another one of our masks as if we know what we are doing even when we don't. Or we say we were caught off guard as if it was never our fault that we did not plan wisely in safe investments. Yes, our broker may have deceived us as well, but were we not warned? Why were we in the shadows?

Can we recover from the losses? Perhaps, if we can learn our lesson. It is like when we are trying to get over the flu. By following the doctor's orders of what to eat, with plenty of rest, taking in the right nutrients, liquids, and medication, we may get back to health. But what was the lesson to be learned? Do not take our health of the body/flesh for granted! We may feel this way for the first few days, but the majority of us quickly forget with the passing of time. Yes, we also do the same with our soul's health. We have good spiritual advisors, we may listen and observe for a while, but generally in time we tend to forget or make the choice not to recall. A flashback of our lives from beginning to current, is this what we need? Do we have to take our life to the edge of no return? Do we need the risk? Some of us do. Problem? A few of us will fall off the edge.

As stated, we are all beggars, all invited to the beggars' banquet. Here we are all equal. Will we go? If we do, how long will we stay?

What will we eat? Will we take food back to others, or will we hoard it for ourselves? The beggars' banquet, my friends, are all of the graces available to us for ourselves and to give out to others. The banquet/ graces are unlimited for a humble, gracious, and sincere heart. It's our pride and ego that keep us from attending, not a miscommunication, misunderstanding, or interference. In spiritual light, all is clear of impurities. It is not like a space station in which anything could go wrong with the transmission. Now try to make sense of one times seven billion-plus. How could we possibly understand this phenomena? We cannot, not in our second journey for sure, but we can, by our free will and 3Cs, try to participate.

The phrases, "lost soul," "poor soul," "SOS (Save Our Soul)," "dying soul," "soul survivor," "get to the soul of the matter," are the vocabulary used by humanity for life and death, but notice that it includes the soul, not the body/flesh. A coincidence? Think again. I believe that our conscience does enter our consciousness when it is a matter of life and death. At the same time, by saving the body/flesh, our soul is able to be helped as well since the two are one. This is mindfulness of our soul for our body/flesh that is needed for our second journey, leading into our third journey. When the time comes, and for sure it will, who will accompany us? There are two angels of death. One is the grim reaper or angel of darkness that takes us into our chosen destination of hell. Do not worry; although the angels of hell are the busiest, no appointment is necessary. In fact, they have plenty of assistance who actually make the appointment for you. You really have no choice anyway at that point. The other, the angel of light, will accompany us either into purgatory and drop us off or continue with us into #10, heaven. These angels have the final draft of our chart. This is sort of like our final report card and final grade. At this point, we cannot change anything. No extra points, no excuses. Yes, there is equal justice for our soul. Take another look at the charts. Dare to test them for purgatory and hell? You will lose, my friends, as the billions of those who dared before you dating back to creation. Since you are reading this, you have time to make the choice of your free will for your destination. For how long, it is hard to say.

This reminds me of the pigs that had to eventually be slaughtered in my hometown of Bagnoli Irpino. The pigs were raised for the purpose of providing pork products that could be preserved up to a year and longer. Examples are prosciutto, sausages, suprasada, pork rind, etc. This usually took place in the winter months to prevent spoilage. Anyway, these pigs were not stupid; they knew the time would come for them to be slaughtered. They were created to be a food source for humanity regardless of what Hebrew, Muslim, and Hindu may think. So come winter, you could hear the commotion of pigs screaming and kicking as soon as they were grabbed because they knew it was their moment. This, my friends, is as close as I can come to illustrating what could become of us in those last moments of our soul's second journey if we are accompanied by the angels of darkness for a destination of hell. We may be like those pigs going down into hell kicking and screaming. But at that point, who will listen? Who will help? We laugh at all of this now here in the metaphysical, but there is no laughter in the descent. We are not pigs, my friends, unless we choose to be similar to the pigs that we are often compared to.

Self-imposed sacrifices and hardships could do us more harm than good. Do we know the needs of our soul? At this stage, we should, at least, have an idea. At times, it becomes confusing since so many voices are calling us from one direction or another. For us Roman Catholics, the rules of law and order for our soul and body/flesh are given to us as a gift by our ancestors. This is the helpful knowledge that does not necessarily need new knowledge to build upon. The Canon laws of the Roman Catholic Church are set in marble. There is no need to add or change anything, no amendment, no subtraction is warranted.

Also, we have the foundation for the 3Rs to process our choices. This is the reason for ordained priests to offer assistance. This is already set up for us. I am aware of a few bad priests that have ruined the integrity of the priesthood and have written about this, but the overwhelming majority are worthy of their vocation. Priests help for baptism, to communion, to marriage vows, to confession, for repentance, reconciliation, and redemption for atonement. They are critical up to our second journey's end. All of this that took two thousand years to build up is mostly being wasted. Another quiz question, as waste comes in many forms—forms such as the gifts of others and all graces. Yes, some of us Roman Catholics have become as wastefully ignorant as everyone else.

The silence and stillness of a good Church serve as a suitable starting point for meditation, reflection, and contemplation. At times, nothing is required of us but to just sit there and allow the Holy Spirit to review our soul's condition. All of our past sins will flash before our eyes. All we can do is bury our face into the palms of our hands and listen. Let out all of our emotions, our *dolori* (pains) that are the conditions of the 3Cs of our lives.

All of the blind ambitions, the 3Fs, and 3Ds come up into our consciousness. Stay this way as long as needed. This is the reconciliation, beginning of dialogue with the Holy Spirit.

The next step is confession for those of us that are Roman Catholics. Yet this should not be a barrier for those of us who are not. Notice that the churches in Rome have confessional priests of multiple languages. I don't know of any priest who will ask you of your religion or any personal information. Confession, as I have mentioned, is a time to unlock and unload. At times, this could be more helpful than psychological and psychiatric therapy by pay for so-called professionals. In fact, this is therapy for where we need it the most, within our soul's heart and mind. Yes, you will be forgiven of all of your sins, even if you forget some of them. But don't worry, what you recall, you can return and confess the following week. There are no limits, and you will not be charged.

Opening the doors to the confessional is opening the doors to our heart's tabernacle. This is a major first step, a little similar to an alcoholic opening the doors to rehabilitation. Note that we have to be reconciled with the Holy Spirit before we can be reconciled with ourselves or anyone else. This is a time to get rid of the false masks, the pretentious fake self. We should not have false expectations as a few of the celebrity type religious commercially profitable businesses out there. The next step is to listen to what our priest advises us to do next, as this is for our own good. We should never think of penance as a form of punishment but rather a form of communication and healing. We should never lose the smallest degree of faith, hope, and trust in the Holy Spirit. It's a long process, almost like training a child that grew up in the wilderness without an education. We should take it one day at a time unless the Holy Spirit moves us otherwise. Each of us is different with a different past and present story. The process for transformation will most likely be tailored to our soul's needs. Anyway, the process for everyone is in the opening of our tabernacle doors and letting the spark/light come out into our soul.

The whole purpose of the 3Rs is for our soul to become enlightened or, in other words, get rid of the darkness. This is all that our soul ever wanted and needs. This is what brings joy to our hearts and peace to our minds. Our soul, realizing what is occurring, begins to be grateful, the 3Gs. Again, a quiz question on being grateful. A grateful soul must express the gratitude to the Holy Trinity and others. Perhaps unknowingly, here we have started climbing up to our summit. Small steps perhaps, but to each according to the strength they have, as it is a long hard climb. What is important is that we have stopped the stagnation, the descent, and started ascension. There are many battles ahead, but the major battle is dealt with. We look up now, not down. At least now we begin to see the reasons for why we lost light. Understanding our weaknesses and how to overcome them will take time. Understanding of the testing process will take even more time. A week, a month, a year, or many years is irrelevant. We climb as we are capable of climbing in the strength we are given for our climb.

What is helpful is the understanding of the false elixirs, adrenaline rushes, and drug highs. The sadnesses of the events that must be unfolded do not occur overnight; they are ongoing. It is okay, and this gives us pauses, breaks, to reflect where we were before the climb. Light within our soul's heart will let love blossom again. This is one of our greatest needs. This is what takes us into eternity. Love nourishes us, our relationships with people, spouse, children, and parents. No more artificial intelligence or self-physiological therapy is needed.

Now in our climbing, our conscience or inner voice becomes audible again within our consciousness. We regain our moral sense of right from wrong. Our moral imprint becomes more visible as well. No more false justifications of our deeds or actions are needed as we are putting a stop to an immoral itinerary. Of these, the most difficult are the sexual activities that are, without a doubt, the most dangerous. From teenagers to adults, there is a constant feed of girls/women, boys/men readily available to sell themselves, body/flesh and soul, to brokers who fill the demands. But it is, as always, the evils working through humanity that destroy marriages, families, and friendships. The images, fantasies, and onslaught as a sometimes daily routine require constant defensive maneuvering. I mentioned this due to the necessity for the sacraments, as evils (knowing our past weaknesses) are relentlessly trying to stop us from climbing. Also as stated, we will have days of relief, but they are few and far between.

Yes, we will be abandoned in our testing, but how else are we to learn? Notice that I wrote *abandoned*, not *deserted*. There is a huge difference between the two words. Abandoned means to be left on our own, to learn to walk on our own two feet, or to fly as a young eagle. Desertion means quitting, to be left and forgotten. We, my friends, are never left and forgotten in our trials and testing, especially in our climb. It is always just the opposite in that we quit and forget about the Holy Trinity. Notice also that in doing so, we easily quit spouse, marriage, family, and friends. For better words, we become quitters in all aspects of life. The sequence is the same—from venial sins to cardinal sins, to mortal sins.

We will, without a doubt, have days in which we question what we have chosen to do. We may get angry at ourselves and the whole process of the climb. This is our immaturity, our lack of wisdom. Notice, for example, that even our pets, dogs, and cats eat grass or other types of natural plants when they feel sick. Who taught them this? Yes, as mentioned, they also possess the instinct for healing and survival. Are we as human beings any smarter? Wisdom comes from being tested in sacrifices and hardships, in failures and success. The process is the same for everyone. When we are synchronized with those who have climbed to the summit, we see the advantages of their wisdom and the disadvantages of our ignorance.

Take as an example how love was consummated by most of our grandparents. There was a moral sequence in the entire process. First came the meeting, visual, touching by hand, fragrance of body chemistry, and hearing about each other's interests. Taste? Perhaps a kiss or two in time. Next came the engagement, dating, getting to understand each other, our thoughts, emotions, beliefs, standards, expectations, seriousness, commitments, and being in union with each other. In Italia, this usually involved years. Finally came the marriage and the consummation of love for family. These steps, as stated, although involving our five natural senses, in true love become elevated into our five soul senses. I am happy to see that this process for the most part is still evident in Italia, although also changing for the worse here.

Fast-forward to modern pop culture in America and what do we have? The entire process has been put into reverse, and nothing is even remotely considered taboo, 3Ns—nothing, *niente*, nada. We meet, even as strangers, quickly move through the five natural senses, and jump in bed or the backseat of a car or anything anywhere, anyhow for that matter and have all types of sexual activities. We do this all on one date. Hmm, we wonder why most of our relationships do not blossom into marriage. We think that we are smarter, but age-old wisdom is crying for us. They know that this is not love, only lust of the body/flesh and limited. Faith, hope, and trust in any moral law and procedures are an abstraction to pleasure at that moment. Sounds familiar? Notice how animals do the exact thing? Do we really want to be animalistic?

New knowledge of darkness in darkness is worthless knowledge to be discarded for the trash that it is. The same holds true for false loves without moral law and procedures. True love after consummation has a lifetime to grow in union with the other. In union with the Holy Spirit, love travels into eternity. Light is eternal, and love rooted in light is eternal as well. Darkness, the opposite, is also eternal. Which do we want? As always, it comes down to our 3Cs positive, 3Gs, 3Ls, and 3Ts or negative, 3Ss, 3Fs, or 3Ds. Look back if you have forgotten their meaning and review the importance of the 3Rs.

In America, we have kept so little of the good culture of our family birthplace, be it Europe, Asia, Africa, or the Middle East. Rather than discarding the bad and keeping the good, many of us have done the opposite. Hence, we brought our criminal elements, superstitious beliefs, barbaric ways, corruption, and even cannibalism into what was supposed to be a new, better way of life. How could the Native Americans see us as better, civilized people? For the most part, they did not.

Civilized people have 1) a democratic senatorial republic; 2) enforced civil law and order; 3) civil freedoms/liberties; 4) controlled capitalism with free trade; 5) freedom in a true religion; 6) a collective healthy moral imprint and conscience; 7) a collective charitable heart; 8) an overall soul's chart tracking above 6.0; 9) an acceptance of the Holy Spirit. I estimate that currently we Americans, Europeans, and the rest of the free world are tracking overall very close to 7.0. But study the chart of humanity overall. We are the 40 percent of the population. The rest, 59.9 percent of the population, I believe is tracking below the threshold of 6.0. This is very concerning. There is an imbalance due to many reasons that need our attention and action.

Study the history of any people/country. For example, Italia, Romans rid themselves of kings in 450 BC. How? By the first peaceful way to force change/corrections in government. The majority of the people warned the senators that they would simply leave Roma without their voices being heard. Without results, they did exactly that, so no more people to plant and harvest crops, bake breads, work the trades, services, marry, and have children to continue the process, etc. The city virtually closed down. The citizens wanted a true republic with uncorrupted senators that listened to their needs. The word itself means "for the public/citizens." Senators were not even allowed to be involved in business transactions. Two counselors were elected yearly. NO more monarchies, NO more aristocratic system in which corrupted senators favored the top 1 percent to 5 percent! Sounds familiar? The people demanded change, and the senators had no choice but to give in. Most so-called historians are not even familiar with this most important event in the history of humanity. It is not being taught in our school world history classes. Due to this, we have had nothing, *niente*, nada—the 3Ns—but problems in civil governments for the past two thousand years and counting. This has been and is the case all around the world. This sharing of a system to future peoples and governments was/is to this day one of the most critical elements in civil governance. The second would arrive in Bethlehem in Christ yet not fully recognized until Roman Constantinople in the fourth century AC as a true religion. When uncorrupted, this is proven to work for the benefit of all, NOT just the top 1 percent to 5 percent. Recall that it worked for Poland in the last century.

The nine essential elements of a people/government have not changed. It is always the greedy, that small percentage of corrupted humanity by evils, that ruin it for all. Study India, China, Russia, and all past monarchies, and you will see the corrupt process repeat itself over and over again. Remember these letters, SPQR: the senate and people of Rome. They are still visible in Rome and Milan, the former administrative city of the Roman Empire. These four letters and their meaning were among the most catastrophically damaging losses of all succeeding governments in Europe, the Middle East, Eurasia, and Africa. There has been nothing but bloodshed and miserable consequences and conditions due to the allowed monarchies, aristocratic governments, and false ideologies of all the isms. A case in point: China with thousands of years of imperialism until 1911 with the last emperor. Why was the Imperial City called the forbidden city? It was only for the privileged tiny percent of Chinese. The rest, peasants, were in their service. What followed the successful revolution? Only thirty-eight years as a democratic republic till 1949. Study the consequences and conditions from 1949 until 1976. For me, the most important person in all of Chinese history is Sun Yat-sen, a true man for a republic to end imperialism. Had he not died so early, one could only imagine what China could have developed into!

Roma and Italia suffered the greatest losses of all European countries with the loss of SPQR. Study the sequence of events. It started with the evolutionary process underway in Rome in the fourth century AC, forced on her by Emperor Constantino into the 3Rs for her soul. Instead, Rome and Italia went back to kings and papal Caesars, aristocratic monarchies! We forgot our past history. Italia survived and became prosperous due to her city states, Liberta and many, but not all, of the nine basic principles listed of successful governance. The Renaissance saw a way back to SPQR and what worked well from 450BC for almost five hundred years. The *Risorgimento* (Rising Again) to 1871 with the Revolutionary War with Austria was limited in scope, giving us another kingdom and monarchy. Again, it was a government that favored the special interests of 1 percent to 5 percent of her citizens. In the early twentieth century, we stupid Italians followed fascist psychopathic ideological craziness. It took World War II and the election of 1946 to return to 450 BC. How much bloodshed and miserable consequences and conditions took place in the almost 1,500 years? Study history. We Italians still did not get it in the second half of the twentieth century with all of the neo-fascists terrorists, red brigades that wreaked havoc on innocent citizens. This was unification? In what ways? What were/are we Italians teaching in our school history classes? We gave the world a system of government that was/is proven to work well, and yet we ourselves have failed miserably to reapply a successful system. Why? It appeared that the full atonement process was not yet over!

The problem goes much deeper than civil matters. They go into our collective summation in losses of light. Try this formula SPQI (senate, people of Italia) + HS (Holy Spirit) = the 3Gs and 3Ls that result in a Pax Italiana with prosperity. The same was/is holding true for SPQA (America) and any other world government applying the same formula.

What was the so-called Northern Europe Holy Roman Empire? It was neither holy nor Roman. It was nothing more than a set-up between Germania kings and corrupt popes serving their own personal interests. The true Holy Roman Catholic Empire in the same time period until the Ottoman period was centered in the Eastern Roman Christian Empire and specifically in Constantinople.

I was puzzled as to why Muhammad. Why Islam? I think that Roman Christian Constantinople stagnated, failed to bring the Holy Spirit into Eurasia and Asia itself. Hence, she began losing her power and provinces in the Eastern Christian Roman Empire. Christian Constantinople walled herself up into high fortifications, as if wanting to keep grace concealed. Sounds familiar? We Muslim, instead, retained the Greek and Roman classics, thus not experiencing the Dark Ages. We Muslim, though, also like Constantinople, were missing a key ingredient, a voice/senate, and had a Sultan instead. Not only this, but we also failed to bridge the gap between Christianity and Judaism. We were given a few centuries to accomplish this but never did. We failed Muhammad and the Mali manuscripts for Islamic practices. The consequences? The barbaric Mongoli invasion. Notice how these barbaric Mongoli, although capturing all of the Muslim territories, became themselves the captured by Islam. With this, we carried Islam into India, Asia, and Eurasia. Yet we also were lacking in a main ingredient for humanity: a civil voice, a senate, a republic. We will see that there was nothing magnificent about the sultans. They indulged in the illusion that by capturing Christian Constantinople and the Hagia Sophia (Holy Wisdom) Roman Catholic Church where the Caesars were ordained, they could become a better replacement. Converting the wonder of the known world into a mosque did not help the situation. The sultans had all of the vulnerable weaknesses of the Caesars. What really changed? Notice that the sultans eventually did what the Egyptian Pharaohs did with grand burial mausoleums such as the Taj Mahal? They took the architecture and engineering of the Pantheon in Rome built by Caesar Hadrian in 125 AC, again one of the greatest wonders of the world whose same engineering went into the Roman Catholic Church, Hagia Sophia, and the great domes of the cathedral in Florence and Saint Peter in Rome to build mausoleums. Graces wasted? Hence, the decline, loss of light.

We Muslims would be expelled also from our territories and all of Spain. Granada, which we cherished so much, would be lost. The genocide of the Armenian would be the end of us. We Muslims had three chances for the unification of monotheist religions. The first is in Spain, where we instead tore down a Christian church. The second is in Jerusalem, where we burned down a Christian church. The third is in Constantinople where we desecrated a Roman Catholic church. We failed to observe the decree by Muhammad saved in the Museum of Istanbul that we should work with Judaism and Christianity. We failed Allah, and we, to this day, are still failing ourselves. Notice our consequences and conditions till today! Who can unite all three monotheistic religions today? Revived Roma with Pope Francisco? New Rome in Washington, D.C.? The revival of the European Roman Empire in the EU? Or all three? The reason that historians cannot figure out historical events is that they are close-minded on the 3Cs and 3Rs.

# CHAPTER *Nine*

Corrections—Kindness—Caring—Charity—
Being Loved and Giving Love Out

In this chapter, after the 3Rs and having started to climb, we clearly begin to see the need for corrections in our second journey. Why? Because now we realize that evil begets evil and that love begets love. We see the difference and the need to change, or I should say allow for the changes to take place within us for ourselves and others. We begin to see how our 3Ss—stubbornness, stupidity, and sickness—in not observing the Ten Commandments in our negative 3Cs made a mess in our lives. This is similar to going against the laws of nature in the metaphysical world. We make a mess and ruin everything for everyone as, for example, the climate change problems. The offenses are against our body/flesh that are followed by the offensive actions toward others for which we need to adjust and compensate. Yes, our 3Fs—foolishness, fault, and failure—were caught in time for the corrections to take place. The loss of peace, happiness, and harmony in our lives is hard, but the 3Ds—disgrace, despair, and death—are worse. It is enough having to deal with our failures, yet despair and death are hell themselves.

We Roman Catholics do not have it as hard to make the corrections; we just need to recall what was lost to us. The mysteries of light and goodness for the growth of our soul's climb was known but put aside foolishly. We wasted precious time and energy in not integrating all that we did for our third journey. We remember that our Blessed Virgin Maria and prayer are available to assist us in our climb. The Holy Eucharist is no longer taken for granted but becomes a priority and a thanksgiving. Our Lord's Prayer takes on a new meaning. Love becomes the purpose of all that we do and live for. A hug, an embrace, a caress, a sense of humor, and companionship are appreciated. All of the moments with friends and family become precious again as when we were children. We only want to cherish this forever and ever.

If we are not Roman Catholics? All of the above are available for everyone regardless of any obstacles. This is what the 3Cs are about, remember? Humanity for the souls of humanity—even with the weaknesses evident in us and others, there is hope. In this, the battle is half won. Being Protestant Christian, let us stop the protesting, and the transition is an easy one in rejoining the Roman Catholic Church, which we lost centuries ago. Greek and Russian Orthodox, what is preventing the reunification? Being Jewish and monotheist, we are halfway there. Let us study our Old Testament and prophecy of the Messiah. Being Muslim and monotheist, it becomes more difficult because we are so rooted in fanaticism of Allah, but it is not impossible. Being Buddhist with our M&M values, it is a real challenge. Being Hindu with all of our multiple gods? We need to start asking ourselves, why so many gods? The Holy Spirit does, indeed, work in mysterious ways. Look for the signs. Out of faith grows hope for love and charity; this is what it is all about.

Yes, love is the reason that we are born, that makes life worth living and working, for in our climb up to the summit in our second journey. But what have we done with love? We have abused, perverted, and traded it in for lust or profit. The 3Fs have proven our stupidity. We see now that there is only one place for the sacred seed of man within the sacred womb of woman in marriage. No, the mysteries of marriage are not so difficult to find, but they involve two, in which one in ignorance could easily ruin it for both. We ask ourselves, why have we waited so long? Waiting and waiting for the perfect person when there is no perfect person—just people like ourselves with various degrees of light in need of happiness. We, our souls, had been falling into hypertension from hyperthermia as we kept dropping down our soul's chart. Yes, it gets colder and colder in the descent into darkness.

We do not want to take people for granted anymore. We see how we could lose them one day. A tiny microscopic virus in their bloodstream and they die, gone from us.

No, we will not take anyone for granted again. We want to reach out to others that we feel are hurting someway, somehow because we realize that light heals the deepest wounds. We want to, at least, instill hope. We want to help turn their tragedies into opportunities if possible. We see that this is what tragedies are about. We want people to see the three destinations for the third journey and the importance of the 3Rs. Life is about the good art in people and their pouring out of grace, not dead art that says nothing and is abstract and colorless.

Our charitable heart began at home within ourselves after we were forgiven. Yes, we have a role to play in creation, in motherhood or fatherhood. We have responsibilities in our vocation and profession. No, we do not have the stigmata, but we have a charitable caring heart. We have been dying to ourselves. We do not want to see the same happen to others in despair and desolation. In helping others, we keep climbing, climbing, climbing.

This is, or could be, a challenge for us, especially helping those that do not want to be bothered.

But think about the millions of people worldwide that want and ask for assistance. Take for example clean drinking water that we in developed countries take for granted. Here we are in the twenty-first century, having traveled to the moon, and yet we have people in countries that have no clean drinking water. What are the words that I am looking for? Ah, yes, unconscious disgrace for all of us aware but failing to help with our advanced technologies and resources. Our good earth is roughly two-thirds water surfaced with depths of up to several miles deep. We have navy carriers that produce their own potable drinking water. We spend hundreds of billions of dollars and euros on military war machinery and yet little to nothing on one of the basic needs of humanity—potable water. We call ourselves civilized Christian people?

A tiny percentage of us have tried to focus on the inequalities in humanity by the one percent, but what have we accomplished? We wealthy, greedy people need to suffer our own losses in soul before we will change. The M&M loss is secondary but does occur in time. If we study the wealth of individuals, families, dynasties, we will see that this always takes place when that wealth is not shared with the most needy. In fact, wealth actually grows when we are charitable toward the disadvantaged, the victims of their circumstances and environmental inequalities. This occurs not only individually but also collectively as a family and a country. An example of this for young readers is the magnificent California redwoods. These trees, although in California, need to be shared not only for Americans but for the world of humanity. They are a gift to humanity for humanity.

For the haves in this world, we one percent may be the top one percent holding 50 percent of the world's overall wealth, but without a charitable heart, where are we tracking on our soul's chart? We should not be surprised if we are the one percent closest to zero at the bottom of our chart. For better words, we are in the bottom and not at the top at all. Yes, wealth is also a gift and a tool to test our 3Cs. What are we doing for the handicapped close to us? Do we avoid them as out of sight out of mind? How are we helping those that do not have even their basic needs of survival far away from us as in Third World countries? Again, study the important figures in history and read of how they gained much more than they gave out. This is not a mystery but a reality.

We have people, children, wondering why they were ever born into the conditions that they endure. We have teenagers that are asking what it is all about. We have an overwhelming wrong balance of wealth, natural resources, food, and even drinking water on our earth of plenty. These people need much more than our prayers; they need also metaphysical sustenance. There are no shortages of any of the above. The only real shortage in the world is the shortage of charity that is rooted in love, which is rooted in light.

We do not need psychological studies of humanity to figure out why the disadvantaged people in our world suffer the mental and emotional health issues that they have to deal with due to poverty. The everyday stress of survival needs take their toll in time. Here we are studying rat behavior from similar deprived conditions when we have humanity as proof of degradation from deprivation. How do some of us sleep at night? Oh, sorry, I forgot about the tranquilizing remedies that we have invented for ourselves.

Notice how the poor in the world may suffer one way, for example, from physical lack of nutrition that is clearly visible to the naked eye. Yet those of us hoarding the natural resources of the world suffer from the inside. It is not fully visible to the naked eye until it surfaces out of us, which in time does occur. We should meditate on which is worse. Our chart is a good start. Now also notice how we glamorize the so-called filthy rich as someone we aspire to be. We make no sense. We even do this with criminals that steal fortunes, as if they are to be admired in getting away with it. Do the words "twisted minds and dark hearts" fit the description of who some of us have become?

When we reward a child for bad behavior, that child's behavior will only get worse. When we compliment the criminally wealthy, we breed more criminals that steal from all of us. When we let large corporations do only what is right for the shareholders and not everyday people, we let them steal from the landholders as in the cases of the fracking currently happening in America. Now notice how we ourselves collectively as an entire nation try to steal from other nations. For example, we have gone into another country, invaded it, overthrown the government, and occupied it for no other reason than to take certain resources such as crude oil.

Again, for the young readers, an example would be a country like Iceland that grows no bananas but wants bananas as they are an important source of nutrients. Iceland could trade with, let us say, Martinique in the Caribbean for bananas in exchange for what they need from Iceland which is, let us say, certain cold freshwater fish.

In this scenario, both countries would benefit in trade. But what happens if either one wants to just take over the other? War, death, destruction, and stealing of natural resources will occur. This is what occurs when the evil of greed works in humanity. We Christian nations need to question how we could celebrate Easter, *Pasqua*, in good consciousness when we collectively do what we do to other nations and their people. We need to seriously reconsider Lent and Good Friday before we can celebrate Easter. Do we remember how? Maybe we need to go back to Christmas to relearn the importance of charity.

For example, in America, we waste more food than any other country. The food that we throw away every day could feed an entire small Third World country. Again, waste is an important quiz question. The words *waste, wasted, wasteful, wasting* describe a percentage of us American and European people. I have witnessed so much waste in every field associated with humanity. Let us look at the ways that we do this.

I am not sure what is worse, not donating excess food and material products to the poor or throwing it away each day. I would think throwing food and material products away. But it is not only this; waste in other areas all adds up. For example, gluttony with overconsumption of food actually is a waste that is harmful to our health. Oversleeping is also a waste that takes energy away from us. We become lazy pig heads that cannot think straight, causing additional waste since we feel out of it and can't be productive. Jail or prison time in America is mostly an awful waste of time, money and energy of the prisoner, and taxpayer dollars. War is 70 percent total waste unless for defensive reasons to protect our freedoms. Illegal drugs are a 100 percent waste that could kill us. Alcohol in moderation is healthy until we drown ourselves in it, causing us to become severely wasteful. Prostitution is a100 percent waste that may not be evident from the start until we end down in the gutter of life. Slavery, one of the worst crimes against humanity, wastes away the perpetrators' souls more than those enslaved. I could go on and on with this list from gambling to workaholics to fictional fantasies. Waste comes in so many forms. Add them all up throughout our second journey, and what do we have? A mostly wasted life of regrets if we ever come to realize it.

Charity changes all of the above. As I have mentioned, charity should begin at home, within ourselves for ourselves. But having said that, we must continue to give out to others that which we receive in grace/gifts/blessings—call them what you will. When done in an altruistic manner, we learn not to be wasteful. We begin to see how much more we have been given compared to the poorest people in the world.

Now study your habits, your bad habits, and study the waste each day for a week, a month, a year. Now multiply that to your expected lifespan. Yes, my friends, we Americans, and even Europeans, are wastefully robbing others of their basic needs. This is sinfulness on our part. Charity is the cure for what ails us, and in this are all good deeds, good works that we are designed for until we let evils entertain us into being lazy, wasteful pig heads. If this is not bad enough, in staying this way, we succumb in time to being the vehicles to bad or evil deeds, works for evil itself.

As mentioned, after seeing the negative effects of our evil side of 3Cs on our life in our second journey, we can see how they would have contributed to the dark destination for our third journey. Review the 3Fs, 3Ss, 3Rs, and 3Ds every so often. They should remind us of the importance of faith, hope, and trust in the Holy Trinity, the Holy Eucharist, prayer, and charity. We human beings could, if we want to, be like an olive tree that never dies but lives forever, giving out precious olives for the countless ways that olives benefit humanity. Or we could be like the almond trees that bear poisonous fruit, in which case we need to be cut down and used for firewood.

Now notice how many of us get bored with life. We get bored with everything, people, our job, our lifestyle, our family, and our friends. Why? Our soul is trying to tell us that we are not really experiencing fruitfulness in our second journey. I remember a genius in school that was quoted as saying, "I wish there were more hours in a day. Twenty-four hours is just not enough for all that I need to learn." This is living for what we have been designed for, ISD (intellectual spiritual design) and ESD (emotional spiritual design). Good deeds, good works are never boring. There is no time for boredom. They are challenging, positive, constructive ways to fulfillment. This is not chasing after illusions and fantasies but acts of kindness, caring, and giving of ourselves with the talents with which we are gifted. Want your boredom to disappear? Try being charitable; it works every time. We need to keep our options open to the guidance of the Holy Spirit who will guide us into where we can be the most productive and rewarded. Forget about old photographs; we need new photos of our accomplishments that help the new needy of life.

It never ceases to amaze me how a simple gesture, a smile, an open listening ear, a kind word of caring can change and benefit another person so much. It changes and benefits us as well. Each and every act of charity is rewarded with additional grace. There is no waste, but we need to get out of the habit of instant gratification for our good deeds. It may take weeks, months, years to witness the results. We may not see them until our third journey. No, we should never take graces for granted. When we do, we begin to lose them. Use them or lose them as is the case with our physical facilities. In losing grace, we are thrown back into the desert to be tested again until we learn to appreciate, be grateful, and be charitable. It's for our own good.

We do not reach 9.9, the platform to #10, on the deeds of old events that in our climb up got us to the summit of 9.0. No, this privileged platform is for the few that have turned over their free will to the Holy Trinity. Again, study the charts of how many of us I think are able to accept this. The number and percentage is miniscule. Our Blessed Virgin Maria, the apostles, and the saints were willing to be in the category. But read about their deeds, good works, and entire second journey. They never lost faith, hope, and trust in the Holy Trinity. Their sacrifices, trials, and hardships were genuine and sincere. They learned the meaning of empathy and sympathy. They worked for the Holy Spirit for the love of humanity. They helped change the course of history.

Again, we have the key to the tabernacle of our soul's heart. Giving up this key to evil could cause the death of our body/flesh and soul. This key needs to be protected at all costs. Read about the martyred saints and what they were willing to sacrifice of body/flesh in order to protect the key to their tabernacle. Who does this today? The estimated figures should tell us that the majority of us have given up on our climb altogether. The super rich of Europe had built their own chapel as if they could purchase absolution, control their own 3Rs of repentance, reconciliation, and redemption. Some of us did and do think that money could buy anything. The old private chapels of the European aristocracy are still here. They are seldom used anymore. What became of those who thought they could buy the 3Rs and grace? Only they and the Holy Spirit know.

Has anything changed with the later generations of Europeans in America? These days we pay for churches, hospital wards, university annexes, etc. Does this buy/pay for grace, the 3Rs, and our climb? Sorry to say that some of us think so. Changes are hard. False beliefs and superstitious thinking are evidenced today as they were with Savonarola's time in Firenze, Italia. The elaborate funeral tombstone and burial chambers for our body/flesh changes nothing, *niente*, nada. NO, but there is complete justification in death for all.

Now the true corrections always deal with the love of light. For example, a loveless marriage, family members' and friends' situations can change. We have the key to extraordinary light, hence love. An inferiority complex does not deter us. We never wait for love to find us, as the spark is within our soul's heart. The corrections can take advantage of our situation's negatives and turn them into positives. Empathy and sympathy for others speed up the process. This, as stated, always requires a degree of faith. Take as an example Stephen Hawkins, our physics genius of the UK. Were it not for the kindness, caring, and giving of ourselves in charity to help him, where would he be today? If we study history, there were times when people of his condition were put to sleep by atheists as an undesirable specimen. I wonder if Hawkins realizes this. Or take as an example some of us sometimes snobbish British acting as though we are more cultured and refined than other nationalities. We need to study our own history. Before Emperor Claudio and his legions came to the British Isles in the first century AC, we were living in huts and animal skins. As barbaric, almost savage tribes, we gradually welcomed the Romans to help civilize us. This was also a somewhat forced sharing, civility, yet was still a learning of engineering, architecture, and Roman laws and order. The cities of Bath and Londonarium/London are testaments of this to this day, resulting in London as a major world first-class city. Sharing, my friends, is about sharing that helps us become decent human beings.

In charity, we see that in loving, we are always loved by the Holy Spirit. So if you are reading this and have love issues with spouse, family, and friends, put this book down and open your heart to them before continuing to read again. Of course, it does not stop there. We are all capable of being the Good Samaritan. Again, notice that even certain pets have an altruistic charitable heart when saving an abandoned baby. Do they also possess a soul and moral imprint? I believe they do. Yet there is no communication of sincerity (honesty); they simply are. Now let us look back at how often we have used or read the word *sincerely* as in "Yours sincerely," "With sincerity," "In all sincerity." Hmm, this is at the top of our to-do corrections list. The word without honesty rooted in truth is meaningless. For example, people say, "I sincerely believe that there is no heaven when we depart." What does this mean when truth was not known? No, a long fasting is not a necessity for understanding truth. With living water, our desert springs forth new life and knowledge.

In our corrections stage, we all have a great deal to make up for. Our past aggressions toward others, even their name, needs to be accounted for. Take as an example Italian composer Antonio Salieri, who was vilified in the movie *Amadeus*. The lies, insinuating BS to interest the public, are evil at work. Some writers and directors will try to get away with any insult to a person's very name after they have passed away and are not able to defend themselves in a court of law. But in time, justice does prevail. Yes, Antonio Salieri, whose pupils included Schubert, Beethoven, and Liszt, is now recognized and remembered in Legnago, Venice, Italia.

It is not about "if only I had done this or that." It is not about self-pity. Corrections are about "What do I need to get done now, today, to make up for lost light, love?" One of the greatest rewards that we have after the 3Rs is a practical heart. No more foolishness or false loves and no more false fantasizing. We see that it does us no good to want to go back in time to correct our wrongful choices because even if we could go back, without the true enlightenment, we would probably repeat the same wrongful acts. There is only the present and future, whatever we have left of it.

The actions of souls descending, for those of us at the summit, are noticed and seen in all their predictable outcomes. We see the corrupt 3Cs that will, in time, in their darkness, deliver them into the desert of despair. An example is the LGBT community, where a war is raging resulting in depression of mind and soul. The 3Fs and 3Ds are clearly evident for seeing eyes. Another example is soul mates that become unmated. Notice that the word *male* combined with the word *feminine* equals female. Notice also that the word *man* combined with the word *womb* equals woman. Notice that the words combined are fifty-fifty as in marriage. We need to stop fighting this formula. When our pride and ego combined with evil interfere, as in modern-day feminism or chauvinism, the result is separatism. When the Holy Spirit is excluded, relationships are very predictable. Two sincere, kind, and caring hearts are never alone, as the Holy Spirit is always there uniting two into one.

An excellent time to question ourselves is during a death, a funeral of a loved one. At this time, think of all the moments we waste on gossip, hate, and revenge. What for? Death should remind us of what will happen to us soon, tomorrow, next year, it is hard to say. The point is, where are we? What light do we have? What love, what peace? Attending a funeral without this may have been mostly a waste of time. Perhaps we are only thinking about who will inherit the M&M from the deceased as we do in everyday life.

Questions, questions, questions of ourselves are what death of the body/flesh need to be. What are our kindness and caring about? Are we just deceivingly trying to get our way? Are the 3Ds and the 3Fs in play? I do not know what is worse—an evil person being outright evil or a person hiding their evil intentions. What do you think?

The color of black does not equal evil. History and Hollywood have placed this misconception on humanity. Evil does not have color as color; all colors are from light. The absence of light is not black by any measure. It is simply no color, just emptiness and nothingness. The color black is actually a combination of all colors but could also give us the different shades of gray. Think back, there was a time when hotels had a Bible in every room for a quiet place and time to read and understand the words. Today, the replacement is all colors of condoms, even black, and porno on demand. What does this tell us? The times have changed, and so has humanity. Meditate on this for a while.

During corrections, we all aspire to be loved. But what is there in us for others to love? What color is our light? Light has different colors, from the brightest white down to various ambers. The brightest light has the highest grace; the ambers have the least. Bright light is what we love in others such as the saints, their enlightened heart and mind. We are not talking about a utopia of peace and love as in 1960s America. This was only an illusion of grace in peace and love. Notice how once the drugs and money ran out, the illusions also evaporated. This had nothing to do with the light of love of our soul's tabernacle. For example, what makes a child naturally sweet and likable even by strangers? Their tabernacle doors are open. The Boy Scouts and Girl Scouts of America were another example of children wanting to keep their tabernacle doors open until they caved in to the liberal, no-standard, tainted values of a corrupt few.

If we stop to look around, all of nature is busy working on that which they were created to be, as in busy bees, nonstop working ants, etc. Humanity is often the exception. What should we be learning? I recall those days long ago in Salerno, Italia, with Ettore and friends being one of the ones who were not learning to climb up to the summit. Those were not bad days, but still they were days of greediness, laziness, and indecisiveness. Ah, but we cannot stay in this stage for long. We are in need of growing up. A eureka moment, an epiphany? Is this what it is going to take?

An extremist club is a club either to the far left or down. Take the Millionaires Club of America, it is a small percentage of us far down (in light) but a growing club of the most selfish extremists of humanity—who are proud of it. This is pop culture's idea of success, self-righteousness, self-worth, self-respect, self-esteem and self-love based on self-determination. This is what a percentage of us are involved in while the percentage of homeless children and poor people in America is also growing. We turn away from the smiling faces of children that remind us of who we were. Yes, some of us are Christian, even Roman Catholics. Our Dio has become the bull of Wall Street that gives us limited editions of designer brands of Fifth Avenue, yachts, castles, and country clubs.

Perhaps we self-made millionaires are anonymous charitable donors? Take a look at our friends and those with whom we associate. Take a good hard look at our virtues. I think not. A few of us will go out of our way to have published anything charitable that we are persuaded to give. This has nothing to do with an altruistic heart. We still think of it as human nature, as if it is naturally correct. Hmm, we do not need to wait until the day of judgment; corrections now save us a lot of anguish later. Hell raises hell's angels ("Hell yes," "Hell no," "The hell with you," "Now go to hell"—these are generally our responses to our critics).

Yet what is to become of our super talents of success? For example, what became of Leonardo da Vinci, Nikola Tesla, Newton, Einstein, Jobs, etc.? Were they charitable? I wonder where their souls are today. One of the Rockefellers was quoted as saying, "I would give away my millions for a healthy stomach." Hmm, millions for a metaphysical stomach, how much for a healthy soul?

This is our trade-off; we are always wheeling and dealing. Charity is not a series of trade-offs. In fact, look up the word. Charity is an act of love for humanity. It is an act of morality rooted in light. So love stems from the conscience, our soul's spark. This is where all truth and meaning exist. A few of us are planning to spend millions to venture into outer space. Give your millions to the truly needy children of the world. You will get far greater returns on your investment. Ever since we Americans started taking Christ out of Christmas and replacing Him with Santa Claus, trees, and ornaments, we have become less charitable and have descended on our chart.

The issues facing the children of Morocco, Syria, Iraq, Libya, and Middle East are of international crisis and challenge. These children, adults, and elderly are fighting for their lives. We developed countries are just not doing enough to help out. These people are taking unsafe illegal boats and rafts across dangerous open seas in a desperate attempt to just stay alive. Where is the willingness to change the current events taking place in these countries to rid them of the tyrants, terrorists, and evils they have to deal with? There is a lot of talk from cozy offices and international meetings, but little is done to help them. Why are not a few safe havens with international aid not being set up? We know how to set up military bases in the desert but not humanitarian safe shelters? These people are in need of an education in overthrowing the regimes of evil itself and taking back their countries. This includes charitable acts for the future of their livelihood. These people prefer to live in their birthplace if it were safe. They don't want to face the race discrimination and nationality prejudices of migration to a foreign country. Are we not all that way?

*Brave-hearted, kindhearted, good-hearted* are all adjectives describing the heart of humanity. Do we truly know the meaning of the words? These words are all associated with goodness in light. They're associated with active involvement, as in World War II, to put an end to the genocidal leaders and their atrocities toward the innocent people who are defenseless. These people already live in poverty and misery. Taking away what little freedoms they have left is despicable. Yes, there will be accountability for all, but in the meantime, we ourselves are always accountable as well. We have the means that only require the will as an international community. The United Nations seems to be a bureaucracy of incompetent people who are paid for what? What do they really accomplish? All of the expenses involved could be put to better use.

We Americans are always talking about team spirit in sports, business, this or that. What became of a collective spirit of will? What became of being our brother's keeper? In Europe, we are not much better. We seem to be more concerned about sports such as football and what we are going to prepare for lunch and dinner. We are all in this together, my friends, throughout our second journey. Our vocation, profession, and soul cry out for participation in world affairs of the needy, the persecuted, and the dying. Children need not go to bed at night hungry when there is plenty that Mother Earth gives out. For example, China—she is the latest wasteful country. People in the last century were starving to death. Now she wastes a great amount of food in the metro-city restaurants. Is a new world collective atonement in order? This begs the question: should communist regimes be supported in sharing the gifts/graces of those of us in Western democratic republics? With the human rights violations of the isms in the East and rest of the world, should we help make their leadership look good? Is this condoning dictatorships and tyrants on our part? Are we doing more harm than good? Or is this the evil side of capitalism exploiting cheap labor and lax environmental laws? Regardless, true justice will still take place. We should not be surprised when, with the implosion of the China economy, it triggers a depression in all of Asia, spreading into Eurasia, the Middle East, Africa, the EU, and eventually the Americas. The 3Rs are not coincidental, my friends. They are given whether we want them or not. How else is an atonement to be given a chance? Again, it is like a high pressure of nature on us with the devils having a field day. Hell has no fury as people become subjected to inequalities, injustice, and false liberties. "Give me liberty or give me death." Who spoke these infamous words? They apply to all humanity, my friends, all humanity! Liberta is similar to figs on a tree eaten by birds in which their droppings plant the seeds of Liberta wherever they fly to. Yes, the Holy Spirit works in mysterious ways.

Humanity is made up of givers and takers. We are at CMM (critical mass of misery) in certain areas of the world, of more being taken by a few at the expense of the rest. The statistics from the World Health Organization (WHO) warns us that some people are not receiving the necessary daily amounts of nutrients. Like the insurance companies, these figures do not lie. Religious fanatics, extremism left and right are trying to steal the very souls of people in all of the various forms that evil takes through humanity. Recall that our tabernacle spark needs oxygen to flame us up. Charity provides the means for the process to occur. If we think about it, this becomes an opportunity for us. We need to be cautious, though, as at times the takers could turn out to be terrorist fronts. We have also learned of leeches that feed off of the generous right here at home.

For example, there are a few that will exploit the givers, especially in metro cities where there are far too many people to figure out who is who. We have discovered people who make a living, fifty thousand dollars-plus, tax free from unsuspecting generous givers. So give only through a reputable no profit organization that is affiliated with an established charity or true church. Monies given to anyone, even if a needy homeless person may only be wasted on alcohol and drugs, make matters worse.

A reminder, though, generosity needs to take place within ourselves first and foremost. Each day we need to look our best, well groomed, with good hygienic habits. From the summit, this becomes automatically generated every morning. When our soul is content, we want to look and be at our best. This doesn't necessarily mean brand-name clothes or the most expensive cosmetics. A content soul simply likes a clean body/flesh without artificiality. Yes, a major correction at the summit is loving our body/flesh and keeping it as healthy as possible. This is one of the best ways to make a good impression on our children and other people. This defines who we are, not tattoos, face lifts, or injections of various fillers into our body. What was the expression, "Cleanliness is close to godliness"? True beauty radiates from the soul, not from the body of makeup artists and plastic surgery. Notice how diamond companies advertise, "Diamonds are forever." Hmm, but not marriage? Another joke? Forever occurs only in union with the Holy Spirit. At this correction stage, we will not have it any other way. This is family, as in the holy family of our Blessed Virgin Maria. Again, a cold-hearted, dumbfounded person will not feel this way, hence all of the bad body/flesh habits.

We Italians have a passion for love and a *bella figura* (a good figure). The aesthetic is valued in everyone and everything. Knowingly or unknowingly, a true passionate nature is derived from light within our souls for beauty as in the beauty of creation. This should not be mistaken for arrogance but an appreciation for the artist. This is a good quality in humanity's gratitude.

Corrections in business ethics? What are they? This also has to do with corrections at work. As employers, we will achieve far greater returns when we give our employees a decent living wage and benefits that we can afford. This is also being lost or, I should say, stolen from employees at many companies. We are going backward in time in how employees are treated as machines or charcoal. We are exporting jobs and people's livelihood. This is top management's collective conscious attitude stemming from an ignored conscience and rather for the bottom line and shareholders' interests only. When this occurs, count on problems down the line of the bottom line. The corrections in the past decade have been mostly negative corrections that in time will come back to bite us on our ass. The BBB and other state and federal organizations have turned into a joke, seemingly bought out and helpless. Corruption/evil goes hand in hand with immorality, be it in corporations, the court system, city, state, and federal government. As employers, we need to check our complaints box or blogs more often if we want to be competitive and stay in business.

I hear people ask, "Why is there so little love and caring in the world?" I have to respond, "Why are we willingly losing light when there is an abundance for the asking?" This brings to mind my golden canary when I was a child. I was responsible for feeding and taking care of our beautiful singing canary. I was very responsible for a while. In time, I became distracted with homework and playing. I figured that our canary did not need daily care of feeding and water, maybe every two to three days would suffice. I was wrong and only realized it once our beautiful singing canary died. It was my fault. I could not correct my 3Cs. I could only feel the sorrow and remorse. This is what continues to happen into our adulthood until we make the corrections that we all need to confront.

Yes, we all frustrate our lives to some degree. The corrections are a necessity after the 3Rs for true change to occur. If we could just keep three priorities in mind—first, light for our soul; second, love; and third, caring—we could make our lives so much less frustrating.

Our second journey is a schooling to learn from our mistakes and grow, but without the enlightenment from the summit climb, we clearly don't mature. The climb is also similar to our regular school grade system, one grade at a time. Graduation comes at different levels as well, from primary to middle to high school. Our soul's chart 0 to 10 is similar as well. In both instances, we cannot go it alone. Notice that the rewards in education for hard work are good grades, honors, recognition, etc. For our soul, it is charity in action for which we are rewarded in many ways. These two parallel each other into our vocation or professional careers and keep working the same way throughout our second journey. It really does work on a merit system.

Charity comes in so many different forms, monetary is only one form. Examples are assisting pregnant mothers in delivery, adoption of a child from an orphanage, helping poor children with education, medical assistance, life with dignity, helping those in prison to change, compassion and prayer for the deceased, etc. The list is endless. We need to look at our strengths and see what the best option is for us to give of ourselves. Again, this is the quickest way to the summit of 9.0 plus. All that is required is a sincere and caring heart. Our soul's tracking is not a game. It is a matter of life and death. Honest rules for honest tracking need to be kept in mind. Light from light, life from life need to be our first priority always. Finding one good role model for learning is so beneficial. Kind, kindness, kindle, rekindle, kindled are the names of charity. For example, in Italia, love is expressed everywhere: in coffee shops, restaurants, churches, parks, beaches, etc. It is infectious and wonderful. This also is a form of charity.

Yes, love is giving of grace and at the same time consuming. In the metaphysical, a natural soft blue flame is the hottest and most consuming. It is known by a tiny fraction of us that the light of the Holy Spirit is also a soft blue and also consuming. This same light also gives us the graces to persevere. As light is forever, love is, indeed, forever. The lives of the saints focused on selflessness for a reason, whereas when we give in to hate, prejudice, profiling, we fail our tests. For example, the most influential and powerful woman in history is who? No, not Cleopatra, not Catherine the Great, these were selfish self-absorbed women. It is our Blessed Virgin Maria. Why? Study her in every stage from the annunciation to her assumption. She was and continues to be the perfect model of charity and love. Austerities and fasting could help us see this. Economic recessions, depressions could benefit us if they could teach us to value and be grateful for what we have or lost. The Great Depression in the early last century did more good than harm to humanity.

We are like automobiles that, with constant timely oil changes, can go for miles and miles. So also in receiving grace, in being interconnected not only with humanity but all forms of life, in charity, we can travel forever. It's hard to be saint-like, but nothing too easy is worth having.

In our metaphysical world, we always need fuel in some form to function. Most of us recall the oil embargoes of the 1970s that wreaked havoc on our economic superpower status. Hence, we started to develop our own fuels. Our body/flesh is also dependent on fuel to function by use of the bounties of earth. Knowledge of fuels is valuable to us. The question is, why are we not able to see that our soul needs fuel to function as well? The fuel is light, that is love, that is renewed in acts of charity. This is truly a renewable fuel from the source of all other fuels.

Charity to the right charitable organizations is important, as there are plenty of fake charities out there that are self-serving and consume up to 90 percent of donations. Giving to some charities is like giving to North Korea; the few in the top echelon would probably take 99 percent of the donations. Notice photos of North Korea from outer space at night. She is mostly in darkness with scattered tiny lights compared to South Korea that is lit up. This is like their collective souls' degree of light, light from light, true life from true life.

Another example would be stents for the metaphysical heart. We put stents into a heart that, although clogged in the arteries, is still capable of functioning after the stents open the arteries. The stents become the tools in the heart to allow blood to flow out to other parts of our body/flesh to function. As a member of families, charity allows us to let grace from our soul's heart reach other members of families in need to function. Again, caution is in order, as there are many false charities out there without heart. There are also charities with false fillers, giving people not what they need but only what they want. For example, free handouts without working for it,

M&M, money and material things rather than an education, skills, and the knowledge of helping them help themselves.

What is most beautiful in humanity is a woman in love and pregnant in her prime of life. Yet some in the world are not able to afford medical care when they need it the most. We in the affluent developed countries are a disgrace for not making this a top priority for our charities. What is more important? We say that we have been through the age of enlightenment. What age was that? I see very little enlightenment in our modern age. True enlightenment and charity go hand in hand. At times, we need to be alone to meditate on being in the same shoes of the person in most need. What would we think and feel about not being helped by those in a position to be helpful. Yes, the needy is a large multitude of humanity and growing larger due to the imbalance in the world. What is to change this? When will this change?

One of the greatest consolations in our second journey is the opportunity to be charitable. It's healthy for our entire well-being that starts in our soul and works out into our body/flesh. We have observed this in various studies but are not taking full advantage of this phenomenon. We should be asking ourselves why? We have these studies, we read them, and then put them aside, forgetting them like yesterday's old newspaper. Everything that happens to us and those around us happens for a reason. We need to ask, what is the reason? As a child, I was told by the Notre Dame nuns about the alpha and the omega, about love and the Holy Spirit, about charity. It was so long ago, and I did not understand because of my age, but I have no excuse today. What is our excuse today, right now?

Notice that with the classic Italian operas, one does not necessarily need to understand the Italian lyrics or libretto. The emotions and passion pulsating from the tenor and soprano in a love scene are easily understood. So it should be with the needy in our world that suffer from the inequalities of humanity. It is there on the news, on our phones, on TV, in the newspapers. It is not a language barrier but a heart barrier. Are we listening? We condemn ourselves when we refuse to listen. Love is of not much use to us without giving it out to those in need. After we learn to love ourselves in a healthy way, this becomes self-evident. Yes, charity begins at home but can't stay home for long. How we allow love to effectively change us will determine how we effectively help change others.

We have discovered charities that are false fronts that fund terrorist groups around the world. It is vital to work through church-affiliated charities to be safe. We now live in a world of very little trust. After all, it's humanity that runs the charities, and all humanity has weaknesses and temptations. Although the ones that run charities with altruistic hearts present a clue for what to look for. Why? The altruistic heart as mentioned works for the love of humanity. Enlightened, we have the knowledge that love begets love. For better words, we knowingly feel loved as we are giving love out to others, especially to the most needy. Again, take the example of Saint Padre Pio, who had the scent of flowers easily picked up by other people who followed his presence. Should we ask why? He had an altruistic heart. Those of us with selfish hearts cannot comprehend this phenomenon. Those of us involved in hate, death, and destruction, along with all other sorts of evils, cannot begin to imagine the phenomenon. It is no different with those of us who get involved in crimes against animals, nature, and all that is of goodness in the universe.

A fall from grace is the greatest fall of all. Study your soul's chart, as grace and light are one. The problem is that the further the fall, the less we are able to understand the phenomenon of charity and love. A charitable heart is a vigilante and safeguards against the darkness of evil. Also, it knows that evil is powerless against a loving heart. At the same time, a closed, dark, and hardened heart cannot feel the difference because the soul's senses have become numb. A charitable heart prays for strength and perseverance. An uncharitable heart thinks that prayer is a waste of time. A charitable heart wants to always be prepared, not knowing the moment of the end of the second journey. An uncharitable heart does not consider the end of the second journey or of the third journey or #10 or of purgatory or hell.

Enrico Caruso sang "*O Sole Mio*" about one hundred years ago. Listen to this song; it captures the Italian way of life, of living and loving. It is as true and applicable today as yesteryear. What has changed? The times? Us? A healthy lifestyle doesn't need to change. Charity and love never change in how they transform us and us others. Another one of my favorites is "Return to Sorrento." This song is a timeless reminder to return to a healthy lifestyle, return home to the beauty of your childhood, your country, your culture, and the *felicita* (happy) way you were growing up. This is the *bella vita*, a *dolce vita*. The metaphysical body/flesh, yes, but also the mystical and spiritual for our soul, as the two are one.

Most of us remember the Scrooge that stole Christmas. We remember the characters in the movie. The movie may be fiction, but it pretty much sums up the spirit of charity. This movie, indeed, gives us a real life glimpse of charity and love with the effects it has on people. The movie is full of moral issues no matter what social levels. It shows us a life lost, a life spent on M&M, and not love or charity. This is only a movie story, but notice how we like to be reminded each year of the significance of the messages. We all seem to find a part of ourselves in this story. The story has a happy ending. The question is, what about our ending?

We are like the grapes of life, different varieties of color, taste, and sweetness. What we decide (the 3Cs) to do with our lives and talents is up to us. We could become eaten up young as fresh fruit by insects, birds, for our sake and for others. We all make mistakes with the 3Fs in life, but until the end, we have the 3Rs to correct ourselves in the 3Gs of grace, gratitude, and graciousness, charity and love toward humanity. Pope Francisco is right. He will not judge us; there is no need, as we judge ourselves.

As wine has alcoholic spirits, so our body's soul is similar with spirit. We do not put wine into a refrigerator to store it. Neither should we store our body/flesh/soul for this world. Both need to be consumed. Notice how darkness can benefit wine in aging. So also, darkness, while being tested, can benefit us in our climbing and aging. Precious wine is stored under lock and key in a wine cellar. Our tabernacle is the storage chamber under lock and key. We have the key. Wine from the best grapes can only be kept for so many years and eventually needs to be consumed or will go flat. Our spark/spirit in our tabernacle must also become consumed (grace) for ourselves and, in turn, given out, consumed by others in charity and love.

We Italians do not want anything added to our wines—no additives, artificial coloring, preservatives, sugars, etc. We want it the same today as when our ancestors made the wine from the same vines in the same earth. No, good things need never change. So it is with our soul that has the imprint of our creator. There are hundreds of fake wines out there, some have a fake "Made in Italy" label. It is scary to see what humanity in union with evil is capable of doing. Yet what I am grateful for is seeing my brother and sister Italians getting involved in every aspect of life in their second journey. From issues in marriage, children, education, politics, jobs, environment, Church to charity and love, there is constant passionate debate. Yes, it is wonderful when most people read their imprint and care to make a difference.

We Americans have become so complacent to a point of not wanting to be bothered about some major issues. Is it due to a collective silenced conscience? We are letting the attorneys and judges decide for us. An example was Proposition 8 in California that was decided by the voters (NO on same-sex marriage) only to be overturned by a not-so-supreme court of judges. What is the purpose of voting? Why have state courts? Waste upon waste. There is that word *waste* again. Perhaps this issue should not even be decided by a civil court? Perhaps by the five mainstream religions? Radical liberals would not like this? We have complicated things so badly that we no longer know right from wrong. Sounds familiar? This should be enough to shut down the Supreme Court that is attempting to shove their false sense of morality down our throats. Where are the mass demonstrations? This is the love of modern humanity? We have become sickened to our very core, our soul.

If only we could communicate and learn something from the saints or, at least, the dolphins and whales. We Americans have lost a lot of meaningful reasoning. What is meaningful? Pope Francisco's words are meaningful. A tiny few Americans such as Warren Buffet, Bill Gates, former president Jimmy Carter, and religious faithful are meaningful and still actively making sense of it all. There are many more important issues in the world, such as the lack of caring for others less fortunate. They understand that when love is missing, the willingness to live could suffer from the miserable misfortunes of life. Human life with dignity is what charity and love are all about. When we forget or ignore this, we all lose. Yes, true light and love never die, but people suffocate, become saddened, and suffer needlessly. It is evident in humanity when the moral senses of the body/flesh have not been transformed into the senses of the soul.

I recall a high suicide rate among young factory workers in China who were required to work long monotonous hours in bad conditions. Being from the countryside, they were exploited and treated as just peasant farm labor, just numbers that could be replaced. Employees that are mistreated cannot be creative or very productive. Out of sight, out of mind is what globalization from corporations can do to their workers. Who is to blame? No one wants to take responsibility. No rules, no regulations, no accountability? Let us recall that knowledge of wrongful acts is responsibility.

Within our soul, none of us like unfairness. But what if we are a part of the problem? Are we being hypocritical in our everyday dealings? If we are in continuous revolt against our imprint, we have a problem. Evil does beget evil, and what goes around will ultimately come around back to us. Take as an example what is heard at sports events. Listen for the three-letter word kill. Take the violence and fistfighting at these events. This is sporting? How are we better than the pagan fans of ancient Rome in the Coliseum shouting the same three-letter word? Another example is gun control. We need an armory to hunt or for self-protection? How many innocent lambs in schools need to be slaughtered and sacrificed? Do we care?

We tell ourselves that we are not gifted to be caring and compassionate toward others. Hmm, have we tried? What were we as children? We all have a moral imprint to remind us to be helpful toward those less fortunate. Has our imprint become a blurred vision? I have witnessed amazing results when people dare to care, even in countries under tyrants.

I recall a time when pop songs were mostly about love. Listen to the lyrics today if you can interpret them. Yes, it is the writers, editors, but are they not giving us what we want? We ask for adulterated, contaminated, sexual, anti-law, anti-police lyrics and songs. This is what we like. Caring and compassion for others are quickly becoming a part of the last century.

What is occurring in this century is an outward attempt to kill love. This is what evil does through humanity. Again, evil spirits in themselves are powerless, especially against light/love. Yet through humanity, evil has and continues to wreak havoc on humanity. Why?

Recall that we enter this world due to love/light and retain this degree of light for about three years after birth. After that, things begin to change. We become less and less protected as we grow up. We, our souls, begin to be tested as in school with education. As children, we are not able to comprehend what is happening, but those around us, those responsible for us, help us. This changes drastically in our teens. Now we make the 3Cs—choices, consequences, and conditions—for ourselves. The moral 3Cs will benefit us. The immoral 3Cs will hurt us. The moral 3Cs involving charity and love help us climb to our summit. The immoral 3Cs against charity and love cause us to descend. This is just a refresher to remind us of the power of charity and love.

Perhaps 99.999 of us are not, will not ever be Christlike. This is okay; even the monks and nuns in cloistered habitats have a difficult time of it. The point is, we are all capable, very capable of charity and love. We just have to will to be and do so. In this is the fountain of youth, our childhood, our living forever in our soul. In this, we are able to travel through the galaxies and entire cosmos in union with light. What could possibly be more important than this?

*O Dio, O Gesu, O Madre Maria*, how often I have heard these words. No, not in the time of death but in everyday living. We are all a little bit like Mary Magdalena, Pietro, Tommaso in modern times, only the names and dates are different. The Word, the truth, and good knowledge are in our faces even more so. Will we deny and refuse this good knowledge or embrace it? To be a sinner and not fully be aware of it due to ignorance is one thing, but to know and not have the willingness to correct ourselves is something else. Who among us is that ignorant? Who among us has no willingness to change? Open your eyes, see the consequences and conditions in India, Africa, the Middle East due to the multitude of unwillingness to correct, change, and contribute in charity and love.

We become liars to ourselves before we become liars to others. Do we know this? Do we deny inequalities, injustices, and inhuman conditions in the suffering people who are not able to handle helping themselves? The greatest returns on investment are the returns on charities and love. Collectively, America was at the height of her mission after World War II. We were standing tall, having helped free Europe and Asia from the evils of darkness. It saddens me to write that since that time, we have declined due to collective losses of charity and light. But it is not just America, no, it is all Christian developed countries that have forgotten their role in world affairs. Again, this is not coincidental; it is the 3Cs collectively. It saddens me because I know that the overwhelming majority of people in these same countries are caring and good-hearted. We have allowed the few, the special interests decision-makers, to decide for all.

There have been past voices, yes, of Gandhi, Mandela, King among others. There are currently voices of Carter, Pope Francisco, Buffet among others. Are we listening? Who are we? Are we the peacemakers? Peace comes at a price of generosity, not war. Should war ever come to Jerusalem and Rome again, we may all be in the end of days.

Charity should begin at home within ourselves in opening our tabernacle doors for our soul to properly function in charity and love. After this, it needs to quickly reach family and friends and after that community and country. After that, all others in need. The needs are humongous in the world. First step first is the process, just as a child.

When we lose our spouses, we lose 50 percent of ourselves. When we lose a family member, we lose a small part of ourselves. When we lose friends, we lose a little light and love. When we lose all others, we lose a fraction of ourselves. When we lose the Holy Spirit, we lose our sustenance and everything worth living for. Only the light of charity and love replenishes our losses. Now imagine having to deal with losses alone. Imagine no help during a funeral of a loved one. Imagine no help during our funeral.

A child in an orphanage—unwanted, unloved—has to be one of the hardest tests of life. For couples unable to conceive a child, roughly 10 percent of humanity, this is an opportunity for one of the best charitable deeds of all. The needs again are high, especially for troubled children. The demand is low. Yet 10 percent is a huge percentage of humanity. Why the holding back? What are the issues? Perhaps charity and love have not started at home within ourselves. Having to give up a child for adoption takes a heavy toll on any couple, but abortion takes a killing toll on all involved.

I am reminded at the check stand at retail outlets, especially in America, of the degree of nonsense that we have reached. I can't help seeing the popular tabloids' headlines. It hurts to realize that some of us read some of the absurdity. Lust sells, try this, try that—as if sex is full of tricks that need to be learned. Love by these trash writers is limited to the five natural senses. Invaded privacy and misinformation are the norm, even at the expense of a lawsuit. If it sells, magazines publish it. Business ethics? What is that? Caring and compassion? They don't sell.

Now see and listen to the classic opera, *La boheme*, by Puccini. This opera has it all: poverty, sacrifices, suffrage, being tested, faith, hope, and trust. This opera puts love into perspective. The love in this opera is undying in the worst of times. This opera endures because it deals with reality and not illusions. We Italians are so blessed, gifted with Rossini, Bellini, Verdi, Puccini, Leoncavallo, Mascagni, and many more artists that have put life into song and music. Study the characters, the protagonists, the antagonists, the winners, the losers, the evildoers, the good doers and find yourself. These operas do not deal with the LGBT, no, but they do deal with morality. We Italians love our artists, our operas, and have given them to all humanity as gifts. This also is charity in sharing.

At times, we all need to stop and ask ourselves, what do we like in ourselves? What do other people like about us? What do we like in other people? If we meditate on this for a while, we should realize that the best qualities always have to do with charity and love.

For example, why do we hold back, even pay farmers in agriculture from production of fertile lands? We have people starving in the world and yet pay farmers to keep lands out of production. Forget about economics; knowledge is responsibility and accountability.

At the same time, I am awed by the fantastic works that humanity is capable of. I see wonders in the museums, in architecture, with paint, wood, stone, clay, and all of the metaphysical world. The cumulative culture, traditions, especially in Europe, amaze me. Yes, when humanity puts their hearts and minds into good works, good deeds, in acts of charity and love, the results are wonderful to behold. Yet in acceptance of evil, all can quickly be destroyed as was the case in World War II. It continues to be the case of war, and a nuclear war would be the worst scenario.

Another of the great gifts handed down to humanity is the Song of Songs attributed to the Hebrew, King Solomon. How we interpret this poem is up to us. It could be eroticism, but in the context of true love, it is a masterpiece. It is an expression of love. To me, it explains sexual activities that are wholesome between a man and a woman, again not LGBT. My question is, what poetry do we have today that is a better expression of love? Again, sex is big business these days, and as so often is the case, it has little to nothing to do with love from light.

In the love of light, a man and a woman in marriage have a lifetime to enjoy each other's companionship and sexual activities. From touch and kisses to foreplay and climaxes of delight, this is also charity and love when in the laws of morality. But notice that these days, a few of us have to schedule loving each other, as in setting up an appointment, sad and sorrowful.

Notice how with modern love sex experts try to weigh in on the subject of love and sexual activities. From kisses to foreplay to intercourse to climaxes, everyone is attempting to profit from the inadequacies in a married couple. For example, why did love fade away? Why is the feeling gone? Why the lost magic? Why is the honeymoon over? I could go on and on with the questions that people are willing to go on talk shows to answer. Others pay for the answers. The answers, as always, are in the soul's mind and heart of husband and wife. The same rules, laws apply in dating and engagement relationships. We need not waste time on other forms of relationships

289

outside of moral law because nothing makes any sense in that area. Let the psychic therapists play with that area with their false solutions.

I have mentioned that the degree of light in any relationship will determine the future success or failure of the relationship. For example, it does occur that one person, or even both, in a relationship may never have had a true love to give to the marriage, partnership, soul mate, significant other, etc. Why? I have also written that love is light that doesn't die or end. When true love grows and sexual intercourse in marriage is the consummation of love, it doesn't diminish. When it does diminish, be grateful for finding out in yourself or your spouse; it tells us that a correction is in order. A cold, hardened heart must have the willingness to change for any meaningful love to occur. We do not fall out of love; we fall out of light as falling in the descent on our chart.

Usually, it is those of us that have everything as far as M&M that tend to have the colder, hardened heart. Is there hope for us? There is if we come to realize who we have become. When arrogant, we are despised. I have explained the process already; go back to refresh. But those of us who have serious doubts yet care and have a true love for our spouse, partner, significant other, what are we to do? A healthy moral conscience does warn us. Prayer and abandonment are, at times, the cures. This is not to say that this will or will not work, as we cannot force the free will of others. It is to say that, at times, some of us need time to figure things out in our second journey. Note that the more we are humbled, the more we will be loved. For the caring, this also is charity and love toward others in need of figuring out the process. This is the reason that negative, quick, drastic actions should not take place. They make matters worse in any relationship. Hate and revenge could and generally do ruin the relationship.

Evil seeks to have us rid ourselves of light. Notice that we tend to hurt those who love us the most when we are tested. Evils try to break the bond between husband and wife, between children and parents. In accomplishing this, evil breaks down the bond between us and the Holy Spirit. It works the same in all meaningful relationships. A healthy moral imprint and conscience remind us of what is taking place with guilty feelings. Charity is the remedy by others for the correction. Charity involves empathy and sympathy toward those that offended us. This, in turn, helps bring about the change in others, which, in turn, helps develop gratitude in them as well.

Outside of charity and love, we tend to make vain attempts that turn out to be futile reasoning and illogical nonsense. In the light of love, we add colors to our lives. The grays and dark colors are okay for certain occasions and funerals, but in the light of love, the bright colors speak to others of warmth, personality, and a charitable heart. This doesn't require a sage to inform us. We should take notice that those of us who are climbing up our summit like colors, even bright colors. At the bottom of our chart are the ungrateful, ungracious grays and depressing colorless, uncharitable, and unloving hearts.

We are not talking about infatuation, phony, pretentious, fake charity and love. No, this is evil's way of imitating charity and love. We scoundrels, users and abusers, know this game for the innocent quite well, whereas true charity and love are not complicated or confidential or confusing. It is not complex, and neither does it play games with others' emotions. It is quick to show genuine compassion and sorrow. Hate is not allowed to enter the relationship. Our charity wants to be a help up, not a help to maintain the same level for those constantly asking for handouts. As an example, we are our brothers' helper, yes, but not when they are loafers and leeches.

In the willingness to be charitable and loving toward others, especially the most needy, our heart receives the graces to do so. Again, this is the power of our free will, an important tool. This is what keeps humanity from becoming extinct. As mentioned, our free will needs daily exercise and in charity and love replenishes us to climb up to our summit. The higher we climb, the greater are the graces available to be more charitable and loving. It appears that we live for others, but we benefit the most in light of our soul. For example, the more darkness of despair that we help eliminate in others, the higher we climb up to our summit. Let us keep in mind that although the needs of people in the world is humongous, the graces available to the charitable and loving hearts are always far greater in supply.

Charity and love need to extend outward to all forms of creation. An example of this was Saint Francis of Assisi with animals. Saint Francis had the grace of knowledge in the importance of animals in how they help humanity in our second journey. The opposite of this would be the example of the Chinese in attempting to kill off birds because they ate a tiny fraction of grains. Justification occurred when the insects that the dead birds used to eat eventually ate more grain than the birds. Yes, there is justice in the world; it only takes time to unfold.

Without charity and love in the world, what is the purpose? What is the meaning of our existence? The three major monotheist religions in the world—Judaism, Christianity, and Islam—all teach the importance of charity and love. In fact, because there existed such a huge divide between Judaism and Christianity, a prophet, Muhammad, was given to humanity to help bridge the gap. If we study the written order and agreement between Muhammad and Judaism with Christianity in the text in the museum of Istanbul, there is proof of this. Yet a few radical extremists have decided to take matters into their own hands to cause the opposite. This is what evil does through humanity.

Imagine that all Christians became united. Imagine that all Judaism became united. Imagine that all of Islam became united. Imagine if all three became united. Imagine the power of charity and love in the world. This is not wishful thinking. This, motivated by a willingness to do so, could become a reality. Take Jerusalem today, all three religions exist peacefully in one city. Why not in the world? One *Dio*, one light, one Holy Spirit in monotheism.

If only humanity could begin to see how evil divides through negative provocations of violence. Charity and love are the keys to correct the disrespect and disregard for the suffering in the world. An altruistic charitable heart can overcome all evils. I know that it is extremely difficult not to take revenge on the wrong evildoers in the world. Yet we know from history that this usually makes matters worse. There is a fine line between enforcement of law and order with weaponry and the persuasiveness by charity and love to achieve peace. We are currently being tested up to our full endurance to prevent the escalation of violence and bloodshed into full wars. Where are the so-called spiritual leaders of love and peace? Not all are contributing to a dialogue to stop the beheadings, killings, rapists, and maddening herd of a small percentage for their choices, consequences, and conditions.

We were not created to kill each other. We were created to be procreation and to take part in the process. We are bombarded from so many evil sources to destroy or be destroyed. A healthy moral imprint and conscience are vital for our continued existence. Again, the key that we have is in our willingness to open the doors to the tabernacle of our soul's heart. It is the beginning of all changes for the better.

Charity and love are infectious in a good way. They help inflame the hearts of others who can spread the flame to someone else like a firestorm. What has become of love in the world? I should say, what has become of the love within ourselves? Do we know? We are one person, but one person is able to inflame many. When we have diminished our flame of love, which is the light of our soul, we need to rekindle and set it ablaze. Only the Holy Spirit can achieve this.

Notice how these days the word *spirit* is used, as in free-spirited, spiritual love, spirit in sports, clothing, automobiles, horses, etc. Is it any wonder that the word has lost its meaning? The word *love* is even worse, as in "I love this or that," "for the love of…" Yes, it's always the precious words that are twisted and turned into meaningless nonsense. How are children not to be confused? This four-letter word, *love*, has become used in conjunction with the obscene four-letter F word. In this context, how could the true-lettered word of love survive? The degradation from love's original meaning coincides with our soul's degradation from our descent.

In our ascension, the opposite is true. We come to see that when we want to be pleasing in the eyes of the Holy Spirit, we are pleasing in the eyes of humanity. As mentioned, this is not acquired genetically but rather offered to us to accept voluntarily. In doing so, we become like a mirror that can reflect out to others the same light. Notice that a mirror can reflect light into the darkest areas by just positioning it at the right angle. But the mirror must be polished and clean. So it is with our soul. Again, this occurs with the 3Rs, to become cleansed of impurities that diminished our soul's light. None of us are innocent, my friends. We are all sinners with a degree of darkness.

Recall that the Crusaders were at one time thought of as heroes until the truth surfaced on the reign of terror, death, and destruction that they caused on the innocent lives of the Muslim people, including children. This was all due to one man/pope who lost the meaning of charity and love. Infallibility? He was pope but also a human with weaknesses.

We know from history that the Muslim communities of the Middle East in the spirit of charity and love actually prospered during the Dark Ages in Europe. They experienced a Renaissance in their own right of the classic Greek/Roman philosophers, arts, architecture, math, astronomy. Or should I say they never lost but instead preserved them. They were in their golden age of prosperity and rightly so. They had the consequences and conditions of their choices in charity and love. Study today the cumulative current conditions in the same areas. Why?

In our second journey, we do not have love that we can produce or provide for ourselves. Again, love is grace from light. All that we have is our free will to accept as a gift the love that we need for ourselves and others. A refresher, three of the greatest gifts to humanity are the soul, with spark, our body/flesh, and our free will. In these gifts, we are capable of love and the means of procreation. Love is for the asking but must be put to work and not be simply stored like grain. What good are any of our talents if we do not put them to work for the betterment of humanity? We knew this at one time in the past in America and the free world. What has changed us? Do we need to download an application to relearn? We help shape our own *destino* to some degree. Putting ourselves, our bodies into a freezer changes nothing; it just puts off the inevitable 3Cs of our soul's second journey. It is like in cards, we have to work with the cards we are handed. Every hand could be a good hand depending on how we put it to work. We could easily fold and quit, or we could make the best of it. This is not luck; it is intelligence at work.

The failure to accept love, be loved, and to love others is the sorrow of sorrows. Our 3Cs could be devastating when it comes to the wrong and negative choices concerning love, especially with a potential second journey spouse setup for us. I recall vividly this being the case for myself. Again, the pride and ego can and do make a mess of things.

Love and laughter are healthy for us overall, but how can there be laughter without the love? It works the same in all relationships in all of humanity. It cannot be fake, fabricated, or artificially produced. No, love and charity must be genuine and sincere. There is only one source for this, as mentioned countless times. Let us accept and call on this source and be grateful for having what we have. Also, as mentioned, a guilty feeling is healthy for us. It warns us that we are making the wrong and negative choices in our lives. We are warned before the consequences and conditions follow, as they always do. Why do we try to silence our conscience? We have it to help us, not hurt us.

One of the best examples of contrasting figures in history is that of Marie Antoinette of the French aristocracy and Luisa of Prussia (Germany), also of aristocracy. Many of us know the story of Marie Antoinette and how the French poor, hungry citizens in eighteenth-century France revolted and used the guillotine to behead Marie and all of the aristocracy. Few of us know of Luisa, in how she used her charming, feminine, and motherly personality to be listened to by Napoleon to stop the fighting, death, and destruction of the German people.

These are two sharp contrasting figures in history to learn from among the countless figures. The point is, one person, caring, loving for her family, friends, citizens, and country could, with a charitable heart, accomplish what she did. It did not end there, as we know from history. The German people were gradually given freedoms and property rights that we deserved. This is proof that those of us who are currently uncaring, uncharitable, and unloving will not survive for long in both body/flesh and soul. It is unsustainable when we are taking away from others their share of sustenance. I have mentioned many times that justice begins with our souls light and that our soul and body/flesh are one. It is only a matter of time before our injustices manifest themselves in our body/flesh. At times, as with the two figures above, the injured could take a violent turn as eye for eye or reparations for all of the past injustices. Could they be blamed? Without the laws and order of the soul, chaos is bound to happen. The heart of humanity is always the starting point of effective changes for the better. Our spark within the tabernacle of our soul's heart is either allowed to help us or becomes imprisoned and stifled.

Some of us think that we can cheat others, the system, and even death itself. We are fooling ourselves, deceiving ourselves, and ruining ourselves. In this, we are never at peace with ourselves or other people. It is not possible, as in darkness, nothing good is possible. In darkness, we are unfruitful, uncharitable, unloving, and unproductive. We are a waste of life, time, and energy. Tranquilizing uppers and mood modifiers are both a temporary fixation and no solution to that, which ails our soul's heart and mind.

Current pop culture is mostly outside of the good knowledge of our soul's heart for our mind, hence all of the confusion, hysterical nonsense, and suicidal tendencies in wanting to destroy the body/flesh. This is, of course, no solution. This is the fastest track to purgatory or hell. We women are just as guilty as men these days. Perhaps even more so due to the fact that we are gifted with the ability to be a part of the creative process but rather become a part of the destructive process of ourselves. We have put ourselves in the front lines of the police department, and even militaries, in combat fighting and killing. We risk being captured, raped, and tortured. This is liberation? What have we really accomplished? Is this what we were created to be? It is bad enough for men taking a defensive role. Study the so-called greatest women in history, the Antoinettes, the Luisas, the Joans of Arc, and the Cleopatras. Study their 3Cs and how, in turn, they effectively changed history for the better or worse. Do we see the pictures?

Even nocturnal animals need a degree of light to function and survive. Notice the ones that do not have eyes that we know of. In darkness, their other natural senses are used to survive and accomplish what they were created to be and do. Without the accommo-dations and being hampered in their second journey, they adapt. Are we humans not as intelligent? At times, we simply do not utilize that with which we are graced.

We all have a calling in our second journey. With a moral imprint unrecognizable, a tabernacle with closing doors, a dumb-founded mind, and worse, an uncharitable and unloving heart, how can we begin to know that calling? With the refusing of our climb, the refusing of spiritual good knowledge, our talents are never fully utilized. Read the annunciation to our Blessed Virgin Maria by Archangel Gabriel. Read the full response by Maria. In the two thou-sand years past, the 3Cs have not changed. There is no fulfillment for anyone without the same response.

We all want to be special apart from the madding crowd that, at times, becomes a herd. Yet by deviating from who we were created to be, we become a part of the "maddening" crowd and/or herd. We could all be special, a tiny fraction of us are. Study your chart. The herd is below 6.0, the crowd is between 6.0 and 8.99. The special are at least at 9.0. The ultra special, the elite are 9.0 and above into the plus. Who, what, and where do we/you want to be? The question is, what recognition are we/you after? Do we/you want to be another face, another number, or another has-been? Do we/you want great-ness? Do we/you want more responsibility? Do we/you want to be a part of the divine? It's our choice, it always has been. As examples, the name of Gesu is recognized on all continents above all other names. Our Blessed Virgin Maria, with her apparitions on all continents is also well recognized, honored, and respected. Saint John Paul II, with his missions, is also recognized on all continents. All three are recog-nized due to their 3Cs—choices, consequences, and conditions.

The laws of nature could be harsh on all forms of life; human-ity is no exception. But this is the metaphysical, the body/flesh, and need not be the soul's deprivation. Yes, the two are one, but our soul and the souls of others should be our first priority. Again, we were given the laws of morality in the Ten Commandments to live by that guide us. We were given a moral imprint to assist us. We were given the prophets to warn us. We are given the angels and saints to help us. We are given the current faithful to show us the way. We have no justification for our failures. This book itself is only a refresher. Enough already with our endless excuses. A one-word answer of yes will suffice. All of the laws of nature have a purpose. The laws of morality, of the Holy Spirit within the Holy Trinity, are even more so.

Evil likes complacency, laziness, and indecisiveness. It uses the same weaknesses against us every time. This is how we let tyrants and dictatorships run our lives. This is how we lose our freedoms of body/flesh and soul. This is how we turn our eyes away from genocide, ethnic cleansing, and all other atrocities against humanity. This is what causes us to become crippled and allow the prophesied events to occur. We can change prophecy when we allow ourselves to be changed. Yes, the Holy Spirit within us can do this and much, much more.

We are tested daily. What we elect to do with our testing is up to us. Take for example the needless suffering of children in our backyard, our community, our country, our world. No, the lambs need not suffer as they do. Charity and love are a remedy. In fact, charity and love help cure many of the ailments of ourselves and others. Yes, we are one person, but one plus one plus another and the multiples add up quickly just like the sparkles on a sea that reflect light.

The opposite is also true. Each small sin plus another small sin add up, and the multiples mount up. They become like pestering biting ants that in multiples can devour us. Multiply this by 365 times a year times ten, twenty, thirty years, and you should get the picture and our position on our soul's chart. You see, my friends, we choose to win or lose. Evil is the perpetrator, but we are the vehicles. What have we learned from the Hitlers, the Stalins, and the Mussolinis of the world? Once again, omission to act is also a sin.

Study history to see where and when we have allowed ourselves to be imprisoned, enslaved, and put to sleep, exterminated like animals. How are we able to be emotionally, mentally, and physically healthy of body/flesh and soul with an inactive positive free will? We are not. In light, we are able to see all this. The question is, how are we to let others see it? A cold darkness in despair and desolation are, at times, the only way.

Take as examples how we have modified genetically plants and animals that did not need it. We also have artificial hearts and body parts, artificial intelligence, and artificial almost everything. Are we artificially modified? Can our very Soul be modified? Humanity is often focused on corrections in our body/flesh that need no correcting. We want to tamper with divine creation that we know little about. We know little about ourselves. This is obvious from our chart. We have acquired much knowledge upon knowledge of the metaphysical world but little of the spiritual soul. For example, mental health—what do we really know? We know more about the moon than we know about mental health. Why does our brain become dysfunctional? How can a soul's mind function in a brain that cannot follow orders? How do we replace a brain section or an entire brain? So many questions but few solutions. Do we have the right knowledge? The brain, the nerve center of the body/flesh, is not as simple as the physical heart. It was designed to be much more complex than we can begin to imagine. Bionetics is just a small step forward but has a long ways to go. Remember the lobotomies performed on the brain. We thought it would be such an easy procedure to correct the brain's issues. How many people did we damage for life? Charity and love do not commit these hideous crimes. *Tutto pasa* (all passes), yes, but not all should be forgotten. Without the spiritual good knowledge for our soul's mind, we are far, far away from the knowledge that we need. In charity and love, we, at least, move closer to the good knowledge for our soul's mind and the metaphysical brain.

Those of us who have a healthy brain and mind, it is our responsibility to help those less gifted. This is charity at the highest level of humanity. Enlightened, this is a no-brainer—pardon the pun—but how enlightened are we in the medical and scientific fields? Turning to euthanasia is a total failure of charity and love. All of us involved in these laws and procedures will be held accountable if we have not already begun to be so.

Listen to the dolphins. They may very well be laughing at our suicidal stupidity and hoping for us to become extinct. It is true that earth without humanity would be a paradise for all remaining life forms. Are we ignorant, proud beings in our creator's image the image of Christ? Are we sure? Or are we becoming the image of evil?

Is a class action lawsuit needed to break the backs of institutions that use people like experimental rats as the Germans did in the concentration camps of World War II? Does Islam have valid arguments? Do they have something to teach us?

CHAPTER *Ten*

The Positive 3Cs, 3Gs, 3Ls, 3Rs,
and 3Ts—True Growth

In this chapter, we will get into what it takes to climb up to the summit in order to learn and grow in our everyday life. We will get into the daily testing that all of us are required to endure. Another obvious question would be: why do evil spirits exist? Why are they not locked up now rather than waiting for a later time into the future?

The climb to our summit answers these questions and many more. It is by far the most important choice (3Cs) that we make in our second journey. Yet as mentioned, it could also be the most difficult without the right guidance. It does take a great deal of our energy. We are tested at every level of our soul's climb up. At times, we simply need to stop, take a breathing exercise, and rest. Fatigue does set in with the battles and evils that try to trip us down to stop our ascension. There are times when we just have to vegetate for a few days. The testing could be unbearable, especially at the near top. No, this is not "occupy this or that" like a hangout where no climb itself is ever made.

These tests, at times, involve major setups of near deaths, like drowning, accidents that are not coincidental, relationships both good and bad, vocational calling, being put into a kill-or-be-killed situation, being asked to be a kamikaze for our country, being put into prison after being framed and betrayed, being forced into concentration camps like animals, etc. Yes, you should get the picture by now. We have mentioned some life experiences already.

There is so much corruption in this world. They test us, our family and friends test us, government tests us, teachers test us, our employer tests us—it appears that everyone tests us until our death. Yes, we are tied in with humanity and all forms of life; there is no good escape route from this as long as we are in our second journey. We think we need to be free, just as all of the liberty emblems throughout Europe and America claim. Even wild animals in a trap will bite off their paw to be free. What is to be expected of us?

I do not think that I could be a saint; I am too much a sinner. I know this, I confess this. I read about Saint Joan of Arc, and it depressed me for a few days. How could an innocent teenage girl be set up to fight against the English occupation of France, win decisive battles, only to be betrayed by her own people? Why was she abandoned, accused of witchcraft, and burned alive into her third journey? Why so much suffering? I asked myself. Why become a lamb slaughtered not of her choice? These are tough, the toughest questions that take days to process. Who can bear such testing? Yes, I read that going out of this world by fire is a good sign. It still troubles me. Why be so hard on us? In the Medieval age, a woman even suspected of witchcraft was burned at the stake alive. Today, a few of us women intentionally get involved in witchcraft for a false sense of power. We think that this will help us break through the glass ceiling set up by men. Instead, we find ourselves in a bottomless pit. What ironies. Yes, the devils hide themselves in various forms, even in animals, especially snakes.

Diversions, we will try diversions in an attempt to escape being tested in our climb, but they make matters worse. They only put off what we have to ultimately face. I believe that I mentioned more than once that everyone and everything happens to us in our second journey for a reason. They are all tests for our second journey's climb up to the summit. We attempt to look for ways to cheat the system. Ah, but it is reflected in our chart in our descent. Some of us pray for this evil or that evil, unaware that we may get what we pray for. We do not see that this also is a test for us to see how we deal with the consequences and conditions of our choices. See our sufferings. We are warned to instead pray for a charitable and loving heart, but we do not listen. We want M&M (money and material things) in this metaphysical world!

We have a hard time finding and figuring out the process of the climb. Yes, it is a process, one of ISD (intellectual spiritual design). We avoid it, deny it, try to escape it, but it is always there. It has been since creation. Even J. D. Rockefeller came to realize this.

We all have a story, setups that we need to meditate and reflect on. What is essential is learning how to study and analytically benefit from the testing because that is their purpose. It depends on the test itself. A daily testing requires an end-of-day reflection. An enduring long drawn-out testing needs a yearly evaluation. Take as example Tesla, who invented wireless electricity a long, long time ago. His dream was not implemented due to a lack of investors. Edison and his cronies saw to it. This was his testing. Another example was the Tucker automobile, which was fifty years ahead of its time. The big boys affirmed that it never made it to the assembly line. Testing, my friends, we are all tested.

What are we to study? The study, every study, involves the 3Cs, 3Gs, 3Ls, 3Ss, 3Fs, 3Ds, and 3Rs. Review these. Ask yourself, what do I need to learn? What have I done wrong? What have I omitted doing? Compared to what standards? Whose standards? For example, a crime against humanity without remorse will be followed by a hardship and a more difficult testing until we choose to change. Get it right.

Take a small child lost for a few minutes. That child automatically begins to cry. Their moral imprint is a defensive mechanism that calls out for help quickly and without thought. It is a sign of health. Good parents respond to this cry and comfort the child without hesitation. Uncaring parents may scold the child for crying. As mentioned, our testing begins at an early age. Those of us who had good caring parents should be grateful for the blessings. We are tested with everyone—parents, siblings, relatives, friends, and, all in all, every relationship. The learning curve of childhood—this is what we adults need to relearn and regain.

We have made the hours and minutes (invented in the Middle East by Muslims during their Renaissance) to be used in a time clock to live by. We Americans are the guiltiest of this. It has become our worst stress factor. A hobo may have a better understanding of this, although taking it to the extreme opposite. An example are the hobos in San Diego that use all the park facilities at the taxpayers' expense. The point is, where is a healthy balance? It should be noted that time itself becomes relevant when a person is climbing up to the summit. Making it up to the summit before the second journey ends becomes a passion. Hence, the stress factor is reduced at 9.0.

Even great leaders have failed to comprehend the necessity of the climb. Take as an example the mighty Chin who united the lands of the future China, which was named after him. He was no different from the Pharaohs of Egypt. His main goal was to build a colossal tomb even with Terracotta warriors, as if they could help him in his third journey! He rid the country of healthy Confucius philosophy, only to be poisoned to death before realizing his worthless dream. What ironic 3Cs!

A free soul in the climb to the summit needs none of the foolishness of the metaphysical world. This is acquired healthy good knowledge, grace for the mind. There is no greater freedom from the absurdities of worthless knowledge. Only a soul in union with the light of the Holy Spirit accomplishes truly great objectives. It is unstoppable. We will see in the next chapter that even the death of our body/flesh is a good thing.

It should be remembered, though, that our climb up to the summit takes us through the desert, as in a desert mountain climb. The desert sun is the hottest sunshine. Recall that with our body/flesh put under a magnifying glass of sunshine, impurities burn off. The hottest purifying flame for our soul is the light blue flame of the Holy Spirit.

Take another example, Wolfgang Amadeus Mozart, one of my favorite composers. He was amazingly gifted, a genius, with a father who nurtured his musical talent. What became of all the talent? It was not fully appreciated during his lifetime. He was buried in a massive grave for those that could not afford better. What ironies! I wonder what became of Mozart's soul. Yes, my friends, some of us are greatly gifted with wonderful talents. We spend a lifetime creating wonderful works that humanity appreciates sooner or later, maybe. The question is, what does it do for our soul? The plaques, dedications, and monuments to our name, what do they do for our soul?

It is no different with those of us that are investment savvy. We make fortunes, sometimes with insider trading, to give all imaginable M&M to our family, and yet what have we done with our souls? I could continue with so many examples of this. Remember those that jumped out of the thirtieth floor windows after the great crash of Wall Street in 1929? What ironies! The saints had no regrets, no despair, not even in death. Do we ask ourselves why?

There is such a destructive amount of evil accepted by humanity. Here in Italia and in many countries, organized crime has ruined the lives of so many innocent people due to the 3Cs of a few for M&M. I will write more about this later on a three-way solution to eradicate this evil. As a child, I dreamed of becoming invisible, as in *The Invisible Man* movies of my time produced by Hollywood. I dreamed of becoming invisible and eradicating all of the evil people in the world. I could be forgiven for my innocence at the time. Reality is a true test of who we are, all of us.

Our testing is continually modified, depending on how we accept and deal with it. Take as an example a college professor testing his/her class. If the professor finds out that someone got a hold of the test before testing, the test could be quickly modified. If the test was too easy, the next one could be made more difficult. The testing of our soul, although involving our body/flesh, is for the benefit of our souls. The majority of us see no urgency to our climb, but time and age wait for no one. The point is, without the knowledge from basic light itself, enlightenment from spiritual light could take a long, long time.

The low levels climb up, like a metaphysical climb is not that difficult most of the time. Take the best example of *Gesu*. The earlier years were not that difficult within family. Starting at the age of thirty, the climb became more difficult. At thirty-three, it became the hardest with finally the last steps up Gethsemane bringing death of the body/flesh itself. Yes, the climb changes us from the inside out. The forgiving part takes place in the mid-range of the climb. It has to because without it, we are not able to continue the climb. True knowledge upon knowledge takes place at level upon level of the climb. As mentioned, evils are allowed to occur in our lives for a reason. Take for example the evils in advertising of lies and deceptive messaging. They remind us of the power of media and how evil works through humanity in media. For example, those in media know that if something is advertised enough for a period of time, those receiving the messages come to believe it as being true and acceptable.

In other words, an immoral act could in time become moral without shame or guilt. Advertising calls this liberation as if the messages in themselves help with a liberalization of our soul's heart and mind. This actually puts us into a cage with someone else having the key to keep us locked up and controlled.

The diabolical term, "*Stanno lavoran*" ("They are at work") in Italia is understood as evils are at work. In America, it is considered somewhat nonsense. Without this understanding, the obstacles to the summit are misinterpreted. The students of Saint Basil at Saint Michael's College at the University of Toronto in Ontario, Canada, along with a few other religious colleges, are thought this. These students need to be grateful; they are at an advantage. Even pagan Roman emperor, Marcus Aurelius, having a healthy moral imprint, put a stop to the games in the Coliseum. He wrote a book about 1,800 years ago on the virtues a man should have. The book is in the library even today. The knowledge is available, but the willingness to read it is not. Yes, readings are available, and the Scriptures, the Gospels all help our climb. For teenagers especially, the time period makes the right readings crucial. For those who doubt this, you have not begun your climb. Recall that those involved in Nazi and fascist ideologies tried to kill the climb itself in people with catastrophic

3Cs. Yes, love conquers all false ideologies. Need we be reminded of the 3Ss—stubbornness, stupidity, and sickness—of the soul's heart and mind? Yes, my friends, we are all part Jewish.

A few of us pray to win the lottery as if this will cure all of our ills or help our climb. We suffer from the knowledge of our quiz false answer that unearned income brings with it all sorts of evils. The losers of this phenomenon attest to having this experience. I have to admit that this century has been the most testing for humanity. The world evening news only seems to get worse with each passing day.

Most, if not all, of us need to start the process of our climb with the 3Rs—repentance, reconciliation, and redemption. There is no alternative. I mentioned *Gesu*, who, although an exception to the 3Rs, still made the climb for our sake. Our Blessed Virgin Maria also did not have to make the 3Rs but did make the climb. The apostles and saints all had to be tested in their climb. None of us are different. If our days are just another day, another dollar, we will probably never start or continue our climb. This results in testing of its own. Again, study true nature, not in a zoo where animals are caged but in raw nature. In their true environment, wildlife does what they were created to do by ISD, intellectual spiritual design. Are we any smarter? When we allow ourselves, body/flesh, to be caged, as in prison, who has the key? Our second journey may involve the test of being caged up for a reason. Although in the metaphysical world, it should remind us of possibility of our soul's imprisonment in our second and third journeys of purgatory or worse, hell.

Our soul never tires, but our body/flesh does, hence the reason for a restful night's sleep. A 24-7 schedule is no help. Again, notice wildlife. They sleep whenever, wherever for a reason. If we want to modify anything in our lives, it should be our bad sleeping habits. We need not worry about modifying seeds, especially of humanity. For example, a smart business manager will modify a work schedule hours to where they are most productive and profitable. In business, each day is a competitive battle, people just constantly trying to stay ahead of competition. Those that stand still and do not plan ahead, in time stagnate and lose. It works the same in our climb; we need to think ahead to the next level.

Original humanity in ISD was to live in the body/flesh for a thousand years. This was modified for a good reason; we messed up the plan. Thank goodness, who could withstand a thousand years of testing and climbing? Ever since the modification, humanity has had to count his/her losses. We continue with the same process in losses at around three years of age. The climb to the summit reverses the losses.

I have mentioned that our free will is the key to unlock not only the doors of our soul's tabernacle but also the cage that we have allowed ourselves to be imprisoned in. In our positive 3Cs—choices, consequences, and conditions—we are also able to make the modification of changing the negative past into positive, productive choices. The negatives could kill us, but the positive is what helps our climb.

When we try to force upon ourselves what our soul does not truly desire, we force our descent. There our soul is never happy but filled with discontent and sorrow. Do we hear the right voice? There could be three voices at work all of the time. One voice, the helpful voice, is from our tabernacle. The second and third voices are outside, voices from the good spirits or bad evil spirits of the demons. In our second journey, there is no escape from this, but this is a part of the testing process to help us to climb and grow.

It is up to us. Do we want to bear good fruit that benefits all? Do we want to be fruitless and a waste? Do we want to bear bad fruit only to be cut down and used like firewood? What do we want? Remember, there are no coincidental, freak, or bizarre accidents in life, just events that test us to our core. What is sad is that most of us have to get burned to learn. Worse, we have forgotten how to cry out naturally as a child for help. We should take the ride, It's a Small World, at Disney Land every so often to remind us of our childhood and how wonderful it was or could have been. Creator, created, creative, creativity, only on the 9 plus platform can we appreciate and understand the differences.

What is our story? Do we know? Take as an example the number of women in the world currently suffering from their own spouses, misguided men, and religion. Do we/they know their story? Unknowingly when misguided, men do make a pact with the devil when they mistreat, abuse, and torture women in the name of their Religion. This is a false climb and false enlightenment. We should never assume a comprehensive mentality of the Holy Spirit. We should rather focus on the losses in our life and study our 3Cs and our testing as a result. For example, take a loss/death of a loved one. What is it that we are mourning about? The loss of not having loved them while they were alive and with us? The loss from not being on good terms? Study the losses and the reasons for the losses.

When our body/flesh lacks certain nutrients, for example, vitamin C, it tells us in a craving for additional foods rich in vitamin C. Our soul is the same in the climb to enlightenment. Since the two are one, the soul always needs the body/flesh to succeed in any endeavor

When our pride and ego tell us that we need to be the wealthiest, the most powerful, and the most of just about anything in our metaphysical world, we are listening to the wrong voice. *Quo vadis* (Where are you going)? Our chart is our guide, study it. Recall that our summit path generally takes us through the desert first. The metaphysical desert is symbolic of our soul's desert path. The desert light will show us our soul's true colors when being tested regarding who we are. The desert tells us if we have become too comfortable in our second journey. If so, it reminds us to be stargazers.

Sports teaches us to be team players, but does it teach us to climb to our summit? The rules are different. For example, in our climb up, we see clearly how certain people try to exploit our kindness and generosity. The climb warns us at times to let certain people enter their own desert. As good natural parents allow children to make their own mistakes to learn by, so the Holy Spirit even more so. At times, we need to be abandoned in the desert to learn. Yes, my friends, even our journey to the moon was easier than the climb to our summit. Do not worry about a language barrier; the Holy Spirit recognizes all languages. We just need the willingness to correct, change, and learn.

There was a time when a few people talked about carrying a cross and learning from it. Modern pop culture thinks of this as being ridiculous. Yes, dumbfounded and dumb—sounds familiar? The demons can work on our weaknesses but also our strengths. For example, here in Italia, we tell each other, "*Buon lavoro* (Good work)" in all that you work on. This really means do good deeds. Better yet, your work should be moral work. In America, I only hear of this in mass. What does this tell us? When our strengths are no longer morally correct, they have been corrupted, and they then become weaknesses. An example is the scientists that used their genius strengths of knowledge upon knowledge to help build the ICBMs (intercontinental ballistic missiles) of mass destruction. The same demons are working in North Korea, trying to get them up to speed. It doesn't require a mystic to figure out their intentions. Yes, the devils hide themselves in the world's most fertile arenas.

Demons are like poisonous mosquitoes, one bite, two, three, six, putting a little poison into us, and unless stopped, it could kill us when they swarm and attack us. As we allow this to happen, we condemn ourselves by our 3Cs—choices, consequences, and conditions—without the 3Rs—repentance, reconciliation, and redemption. All of us, even the strongest, are a little like Achilles of past Greek heroes. The point is, it may be in so many other areas of our body and soul than just our heel. Stressful reading, I know, but stress is not all bad when it moves us to climb our summit. A bucket list before we pass away? It depends on what is on the list. Without the 9.0 plus on the list, what purpose does the bucket list serve? Our soul craves to climb our chart—nothing else will suffice, as our soul seeks light.

The natural oxygen decreases in the metaphysical mountain climb, causing us to take small steps in climbing. For our souls, the climbing also requires more oxygen, but the oxygen is that of the Holy Spirit to inflame our spark. The summit is not possible without the right measured oxygen. Unlike a charismatic demon telling us to follow him/her in some worthless quest, the Holy Spirit guides us with what we can handle in our true path and climb. Our needs are known, our demands are supplied as long as we don't quit.

A true guide on the right path will not turn on us like a mad dog in our climb. We could stop for a rest, replenish our energy, and get our bearings of where we are. A false guide tries to speed up wherever he wants to lead us, which is usually a descent. They tell us that there is no need to rest or rethink our direction. The self-righteous tend to be the most dangerous, as in "I know best." It is similar to the Washington, D.C. to Wall Street people who know it all and want our faith, hope, and trust in them. Yes, they are well-dressed, well-groomed with only an external good appearance. Inside, they most often are rotten to the core. A good guide is like a classical music conductor, true to the composer and understood by all music lovers.

A true climb gives us the right combination of tests, trials, hardships, and sacrifices. When accepted, we feel similar to that contentment after a good hard day's work, tired yet satisfied with our progress. This is growing in our climb, unlike an easy false satisfaction that is shallow. Let us look into our chart, what do we see? Recall a day, one of the very few days in our climb, in which evils are kept at bay on the sidelines. Relish it, they're few and far between. They are just a refresher course of the peace available in the Holy Trinity and #10. Again, this is more than becoming a BOC (Born Again Christian). A BOC may have a willing soul to climb, but a weak flesh is a real problem. The anxieties are present in our second thoughts of the path that we are on. Also, notice how trying to reach perfection in our body/flesh leads to the anxieties that we have to rid ourselves of. Rather, wanting to achieve perfection of our soul's heart and mind leads us to peace.

For me, the Roman Catholic Church has all of my needs for the climb. The 3Rs, Eucharist, and sacraments assist with the entire climb. These, as mentioned, are given at no cost to us and are priceless. The only requirement is a little bit of our time. As a five-year-old child getting ready to leave Italia, I remember being told by older kids how lucky I was in that there was gold on the streets of America. What memories, what nonsense for a young child. How we affect others will depend on how we accept and are effected by our peers, friends, and family. Do we know what to accept? Even the demons, without light, are dumbfounded to realize that they have been put to work in tempting and testing humanity. A classic example is Good Friday. Why is it a Good Friday and not a Bad Friday? Consider the 3Cs of all involved. Now consider the final outcome of the entire three days of *Gesu*. I hope that I do not have to explain the resurrection of Christ. The event puts everything into proper perspective concerning evil and humanity. Is the climb worth it? Is love worth it? Is conquering death worth it? You decide.

There are those of us who think the passing of our soul after the death of our body is automatically received into #10, heaven. In thinking and believing this, we are either dumbfounded, ignorant, or plain stupid. I have mentioned that reaching #10 works on a merit system. Stop being deceived otherwise. We can be so gullible. Take for example those of us who are fashion fools. A pair of old worn-out blue jeans with holes in them, which at one time went to Goodwill for the poorest people, has become fashionable at one thousand per cent markup. Yes, there are plenty of buyers.

The shortest distance between two points is a straight line. So it is with our chart from whatever point we are on our chart. A straight vertical lineup is the shortest and fastest way to #9 and #10. The martyred saints may or may not have figured this out. Stressful? It is, but as mentioned, some stress could be healthy for us.

I recall my good-hearted father telling me that the problem with America was that people had too many freedoms. I think back now, a little bit more mature, and have come to realize what he was trying to tell me. It is true. America does have the most freedoms in the world. The problem is that so often they are abused. Again, a great example is the formation of a new church. Anyone can start up a new church, even one that has a climb up to aliens. It is tax-free and has no rules, regulations, or standards to follow. It has no laws, no teeth needed to enforce anything on anyone. This is a setup for a perfect storm filled with darkness.

How many people have been burned in the past and currently are unknowingly being burned by a false climb? For example, 100 percent of women really want happiness in life. About 1 percent may find it in a marriage to a religious vocation. But 99 percent will get married to a man and hopefully have happiness in the marriage. What only a tiny percent come to realize is that the happiest time is when they are pregnant and barefooted. I will get a lot of angry mail back regarding this remark, but the women living in faith and climbing to their summit know this is a fact. It is called EI (emotional intelligence).

A sinner, male or female, after the 3Rs and climbing, sees all sin for what it is. In not quitting the climb, all of the mysteries, good and evil, are gradually revealed. The reconciliation of our soul to the Holy Spirit in the Holy Trinity is the most essential part of our climb. Without this, we are like a plant that takes in nutrients, water, and sunlight only to waste it. It is hard dealing with evil angels in daily life, but I believe that there are good angels near us to call upon. I also believe that if we were allowed to, we would see millions of angels at work all around us, maintaining an acceptable balance between good and evil for the benefit of humanity, the animal kingdom, and for all plant life to grow and flourish. Do we really need to see this? I do not think so. A glimpse of heaven, purgatory, and hell by a few witnesses should suffice. Again, I believe that the testing of our body/flesh in our climb is for our soul. The two, being one, go hand in hand in our climb. It is normal to feel sadness and sorrow when receiving certain testing, especially being abandoned to deal with them, but only the Holy Spirit knows what we need in our climb in order to grow.

For those of us in the gutters and sewers of life, only when we get sick and tired of our condition may we begin to climb up out of our position. Yes, a pain in our body/flesh may hurt us, but a pain in our soul is far more painful and fatalistic. For example, in going from natural light into darkness quickly with our natural eyes, notice that we lose our bearing. Our eyes search for natural light, any light, to find our position. In coming out of darkness quickly, it is even more difficult for our eyes to adjust to the natural light. It is similar with the eyes of our soul changing to and from evil's darkness and back into spiritual light. Changing back hurts our eyes for a few seconds, but slowly we see things for what they are.

The descent of our soul into darkness is normally due to blank ignorance or blank stupidity. Study your chart and try to recall what caused the drops and climb. Now notice that the lower we dropped, the dumber and crazier the things that we did. But we cannot see any of this without the climb itself.

When we make the Ten Commandments the constitution of our soul's heart and mind, the Gospels will do the rest in our climb up to the summit. Some of us refuse and decide to go contrary to this. Again, the example of a woman deciding to go with witchcraft for a higher knowledge or power turns out to be a blank stupid pussy. There is no good knowledge or good power in darkness.

The longer that we languish in darkness, the more time we waste for our 3Rs to occur and start our climb. An example is a married couple suffering from infidelity by either or both. As long as each spends languishing in infidelity without the 3Rs, the greater the chance of divorce. Mussolini is a classic case. In the end, both he, a married man with children, and his adulterous mistress were shot to death. Mussolini was hung head down like a pig just slaughtered. He was another fool in history believing in himself (pride and ego) and false ideologies.

Our brain should serve our soul's mind, but most importantly, our mind must listen to our soul's heart. When this fails to happen, we condemn ourselves. Condemnation is evil, having penetrated our soul's mind within our brain but not necessarily our soul's heart. This is one of the reasons why a few of us enter a monastery to reduce the risks while in prayer for ourselves and others.

A few of us think that we could hijack our way to 9.0, and even #10. This is a grave mistake. We cannot force a climb up to the summit. We can force our soul's descent, though. This is what happens when we kill the body/flesh. There are many ways to die in this world, yet when we choose to die siding with evil, it turns out to be a terrible death. We do not know better than our creator the right way, place, and time. This is true for all of us, the privileged and unprivileged. Reaching the summit is a logical progression of events and relationships. We simply need to let them take place in time. This is not to say that we should give in to evils, as we should always be vigilant and fight a good fight against all evils. But at times, they could be beyond our control.

Now we are trying to figure a way to erase our bad memories, mistakes, and regrets. We are too stupid to realize the importance of having what we have stored in mind and brain. This is the senseless becoming the norm. Not only that, what makes us think that we can erase what is stored in our soul's mind? We are getting into dangerous territory.

Another mistake is sulking in anger and self-pity.

This only compounds our testing, preventing our climb. Thomas Merton, a monk of the last century, was one of my favorite writers. He was from a different generation, but what he wrote concerning his faith and conversion to the Roman Catholic Church holds true to this day. He was a gifted writer that went into his third journey by fire (electrical shock). A coincidence? Think again. One man made a difference with his books in acceptance of his calling and climbing. This is prayer and charity for humanity. Imagine with the multiplier effect what is possible.

We have our customs, traditions, and superstitions. How do they serve us in our climb? Do they help us out, or are they obstacles to overcome? What were the results of those who journeyed before us? Do we know the truth? Is Christianity today what it was two thousand years ago? Five hundred years ago? The last century? Does Pasqua, Easter, and Pentecost change? Does they evolve? Do we care to know? When did we start to descend? Are we hurting? When will we resume our climb? These are questions to meditate on.

We fill our lives with distractions, distancing ourselves from our Church, the Holy Spirit, and our climb. We become like all man-made art that is somewhat really dead art, not living art as in all living matter of this world in light. As Reggie Jackson, baseball Hall of Fame star, was quoted saying, "We could give thanks in gratitude from the moment that we wake up till the moment we go to bed again, and we will run out of time before giving thanks for all." This is an example of climbing, my friends.

Note that a moral army general will defend the life and liberty of humanity. At the same time, he will try his best to end the conflict or war as quickly as possible in order to reduce the death and destruction of war. Examples are Douglas McArthur and Patton, along with a few others. This also is good knowledge of climbing up to the summit. Now notice what the outcome was in history when this was the case. Evil has less chance to penetrate a man who lives his faith and climbs his summit. Study the good generals in history who respected humanity and religions to see the outcomes of peace and prosperity. A coincidence? Think again. Now study history and the generals that were immoral, wanting to win at all costs. The outcomes hold true throughout history. Our precious freedoms of body/flesh and soul came at a heavy cost to those who cared to climb and were tested in war.

Our true ID is determined by where we are on our chart. This reflects our actions and deeds. Is our ID one of goodness or evil? Often, other people know better than we do. From childhood to death, this is always the case. "*Tutto passa*," I remember my father saying this often, especially when nearing his death. This was as if to say our time here will pass and end, that it is only a matter of time. It was a reminder for all of us that the testing of trials and hardships could end at any moment. Will we be ready?

Ever find out that something that you were doing a certain way for years and years turned out to be the wrong way? We all have encountered this, I think. It makes us feel dumb, stupid, for not realizing what was obviously a better way. This is what the climb to the summit does for our soul's heart and mind. In this, all of our priorities change for the better. This differs from pop culture phrases like "Do your own thing," whatever it may be, or "If it feels good, do it," a way of thinking only related to the body/flesh. Or how about "Try anything once." Hmm, try asphyxiation, suicide once? Or "Anything goes," hmm, a life without any moral standards? This is where we are in America and many so-called developed countries. Add it all up, and you could hear a flushing sound for souls.

Now consider the phrases in sports: "sacrifice for winning," "passion for the game," "*sportivo*, sportive," guidelines for fairness, no cheating and teamwork. This is what makes great men and women in their climb up to the summit. For better words, we do NOT "throw caution to the wind" in hoping for positive results. Those of us that climb know of the downdraft that is possible at any time, which could plunge us down dangerously. We cannot control evils by ourselves. No matter how high we climb up our summit, we are always dependent on a higher spiritual force. In thinking we can go it alone, we are playing with fire. Again, we should not fight ISD, intellectual spiritual design. We need to know our limitations. The best possible example is the knowledge of the only name by which evil demons can be expelled. Meditate on this for a while.

There is an abundance of good knowledge in our climb, so much so that it could exhaust us mentally and emotionally. This is good exhaustion that enriches our soul. This is true liberalization from the evils of the world. Take for example the women in the Middle East. What liberalization have we experienced in history? Millions of us Muslim women are hurting.

Watch the news to see our 3Cs—choices, consequences, and conditions—in ourselves and the men in our lives. In the twenty-first century, we are still in servant and subservient status. The men are still trying to keep the status quo of superiority. It is a form of enslavement while they pray five times a day to Allah, facing Mecca. In our climb, it is not a test when we get our way but rather when we do not get our way. Who would pray for a difficult testing? What religion encourages brutality, rape, and beating women to death? This is love between a man and a woman? This is observing the Ten Commandments? This is the Song of Songs in the Old Testament? I think not. I also think that time does not heal everything. Time doesn't heal infidelity, unfaithfulness, and distrust. Time doesn't heal the betrayal of love and a soul's broken heart. Our soul may not get tired, but our body and brain do.

We cannot legislate love, charity, or the climb. It would fail the same way that we tried to legislate against racism, prejudice, and discrimination. The climb teaches us this. It teaches us to do some soul searching. If we pass away in our sleep, will we have those precious three minutes to figure things out? Or will the devils come after us with a vengeance? Sleep on it? Ah, we live for and in the moment, but we know not our moment to pass into our third journey. We live in the moments of gratifications of sex clubs, of power, of reputation, of aggressiveness—but to what end? Or should I say, what drop? Yes, it's enticing and easy to succumb to the pleasures of the body/flesh until they lose all meaning. People tell us to "put our heart into this or that," but what if we have no heart? There it is: reality. We hear,

"Don't sleep your life away," but what if we have no life? This is "falling from grace," falling on our chart after losing light.

It is work, my friends, just trying to make the right moral decisions each day. We seem to be living in a time when being morally right tends to be thought of as being an idiot. Evils exist everywhere, taunting us, laughing at us as if we are out of it, out of the circle, that huge corral of humanity that has been rounded up like cattle to be sold at auction. A healthy conscience is invaluable, and we come to appreciate it not in our descent but in our climb up to the summit. If only we could stop being treated like animals. For example, test after test, countless tests have been done comparing us to monkeys—monkeys that practice incest within their clan. Is this what we children in the image of *Dio* are comparable with? Humanity that built the amphitheatre, the Acropolis, the Parthenon, the Library of Alessandria, the Hagia Sophia, the Colossus of Rhodes, the Aquaculture, the Empire State Building, the Golden Gate Bridge, etc, compared to monkeys? Hmm, no wonder we have the problems that we have. A close DNA is NOT 100 percent DNA similarity. I recall a few imbeciles in the last century attempting to raise baby chimpanzees in a similar way to raising human babies, as if duplicating the process would attain the same results. I often wonder what became of those imbeciles and their grownup monkeys. Perhaps they are all in college working on their PhDs?

Our soul's heart and mind hunger for healing knowledge—knowledge that is pure and clean, not garbage. We hunger for knowledge of light and the mysteries of light. Only in our climb could our anguish be relieved. A test in our climb up could be one second, one minute, one day, one week, one month, one year, or thirty years. We do not know the results until the testing is over, and we can analyze if we moved up a notch, stood still, or fell on our chart. At times, all we could do is to be quiet and still till the test itself is over. Sometimes we want to just pray for the testing to pass, but it is not entirely up to us. I recall that as soon as I became an altar boy, the testing started in earnest, even if I didn't know it at the time. In hindsight, from the summit, our failures and successes are so visible.

A sign of our failures is the degree of corruption at all levels of society. We witness all sorts of corruption in the news daily. Most of it is blue collar, but the hidden corruption, the white collar corruption, is perhaps up to a thousand times more so. Also, behind white collar corruption are serious crimes against business, city, state, federal institutions, the economy, and humanity. This has to be accounted for sooner or later. For example, look at the portraits of past monarchies. How often do you see a smile on any of the faces? Famous paintings worth a fortune with centuries of smile-less portraits of leeches that sucked the very life out of peasants they ruled over. The chosen by *Dio* to rule over humanity?

The biggest problem in modern times is that white and blue collar criminals are combined. Here in Italia, almost no day passes without a tiny fraction of all of the corruption being exposed. The joke is in how it is dealt with. For example, it has taken almost a hundred years to learn how to deal with a part of the organized criminals, the M&M (money and material) things. We Italians could be slow at times, not only with eating good food but also learning from other countries regarding how to improve what ails us. Maybe we cannot think after eating too much. Take as an example Al Capone that tried to rule Chicago in the last century. Why did it take us until just recently to learn the same method that put Al Capone out of business and behind bars? The tentacles of evil are far-reaching, as in the political and judicial systems that need to be purged. In the 1920s, this was well recognized by Mori Cesare as appointed Sicily Prefect (The Iron Prefect) as an iron hand. Sounds familiar? The iron hand/claw of law and order, as in Caesar and the talons of the eagle? Mori wrote two books on how to deal with organized criminals. Does anyone care to read them?

Organized crime requires a three-pronged approach in which the criminals are kicked in the balls each time. This handling of them with cotton gloves is idiotic. Mussolini gave organized criminals an option—get out of the country, or the black shirts are coming after you with clubs and guns. No attorneys, no judges, and no court trials at the expense of the taxpayers. A dictatorship with strong men could accomplish this. This is what makes a charismatic personality inviting, yet in time, it also could become corrupted and become a worse problem, same as Mussolini and the fascists. He got the job done, even though most of it got shipped out to other countries. But think for a minute, if every country did the same, where would the criminals go? A true democracy works better unless those making and enforcing the laws get bought off. Study Mori on how to deal with the buyouts fast and effectively by immediately investigating them and dealing with them harshly.

To be effective, the first step for all associated criminals is to freeze all of the assets of the entire clan at all levels. This is the first kick that hurts because they have no M&M to work with. They cannot make more payoffs, no more favors, the 3Ns—nothing, *niente*, nada—isolate them. The second step/kick should be to take away most of their civil liberties. Criminals don't deserve civil liberties. This hurts them in all of their business dealings and bank accounts. In the worst cases that involve murder of the innocent, throw the entire clan into the cells of cold darkness or, at least, for the less guilty, the cold dark streets. The third step/kick is to create Church rules, laws to take away their religious graces without remorse, without the 3Rs—repentance, reconciliation, and redemption—of atonement. Graces also should be lost to them. This would include most of the sacraments of the Church. I know that this sounds harsh, and maybe even naïve, but think again. The needs of our souls are more serious than that of our body/flesh. Those of the body/flesh are minor basic needs. Those of the soul are much more serious and long-lasting. Take as a perfect example the murder of priest, Don Pippin Diana, of Italy. He was murdered because he put this rule (not giving known criminals certain sacraments) into practice in his church. He knew the criminals, as most are known even to priests. The Roman Catholic Church should seriously consider creating and putting these rules, laws, into effect in all dioceses in the world. It would work because it kicks criminals in the balls of their soul where it hurts the most. Criminals cannot control this. They can't force or buy the sacraments. The thought of losing most of the sacraments does put a healthy fear into their soul's heart and mind where it matters most. Think for a moment, no Church sacraments in marriage, in last rites, in death, in a funeral or cemetery. Worst-case scenario? There is always the tool of excommunication for criminals with the unwillingness of free will to accept the 3Rs.

As Christians, it is our duty to help in the process of justice. *Dio* always comes through 100 percent of the time in having the loss of grace/light in a criminal's soul take place. But this is a slow process. We are a responsible part of the creative and judicial process in humanity. We are also a part of the maintenance process. When we fail to accept and act, we have ourselves to blame for the 3Cs, choices with consequences and conditions getting worse. They do get worse, my friends, just like a cancer in a patient that isn't burned out. Study history, it never fails to happen.

The motto for American elected officials, although unspoken, is "Steal as much as possible, just don't get caught." I would estimate that 60 percent of all officials practice this behind closed doors. In Italia, the motto is "If you don't steal as much as possible in the time you are in office, you're a fool." This is also unspoken but taken for granted. I would estimate that in Italia, it's as high as 80 percent of all elected officials. What happens when this goes uncorrected? We become another Mexico. Our law and order, economy, money value, gradually all go to hell. Hence, it is a degradation that affects all of us. This is what makes it the responsibility of each and every one of us to be a part of the correcting process. Yes, this is climbing up to the summit as well.

Being grateful in charity and love is only a part of the climbing process. When a part of humanity is suffering from injustices, it affects us all. Think of all the innocent lives lost due to corruption. Think of all the families, the children affected by institutional and organizational criminals. Any more questions as to who, what, when, where, and why? Yes, my friends, next time you meditate and pray, reflect on this. Science tells us that we benefit, body and soul, from meditation and prayer for ourselves. At the same time, we also benefit from helping those families who have lost family income and earnings from organized criminals. They need to be compensated from the recovered stolen assets and monies of criminals.

Do we have the willingness? We know the problems, the issues involved. What else do we need? The 3Cs are ours, yes, they affect all facets of our lives but also those of others. Are we more concerned only about ourselves? Take as an example the dentist who doesn't speak out to clients about the causes of tooth decay from, let us say, white refined sugar products. If the dentist is more concerned about office visits and his/her bottom line on the books, there may be silence about preventative care.

Those of us that have climbed to the summit are able to clearly see what we had to endure. We will not judge anyone for their unwillingness to correct injustices and climb. We have been there ourselves. At the same time, we will not remain silent. This would only condone what we already know to be wrong. Pacifism without a voice compounds any existing problem. Who else will speak out? At the same time, giving testimony as a witness doesn't necessarily move the free will of others. Yes, we human beings have our weaknesses that are exploited by demons daily. It remains so throughout our second journey.

Take another example that affects everyone: the way that humanity is polluting our oceans with plastics, garbage, hazardous chemicals, etc. We are the educated, green, scientific community? Clean oceans are vital for survival of all sea life. They are vital for our survival as well. Not caring is a sign of disregard and disrespect that are rooted in the disregard and disrespect of our soul and the souls of others. All disregard and disrespect are rooted in the loss of light of the Holy Spirit.

With a willingness, we could easily use the clean oceans to turn our huge deserts like the Sahara in Africa into millions of productive acres. Again, it doesn't take a mathematician to realize that our earth, which is two-thirds saltwater, surface can go through desalination. Expensive, yes, but how many hundreds of billions of dollars have we spent on the wars of destruction in the past fifty years? The world is in need of positive creativity for jobs and sustainability, not jobs in death and destruction. It should be noted that Cleopatra, the last of the Pharaohs did not build a wasteful tomb as her predecessors. The country was in recession, and people were in need of jobs and income. After centuries of wasting resources, the days of the Pharaohs were coming to an end. Caesar Augustus and the legions of Rome would put the final nail into their mummified coffins. Where has Egypt been for the past 1,500 years? Where is Egypt today? One of the quiz questions involves waste, all forms of waste. So much for self-proclaimed human gods. So much for fools as Mark Anthony, who became trapped in a widow spider's web. A moral lesson for humanity? Meditate on it.

What is the moral of this epic triangular story? Cleopatra, a young sexual creature, started off by seducing Julio Caesar, a married man. She had his child and started to devise a plan for her son to inherit power—as if the Roman senators were going to be fooled by such a scheme. In a way, she is partially to blame for the assassins murdering Caesar on the senate floor. The killings of the rounded-up assassins only brought more chaos and bloodshed. Next, her seductive charms polluted the mind of Mark Anthony, also a married man. Again, she devised a plan for her first son to take control and power from the Eastern Roman Empire. Again, she infuriated the Roman senate. The final outcome of the triangular affairs? Another Roman civil war, Romans killing Romans with blood being spilled and the suicide of Mark Anthony and Cleopatra after their defeat by Roman general, Agrippa. One immoral-woman-turned-bitch helped ruin the lives of so many people, Roman and Egyptian. A moral lesson for women? Meditate on it.

What has changed in modern times? We still have triangular immoral relationships of lust that so often end in murder and suicide. Infidelity and desertion of marriage and family have become the norm in modern times. Yes, my friends, the 3Cs, 3Gs, 3Ls, 3Ss, 3Fs, 3Ds, and 3Rs are just as active today as two thousand years ago, but the 3Rs are less utilized. It is true that love never dies, but we are mere mortals that have difficulty forgiving and compromising the immoral behavior of others, even if we were such ourselves.

Immorality is such a destructive issue as we have or should have learned. It is a negative choice, one that angers the Holy Spirit and gives us the hardest tests of corrections. It leads to tears of sorrow instead of tears of gratitude in joy. We could take long showers, baths, saunas and sit in a Jacuzzi all day; still it does not clean the soul. All of the threes of words are so important, as they tell us and give us a description of who, what, when, where, and why for our soul's position on our chart. Let us review them again. In this chapter, we are reviewing the lower ranges of our chart. In the next chapter, we will focus more on the upper range.

The 3Cs—choices, consequences, and conditions—are of our free will to make in life. When positive—for example, the vaccine for polio—the consequences and conditions are wonderful for everyone involved. When the choices are negative—for example, Roman Emperor Nero blaming the Christian community for starting the fire that burned down half of Rome—it could be devastating. Again, study history. This was the beginning of Christians being used as scapegoats and being burned alive at the stake. After the Colosseum was built by Roman Emperor Vespasian, the choices of subsequent emperors put on trial all of the Christian community. History is filled with examples of both positive and negative choices that affect ourselves and others.

Here is a classic example of a famous figure in history that includes all of the word combinations. The positive 3Cs, choices, bring the 3Gs of graces, gratitude, and graciousness and also the 3Ls—light, love, and life—as witnessed by King David of Israel thousands of years ago. The negative choices with the 3Fs—foolishness, fault, and failure—also by King David brought disgrace and the loss of light. The choice by King David to have an adulterous affair with a married woman, Bathsheba, was definitely a negative choice. Having her husband put on the front lines of war, causing his death, was even worse, the 3Ds—disgrace, despair, and possible death. The testing of trials, the death of his son with Bathsheba and family problems that followed brought sadness and sorrow. This made King David realize his 3Ss—stubbornness, stupidity, and sickness. This gave him the choice of the 3Rs—repentance, reconciliation, and redemption. This is the process, my friends. It is today as it was three thousand years ago. In our climb, we see the reasons for the process in our soul's loss of light. We were created to be children of light, our true ID, not children of darkness with a false ID.

Again, a modern example of this is the LGBT community. This is a false ID. Notice how this community has tried to put the straight (heterosexual) community on the defensive with propaganda of being homophobic for speaking out on their immoral behavior. A true ID always rejects a false ID. This is not discrimination. This is the right of expression of beliefs. An example would be a spoiled child's bad behavior needing correction. A verbal lashing could be beneficial when not abusive. Everyone has a moral imprint to become who they were created to be by ISD, intellectual spiritual design.

My own second journey has endured the best of times with the positive 3Cs that brought joy and happiness of the 3Gs and 3Ls. It also has, with the negative 3Cs brought the hardest, worst of times with the 3Fs—foolishness, fault, and failure—due to the 3Ss—stubbornness, stupidity, and sickness. The 3Fs took me into the arid desert once for the 3Rs—repentance, reconciliation, and redemption—to occur. Due to the 3Ss—stubbornness, stupidity, and sickness—the next time it took me into a sea fog, lost, for the 3Rs to occur. Thank goodness, without this, the 3Ds—disgrace, despair, and possible death—take hold on a soul. My soul has been in a safe home only to become lost in a descent and a desert. I have also been in a safe harbor only to become lost at sea in a storm. I have been in a comfortable position and in difficult climbs to the summit. My friends, there is no better place than the summit of 9.0 except 9.0 plus and finally, I believe, #10. It has taken me around the metaphysical world into foreign countries with different cultures and religions. All in all, I am forever grateful for the blessings and education of heart, mind, and soul. I have met good people that influenced me in a healthy way and vice versa. I also met bad people that tried to influence me in an unhealthy way. But this book is about you, the reader, and your second journey. As a refresher, if you haven't already taken action of *voluntia* (voluntarily, willingness) to express your free will at this point, now should be the time.

Think back on your good years with family and friends, happiness, and joys. Recall your hardest and worst of times with sadness and sorrow, loneliness and isolation. Think of the days of light and the dark days. Remember the times chasing after illusions only to be lost at sea and not knowing north, south, west, or east without a compass or being able to get a position by the stars. Now try to recall your 3Cs, 3Gs, 3Ls, 3Fs, 3Ss, 3Ds, and hopefully 3Rs. Depending on your age, family, friends, education, religious affiliations, and country you were raised in, the above will vary. The climb will also vary but will still be a climb. The testing will vary depending on who you are becoming or have become depending on your 3Cs.

Recall that grace is a blessing, a gift for our soul from light, the light of the Holy Spirit. Recall your soul's heart tabernacle doors and spark within that sanctuary. Remember that our spark needs oxygen to inflame our spark for our soul. Learn to listen to your inner voice, the voice of good conscience in your vocation, profession, and role in society. Remember that our true purpose is the spiritual knowledge for our soul. It is in direct relationship with the climb up on our chart. Through acts of love and charity, the climb starts. Yet the higher the climb, the greater the responsibility. Your chart is your second journey and only lasts for so long in this world. Recall that the only healthy fear is the fear of losing light. Our soul never rests or has peace without light.

Take the example of Marilyn Monroe. She is perhaps the best example for young women of who not to become. True, she became an icon of sexuality, Hollywood success (a false success), fortune, and fame. She pleased the American troops in Korea, the politicians, producers, directors, and friends. Now read the facts about her second journey. She was from a broken family, experienced three broken marriages, and mentally, emotionally burned out at the height of her career. She was exploited by almost everyone around her and could not figure out who sincerely loved her. She turned to psychiatric therapy to someone who was supposed to be ethically safe. She instead was only sexually used and abused. What were those doctor-patient moral ethics of conduct again? According to researchers, there is a high probability of her having been murdered for her diary and silence. Sounds familiar?

Marilyn Monroe is still famous and still making money for others. She is what many young women aspire to be. Yet again, study the negative 3Cs, 3Fs, 3Ss, and 3Ds of her life. She became a tragic figure without the positive 3Cs, 3Gs, 3Ls, and 3Rs. History is repeatedly warning us women, but are we listening? In an SOS, it is customary to save women and children first. Children are understandable, but why women? Why not men before women? There was a time when men knew how to be men, and women appreciated it. In role swapping, this is no longer the case.

In America and most of the so-called developed countries, we have developed false concepts of manhood, womanhood, success, failure, family, happiness, and even death. We have put aside foolishly the needs of our soul based on false prescribed truths. How do we make up for lost light? This is what we should be asking ourselves. Study your chart and ask yourself: who, what caused you to be in your chart position and condition and when, where, and why? It always comes down to a loss of listening and communication. Listening to our inner voice, conscience/communication, and prayer with the Holy Spirit. The 3Rs are an essential part of our climb that needs to be realized. Without this, we remain in our position or keep descending. It is a maddening cyclone that pulls us into insanity.

Study the testing you are given. Embrace and learn from it. This is climbing. Each test is given for a reason, so find out the reason. It may be for the pride and ego, humility, a correction of some kind. A few tests are obvious—for example, physical handicaps. All require meditation and prayer. Some are emotional, some mental—all are related to our soul's purpose, all are for one. There are literally thousands of tests at every stage of life. From family and friends to teachers and employers, to religious guides, we are always being tested. All too often we bring the tests upon ourselves. How else are we to learn and grow? We could easily become inundated at times and need to simply stop everything, stop the time clock, and get off the merry-go-round. We need to study and see the participants in our lives. Why are they there? What is their purpose in our life?

The Lord's Prayer, sung in unison, in high mass in Italian is wonderful to the ears. The point is, we are all in need of sanctuary at times. It is a small yet absolute necessity of our lives. The overall Roman Catholic Church mass reminds us of our 3Rs. It reminds us of the beggars' banquet for sustenance. The "Ave Maria" sung in

Latin is living art. The twelve key last words, "Pray for us sinners now and at the hour of our death," remind us of who we are. It reminds us that we are not alone and that grace, the 3Gs, helps our climb. The Gregorian chants remind us of a true charitable life in gratitude and humility.

There currently exists a huge amount of spam in communication and not just in technology but overall communication in humanity. This is the result of people worldwide putting faith, hope, and trust in faithless, hopeless, and untrustworthy people and their false ideologues and religions. All of the true answers to what, when, where, who, and why are in the approved gospels of the Roman Catholic Church. They have been there for centuries. Humanity, with our science and technology, does not change this. The Gospels are not for the changing, like changing a failed constitution. They are a road map for our climb up to the summit. Alongside is our Blessed Virgin Maria, the angels, and the saints, and the 9.0 plus is not only possible but doable.

Truth, as the Gospels are, never has to prove themselves. Yes, there are scoundrels among us that try to use the Gospels to exploit people, but if we are able to chart them from the quiz questions, we will see them for who they are. We can, to some degree, do this, at least enough to position them. If we reflect on the what, when, where, and why of who people were based on their past and present, we can begin to see the persons in possibly a different light if they have not climbed their summit. Sex, M&M, and power are the three major tests of humanity. How these three are handled truly defines a person. All is fair in love, profits, and war? Within which standards? Whose standards? Not divine standards.

For example, we may know a few of their tests—let us say marital fidelity. The serious failures are obvious and drop people quickly on their chart. They cannot deny this. This has to do with faith, hope, and trust. Without the correct values and virtues, what is a person, any person? Many notable famous figures in history, after I read their biography, made me wonder if they only deceived the public with an artificial image of goodness. When people are not climbing to their summit, they often have excuses for not doing so.

They fool some but never everyone. At times, the reasons for not exercising their free will in a positive way, accepting their test and being proactive, may not surface until after their death of the body/flesh. Stalin of the imploded Soviet Union is another classic example. Although he made the right decision in joining the Allied Forces in World War II, his real hidden intentions surfaced immediately after the end of World War II. Study his history. Here was a man responsible for the deaths of up to twenty-five million people who did not or refused to see things his way. It took some time, but when the truth surfaced, as it eventually does, he was seen in a different light. The Russian people, finding out the truth, tried to wipe his name off of Russian history books or keep him as a footnote—as if this was going to change what had already transpired.

Again, all testing is for the soul's future, even though and while the soul is in the body/flesh. Just as an education from K through a PhD is in institutions through the physical brain, the mind is what needs and benefits from the knowledge. The diplomas, degrees are just byproducts. The careers and compensations are but rewards for the hard work. The future of the mind within the soul is all that is truly relevant.

Few people, just a tiny fraction of humanity, are willing to accept the process of the climb to the summit. It requires testing, humility, charity, forgiveness, and love. In most of humanity, this is in short supply and for reasons already discussed. The majority of us will study the climb and say, "Forget about it." A few of us will start the climb only to stop at a comfortable level and establish a home base camp. At this point, we say enough "knowledge and enlightenment," sort of like a person who learns to read and write and thinks it is enough. But when is enough, enough? This is like asking when we should stop acquiring good knowledge.

A good barometer would be asking a monk, possibly a living saint, when to stop climbing up to the summit and 9.0 plus. He would have a hearty laugh with us and at us. "Poor soul" would be running through his mind. It is the process that confounds people. Why, why this process, we ask? We question divine providence, we question ISD, intellectual spiritual design. We are not much different than the Hebrew people giving Moses a hard time with all of the questioning and complaining. Some of the biggest stumbling blocks are religions themselves, the ones that claim an easier way.

To be blunt, some of us need a whack over the head with a two-by-four to wake up or be struck by lightning. We could all be the 3Ss as the Jewish people. We could take all of our diplomas and degrees and use them as toilet paper if they are not helping us with our climbing. The final graph of our soul's chart is the only true purpose of our existence. What is your current position? Notice the graphics outside and inside of this book. They are reminders!

We admire a conductor that attempts with the rest of the orchestra to perform a piece as perfect as humanly possible, the same with the Olympian at the world games. Yet we are afraid of doing this for our soul and our soul's survival? What irony of ironies. Sleeping problems? True peace requires no sleeping pills. In China, Chairman Mao's dependence was well recognized and recorded. Why? Was he always afraid of being assassinated? Does a healthy moral imprint, conscience need sleeping pills for the body/flesh? Are not the two, body/flesh and soul, one?

Notice that our earth is never completely in darkness, without light. The sun is always shining somewhere on earth. Even when our time zone is in darkness, the sun's reflection off the moon and the stars' light are always there, as if to say, "I, Light, am always here. Now go to sleep." Being conscious of a healthy conscience, we can sleep without sleeping pills or tranquilizing medication. A soul climbing up to the summit is conscious of an acquired healthy conscience. Yes, good and bad spirits can and do enter our dreams, causing us nightmares, sleepwalking, etc. Do medications shut down our conscience? Why do we wake up remembering only a few seconds of our dream? It's a lot of mysteries, but we have enough to deal with in being awake consciously with our 3Cs.

There is currently research of mind-to-mind communication in humanity. Hmm, as in the soul's mind communications with the Holy Spirit? Now let us researchers try this process, brain to brain, when the soul's mind has vacated the brain as in out-of-body experiences. What are the results?

The answers to the quiz questions are from the conditions of our free will's choices, 3Cs, negative or positive. The condition of our soul is based on our 3Cs positivity or negativity in relationship to the Ten Commandments and the Gospels. There are no higher standards. Study your chart, as there is a timeline and limit for each of us. The horizontal baseline of our chart is the number of years that our body/flesh has in our second journey. We have a little control over this but do not fully control it. It reminds me of Genghis Khan of Mongolia, bringing in a famous sage to tell him how to further his life span. The sage said, "I cannot help you with that!" No, even the mighty warrior, Genghis Khan, another proclaimed man god, had a baseline measured in years.

At times, wealth and power, especially when inherited (unearned), another quiz question, could hurt us in our climb up to the summit. Unknowingly, the wealth turns us into pack mules when we attempt to climb. This is the reason that most of us, the wealthiest people, never attempt to climb. We stay at ground zero. A classic example of a person who escaped this was Saint Francis of Assisi, who, unloading all of the weight off his shoulders, was able to climb to 9.0 plus, and I believe the 3Ts—*tiramisu*, transformation, and transfiguration. You might say that he removed the yoke and became free to climb. This, in modern times, appears to be laughable. Yet take as an example someone whose boat is in a storm, taking on water and sinking. What M&M is worth the weight if it's causing the sinking? The 3Ns—nothing, *niente*, nada—even more so if the M&M was stolen in criminal activity. There is no escape from the injustices of our soul except for the climb that involves the 3Rs.

All of us, being mere mortals, will question our climb at each level, especially when feeling fatigue. Doubts will enter our mind, this is normal. Only grace from faithfulness, vigilance, and perseverance can strengthen our resolve. What is being asked of us? It becomes ever more important to keep the tabernacle doors open and listen. Not only that, what do we do once at the summit? We will cover this more in the next chapter.

What is wisdom? A good question to ask whom? A college professor? A monk? An elderly ninety-year-old? Wisdom of the metaphysical? What is that without the wisdom of our soul's heart and mind, of light, love, and life? The climb gives us the true answers we need for ourselves. They must be experienced and not just be heard from others. It would be similar to reading or listening to the Song of Songs without the experience from our spouse and lover. This is what the herd mentality does—it reads and hears but does not experience. As Saint Pope John Paul II is quoted as saying, "It is hard climbing, but even harder going back." *Gesu* spent forty days in the desert being tested. He was put on a fast track of three years to accomplish his mission, from the age of thirty to thirty-three. His climb was a vertical climb—brief but still vertical. The Gospels are wisdom for our soul, my friends.

We know that when a person physically has been in darkness for a long period of time, being brought into light requires a blindfold in order to allow a slow gradual adjustment. The light of the Holy Spirit works the same way for our soul's eyes. It takes time. It is better not to jump to conclusions, judge, or ask for instant responses and explanations. Just as in school homework and assignments, at times we have to take a break, get some fresh air, and digest it all before getting back to our project. Giving our mind a break will help our mind gain clarity. As a freshman, it is a long way to graduation, but one semester, quarter at a time, gets us there. The same holds true for our soul's climb.

Without the International Date Line, what is time?

We have set up so many boundaries for ourselves, for our metaphysical body/flesh, but what of our soul's climb? Do we need mystics to remind us? A sage? A saint? We need to experience the mysteries of the climb ourselves, become a mystic. Recall that the so-called barbarians and Genghis Khan of Mongolia wanted trade and peace with Persia. Genghis Khan sent an ambassador to that effect. The ambassador's head was cut off and sent back to Genghis Khan. In revenge, all of Persia was invaded and paid a heavy price. But after that, notice what happened. The Mongol invaders became transformed into Muslims and continued to spread Islam into India and Eurasia. Yes, it takes time to understand how events unfold, and for what purpose? This is another classic example of a dumbfounded people becoming absorbed and enlightened. History is filled with examples of this.

We measure distance in space in light years. We measure the climb to our summit in Julian/Roman calendar years because our soul is in the dying body/flesh. It is okay, the time sequence almost forces us to climb. When we do and make it to the summit, we will kiss this sacred ground as we will see that there is the platform to #10, heaven. From the platform, we need to earn our wings to transition and fly—fly to explore the heavens. Yes, we leave our body/flesh behind. For how long, it is hard to say, but with our soul in union in light, does it matter?

CHAPTER *Eleven*

Tracking Forward—Horizontally and
Upward—Vertically Stagnating—Three
Destinations—The Summit and Tiramisu

In this chapter, we will further explore the upper range of our chart, the 9.0 plus. For a race car driver, it is the last lap; for a mountain climber, the last leg to finish the climb. Those prepared can make it, and those unprepared may not. Take as an example Steve Jobs; in the end, he seemed more focused on finishing up unfinished business, work, before leaving this world, as if it would make any difference for him. I wonder where he was tracking in the final moments.

What all of us need to understand is that each of us, regardless of our climb to 9.0 plus, will most likely have a stain on our souls until we are accepted into #10. Although our soul is given to us without a stain, the overwhelming majority of us will acquire a stain of some kind. This is okay in having reached the summit of 9.0. We have willingly allowed for the worst stains to be washed out. Our moral imprint is visible now, and our conscience is audible. It was not instinct being a caring mother/father; it was listening to our inner good voice. It is true that moral law does not change, but rather we change generally for the worse. Charity and love have helped us get to the summit. We are conscious of not only our reality of body/flesh but also subconsciously of our soul and spark. We are aware of not only the sea level but also below sea level, into our conscience and subconscious.

There is no turning back from the summit. We are forever grateful that we, the worst sinners of all people, were helped to reach this platform. We can never be grateful enough to those who cared about us in our climb. We reflect back to all the creative minds, yet none were as creative as those who made the climb before us, our guides. They were right, as the molten lava travels from the center of the earth, so also the light of the Holy Spirit travels from our tabernacle into and through our soul's veins.

Of all the ideologies, philosophies, and religions that I have studied, I see none better than that of the Roman Catholic Church to reach the summit of 9.0 and plus increments. The few of us know because we recall being those stupid assholes or stupid pussies, the 3Ss—stubbornness, stupidity, and sickness. We recall the struggles and hardships. We look around and see the collective summation of who we were a part of. We look back at the '60s, '70s, '80s, '90s up to our current decade and clearly see the decadence and turmoil of souls. We see the difference between the poverty in darkness and true prosperity in light. We see how all the resources that went into the ICBMs (intercontinental ballistic missiles) hurt us regarding trade with certain countries. Poor President Kennedy and Robert Kennedy, wanting to eliminate the weapons of mass destruction and wars was a part of the reason for their assassinations.

It should be noted that scientist Wernher von Braun of Germany did not have intentions of putting a nuclear bomb at the end of a rocket to send to other countries and cause death and destruction. His dream was outer space. His dream became reality in America and not Germany where he was imprisoned for being suspected of not playing along with the Nazis. We have him to thank among others for today's technologies developed by traveling into space. Notice the difference between achievements from goodness compared to evil.

Regardless of the size of an entourage, an evil leader, even with the most intellectual followers, still bears bad fruit. The metamorphosis of our soul out of our body/flesh is even more consequently critical of the 3Cs. Is there an escape from the Antichrist, Armageddon, the Apocalypse, the beast, and the serpent prophesied? How else is the new millennium to take place? Are we the few hoping to reach #10 and be a part of the spiritual battles in our third journey? Let the theologians write about that. We have enough to think about. Those speaking in tongues interest me more. What our Blessed Virgin Maria has to say today is more relevant. I recall that my good-hearted father celebrated her feast day each year. I only hope that he called on her intercession in the hours of his passing. I most certainly did.

We should not lose sleep over prophesied events in the Middle East. I have often wondered why Islam developed out of the Muslim world roughly six hundred years after Christianity. I first thought that through Muhammad, the prophet, a monkey wrench had been thrown into the religions of humanity. I have come to the realization that due to the unwillingness of Judaism to accept Christ and Christianity, perhaps Archangel Gabriel was sent to Muhammad to bridge the divide, the gap, to combine the Old Testament with the New Testament. Where did things go wrong? Think about this for a moment. The Muslim world was in the middle of Judaism, of which they believe practically all of the Old Testament, including the prophets—Abraham, Moses, etc. They also believe in Archangel Gabriel and our Blessed Virgin Maria in Christianity. In other words, they are in the position to help combine the two into one. Including themselves and Islam, the three religions, all being monotheist, were a good setup. The problem was that someone got lost in translation—Christ. Christ in Islam is considered just another prophet. Again, consider this: how could the Muslim world in Islam believe in our Blessed Virgin Maria and Archangel Gabriel but not Christ as the Messiah? This is a contradiction. In this, we Muslims have further caused a separation between all three monotheist religions. We have become divided and subdivided amongst ourselves. We have killed each other as was the case in Andalucia/Spain. Sound familiar? The negative 3Cs have given us the 3Fs, 3Ss, and 3Ds. We have turned against both Judaism and Christianity, another contradiction since you cannot be anti-Judaism and still believe in the Old Testament and the same prophets. You cannot be anti-Christian and still believe in Archangel Gabriel, the annunciation, and our Blessed Virgin Maria. Do we Muslims simply want a religion of our own? We have to consider why the reconquest was allowed to take place in which we were forced out of Europe by Christian forces. We did not accept the 3Rs. We are each part-Hebrew, Muslim, Arabic, Greek, Roman, Turk, etc. Monotheism is one *Dio* with one people.

From the 9.0 plus platform, this is visible. How do we measure the light of a people of a religion? Study the collective summation of light within the people and their treatment toward people of other religions. Study their laws and rules as far as interfaith marriage. Study their rules and regulations toward those outside of their religion. One of the best examples is the genocide by the Muslim, Islam of Ottoman rule, the Christian Armenian community of Constantinople. This was early 1900s before World War I. The laws and rules of any religion and government of any country work in a similar way. So what are the laws of abortion and the death penalty, capital punishment in your religion and country? Again, from the platform, these issues, positive or negative, are clearly visible. The natural senses become infused into the higher level of the soul's senses. They become more acute to all of the evil problems and mysteries of the metaphysical and spiritual world of humanity.

What are the signs of the increments off the platform? 1) a major focus on the 3Ts—*tiramisu*, transformation, and transfiguration—of #10, heaven; 2) no doubts about the faithfulness, hope, and trust in the Holy Spirit within the Holy Trinity; 3) a prostration of body/flesh and soul of our free will to the will of the Holy Trinity; 4) the daily appreciation for the tiny details (i.e., bird songs such as the golden canary and their numerous songs) and a deepened gratitude for the graces/blessings of the Holy Spirit; 5) a heightened overall concern for charity and love for humanity; 6) all M&M is put into proper perspective. It is seen as simply a means for our second journey; 7) pro-life for all forms of life in creation; 8) anti-hate, revenge, offensive wars, and all evils of the world; 9) observance of all the Ten

Commandments, especially the first; 10) acceptance of all the holy sacraments; 11) a firm belief in immortality of soul into light and the maintenance and governance of the galaxies and universe; 12) a love for being among children, observing and listening to them at play; 13) a love for our Blessed Virgin Maria, the angels, and the saints. These are in no set order but are all inclusive each and every day. I could list many more, but you need to experience them for yourself. This is my dare to you all.

What is our body/flesh without the soul or vice versa? Take for example the current terrorists waging war on innocent people. Do they not realize that they are only killing the body/flesh but not the soul? Do they realize that their own souls are held accountable? Apparently not. There are no rainbows over the Middle East or Northern Africa? They should be aware of the book of Revelation, or are they too dumbfounded to interpret it? The rapture of the faithful, the tribulations of the unfaithful being put on trial—don't they read? World War III, Armageddon, the second coming of Christ—what are they thinking? What form of enslavement do they have? Think about what would happen if self-righteous so-called Christians were to become offensive, retaliate, and start killing those of Islam? Think about the negative 3Cs, 3Ss, 3Fs, and 3Ds! Attempting to win wars at all costs usually ends up costing lives, including our own. Now think for a moment if every country put their military budget into good works. At 9.0 plus, one is able to imagine the positive 3Cs—choices, consequences, and conditions—for all humanity.

All in the universe is a good work in progress. On earth? Earth has humanity turned terrorists, whose souls are moving in a vertical direction, but it is down, the shortest distance to zero, not up. Only the negative dumbfounded, 3Ss, 3Fs, and 3Ds, are not aware of their soul's chart position. There is nothing to fear in prophecy as long as we are on the positive right side. Imagine not ever seeing our loved ones after prophesied events. We should think of our second journey as a means to a better destination. A peaceful transition in our sleep is worth praying for. The end of days is actually taking place within our being today. As the laws of physics are in constant motion, so today our life also is in constant motion. The metaphysical have natural laws; our soul has divine laws. All laws are from one source, light, that of our creator.

Even at the summit and 9.0 plus, the platform, we are tested. We could be blown off the summit by a strong gust of wind, a down-draft. This is a reminder of our need of the Holy Spirit until we pray, *tiramisu*, pull me up.

Christmas, the crucifixion, resurrection, and ascension of Christ these days are being thought of as mythological ancient history. Only at 9.0 plus will we ever have an understanding of *Pasqua*, Easter. The mysteries of *Pasqua*, Easter, are a matter of life and death due to one man, *Gesu*. It becomes the same for us in our second and third journeys. Without faith, hope, and trust, how could the increments of 9.0 plus occur? They do not. It doesn't matter if this most important holiday of all holidays is celebrated in Jerusalem, France, or Rome. It depends on how we celebrate the holiday within the heart and mind of our soul.

I think about Tibet and the mostly pacifist people who escaped to other parts of Asia for religious freedom. I think about these people and the self-emulations. I think about these people who, in old age, only want to return to their place of birth to be buried there, as if it is sacred ground. I think of these people who only want to live a peaceful life of prayer. I think of their moral imprint and wonder where they are tracking on their chart. I believe Tibet does have rainbows.

Notice the difference in mentality between people of the world. I think of the people of Tibet past compared to the people of Jerusalem past. One people, the Tibetan pacifists, are willing to be sacrificed for their faith. Another, the Hebrew, will wage war yet hide in caves like animals only to be smoked out and slaughtered. Such sharp contrasting people in history and what they are willing to do for their faith. People walk, talk, and write about the divine, the supernatural, but what is that? Suggestive thinking? Vague generalization? I believe that without the light of wisdom of the Holy Spirit within the Holy Trinity, all is a waste (the 3Ns—nothing, *niente*, nada) more than temporarily ending pacification for the soul. From sea to clouds to rain to snow on our mountaintop summit, all is grace, my friends.

Rivers and fertile lands have always been a part of most great civilizations, the greatest rivers—the Nile River of Egypt, the Euphrates and Tigris rivers of Babylon, the Yantzee and Yellow rivers of China, the Danube and Rhine rivers of northern Europe, the Tiber, Arno, and Po rivers of Italia, the Seine River of France, the Colorado, Columbia, and mighty Mississippi rivers of North America, the Amazon river of South America, etc. These civilizations, these people, were/are the recipients of the graces of the rivers of life and sustenance. Any people who lived/live within reach of these great rivers had/have with gratitude, prosperity. Now study history and see what happens when people are not grateful to true light for the river graces. Study all of the above civilizations when they began giving thanks to man-made gods, self-proclaimed gods, false gods needing human sacrifices or taking the river for granted without any appreciation. These civilizations all encountered problems, were conquered, enslaved, and persecuted somehow. This is the outcome of false idols, false priests, and all false ideologies. All true wisdom is in true light.

There is a reason for poverty and poor prosperity in the world. Take as an example Italia. There are sharp contrasts between the north and the south, depending on the time of history. This is not coincidental. It all has to do with the degree of corruption accepted by the people. The greater the corruption, the greater the poverty. What corrupts? Evil—accepted by people who do evil deeds and bystanders who do not care. It is that simple. There is no need to spend a fortune on various economic models and statistics. Rid evil actions, work on good actions, be grateful, and prosperity follows. It is not that complicated as political figures walk, talk, and write about. A great lesson in the history of Italy is the way that the country came together after World War II. For example, immediately after the disastrous war, as all offensive wars are, the number of suffering children in the South became a new epidemic. The kindhearted families of the North welcomed the children to help their situation. The children were taken care of, got an education, and in time returned to their original family. Again, this is charity and love that benefit the receiver and giver. This is climbing up to the summit and into the 9.0 plus level.

People don't need a Napoleon, a strong totalitarian military leader, a great army of legions, nuclear weapons, a treasury of huge quantities of gold, etc. to be liberated. The revolutions against the leeches of the monarchies, the aristocracy, emperors, kings, and queens are mostly past history. America showed us the way. Notice the sequence of events from America to Europe, to the Middle East and Africa. Eastern Europe and Asia are next. The moral imprint of the majority can only tolerate evil in a tyrant for so long, especially these days with the World Wide Web. Current history is taking place now, today, in us, in the immediate present. All current issues have to do with inequalities, injustices, and inhuman conditions (the negative 3Cs) of tyranny in the suffering people who are victims. Study the collective summation of the souls chart for any country. The greater the corruption and percentage of people near zero, the greater the overall performance issues and problems with false propaganda, poverty, and non-prosperity. The higher the percentage of those who have climbed to the summit in any community, society, and country, the greater the chance of prosperity. We are not talking about normal if normal is a part of the negative herd mentality. We are talking about the not normal as in those that reject a base level of humanity, almost animal level. We are talking about men and women created for good works, not about mice and monkeys.

Want proof? Study the free trade of a country with other countries. Free trade is prosperity. Study their gross domestic product (GDP). Study the value of their currency. Study their inflation rate. Study the negative 3Cs, 3Ss, 3Fs, and 3Ds of their government leaders. The less spiritual knowledge of light, graces, the less the freedoms, creativity, and prosperity in the people. Put aside the PhDs. Even the illiterate with a good degree of light have a better sense of the situation.

At the summit of 9.0 plus, we are not all asked to become martyrs. Take as example the apostles—only a small percentage went into their third journey as martyred saints. Now think again, does it really matter? Death of the body/flesh is death. At the summit of 9.0 plus, death of the body/flesh becomes a nonissue. I believe it would be better to be martyred and die a quick death than die slowly with a crippling disease or languishing in some rest home.

This also brings to mind the Rosselli brothers of Firenze, Italia, who spoke out against fascism before World War II. They fled to France to be free to express themselves, only to be followed and murdered there. Were they martyrs? It is hard to say. I can say that they were not a part of the herd mentality following a "pied piper" fanatical lunatic to drown in a river of sewage. Let us remember that 9.0 plus and #10 heaven could be a long winding road uphill needing middle gears or a vertical straight up climb needing low gears. Purgatory is like being in a locked parking garage in idle without a password to exit. Hell is a six-lane highway down needing no fuel or gears, just neutral.

Another good person's martyrdom becomes our loss. Yes, if their death of the body/flesh did not move us to correct the injustices and inequalities that they spoke out against, then we are the real losers. Again, as mentioned before, count your losses in life. This positions you on your soul's chart. A person who is at 9.0 plus will want to prostrate himself/herself on the bare earth naked in humility and be grateful for being helped to reach that level through charity and love. At 9.0 plus, the soul's mind communication with the Holy Spirit happens before the words are even spoken. This only occurs when two hearts and minds are in union freely. Yes, the image of humanity is in likeness to Christ and not the images of artists' abstract imaginations. Blessed are those that see His face in humanity in need.

"Time is of the essence"—how often we hear this phrase. But essential to what? Work? Profit? War? If not toward the last three minutes of our earthly second journey, what is the essence? There are so many dimensions of our soul's second journey, but the summit platform is, without any doubt, the most essential.

What are some of the current signs for ourselves, our country, and the world? We covered for ourselves in our chart and the cumulative signs of our country, but the whole world? There are a number of ominous signs throughout the world currently shaping up. Add up the countries losing light, and the foreseeable future does not look promising for the world and humanity. Study the negative 3Cs,

3Ss, 3Fs, and 3Ds. They are alarming. This includes America and all developed countries. Of course, until humanity flatlines, there is always hope. From the summit, I believe that there will continue to be a spring after winter.

The most ominous signs of our time are out of the Middle East and Africa as usual. The events make me wonder about us Muslims and our Islamic faith. Take for example the the number of men, women, and children drowning in the Mediterranean Sea in efforts to escape the maddening mentality of the extreme overzealous radicals causing so much death and destruction in the region (the 3Cs, 3Fs, 3Ss, and 3Ds). Some of this is human trafficking for profit. My question to all the rest of Muslim, monotheist Islamic brothers and sisters is: what are we doing about the evil events? We currently have sheiks in the region with billions of oil profits, and yet what are we doing to help fellow Muslims? We hate the despicable actions of the Christian West, yet we want to ship out our problems to them to deal with. This is our faith, hope, and trust in Islam? We Muslims keep bringing up the Crusaders into the Holy Land, but we fail to mention the Christian Church we set on fire and burned down by a fanatical mob that started the conflict. How could two wrongs make a right? They do not. The current omission to take action should tell us that we have not changed much in the past centuries.

Trust is the key to the Middle East issues. When people would rather risk their lives crossing dangerous seas without life vests, it tells us that Muslims do not trust Muslims for help. Notice that with faith, hope, and trust, the absence of trust, faith, and hope does not occur. In other words, leadership that is not trustworthy loses the faithful and hopeful. This leads to a deterioration in confidence, which ultimately leads to an implosion. As a refresher, what was trust rooted in? Truth. And what is truth rooted in? The light of the Holy Spirit within the Holy Trinity. What are we Muslim so-called religious leaders thinking? Again, the 3Cs, 3Fs, 3Ss, and 3Ds are in play here. Notice the chronic sickness of the soul in the 3Ss—stubbornness, stupidity, and sickness. The denial is what leads to the 3Ds—disgrace, despair, and death. This is nothing new in the Middle East. Read history about the genocide of between 1 to 1.5 million

Armenian people in the last century under Ottoman rule. This was the first genocide of the twentieth century. This was Ottoman law and order? We build all the magnificent mosques for what purpose? This was the magnificent sultan? This was charity and love toward humanity? Current events appear to me as the works of the devils in humanity more than anything else.

Study the course of events under Ottoman rule. First, we import the use of gunpowder from China. Next, we use the cannons against the walls of Roman Christian Constantinople. Next, we take over one of the largest wonders of the known world, a Roman Catholic Church built by the engineering and architectural designers of Rome's Eastern Empire. Next, we turn the same church, the Hagia Sophia, into a mosque. Next, we turn Constantinople built by Roman Emperor Constantino into Istanbul? All of this as if to say we deserve credit? Notice that the following so-called great mosques of Asia all have a similar architecture. So much for Ottoman ingenuity. It should be no surprise that the same thing occurred in Spain, changed to Andalucia after the Ottoman arrived. The original *La Convivencia* ("The Coexistence") in religion in Cordoba, Spain, benefited both Muslim and Christian in a half-Christian, half-mosque structure on one lot. The tearing down of the church half by the Muslim resulted in the great mosque of Cordoba. It should have been no surprise that after we Muslims were driven out of Spain entirely by EU forces that the great mosques of Cordoba, Granada, Seville, and all of Spain were converted into Roman Catholic churches. This was in retribution for a false sense of *La Convivencia*, living together in faith in monotheism. The magnificent sultan cried in leaving Andalucia, but there was nothing—the 3Ns (nothing, *niente*, nada)—magnificent about the lost opportunity for having Christian and Muslim people living together in peace and harmony. History does not lie, my friends, it is all well-documented. Now also notice that gunpowder and cannonballs were used in the two major wars at sea by Europe to annihilate the Ottoman forces. This was the beginning of the end in which the extravagant decadent lifestyle of a few would lead to sovereign default and put an end to Ottoman rule. The sultans wanted perfection, but perfection does not exist in the metaphysical world of humanity. The only perfection possible is in the soul's climb up to the summit of 9.0 plus.

The Holy Spirit does not necessarily always dwell in a church, mosque, or synagogue of brick and mortar. It dwells first, when welcomed, in the hearts of humanity regardless of how magnificent the structural design, artworks, and gold leaf ornamentation. So much for the magnificent Pharaohs, sultans, emperors, kings, and queens of the past. Even the Chinese got rid of thousands of years of dying dynasties, but what is the replacement? Perhaps they need to study the Republic of San Marino in the Italian Republic. Here is a true constitutional parliamentary republic, the oldest in the world, dating back to 301 AC. It was a tiny republic, yet it is based on the Roma Republic of 450 BC. This republic has seen it all in the past roughly 1,700 years—imperialism, monarchies, fascism, and all other false ideologies. This republic remained true to the principles of a true republic. This republic has been prosperous through all of it, even the Dark Ages. This republic has one of the highest GDPs in Europe, highly educated citizens, and a high per capita income. Also, YES, a surplus, NOT debt in the treasury. Astonishing? Recall what I wrote about corruption/evil in government, it gradually brings debt, poverty, and the 3Ds to itself and the citizens. In a way, we kill ourselves.

Humanity has so many reminders of the metaphysical to reflect on—decaying monumental structures, paintings, and books of humanity's 3Cs that go back thousands of years. We even put these things into museums. They are constant conscious reminders of what humanity did right and wrong in the past centuries. But what is really important?

For me, it was going home the long way, around the world. From Italia to America, Ohio to California, New York to Shanghai, Hong Kong, South Korea, Japan, Toronto, Canada to Florence and Genova, Italia. Finally, I got back to a lost traditional way of life. I went home to write this book for silence and a solitary way of life immersed in a cultural heritage of my lost metaphysical world of Italia. But this was all secondary. Primarily one needs to go home, first to the summit and then home where we all started out before our first journey. This, my friends, none of us should ever forget.

It requires many tests, trials, hardships, suffering, and education. It took me years, decades to regain what was lost. As a country, a people, it works out the same way. For example, for Italia, it took a good twenty-five years to regain what was lost from the disastrous World War II. The metaphysical was rebuilt but the dolori, the pains of the heart for those who died or were severally wounded mentally and emotionally last a lifetime. These are the ravages of hate, revenge, and war, negative 3Cs, 3Ss, 3Fs, and 3Ds. If only we could learn from them.

How important is it to get along with each other? Again, take free trade as a great example. Corn, tomatoes, and yams among others were not available to European people until they were shipped to Europe from the Americas. Now imagine Italia without tomato sauce. Corn, a major grain and food source, has only been in Europe for the past few centuries. Now study the rogue countries in which free trade is restricted by trade embargos. Study their loss after loss after loss. It is always the loss by the multitudes of people, the Cubans for example, that hurts more than the losses to a few so-called leaders. The losses get started from within as in losses of freedom that manifest themselves into losses of the metaphysical. A country could become like an eight-cylinder automobile engine. With a democratic republic system and without corrupted officials, free trade runs smoothly on all cylinders. A small degree of corruption causes it to run on six cylinders, become lethargic, and waste fuel. Major corruption causes it to stall, hard to restart, and ready for the scrap yard, a major waste. There is that word *waste* again, as in *wasteful, wasting, wasted.* This brings to mind the waste of fuel with all the unnecessary STOP signs in America. A three-way stop at a T-intersection? Stop and go? We could easily eliminate 50 percent of the stop signs in America by putting in as in Switzerland, drive through go-arounds. Stoplights? How about eliminating 30 percent of them. The stop and go only benefit big oil in consuming more fuel and only add to the carbon dioxide footprint. It is also a waste in waiting time.

Our soul's climb works in a similar way. We Americans and Western Europeans waste so much. From Abraham to Moses, Christ to the Apostles, the saints to the popes, the summit climb is similar. Yes, there is waste, injuries, bleeding, and a desire to quit at times, but the highest climb has the highest rewards. The mysteries of the 9.0 plus are limitless, as are the mysteries of our galaxies and beyond. At times, we are taken out of our comfort zone for a good reason. Imagine we Americans losing our freedoms. It has happened in the losses of our privacy. Imagine we Italians losing our democratic republic system again. It did happen in the last century. With major corruption, a strong authoritative figure is welcomed to take the reign and dictate. Sounds familiar? Could another genocide, holocaust happen again? Does humanity repeat the negative 3Cs, 3Ss, 3Fs, and 3Ds in history? Is antisemitism active today? Is racism active today? Is the apocalypse possible? Yes to all of the above. You see, my friends, not only do we have a free will and a key to our tabernacle, but we also acquire a key to purgatory and hell if we refuse the key to #10, heaven's gate. What will our epitaph say? For whose benefit? Of course, we may figure out the process of immortality like the Turritopsis dohrnii jellyfish, which is capable of reversing the aging process. The temptations are there until the last mental thought of our mind. But who wants to be in a physical body without end? It is so tiring. Besides, how many people have come out of the doctor's office with a good bill of health only to drop dead before reaching their car?

Both Italia and America are democratic, parliamentary/congressional republic constitutional countries with graces from sea to shining sea, mountains of wealth, prosperity of free trade, and fertile lands. All graces are in light of light and from light that we should never forget. There was a time in America when people would clean their food dishes with bread; today we use disposable dishes and throw everything away, including the plastic forks and spoons. All that is good in any country comes to an end when the collective cumulative sparks within its citizens become an amber. Thousands of years ago, the majority illiterate needed parables and metaphors spoken to them. Today the majority literate of the population want proof by us scientists of which all humans are part of. A metamorphosis of being from the summit of 9.0 plus was easier among us illiterate. What became of dedication and devotion to a higher realm of enlightenment?

*Dio* is always hiring those who are willing to do His will in governing the earth and entire cosmos. This is not science fiction, my friends. The good earth was created as a playground filled with all sorts of wonderful creatures for us and *Dio* to play with. Who is the creator of physics, the cosmos, the body/flesh, and the soul, including the evolutionary process? Who can allow the mind to return into the brain and function again after the brain was ravaged from various viruses? Tough questions with unknown, unexplainable answers for those who have not climbed and are dumbfounded, but for the tiny few at the 9.0 plus level, the answers are known in light.

A snake, a poisonous snake, has a lot to teach us. It was created for many reasons. The lowly snake eats rodents but is also a food source for other creatures. It is an important part of the ecological system. Study history, this lowly creature figures into the history of humanity from inception. Its influence, its affirmation, is recorded in Genesis through Moses for its practical and symbolic design, even in modern-day medicine. The poisonous venom it contains could be used as an antidote in the body/flesh of humanity. The snake has and continues to take a bad rap, especially in the spiritual senses. But from the summit, we see that the snake is just another means or vehicle for evil spirits to tempt and influence humanity. The same holds true for poisonous spiders and other various creatures, including men but especially women. This also is ISD, intellectual spiritual design. Only a tiny percentage of humanity sees and appreciates how the process works and is able to learn valuable lessons from it. The poisons accepted in our soul's heart and mind need to be extracted with the 3Rs.

Take another look at humanity, man and woman. Take a look for the first time at ISD of the magnificent beauty of the raw naked form. The Victorian and Asian nonsense of nudity is understandable given their soul's climb on their chart. These truly wonderfully designed, living, breathing, and evolving forms of light never cease to amaze me. Yes, the Greek, Roman, and also Italian artists of the Renaissance saw what I see in the beautiful human anatomy. It is our positive 3Cs, 3Gs, 3Ls with 3Rs that determine our successful life for the 3Ts. Or our negative 3Cs with 3Ss, 3Fs, 3Ds without the 3Rs determine our unsuccessful life. We should make the most of that with which we are blessed.

Take the Statue of Liberty in New York—a great symbolic figure, a replica of a smaller version in Paris. It has become a tourist attraction, but study the original meaning for the statue. Study the torch of light. It has to do with the metaphysical liberties of humanity but more importantly the freedom of the soul's liberalization from the darkness of evil. Again, in World War II, we Americans knew the meaning of civil freedoms and civil liberties. We were the saviors of Europe and Asia. Our men spilled their blood on foreign lands; some never came home. What has become of us since that time of helping humanity? What has become of our great generals? What happened in the Korean War, the Vietnam War, the Middle East wars? Did we Americans sell out to the warmongers, the war machinery of profits? Where are we today? Where is our conscious collective summation of our conscience? Study the soul's chart of America if you dare to. We saviors these days are considered the evildoers, even Satan, by certain people. Why? How did we get here? How do we change this view of us? The answers are in the collective summation in the soul's 3Cs, 3Gs, 3Ls, 3Ss, 3Fs, 3Rs, and 3Ds. From the platform, we see it all. Meditate on this for the next Fourth of July.

In Italia, it was similar with the partisans, the men and women who spilled their blood for our civil liberties and religious freedoms in this wonderful country. The Italian soul's liberties run parallel to America, let us never forget this. In youth, we have fantasies of freedoms and liberties mostly associated with the body/flesh. Without the climb itself, we cannot begin to see the needed liberties of the body/flesh/soul. The liberties at the summit or the liberties on the platform of the summit 9.0 are in a cloud for our soul until we climb up the increments to 9.9. Until then, we cannot even imagine the beauty of a rose garden, far less our orb and light of the Holy Trinity.

From the platform, death of the body/flesh is seen in an entirely different perspective. No, we do not have to go visit purgatory or hell; watching the BBC or CNN news is sufficient enough. Although a few of us test ourselves in choosing hell for our third journey as a joke only to come to the realization that the joke was on us. We see that our third journey must, at all costs, be to #10, heaven. Reincarnation? What for? It is not up to us anyway. A fourth journey? It is hard to say, but we do see the imperfections in ourselves and all humanity. Hence, we seek perfection in our third journey in the 3Ts—*tiramisu*, transformation, and transfiguration—into #10, brilliant light. In the meantime, this causes us to become like busy bees, engaging in non-stop thinking about the increments of our soul's climb. Time itself, although important now, will eventually have no value. A sign of climbing up incrementally from the platform is an incredible increase in our appreciation for the tiny details of all living forms within the light of the Holy Spirit. At the same time, our empathy grows for all brainwashed humanity outside of light that listen to the drumbeat of imbeciles of superstitions. They are told that they are at the top of a summit—though the summit is inverted—and not knowing up from down, are actually in the process of *tiramigiu* (pull me down) by evil toward the bottom to near zero. We cannot condemn them; to do so would be to condemn a part of ourselves as a whole. Yet after reading this book, we no longer have any excuse or alibi, do we?

From the platform, we want to follow the beat of our soul's heart tabernacle. We want to leave behind the bad memories of evil itself. We want to only keep the good memories of those times past. For me, those days were years ago in my youth as a child filled with wonder and not too long ago in Salerno, Italia, with Ettore and friends. It was those days at the Immaculata in the University of San Diego campus listening to Father Gallagher and the kindness of Father Susko at Our Lady of Mount Carmel Parish on Summit Avenue in Youngstown, Ohio. Let our body/flesh become dust after it has served our soul well, a necessity, working as a team. We see that dust itself is of light. Even after all the evolutionary process that has occurred, our moral imprint is left the same. Let our creator gather our dust into light at the appropriate time. We recognize that our body/flesh is like a computer hardware. Our soul wants to be a part of the server, a part of the third and possibly more journeys. Even those of us who are physically blind can see from the platform and want the same. This has nothing to do with technology that remembers my words and helps finish my sentences. Spelling and writing itself could become a lost art, but our soul continues, my friends. This is not limited to Christians. There are those of us with no religious affiliations, and yet due to our charitable heart and love for humanity, they are unknowingly climbing up to our summit and platform. Everyone living in the second journey is always tracking whether we know it or not. We are not forgotten, no less than a priest, rabbi, or other types of religious leaders.

Government cannot really cure what ails the souls of its citizens. The civil liberties in America and Europe help compared to a country like North Korea, whose citizens are always in crisis with South Korea. They are like the shadows of humanity due to the hideous criminal tyrants controlling them. All governments are capable of doing harmful acts to its citizens. Take the example of the Reagan Republican Administration that threw mentally ill American citizens, of whom many were war veterans out on the streets. This was an administration draped in a facade of Christian values. What hypocrisy—America dropped a degree of light on the country's soul chart that year alone. The Bush Republican Administration in the second war with Iraq to find weapons of mass destruction (WMD) was a total sham that cost the citizens of America a fortune from which we have yet to recuperate. The Clinton Administration, using the White House for personal business and sex, was despicable, to say the least. This is what America has become. For all public officials, study your own personal chart. Study your positive/negative 3Cs, 3Gs, 3Ls, 3Fs, 3Ss, and 3Rs to prevent the 3Ds in public office. We seem to have become a melting pot of swine rather than a melting pot for all races of humanity. Babylon was made confused and dumbfounded and to be dispersed under similar conditions. The corruption/evil started with the Nixon Republican Administration of Watergate, next Irangate and Contra-gate. Next, next, next? It's hard to say with so-called classified top secret documents. Again, we really do NOT need a president or vice president that tries, along with his/her cabinet, to do things without transparency. It should only be the senate open to all citizens with the 3Ns—nothing, *niente*, nada—hidden. The collective summation of a country's soul light can reverse itself from a descent to a climb with the collective summation of her soul's 3Rs. There is such a thing as going into darkness slowly, but without the corrupted/evil officials' corrections, it is a hard landing to the bottom.

The new gods replacing Christianity in the New Rome of Washington, D.C., America, and Italia governments are bulls with gold over leaf and M&M (money and material) things. The more darkness that we Americans and Italians accept collectively in our soul as a government and as a country, the uglier we become. Economic crashes and recessions are good for us. They remind us of who we Americans and Italians, under false, corrupt leadership, have become. In all governments, it is no different, hence the necessity of austerity programs, even though they affect more the middle and lower classes. In all of Europe, it is similar. In Italia, real church bells call us to reenergize, the 3Cs and 3Rs. In America, although having fake church bells, Sunday services still call people to do the same.

In Italia and Western Europe—the past, the old, and the current—the new all come together to try to become a harmonious deja vu of the *bella vita*. There is a nostalgia for the culture and history of better days. It is evident in the voices of people who are at 9.0 plus on their souls' charts. The percentage as a collective summation appears to be higher than most other countries. There appears to be a higher appreciation for the blessings of graces. In America, the same percentage, although still high, is dropping. The younger generation as a whole is becoming more interested in M&M rather than counting their blessings.

Now meditate on this. Seven billion-plus people in hundreds of corrupt countries with false leaderships and ideologies, and what do we have? A nightmare. How on earth could there not be wars? Study the collective summation of darkness in any country's government officials and its people, and you can begin to appreciate the work needed by the Holy Spirit to help correct the consequences and conditions of that country. Perhaps we should start cloning decent moral leaders for our future? Just joking. Let us never be negative, my friends. Where there is a willingness in light, there is a way. Having been to countries with various government leadership, I see what can work and what will never work. Forget about all the economic models, and even constitutions, of any country. It is the collective summation of light within people that determines poverty or prosperity. Want proof of this? Take the Middle Eastern countries and study their history and current conditions. Try to take one country such as Iraq and study it in relationship to light. The results are undeniably accurate. The same holds true for all of the Middle East countries. Take another example of Israel that dates back thousands of years. Recall how two thousand years ago, in 130 AC, Caesar Hadrian of pagan Rome sent thirteen legions to restore law and order in Jerusalem and Israel. The rebellious solution led to the slaughter of hundreds of thousands and expulsion of all us Hebrews out of Judea. It restored law and order, establishing Palestine. After almost two thousand years, a Christian president, Harry Truman of New Rome, against the advice of almost everyone, gives a part of the territory back to us Hebrew people, along with billions of dollars. Yet study the consequences and conditions of our region. There was/is enough hate and revenge in the region to kill a million camels a year, every year since 1949. Complicated? Study the collective summation of light within Israel and her neighbors. How could there be peace in a region without true law and order of the soul? Where does true law and order begin? Within the soul's heart of humanity. Take India for example, study her history and the mostly Hindu-practicing people there. Even after the peaceful revolution with Gandhi against the British, study her discrimination against women, class levels, a class structure that tells people poverty needs to be accepted for their class levels while people put their faith in cows and beasts of burden that are considered sacred. What does this tell us? What is the collective summation of light within the peoples' souls? Is this the enlightenment of Hinduism?

Now what do we do with the millions of people attempting to escape their conditions? Acceptance of them into an already highly saturated Europe is not the solution. It is no different than after World War II when European people had to immigrate to other countries. What countries can handle the millions of people needing

353

help? Countries with large land mass such as the Americas, Canada, sub-Sahara Africa, Russia, and Australia. Of course, this requires charity and love for suffering humanity. Where is the willingness? What could be worse than the feeling of being rejected when desperate needs set in? For those of us blessed in a mostly free and democratic system of government, think of what it would be like exchanging places with those hurting for help.

What defines us as a government, a country, a people? Our technology, medical advances, educational system, democratic system, etc., yes, but what is the most important? Without the humanitarian willingness to help others help themselves, we will keep repeatedly making the negative 3Cs due to the 3Fs, 3Ss, and 3Ds. The higher the percentage of positive 3Cs, giving us the 3Gs, 3Ls, 3Rs, and 3Ts, the higher the peace and prosperity for all. It starts with our climbing to our summit, but the platform offers the greatest rewards. Why wait?

There are greater rewards in constructive implementation of our graces in labor for humanity than destructive actions of wars, funeral parlors, and cemeteries. Death and destruction have become big business in the world but at a humongous humanitarian price. The body/flesh dust is dust no matter how much we spend to prepare it. Even in a mass grave in the company of others, the soul's departure is the only true concern. We cannot learn the true needs of the metaphysical body/flesh of humanity without first learning in light the needs of the soul of humanity. A government, a country, and a people need to compare to each other which offers its citizens a lifetime of freedom and liberties of peace and prosperity. We will see that it is always those that are tracking high on their collective summation of their soul's light. It is groups such as white supremacy racists that drop a people down on a country's chart. I figured that the tracking of the world as a whole these days is at around 6.0. It is up to us to change this for our children and grandchildren. "*Con Dio tutto e possibli,*" as in "In light, all is possible." Nothing, *niente,* nada—the 3Ns—good is possible in darkness.

A current sign of the times is toxic people, groups exploiting those who are charitable and caring. Evil again always works through humanity. Toxic people are seen in the amount of lies they tell. The greater the lies, the greater the toxicity. The chronic liars are, indeed, sick, the 3Ss—stubbornness, stupidity, and sickness. They are not trustworthy, as they do not trust their own thoughts and actions. They may know what truth is, but ignore it, as ignoring our inner voice of our tabernacle. Rather, we listen to the negative voice of the pervasive evil tempting our minds. From the 9.0 plus platform, we are fully aware that all truth is rooted in light. Without the 3Rs— repentance, reconciliation, and redemption—by the light of the Holy Spirit, we betray ourselves and everyone else as well. It reminds me, growing up, of kids that were constipated, needing castor oil in order to rid themselves of the toxins within their bodies/flesh. For our soul, my friends, the toxicity could be deadly, the 3Ds—disgrace, despair, and death—without the 3Rs being accepted.

Show me a government, a constitution, any set of civil laws with a collective summation of people who are not listening to their inner voice from their tabernacle of ISD (intellectual spiritual design), and I will show you the degree of toxicity and darkness within the same people. Take as an example women's rights. It took America until 1920 and Italia until 1946 to give women the right to vote. Why? Recall in previous chapters what I wrote about regarding how women need to be treated by men? Notice how women are treated in the so-called religious Muslim, Islam, Hindu, and Buddhist governments and regions of the world. What does this tell us in the twenty-first century? Toxicity, high levels of toxicity in humanity. The toxicity of American governments, city, state, and federal? With an approval rating by the people of less than 30 percent, what do you think? In Italia, it is even worse.

Notice that there is a flip side to just about everything. The flip side of light is darkness, good/evil, the positive 3Cs/negative 3Cs, positive 3Gs/ negative 3Fs, positive 3Ls/negative 3Ss, positive 3Rs/ negative 3Ds, ascend/descend. This holds true in all facets of our lives, in vocation, profession, and lifestyle. Again, this positions us on our soul's chart. Individually, this is always the case. When we add up the collective summation of positive and negative, what do we have? Is there a higher degree of positive or negative? A great example was the end of slavery in America. Study how the South under slavery (the negative 3Cs) became impoverished. With 1 percent of the population and the plantation owners taking all of the profits, the slaves suffered all of the injustices. Sounds familiar? Again, all true justice first takes place in our souls. Now study the destruction, death, and suffering in the South mainly due to plantation owners and their constituents due to their negative 3Cs, with the 3Fs, 3Ss and 3Ds during the American Civil War. A coincidence? Think again. The South, without the higher degree of a collective summation of 3Rs, still has a lower overall wage and prosperity rate compared to the North, so the North, with President Lincoln and Congress, did their part, but with their pervasive discrimination and prejudices, the South has as of yet not fully recovered. History tells us that only after people become sick and tired of death and destruction do they willingly accept a change for corrections—the 3Rs. Until then, people who do not value the freedoms and liberties of other people will not change and track low on their chart.

Positive and negative 3Cs are recorded throughout the history of humanity. One of the greatest positive 3Cs is how America helped Europe after World War . Study the Marshall Plan by America that helped with the recovery of Europe. This positive 3Cs ushered in the 3Gs, 3Ls, and 3Rs by European people and one of the most prosperous decades, the 1950s, in American history. It was a good investment with amazing returns. It also helped everyone involved in their summit climb. Another wonderful positive 3Cs in history is the development of the Red Cross in many countries. Study the results of the consequences and conditions of humanity in history, my friends. Justification takes time to unfold, but it always does.

Once more, currently one of the basic critical needs is for potable water in many countries that needs to be filled. With only 3 percent of clean drinking water on land and 65 percent of earth's saltwater in our seas, it should be a no-brainer and yet is still true in the twenty-first century. Where is the willingness? Where is the creative process? Where is the charity?

What transpired in America paralleled in Italia and Western Europe during the same time period. Now study what happened in America during the 1960s. The negative 3Cs with laziness, illegal drug use, and people dropping out and down of hardworking America. With the 3Fs, 3Ss, and 3Ds with ODs (overdose death from illegal drugs), evils were accepted and took hold of lost generations. Study Italia after the metaphysical reconstruction. In the 1970s, study the neo-fascist cells with communism and the red brigades wreaking havoc as terrorists on innocent people and eventually killing Moro. Study the acceptance of evils in abortion laws and divorce laws. Study the assassinations of Giovanni Falcone and Paolo Borsellino. The negative 3Cs with the 3Fs, 3Ss and 3Ds took hold of lost generations. We were lost generations who refused to get a life from climbing to our own summit.

Another example was the war in Kosovo, the former Yugoslavia in Southern Europe. As war was raging again in the backyard of Europe due to the 3Cs, little to nothing, nothing, *niente*, nada (3Ns) was done there by us European people. Again, the negative 3Cs resulted in the 3Fs, 3Ss, and 3Ds. It took America, in NATO, to resolve the issues. When will we learn the similarities today? The crisis in the Middle East and Africa are close, very close to us. I recall my good father almost drowning in a lake that we were picnicking at when I was a child. He did not know how to swim. Another American, a total stranger, without thinking, rushed in to save him. As of the writing of this book, the Mediterranean Sea is becoming a graveyard for thousands of people who don't know how to swim. What are we European, American, Russian, Arabic, African, Australian doing about it—seriously?

Also, we have in both America, Italia, and Western Europe young lost generations joining evil terrorists, and they have no clue as to who they are dealing with. We have lost generations who would rather spend countless hours of the day and night on social media for gossip garbage, the negative 3Cs with the 3Fs, 3Ss, and 3Ds. Add to this, in Italia, young generations that would rather take part in constant mass demonstrations for employment but not accept thousands of jobs available throughout the country, and what do we have? A bloated fat lazy super pig of pigs—a super pig larger than the three pigs of Portugal, Greece, and Spain combined. There are more lost generations that are refusing to get a life from climbing to their summit. Will more job legislation pushed by Sergio Mattarella, president, and Matteo Renzi, prime minister, improve the unemployment rate in Italia? Does feeding a fat lazy pig change the willingness to accept the jobs already available rather than want only cushy, gravy jobs? It's all about the willingness to work and light stupid people. Meditate on this for a while.

As soon as a mother hears the sound of her child crying, her breast nipples start to drip milk. This is ISD, intellectual spiritual design, of motherhood. For a mother at her summit, she comprehends this without needing scientific research of the phenomenon. A mother is the vehicle for our first journey measured in a sequence of time. Our body/flesh is the vehicle for our second journey also measured in a sequence of time. Our body/flesh will move in a horizontal sequence of time until it dies, as it was created to do, again ISD. Our soul's vertical descent or ascension to the summit of 9.0 is a sequence in time. On the 9.0 plus platform, time starts to become less relevant, and in our third journey, time becomes totally irrelevant. We need not worry about it if we processed the 3Ts—*tiramisu*, transformation, and transfiguration. Study all of creation, all has an understanding of ISD except humanity due to our negative 3Cs, 3Fs, 3Ss, and 3Ds. We have the gift of our free will, and what do we do with it?

Let me give an example of what occurs within our body/flesh and soul in an age sequence of time. Let us take the age of sixty, as was figured out by us Muslims centuries ago as a good number for time that is easy to work with. At sixty years of age of our body/flesh, if we are ascending on our soul's chart, especially on and above the platform of 9.0 plus, we become more childlike, younger emotionally and feeling like forty years young. Mentally in the same position, we gain wisdom like an eighty-year-old, due to seeing the mysteries of ISD in light. Physically, our body/flesh benefits as well since the two, soul and body/flesh, are one. We feel and may look like a healthy forty-year-old. In a vertical descent at the same age of sixty on our chart, the opposite occurs. Emotionally, mentally, and physically, we could look and feel eighty years old. In union with light, the Holy

Spirit, and in works of charity and love, we benefit immediately and immensely. In union with evil, darkness, the opposite occurs. This explains the phenomenon of a few of the saints whose body/flesh was not rotting or decaying when their tombs were opened to view years after the death of their body/flesh.

So, my friends, the positive or negative 3Cs are for us to make with our free will. Once more, let us use Mussolini as a classic example because he was about sixty years of age when he was executed, shot dead. Mussolini, rumored to having the balls of a bull, had numerous extramarital affairs as dictator, the negative 3Cs, 3Fs, 3Ss, and 3Ds. Stupid pussies, the 3Ss, lined up to be ravished and have sexual intercourse with this man. It was all physical lust, of course, and not love, the 3Ns—nothing, *niente*, nada. He admitted this himself. True love is known by the moral standards a couple—man and woman—lives by. A false love has no standards or false standards. Now study the photos of Mussolini at the age of sixty. He looks like an eighty-year-old man. This is a prime example of how the evils of darkness age a person due to the negative 3Cs, 3Fs, 3Ss, and 3Ds. In current Russia, there is a very similar man that reflects past twentieth-century Mussolini. That man, having taken control of government in fraud elections, became a so-called leader. Sounds familiar? As a people, change does not take place usually until the same people being governed have reached critical mass of misery (CMM). It doesn't matter where or what country. The problem is the same. A tyrant will take its toll on the people emotionally, mentally, physically, and spiritually. Notice that this so-called leader is already talking about the use of nuclear weapons. World War III? World War II cost humanity around fifty million lives. A nuclear war could cost an estimated five hundred-plus million lives if a limited war. A full-out war? Will anyone or anything be left afterward? Action to change the CMM will be too late at that point. Action needs to be taken today as of yesterday. Is there a willingness? What have we learned from the Polish people in their success to overcome a similar tyranny? Are we developing Alzheimer's disease? In the twenty-first century, we still have tyrants with a Niccolo Machiavelli philosophy of the medieval age. Have we Italians forgotten what the followers of a mad dog did in Marzabotto,

Italia in war World War II? The retreating Nazi murdered 1,800 people in the city in 1944. As a part of the EU, we need to have a say in what is shaping up in our backyard once again. What became of Mussolini's body/flesh and soul? What became of all his mistresses? What became of all his brainwashed followers? Meditate on it.

Yes, my fellow European people, if we do not want a repeat of the deaths and destruction in a World War III in Europe again, we need to act now. A nuclear war could destroy our culture and heritage. A few extremists anxious to push a few buttons is all it takes. It is time to demand a supervised dismantling by the United Nations of all ICBMS, nuclear weapons of mass destruction, nerve gas bombs, biological poisonous bombs, etc. It is possible if only we, the moral majority, will not take no for an answer. After all, it's the few, those tracking near zero on their chart, that object. We have to demand that world leaders come together on the issues and set up a time frame. I believe that America should take the lead on this most important issue. Yes, we are leading in R&D (research and development), new cyber, nanotechnology, bio and energy, but what good is this for humanity in case of an all-out nuclear world war? All of the Clara Bartons in America would be of no help, the 3Ns—nothing, *niente*, nada. Capitalism, along with all of the isms, would lose. All life forms would lose. We could only imagine the losses at every level.

A Democratic Republic with controls on capitalism and a degree of charity for its citizens works and brings prosperity if there is a moral majority making the decisions. The immoral majority part has become the greatest obstacle to overcome in America and the free world. The rest of the world is in even worse shape. But how do we reach and legislate morality? We can reach it but not legislate it. Attempting to do so actually makes matters worse. I am sorry to say that the CMM process almost always, yet not 100 percent of the time, has to take place individually as persons and collectively as a people in any country. Why not 100 percent of the time? Study the arts. The artworks of the Muslim people combined with the artworks of Christian people are what gave humanity the magnificent works in Alcazar, Granada, and Seville, Spain. Study the combined artworks of the Mongolian, Muslim, and Indian people for the mosques and other structures. Study art in history to see what is possible when the soul's heart and mind of humanity come together in harmony to see what is possible for peace. Now study the book of Job in the Old Testament of the Holy Bible. I hope that you can begin to understand the testing process.

The sooner that the collective summation of the inner voice of the tabernacle in humanity is listened to to activate our free will in positive 3Cs—absorb the grace, aid, light of the Holy Spirit— the sooner we can correct and make changes, remove tyrants, and achieve a degree of peace and prosperity. This is hard but not impossible to accomplish because of the 3Ns; nothing is impossible for the Holy Spirit within the Holy Trinity. Now what religion speaks of this? Hinduism? Buddhism? Islam? Judaism? Christianity? Now of the major religions, which religions are false ideologies attempting to disprove with propaganda, drama, and suspense? Christianity, specifically the Roman Catholic Church. Why? Meditate on this. It always has to do with evil.

Let us lighten up a little (again, pardon the pun).

A French kiss between a man and a woman activates three of the natural body/flesh senses, which are that of touch, taste, and smell. This, from the 9.0 plus platform, is also understood as ISD of love. A simple kiss could be, when positive, the 3Cs with 3Gs and 3Ls— the beginning of taking part in procreation, EQ (emotional quality). When negative (3Cs), it is nothing (3Ns) but a casual physical encounter. It all has to do with morality based on true standards, my friends. Notice how animal owners kiss their dogs, human to animal, mouth to mouth with animals that lick and clean their not-so-private body parts. This is EQ? Also, again, this is what makes the LGBT community, by their negative 3Cs, result in the 3Fs, 3Ss, and 3Ds. Without the 3Rs, what else is to be expected? I am fully aware of the issues with the LGBT community, but without true guidelines and standards to follow, what are we accomplishing? Are we not only making the issue worse in which people need psychiatric therapy, especially after a surgical procedure? We need to remember that the soul and not the body/flesh needs to be our first priority in our second journey. Take the example of the Elephant Man disease of the body/flesh. Without a cure or focus on the soul's heart and mind in the summit climb, the 9.0 plus and possibility of the 3Ts—*tiramisu*, transformation, and transfiguration—the entire second journey could be miserable. We in the LGBT community need to meditate on this. We went from being in the closet with the negative 3Cs, 3Fs, and 3Ds to being out with a false liberalization, becoming at times brazen, even obnoxious. Notice the consequences and conditions. We have evil working through humanity, as always, wanting to take baseball bats to crack our skulls open. Evil does hate and discriminate; it even kills for minor reasons.

The opposite of enlightenment is dis-enlightenment, engagement, disengagement, participation, nonparticipation. All of us are, knowingly or unknowingly, choosing one side or the other. With our free will, we choose the positive 3Cs for enlightenment with engagement and participation of creation and maintenance of creation. With the negative 3Cs, we choose dis-enlightenment with disengagement and nonparticipation. Think about this: study the chart and see that at birth, we could have more light than in old age. Why? Because as children, we are still engaged and participants in light. As we grow older, the majority of us become disengaged and nonparticipants in the light of the Holy Spirit. Hence, we become dis-enlightened and dropped on our chart.

Again, history is filled with examples. Take the example of the Italian entrapped in the last civil war that started in 1943. After the Armistice in Napoli with the Allied Forces of America, the Italians that engaged in and participated, the Partisans, became embroiled in a civil war with the Fascist Italian forces—Italian killing Italian. If this was not bad enough, the Fascist Italians were also at war with the American Italian troops—more Italian killing Italian. This had to have been one of the darkest three-year periods in the history of the Italian people. Recall that I wrote about how evil works through humanity: separate, divide, and subdivide. Have them turn on each other with hate to have them kill each other. Study history to see how often this happened and to this day continues to happen in the Middle East and Africa.

When humanity is not willing to be engaged and participate in the light of *Dio*, the orb, the Holy Spirit, however you wish to think of receiving enlightenment from the climb to the summit, the opposite occurs. Take another example of rich political figures paying millions of dollars or euros of their own money to win an election. Why? Because they are responsible concerned citizens? Hardly. They are trying to fill a void within themselves, within their soul's heart and mind. Instead, they pay for influence, power, and a chance to make one hundred times their investment. Of all the ways to legally make money, dis-enlightenment causes people to turn to illegal corrupt/evil means to make a fortune. Yet the void remains without the 3Rs. "Forgive them, they know not what they do."

Like Martin Luther, Savonarola of Firenze, Italia, also was excommunicated by the pope for expressing his views on the corruption/evil of people in Florence. He was another martyred man burned at the stake in the grand piazza in the very center of Florence. Again, another man forced into his third journey by fire. A good sign, but how much it helped change the corrupt people is hard to ascertain. Again, no, the popes do not have infallibility status. This is reserved for the Gospels of Christianity, Christ, and our Blessed Virgin Maria. *Gesu* and our Blessed Virgin Maria only experienced the positive 3Cs, 3Gs, 3Ls, and 3Ts. They were tested, yes, but they did not experience the 3Fs, 3Ss, and 3Ds, hence the 3Rs were not necessary. Immortality is represented in the resurrection of Christ and the ascension of Christ and our Blessed Virgin Maria. Popes are human beings with all the same weaknesses of humanity, so they could—and a few have been known—also be the worst sinners. When popes live and teach the Gospels, guided by the college of cardinals and the Holy Spirit within the Holy Trinity, it is about as close to the summit of 9.0 and the platform that they can achieve in being a teacher, guide, and model Christian for humanity. There are no risks for popes or any of us when our soul lives in union with the will and light of the Holy Spirit. This is the highest level of ISD (intellectual spiritual design). Those who attempt to disrespect and discredit the Gospels, Christ, and our Blessed Virgin Maria always discredit and disrespect themselves in not being who they were created to be, hence the drops on their own chart.

In being tested in our climb, we all experience a degree of hell. It is a part of the learning process. The hardest testing is from under-utilization of our blessings, graces. What have we Americans and Italians learned from our civil war and paradise lost? Civil unrest follows the soul's unrest. The process of corrections, the positive 3Cs and 3Rs, is by far worse when we let tyrants and false political figures take control of our democratic institutions. Study what is currently happening in congress in America. The negative 3Cs give us American people the 3Ns positive. We have a majority Republican congress that wants to see everything deteriorate for political gain in the next presidential election and, in the meantime, wastes time. There is that quiz question of waste again. A congress that doesn't work together and with the president accomplishes little to nothing. We have a current president that is working alone, trying to get anything good done. In Italia, it is a total joke with the daily rhetoric. We have forgotten the blood spilled in the Revolutionary War and Civil War in America. We have forgotten Washington, Jefferson, and the words of Lincoln. We have forgotten our Christian roots. We have forgotten the Risorgimento, Mazzini, Cavour, and Garibaldi in Italia. We have forgotten the words of Pertini. We also are in the process of losing our Christian roots. In the last century, we finally got rid of the monarch to form our republic in 1946. After almost two thousand years, we finally got back to our republic. But what are we doing in this century?

What is becoming of our prosperity in America, Italia, and Europe? Put aside all of the economic models, indicators, and predictions by economists. They have a hard time predicting anything right when they fail to take into account the light degree or darkness of all the players involved. Recall that the prosperity of any country has to do with the collective summation of light within all people involved. This includes government workers, unions, management, employees, and those who try to manipulate the stock market. When there is unfairness and a negative imbalance and the inequalities that exist today, there will be and already are serious problems. We currently do not have a fair playing field for all. All sides are not working together in a positive way, the 3Cs, hence the negative consequences and conditions of the people overall. We are fighting each other and not helping each other. Sounds familiar? Study history, my friends, to see what evolves when this is the case. Recall the guillotine?

In country and world situations, only the true wisdom of honest leaders and generals should prevail. When we allow corrupt politicians to take control, the negative 3Cs bring miserable consequences and conditions. Without the positive 3Cs of engagement and participation in current events in our country and around the world, we all lose. I am sorry to say that we have not learned much from the past. Inequalities, injustices, and civil war anywhere in the world affect us all sooner or later. It gives us an unhealthy negative imbalance. For example, the Native Americans that sacrificed the body/flesh of humanity to some pagan man-made god had to have the Spanish conquistadors balance the region. It was a lesser evil to overcome a terrible evil in humanity. It is hard to say, but perhaps even the plagues of Europe were allowed to penetrate humanity for a balancing purpose. Was the AIDS epidemic in Africa the same? What have we collectively really learned?

Even at 9.0 plus, the platform, there is a degree of peace, yet what little enlightenment we acquire is still like a grain of salt. Anywhere else on our chart, even less, near zero, the 3Ns—nothing, *niente*, nada. Blind faith in climbing is still better than no faith, as small steps to the summit are better than no steps at all. Yes, even at the summit of 9.0 plus, we have moments of abandonment. The moments are painful but for our own good to learn from. This book is a grain of salt. It is only a refresher, a reminder of that which has already been said and written in history thousands of years ago. We are one people on one earth from one seed and one source and all related to each other.

Eastern Europe was a great example of letting political figures decide the future fate of millions of people. The system of communism was doomed to fail and fall. This was a tough love of fellow Western Europeans. At times, it is the darkest times that bring us to listen to our inner voice. Yes, everything is always evolving, yet the true needs of our body/flesh and soul do not change. How much time do we have—three minutes, three days, three weeks, three months, three years, thirty years? Do we know? Are asteroids a concern? Is it not possible to have a full appreciation of the metaphysical world without appreciation for our creator? Tracking at 6.0 and below, it is hard.

How much time do we really have? It depends on how we define time and for what, when, where, why, and whom. For our body/flesh, it is definitely an age horizontal timeline, as in your chart. After that, we have no control over it. For our souls, it is a vertical time period of our soul's second journey on earth. But after that, it depends on our soul's destination on third journey. Again, hell is a non-ending dead-end journey. Purgatory should be a period of the twilight zone just waiting for others to figure out what is to become of us. At #10, heaven, we cannot be sure until we get there. It is like an open-ended infinite question that may involve more journeys, all in different dimensions of light.

We scientists are attempting to find out the beginning of time— the time and date of our earth, when our galaxy began as well as other galaxies, the universe, and entire cosmos. So the question is, how old is Mother Earth? We have an idea, but is the figure inaccurate? We have been wrong many times. For example, the Shroud of Torino, we just can't get the data correct. Why? Of course, as mentioned, there are two parts to this mystery. One part, a smaller part, is in Spain—the face shroud that is an exact replica of the facial part of the Shroud of Torino. A coincidence? Think again. For example, the blood markings of both pieces have been proven to be of real blood. We got this part right, but the rest of the two-part shroud? Consider this: we physicists, as mentioned, already know that all in the meta-physical world is of and from light. So the shrouds themselves are of light. Now the question is, how do we date light? How do we date the light source that the entire earth and cosmos derived from? Can we get a definitive answer?

Let me make it easier for the young readers. An olive tree could live forever from the offshoots as long as it has the water and earth and sun to be able to grow. A tree grafted one after another is the same. So are we ever able to get a date for the trees if they never die? A much more difficult question is this: since the original seed of the trees are of light and from light, are they not forever, as light is infinite and forever, without time and date? For better words, in light, time and date do not exist. This being the case, how could we ever get a date for both shrouds? We cannot. We are talking about the metaphysical, yet the metaphysical light is an extension of the spiritual, supernatural light. Hence, as mentioned, the light waves from the Big Bang are still traveling and expanding without end. How could we possibly ever try to put a time or date on this phenomenon? We cannot. How about our soul's life span? We cannot. In faith, hope, and trust in the Holy Spirit within the Holy Trinity, we may, in our third journey in #10, heaven, get a better idea. ISD, my friends, keep these three letters in mind when trying to explore dates and time. Even with the question of the Alpha and Omega of the Holy Spirit within the Holy Trinity, we cannot even imagine an answer. We can only pray to be a part of in union with this light. This is what makes our souls' third journey into light infinite.

I think of the 3Ts of the crucifixion of *Gesu*. *Tiramisu*, the first day, was for His soul into discovery. On the third day, the transformation and transfiguration of *Gesu*, I think, appears reflected in the Shroud of Torino. I also think that the shroud is an affirmation of the resurrection of the body/flesh. It is like a sign-off left for humanity to say, "I was here and will continue to be among you." There are three parts to this mystery. The first is the cloth itself that was just explored, of which is not possible to get a definitive date. The second is the bloodstains that we have proven to be actual human blood. Can we get a definitive answer to the blood date? Like the cloth, I think that it is even more impossible. The third is the image of a human being. I think the transformation of the body/flesh by a radiating light coming out of the body/flesh can cause the image. Again, how could natural light, an extension of the spiritual light, be dated? As for the transfiguration of *Gesu*, it should be noted that children who have seen Christ in the present are witnesses to a *Gesu* different from the shroud. I think that this is the transfiguration written about in the Gospels.

The apparitions of our Blessed Virgin Maria are very similar. Although we know that she passed away, body/flesh and soul in her ascension into #10, heaven. Yet, although at the time, an elderly woman, the apparitions are witnessed of her at a very young age. With the saints, there are many variations, but they always have to do with spiritual light. Notice that all of the above never quit their climb off the platform. Even abandoned by a measured length of time, they all achieved the last increments into #10, heaven. Notice also that none just sit on their laurels. They are constantly reminding humanity that during our test climb up to the summit, we need to follow directions and keep our soul's senses awakened. None of this is new, as there are the 3Ns—nothing new under the sun. We just have to get above the clouds to where the sun is always shining. We do not need to be astronomers to see this. Yes, light is always evolving, always expanding, and always being renewed but not recreated. It is not Church doctrine or Canon Law that holds us back; it is our free will. The Inquisition and reformation are centuries past.

Why do we need reunification of our body/flesh with our souls? This promise completes us. We become like a saint, a crystal that throws out light and is able to be in more than one place at one time. We do not need the Holy Grail that humanity is in search of. We don't need to be fictional beings in someone else's fictional soap opera. We do not need to choose to be unconscious of our climb. We do not need to be like animals in cages, zoos, aquariums—or worse, develop a "survival of the fittest" mentality. Complacency degenerates into laziness, which results in apathy, which results in hopelessness and despair.

A brain blood cloth or broken vein hemorrhage has always scared me upon hearing of the news in friends and relatives. I witnessed the event twice in a friend and a relative. It happens unexpectedly. A tiny vein can cause such serious issues and death. One, a friend, survived. The other, my cousin, the doctor gave his wife the paperwork of cause of death to be filled out, but miraculously at the last minute, he pulled through and survived. What did humanity do in similar situations before the Christian monasteries began to open hospitals? People simply died. I wonder, was it the last three minutes and the 3Rs for my cousin? Was it the prayers of family or both that helped my cousin come through? Death could be scary. The flesh, face, takes on a different hue. It's like a warning for others to consider their own time for departure.

I recall my parents going back to our hometown in Italia after being gone for a dozen years. The memory is so clear of their return to Youngstown. They complained that people were getting lazy, did not want to work the land anymore, and let it go to weeds. The hometown people all wanted to be on pension, even at a young age. They wanted to hang out in the piazza drinking coffee, walking, and talking. My good parents did not have to work the garden but did. They gave much of the vegetables away to neighbors. What is the moral of this little story? We are in constant transition, my friends. The sooner we work our way up to the platform, the less we have to worry about unexpectedly dying. Forget about nostalgia and feeling melancholy about past events. The future of our souls is all that matters.

Far too many of us have become immune to shocking news. The past fifty years in which humanity has been enticed, seduced, and exploited by evils required little persuasion. Satan and his cohorts are now on cruise control in many parts of the world. People are being set up for their last shock into the abyss of oblivion. Will we get to the same days as the time when Jewish people were killing Jewish factions, killing as zealous terrorists their spiritual leaders before the total collapse of Jerusalem? It is hard to say. I can say that I remember a time when we Americans believed in the pledge of allegiance to our flag, Old Glory. I can say that I remember singing "America the Beautiful" and feeling grateful. I can remember singing our national anthem and feeling proud. I can remember the words, "Shed His grace on thee." I can remember the words to the oath, "Under God," and "So help me, God." I can remember so much until we let atheists get their way. Study Mount Rushmore, my friends. Don't just go there to hike and take photos but also appreciate what these faces of great leaders stood for in America.

People from the platform are asked, "If you had to do it over again, what would you change?" The best answer, "Start the climb to the platform as early as possible." The final chart/graph, your report card to take with you on your third journey could take place at any moment. The desert awaits you, my friends. Yes, it is arid, there are mirages, scorpions, and temptations, but there are also silence and solitude. There is also an oasis and a spring.

I have written a good deal about ISD (intellectual spiritual design). Perhaps as high as 50 percent of scientists will argue with this as being unproven. In closing this chapter, let me give you the two best possible examples of ISD. With ISD, it all depends on the interpretation. Take the example of polygamy versus monogamy. In the Koran of Islam, ISD of marriage between a man and a woman is interpreted as that a man could have up to four wives as long as he can afford them and treat each one fairly. It drastically differs in the Holy Bible, specifically the latest updated ISD on marriage. In the holy gospels of the Roman Catholic Church, the same ISD of marriage is interpreted as one man in marriage with one woman to cherish "until death do you part." Now which interpretation is the right, correct one? Allow me to give you a little updated medical information on a study done in the Middle East, in the middle of Islam, by medical doctors. The heart health of men living in a polygamous marriage compared to the heart health of men living in a monogamous marriage also differs immensely.

The findings were that men in a polygamous marriage with four wives had five times a severity rate of coronary blockages compared to men in a monogamous marriage. This is serious life or death 3Cs. Furthermore, men and their four wives living in a polygamous marriage had a much, much higher rate of violence, poverty, and gender inequalities compared to men and their one wife in a monogamous marriage. How many wives did the prophet, Muhammad, have? Also, what is the rumor, propaganda, information about an engagement to a six-year-old girl consummated in marriage when she was nine years old? Is this even remotely possible or just mythological nonsense? What proof is there?

This begs the question, putting finances aside, of how one man could be fair to four wives without causing resentment, jealousy, hate, and revenge. How could he be fair to each one without showing bias, favoritism, fair and equal treatment to children, etc. Also, the same man is giving 25 percent if that, to each wife while expecting 100 percent from each wife of affection and love. This is fairness? Do the math, it simply doesn't add up. Consider three, or even two, wives—it doesn't add up, period. In a monogamous marriage, each person enjoyed much better overall healthy living and loving each other and their children. Also, those same men living with one wife enjoyed the blessings, graces of more children than the men with two, three, or four wives. Again, do the math. Not convinced of ISD? Fellow scientists, this does not help resolve the issue of ISD?

Need another example? Consider this, the death of our body/flesh. One of the Ten Commandments is "Thou shall not kill." Now this is from the Old and New Testament of every Bible. Allowing one to kill others unjustified is a crime punishable by law. But the killing of the body/flesh of oneself is far, far worse yet not able to be punished in a civil way but in a spiritual way. This is also by ISD.

Now the killing of others in self-defense is understandable and acceptable as, let us say, a serial killer. It is justifiable and stops the killer from killing others. But how are we interpreting ISD in killing oneself—suicide? Of course, people could have a very difficult time preventing a person who wants to kill himself, herself of their own free will. But what about those now assisting in the killing of a suicidal person? This is still taking part in the killing of another human being. It is still assisted murder, as an accomplice, which is much more serious than a felony. The Roman Catholic Church sees from the platform the interpretation of this ISD for humanity. There is palliative sedation available for those suffering, so there is no real excuse. Not only that, there is a reason for the sequence of events, also ISD, that may involve the 3Rs in the final moments of the second journey. It is just that humanity wants to use their own unjustified interpretation. The same ISD holds true for abortion and all killing crimes against humanity.

ISD exists in every aspect of our soul's 2nd journey. The who, what, when, where, and why require those from the summit platform to interpret for humanity the correct meaning based on the highest moral standards. This is cause and effect, the 3Cs, for humanity to live by. The scientific and medical fields are becoming not open-minded but rather close-minded on these most serious issues. All of those involved in a negative 3Cs way are simply not climbing to their summit platform and yet will be held accountable. Their chart/graph of their soul's light will reflect all, count on it.

# CHAPTER *Twelve*

Unification—Church and State—A
Collective Summation of Willingness in
Light—Contribution—Involvement

Final chapter, we want to explore unification, if you will, within ourselves, religion, and state. This includes scientists and academia. We are all a part of humanity regardless of position unless we become like lost astronauts in space. A positive unification of humanity is only available in the Holy Spirit. Study history to see what occurred when this failed to take place. Study the false lights of conquering armies with their self-proclaimed kings and emperors. Study the religions that failed the interpretation of ISD. Now study what happened when humanity put their positive 3Cs to work in helping each other. For example, we use the Arabic numeric system, time clock system with 60 seconds and 60 minutes and the 360-degree measurement system. Combine this with the Roman alphabet and calendar systems still used internationally today. Study how this brings humanity together in using one language to communicate online. And so it is with ESD (emotional spiritual design) that could bring humanity together, united in and with one light. The problem is that far too many of us are all brain, body/flesh and no brains/mind. I am sure about the mathematic part in unification because the higher the collective summation of humanity working with positive 3Cs, the higher the prosperity. This, of course, depends on their collective summation of light in unification. The light part of humanity is the hardest part to overcome due to acceptance of false luminosity that evil offers. The darkness of evil has no true light. There are Antichrist people everywhere in the world. Read the news of Christians being persecuted in heathen countries. The Egyptians did not learn from Moses. The Hebrew did not learn much from Christ. We are not learning much from Pope Francisco.

Very few people know of an event that took place in Rome in the eighteenth century. I happened to stumble upon it myself. It all started one day when a person noticed that the eyes of our Blessed Virgin Maria were moving in the paintings of her. This was a phenomenon that continued for months with her eyes moving in many of her paintings. The Roman Catholic Church brought in so-called experts to examine the paintings, but they could not give an explanation of the event. An unresolved mystery? Think about it. Our Blessed Virgin Maria has given humanity warnings about future events in her apparitions many times. Take for example the outbreak of World War I and World War II. Her apparitions are warnings of what will happen when people are no longer willing to change their acceptance of evils and refusing the 3Rs—repentance, Reconciliation, and redemption. In this, humanity suffered the negative 3Cs—choices, consequences, and conditions—with the 3Ds—disgrace, despair, and death. Men were put into the trenches, the bowels of the earth in World War I, experiencing hell itself. This was the famine of war. The feast that followed after a superficial peace brought with it an extremely exuberant lifestyle. Enter the roaring twenties of indulgence and the collapse of the stock market in 1929. Enter the Great Depression, famine again. Enter the Nazi and Fascist regimes with false leadership. Enter Imperialism in Japan and Asia. Enter the hype, propaganda, and false exuberance and exultation. Enter World War II on a much larger scale. Evil, through humanity, works on more death and destruction. Enter famine again in Europe. Does this sound familiar? Do we see the maddening cycle of events that repeat themselves? This is always, always the result of the negative 3Cs with the 3Fs, 3Ss, and 3Ds. We become so sick, body, and Soul that even the vultures refuse to consume our carcasses. We become toxic. Our body/flesh is mostly fluid that consists of hydrogen and oxygen/water. What we fail to grasp is the ISD of our body/flesh in relationship to our soul and light. We have not figured out the formula of who, what, when, where, and why. The huge drop in religious vocations in America is an indicator of a huge drop in the collective summation of light.

There are three components needed for unification in humanity for the greatest good—first, the freedom of body/flesh, which in our developed democratic countries we have; second, civil laws and order, which we have to a large degree but not strong enough; third, freedom of religion, which again we have. So why are we not unified against evils? Again, I believe it is the misinformation and misinterpretation of ISD. All three of the monotheist religions—Judaism, Islam, and Christianity—are separated, divided, and subdivided. Sounds familiar? What evil does in warfare, it does to humanity in religion.

How is this to change? With the willingness of the free will to focus on positive 3Cs, 3Gs, 3Ls, and 3Ts. Another issue is Church and state. Again, study history. When Church and state coexist with the right moral soul's laws and civil laws, harmony is the result.

From Sodom and Gomorrah to modern-day Europe, America, Asia, with everyone and everything in between, history has always repeatedly given us the results of our 3Cs. We are currently on the negative side of history. This was/is all due to the injustices and inequalities of humanity toward humanity. It's our immorality that is causing the deterioration. It's the lack of transparency in some Church and state actions. This occurs in capitalism, socialism, and worst, in communism. Regardless of empire, kingdom, republic, or commonwealth, it does not matter. Notice what transpired when the scourge of evil scoundrels of Nazi and Fascist forces combined in Europe, the Middle East, and Africa. Added to this is imperialism with evil in Asia as well. The combined forces of evil in World War II were foretold a warning by our Blessing Virgin Maria. No one, the 3Ns—nothing, *niente*, nada—was done to try to stop it. Notice that the above false leaderships all controlled their citizens. In Germany and Italia, democracy was allowed to be broken down. In Japan under imperialism, it only took one man still being treated in the twentieth century as a form of god to allow the Nanjing, China massacre of thousands to take place, torturing and killing a civilian population. From pagan Roman emperors Caligula to Nero in overriding the senate to twentieth-century sultans in Ottoman rule in not listening to their advisors, imperialism was/is an overall failure.

A government, regardless of ideology, that fences up and walls in its citizens is a government that needs to be abolished. This begs the question: do we really need a president, a vice president, a prime minister, a vice minister? Do we need someone to veto the majority-elected authority, voices of the people? Study Rome 450 BC, a republic with senators as SPOR, Senate and People of Roma. It functioned well for five hundred years until one man took over full power. Julio Caesar wanted better compensation for his legions and the citizens of Roma. The senators were milking the treasury, hence the corruption/evil, injustices, and inequalities toward the citizens. Sounds familiar today? A civil war with Pompeii, an assassination, and the republic disappeared from Rome for almost two thousand years. At least, the peninsula evolved into strong city states with Liberta. Now study the most prosperous ones: Venice, Firenze, Pisa, Genova, Siena among others that maintained Liberta. Study their combinable state and Church systems. There was a reason for their prosperity that even today brings in the tourists to admire their contributions to the arts. Read about the power struggles that ensued. Notice today, in congress or parliament, the gridlock. Remember the communist Red Brigades in Italia? The Italian soil is saturated with the blood of millions of people of the past, more so than any other European country. Remember the political assassinations both in Italia and America? Recall Watergate, Contra-gate, Irangate? Who knows what was not discovered from the out-of-control executive branch. Notice the classified documents hidden with no transparency. Hidden for what reasons? Hidden from citizens? Why?

Now notice what happens when the constitution of any country lacks values and virtues. Notice that they are there in America, but we allow them to be ignored. The American Constitution was/is the model for the rest of the world. It was at one time until atheists chipped away at its foundations. This is what causes the abuses to citizens, in conspiracies, classified information, loss of privacy, disrespect for the unborn, the deterioration of the marriage institution, corporate greed that ships jobs abroad in deplorable conditions and wages, marking it up by 1000 percent to sell back to the American people (that don't pay taxes being an offshore company). Again, history tells us what happens to abused citizens. You see, my friends, the collective summation of healthy moral imprints and inner voices only tolerates abuse and corruption for so long. Then there is hell to pay.

In time, entire governments falter and go through sovereign default. For example, this happened under Ottoman rule, the Soviet Union, and Russia. We, those of the free world countries, need to be defensively ready, yet corrupt governments in time all implode. The current events with Russia going back to the Cold War era and North Korea fencing in its citizens will falter and fall, just as so many countless countries before them in history. Let us keep the B52 bombers ready. Let us strangle and put a choke hold on these tyrant criminals. In time, their money becomes worthless, and they incur sovereign default. Yes, my friends, true justice always, always begins in the soul of evildoers, yet we can and should help it along.

A collective summation of healthy moral imprints is not enough. This is basically surviving through instinct. What is essentially the key is our collective summation of healthy inner voices that need to be heard and followed. Recall that this is from the spark of our souls' heart tabernacle, lighted by oxygen, whose doors open due to gratitude, charity, and love.

I often wonder how historical events would have changed had Rome not stopped her defensive expansion into Northern Europe. She used natural barriers, the Rhine and Danube rivers, as an end.

Yet the barbaric tribes from the north entered the Western Roman Empire. They wanted to become civilized and infused into the culture. They just didn't want to be forced instead of exercising their free will. When they did enter, they absorbed a good law and order system and infrastructure, but they also absorbed the pagan gods and decadence. The evil outside voices were there. It took time to transition to Christianity, hence the Dark Ages.

The same happened to the Muslim world, as they were invaded by the Mongolians with Genghis Khan and the barbaric hordes from the East. Yes, we were infused into Muslim culture and Islam, but here it was a faster transition. In fact, culture and Islam were quickly absorbed and brought into India and Eurasia. As mentioned, Genghis Khan did not want war. He sent an ambassador to negotiate free trade. We Muslims cut off his head and returned it to the Mongolians. Our Muslim world could have saved a lot of anguish if we had been open-minded and open-hearted, listening to our good inner voice. We current Muslims of the Middle East, Africa, and India are all intertwined with the Asian blood of Mongolia—a combination that brought free trade and prosperity to our region. In China, we built the greatest waste of a great wall in history. People were actually entombed in it. We Mongolians simply went north and around it. We barbaric Mongolians wanted to become civilized and cultured. We Chinese imperialists refused, so we Mongolians laid waste to the arrogant dynasties. Yes, my friends, history is filled with examples of both the negative 3Cs and the positive 3Cs. A lot of bloodshed could have been prevented from the positive 3Cs. Will we ever accept ISD, the intelligence to get it right and keep it right? For example, we know that a little new blood, barbaric or not, improves the genetic makeup of a people, or else we suffer from inbreeding. We have now come up with artificial intelligence rather than accepting ISD. As if humanity did not have enough to worry about with non-artificial intelligence. Enough already.

In the meantime, we are in a reverse mode in the Middle East and Africa. Collectively, we have lost so much light that we are, as terrorists, returning back to being barbaric. What we fail to comprehend is that we can destroy the body/flesh and metaphysical surrounding but not the evil spirits. They remain; we can only neutralize them. Do we need to let the younger generation start to control what we unwise, 3Fs, in charge just cannot seem to get right? Or are they corrupted already from our propaganda? In world news, it appears that there is still a little hope in the majority. Everyone going against ISD sooner or later suffer the consequences and conditions. For example, in Israel, there is little, if any, free trade with her neighbors. There is less prosperity and very little peace. What do we Hebrew people want? More time in order to occupy more land and build more settlements? Are we feeling nostalgic for the days of King David and the great Temple of Solomon in Jerusalem? The monotheist Muslim and Christian have already established churches and mosques in the area. Saint Helena, Emperor Constantino's mother, started with the Holy Sepulchre Roman Catholic Church in Capitolina/Jerusalem after a three-hundred-year void. She initially wanted to find the true cross of Christ. Did she? It is hard to say. It was like trying to find a needle in a haystack. Carbon 14 analysis was done on one supposed sample of the true cross but was negative. Carbon 14 analysis could take us back fifty thousand years, but is it even relevant? Recall light and transforming light into the metaphysical?

We need to recall the forty years of prosperity under King Solomon, forty years of prosperity under Caesar Augustus. Why? What were the reasons? Do we people of Israel know our own history? Do we know the reasons for our exiles into slavery in Babylon, Egypt, and Germany? Yes, my fellow Jewish people, recall how we also were thrown out of Spain, along with the Muslims of Islam. Why? What became of our so-called olive branch, along with the so-called Pax Ottoman? The negative 3Cs with the 3Ss and 3Fs!

As great a general as Napoleon was, his biggest mistake was to put embargos against Britain. This was the beginning of the end that started in 1813 to 1815. Napoleon did or did not fully understand free trade or economics. He wasted military men on the Rhine and Danube trying to control the contraband. After the Russian winter and unified forces war that crippled his Grande Armée, wasted, he ended up on the island of Elba. Escaping, severely weakened, he suffered his final defeat by Britain in Europe. He was offered but refused being shipped to America. Instead, he ended up on St. Helena alone, in his darkness, and was probably poisoned to death in 1821. The monuments to him say nothing about his negative 3Cs of imperialism!

Study slavery in history. Humanity was not created to be put into slavery. People that allow for this evil eventually pay a heavy price. It is no different with all extreme evils. When humanity goes against ISD and ESD, humanity always suffers in the process of the 3Rs—repentance, reconciliation, and redemption—atonement. It is the unification, individually with our souls' spark and collectively as a people in positive 3Cs stupid people.

We need to study the waste in our own lives. The absolute worst waste of all is the waste of graces, blessings. Again, a quiz question, as waste has many forms. One of the best examples is the lack of appreciation and gratitude toward good-hearted parents. So often we do not show appreciation and gratitude until they have passed away. Then we visit them out of guilt in their cemetery graves, bringing them flowers that do 3Ns–nothing, *niente*, nada. Does this relieve our guilt? It doesn't without a sincere confession, but if we do not want it to be a complete waste, we can, at least, pray for them if they need to spend time in purgatory. For us Roman Catholics, a church mass in their name is also of beneficial value for the named deceased. This is also charity and love.

For the sake of our young readers, parents are like pine trees. Pine nuts or seeds started as all seeds start—from light, our creator. Although we were taught to call our creator Father, light, orb does not essentially need a male, or female gender. This was established for the mostly illiterate that needed parables to comprehend what was being taught them at the time by Christ. Seeds, all the seeds of humanity, of each and every race trace back to one man. We biologists have proven this in the metaphysical sense. So the seed of our natural father goes back to the same seed. Now how are our parents like pine trees? Their reproduction is similar in what ways? Seeds, all seeds, are the natural, metaphysical transformed from supernatural, spiritual light. This was the case with Adam and is the case in all of the metaphysical universe. We know what happens when pine trees burn down from a natural forest fire. The heat from the fire helps open up the pine cones so that the seeds can go through the conception process with Mother Earth. ISD again. Notice that the pine trees themselves, if not fully burned out, can recuperate and grow again. If completely burned out, their ashes remain. Their ashes—along with the soil, rain, and sunshine—nurture the new seeds to take root and grow.

The question is, what became of the reverse transformation of the pine trees from the natural, metaphysical back into the supernatural, spiritual light? It is a matter of the interpretation of ISD. Since all natural, metaphysical matter is of light, from light, all is able to return to their original source. For trees, this is an easy process. For humanity, it is a more complex process due to our free will. Now study the chart/graph in this book that describes the reverse process back to home for our soul. *Gesu* went through the entire process from inception, conception, death, resurrection, and ascension in thirty-three years. This is the reason that going into our third journey by fire as the pine trees is a fast purifying process. This, of course, depends on our soul's chart position. Salt, thrown back into the sea, becomes liquid again, a reverse transformation process.

This is also the reason why carbon 14 dating is limited at best to a time period of transformation from the supernatural light to metaphysical light. Dating further past that into the supernatural, spiritual light is simply not possible, at least, not in our second journey. The third journey? Maybe. The supposed approximately fourteen billion years since the Big Bang is the best example of humanity attempting to date light. Since natural light is part of the supernatural, spiritual light that has no limitation of time, a time period or date does not exist. We cannot put a date on the alpha of light or the Holy Spirit within the Holy Trinity. Humanity has a difficult time fathoming this.

Going back to the Shroud of Torino, how is it possible to get a definitive date on the image of the shroud? Being original, authentic, and without human intervention, we do not have any equipment that can go past the transformation stage in reverse. For better words, we do not know the reverse time and date because we do not know the beginning of time because we don't know the beginning of light. With the negative film, what stands out is radiated light. What paint pigment or other solid matter can radiate such light on a negative? Perhaps it can occur on a miniscule scale but nowhere near the amount of the Shroud of Torino.

"*La vecchiaia é brutta*"—old age is ugly. I remember my father saying this often. It could be true depending on our position on our soul's chart. Our chart is the determining factor. Collectively, as a summation of a people and a country, it could alter our history. For example, in this century, Japan, Italia, France, and many more countries are experiencing declining birth rates. There are many reasons for this, but it comes down to the percentage and collective summation of us childbearing, pro-life, pro-family, and pro-light in decline. These are all signs of deterioration in a people of a country. Who is to take care of the elderly? Who will work our factories? Who will power our green economy? Notice how humanity tends to always wait until reaching a crisis mode, CMM (critical mass of misery), to take serious action? Why? Again, take the collective summation of people who don't care about their own soul's health, and you can see the reason for the above results.

This is capitalism out of control. How? Capitalism helps create inequalities with low wages, no benefits, and part-time jobs where both parents have to work to get by. Capitalism becomes part of the problem. For better words, it hurts itself when it hurts humanity. If we again go back into history, we see this happening over and over. Take the example of the slave trade started by so-called Christian Western Europeans. African people were captured like wild animals, sold, and traded like just another commodity in order to work the land of barons for free. This is capitalism at its absolute worst.

Also, study the drug trade, for example, opium. This also was capitalism polluting the body/flesh of humanity for profit as in China by so-called Western Christian countries. Sounds familiar today? How about the takeover of the Americas from the natives? This was capitalism for land commercialization and profit. Should we question why other ideologies wanted to rid Western entrepreneurs and capitalists off the face of the earth? Study child labor in history, cheap labor for the investors in capitalism. Study child and teenage prostitution in any country. Legally or illegally, it is still a form of capitalism for supply and demand. Here we are in the twenty-first century still dealing with some of the worst evils in capitalism for profit. We say and think we are civilized? We are the educated? Educated in what? Civilized how? According to what standards? Whose standards? The standards of darkness.

Ms. Yellen of the US Federal Reserve has recently mentioned that "the inequalities in America to the middle and lower classes pose a risk to the American economy." At the current rate, "in five years, there will be a large increase in the number of millionaires in America." Hmm, at whose expense? The expense of us people living with poverty rate wages and broken unions? This is the fruit of capitalism? We middle and lower classes are the ones that run the economy of the stupid capitalist. We represent by 95 percent those that spend and pay taxes at city, state, and federal levels. We need for CFOs and all of the above millionaires to be millionaires and billionaires, to not only take a few classes in economics but also check themselves on the chart position of their souls. Remember, we will not escape accountability no matter how sly we are. Satan shows no one sympathy. Compare your monetary gains to your losses in love and overall good health. Is it worth it?

One of the advantages of technology is to be able to capture evil actions in humanity quickly and expose them to the rest of humanity. Enlightened, we are able to see evils for what they are and how they work through humanity to our demise. It takes more than one or a few people to confront the injustices and inequalities toward humanity in the world. Again, the collective summation can and does make a huge difference to neutralize evils in humanity. We are not able to eliminate evils, but we can incapacitate them by discouraging people from indulging in them. It doesn't happen when a majority of us are living in the sewers, bowels of the earth. We are all politicians, my friends. We all need to confront people each day and help deal with the issues that affect all of us. We all have our demons to deal with and the demons of others as well. With unification of positive 3Cs, we have a higher success rate to neutralize and even help change people that chose to accept the evils. Life from conception, liberty, and the "pursuit of happiness" for all needs to never be forgotten.

Notice that when we human beings voice and try to prove our happiness and contentment, it turns out to be the opposite. This is another sign, as from the summit and platform; we do not have to prove anything to anyone, 3Ns. Light is simply emitted out of our eyes. Again, I mentioned that we are able to get an estimated position of a person on their chart when we know a little about them. Quiz them. For example, chronic liars are not trustworthy; it drops them on their chart. Take celebrity figures such as Elvis Presley, Jimmy Hendrix, Jim Morrison, and countless others with their tragic departures. Could we have gotten a read on them to help them?

What is the difference between Russian roulette and an unchanged descent on our chart? No difference, they are about the same. Meditate on this for a while. We do not know our time of departure out of this world. We are given warnings. For example, at about the age of forty for men, our inner voice is much louder or, at least, tries to be if we do not drown it out. We men are warned that our body/flesh is about 50 percent through our second journey. What is done? What needs to be done? For us women, the age is around thirty-plus. The reasons are much more profound. Remember, our body/flesh is different from men regardless of all the nonsense to the contrary. The point is, if we deny the warning, we are in denial—dumbfounded, ignorant, cowardly, plain stupid, or a combination of all. This is not just about marriage, motherhood, or vocation. Like men, this is about our ID, of who we were created to be and do. Only in our climb up to the summit and platform will we proceed in the right direction. It is somewhat like an astronaut having to take the needed steps to the spacecraft to get to the space station, to continue from there the platform to another planet. The risks are in not taking the right steps or no steps up. In this, as a collective summation, we change what? Nothing, *niente*, nada—the 3Ns. The greater risk is that we are only dying and not living. We have until that electromagnetic wave tells us that we have roughly three minutes left. What a horrible thought.

Now what happens when the overwhelming majority of us fall into the above category? Disharmony at all levels of society. Again, what are we waiting for, to develop Alzheimer's disease and forget to remember? A brain wasting away is not going to be of much help, people. We need an iron will, iron claws to climb up to the summit where eagles turn to doves. We can help ourselves and each other. Collectively, we can make an impact on humanity. For example, we no longer really need guns to take back a corrupt government. Unified with the right reasons, we can easily shut it down. The ancient Romans showed us how easily this is doable in 450 BC. Scipio Africanus was one Roman general, but backed by the right men behind him in Carthage (modern-day Tunisia, Africa), he determined the course of history. In the final Punic War, Hannibal simply did not have the same men behind him.

Facing the future collectively as a unified force, my friends, is what changes the course of history. America is not figured into prophesied events. Do we need to ask why? Read history. Make this comparison. Ancient pagan Rome started out pagan and remained so for roughly the first eight hundred years in the West before becoming Christian. In the East, she started as pagan and continued to be for about 380 years until turning Christian and remaining so for roughly another thousand years as the Eastern Roman Empire. It continued to spread Christianity within many countries in that region to today as the Roman Catholic Church. Yes, Rome, Eternal City, is and will be a major player in prophecy. Now consider this, America, the New Rome, starts out Christian and remains so for about five hundred years but gradually, slowly is turning pagan. The new gods are M&M (money and material) things. Sounds familiar? Unless there is a major correction from a unified moral front, we Americans may become irrelevant in future world affairs. Has this already started? We need to learn to listen to men such as Pope Francisco; he knows what he is talking about. He sees the bigger picture of humanity and how to keep vigilant on the front lines of battle. Each of us is a fraction of humanity or one over roughly seven billion. As a unified numerator, we Americans should be a major player in future events.

Let us study the sequence of events. From Africa, the beginning of humanity, to the Middle East, to the East, to the North, the EU, to the Americas and back to the Middle East and Africa—it is a full 360 degrees of humanity on earth. Collectively, what have we learned? I am sorry to say—very little. As cavemen we were far less destructive and self-destructing. Under the harshest metaphysical conditions, we were pro-life, pro-work, pro-green, and got along great with all other forms of creation. Study who we collectively have evolved into. Study how we today get along with nature and all life forms. Paradise lost? We most certainly have a lot to meditate, reflect, and contemplate on.

Notice how often the words *faith* and *trust* are used in America, especially in government, the federal treasury, and in so many documents. What do these words mean to people? Anything? Why are they even in the documentation if they have no significance to us? They were originally put in when we believed that Church and state could and should coexist and work as a team. Not the Niccolo Machiavelli way of state as if Church morality need not interfere. There is a shortage these days in all parts of the world for the willingness to let Church and state work together to help resolve many of the illnesses of humanity. For example, it is not about anti-homosexual people, anti-lesbian people, anti-bisexual people, anti-transgender people, anti-feminist women, anti-gun people, anti-capitalism people, anti-socialism people, anti-communist people, anti-war people, or any other anti-anyone people. It is about anti-immorality overall in people that accept with their free will the evils in this world.

For example, capitalism with controls is important to any economy. What do we do without capital? It is about the evils working through humanity, through uncontrolled capitalism, that is at the core of the problem. We have people throughout the world risking their lives every day, trying to get entry into a capitalist, free, democratic republic system with freedom of religion. Why? How many people are attempting to get into a country like North Korea, Syria, Libya?

What voices are we listening to? In America, at the beginning of the last century, early 1900s, some yoyo, an educated idiot, determined that newborn babies should be left alone without being hugged or given much attention. This was supposed to make them stronger children and adults. People listened and followed his advice. The results? The mortality rate among newborn babies skyrocketed immediately. After thousands of deaths, people figured out that love, a major component of ESD (emotional spiritual design) was import- ant for the healthy development of a newborn. Combine ESD and ISD (intellectual spiritual design) for our souls' mind with our souls' heart spark, and what do we have? A combination of overall health emotionally, mentally, and spiritually. This is all from light, my friends. I recall studying another similar person also in the last cen- tury, who told people that we do not need the fiber/pulp of fruits and vegetables, just the juices. Many people quickly followed this advice as being practical. Do I need to write about the results? Our free will, my friends, determines our success or failure by choosing the posi- tive 3Cs or negative 3Cs. Choosing the wrong philosophy stifles our soul and body/flesh. In this, we cannot be pro-anything. This doesn't require brainstorming on a positive plan; it requires an open soul's heart and mind. Evil does have a plan. It has been in effect since the creation of humanity. Meditate on this.

Humanity without ISD and ESD as guides is bound to fail and fall. Again, a great example is the Italian people in World War II that heard and followed the voice of the Nazi SS. The diehard Fascist ended up committing war crimes in Europe, Greece, Yugoslavia, and Africa, the same as the Nazi SS. This was being Roman Catholic? The Nazi retreat north through Marzabotto, Italia, resulted in the death of hundreds of innocent civilians, including children. This was German Protestant Christianity? The Portuguese entering India during the inquisition, torturing, and killing civilians, this was Christianity? The recent slaughtering of school children in their schools, this is law and order of a democratic Republic? This begs the question: can civil laws in themselves prevent the evils throughout humanity? Study history, it does not work. What combination of Church and state works? Study the temples of ancient India with sculpted figures of men having sex with beasts. It should be no wonder that we have meteorites very active in outer space. Recall Sodom and Gomorrah?

Now study the oldest active true democratic Republic in the world—San Marino in the peninsula of Italia—that has been a model for the world for the past 1,700 years and counting! San Marino combined the civil laws and order of the state with the law and order of the Church to achieve Pax Marino for us citizens.

Law and order with the teeth of uncorrupted law enforcement agencies, along with Church law and order, works against evils. Collectively, consciously working together country to country, this works as well. This holds true for every level of humanity for the evils against our body/flesh and soul. The state level we understand, yet the Church level we do not. Body and soul always require the institution of state and Church working together against all evils. Nationally, this works; internationally it works even better.

The best possible example in history of a failure, the 3Fs? A flashback to Jerusalem, John the Baptist beheaded, *Gesu* rejected by His own rabbi as the Messiah, crucified. Titus, the revolution by us Jews crushed, roughly 3,600 of us killed; Masada, all men women and children killed, mass murder/suicide. This was faith in Judaism? In whom? Flashback, 130 AD, another Jewish revolt, we followed a false Messiah, accepted war and not peace, roughly six hundred thousand of us slaughtered. The few survivors fled into Africa, Russia, and Spain. A lost Jerusalem, Judea, Israel; Caesar Hadrian, new name, Palatine, Palestine, Arian. This was Judaism without state law and order that the Romans offered but was refused. We also refused to pay taxes. It cost us Jews nothing (the 3Ns) but bloodshed and misery. This was true Judaism?

This has been going on century after century after century with all religions in all states. Humanity has had a hell of a time of it as far as getting it right. It's about a unification of Church and state, working together against all evils. Recall how evil works: separate, divide, and subdivide. Have them turn on each other and kill each other. The rest is easy. It's not about seven billion people over one religion. That is nearly impossible. It's not about seven billion people over one free democratic Republic, which is also nearly impossible. It is about a positive collective summation of billions of people over a free true religion combined with a free true democratic Republic working together. This is the challenge. On a scale, the more people on the negative side, the more the imbalance and drop on the soul's chart of humanity. This is the negative collective summation numerator over denominator effect. We should not be surprised if an atheistic country such as China sets off a global depression in the near future. Perhaps it is time for another dark period for humanity for the 3Rs to take hold. The atonement process does repeat itself throughout history.

Individually, in love time between a man and a woman, it's not about one hour over twenty-four hours. It's about twenty-four hours over twenty-four hours. It is not about a percentage of 100 but 100 percent of the time. This is the individual challenge of challenges. I have seen so much, at times I wonder how I survived to this point. It has been such a long and difficult second journey thus far. I study people in history: Moses, Christ, the apostles, Saint Paul, Augustine, Thomas Aquinas among others. I read Merton and countless others. I study religions—all religions and philosophies. I see those disillusioned, misguided asking questions, questions, and more questions. I see the separations, the homeless people wandering, searching, not knowing what they are searching for. I see people mesmerized and confused. I see female prostitution, male prostitution, and child prostitution. I see people putting poisonous drugs into their miracle body/flesh. I see all of the above that we bring on ourselves. Yes, we help bring upon ourselves the testing of our souls when we accept evil. It is about Spiritnetics, ESD and ISD. It always has been from creation.

I am here, in Rapallo, Genova, Liguria, Italy, finishing up on this book. I could easily just retire here in this heaven-on-earth, aesthetically beautiful medieval city. The food, climate, people, churches, and sea are wonderful. I am tired, exhausted from writing this book, but it still needs to be published. I have to remind myself of the work that needs to be done. Was it worth it? I often ask myself. What difference will it make? I just finished studying about William Wallace of Scotland, another tragic figure in the vast pool of human tragedies. Another brave heart betrayed, suffering, and murdered. I wanted to cry. A massive monument was built afterward dedicated to his name. Did he make a difference for Scotland? He did, "*Liberta, liberta, liberta.*" I see that each of us are obligated to make a difference according to our blessings/graces and abilities. There will be time, plenty of time, to rest in the right third journey.

In the meantime, foreigners are destroying the very fabric of our free democratic states. They are bringing in drugs, guns, and criminal elements that are ruining us. The question should be: why the demand in us for illegal drugs? Where are we tracking? Criminals supply demand, legally or illegally. Recall that evil exploits the unsuspecting charitable hearts. In some foreigners, trying to help their situation, we bring onto ourselves an evil nightmare. It is time to pick up and deport these people into the Sahara desert without water to reflect on who they have become. Let us see if Allah helps them.

Education? How are we zealous radical terrorists to be educated? Can we read and write? Can we read history? Can we put aside our hatred? Can we learn to become open-hearted and open-minded? Can we learn that our free will can determine our success or failure? When will we become responsible? When will we stop blaming others for our failures? When will we stop glorifying war? When will we study the despair in the artwork of those who survived war?

We all need to be much more proactive for the right results. For example, the mostly teenage graffiti and trash issues need to be worked on. In Europe, these issues make us look like Third World countries. Boys and girls need to be taught at home, in schools, and at church to respect themselves, others, and private property. Whatever became of the Scotts? Gratitude helps us all, but are we grateful? Who are we grateful to? I see a great amount of apathy in people these days. As for graffiti, a worthwhile program by responsible officials to start is the program in Southern California, America. It works.

We need to remember the "eye of the needle" that our soul's degree of light needs to pass through. Yes, only our soul's bright light is able to pass through the "eye of a needle" that is heaven's gate. An amber soul cannot pass through. It needs to regain light from others. Souls that lost far more light in darkness, well, what else was/is there to help them? They spilled/spill more blood than milk. They were/are the Hindu-killing Buddhists and vice versa. They were the Hebrew killing Hebrews. They were the Christian-killing Christians, Hebrews, and Muslims. They were/are the extremist Islamic state, Muslim and others killing everyone outside their false standards. They chose their destination of hell for their soul's third journey. Did the martyred saints die in vain?

This begs the question: what of those of us who donate body/flesh parts to others? An atheist kidney in the body of a Christian? Christian body/flesh parts to an Islamic terrorist? Actually, this happens every day with blood donations. Does it matter? It is the soul and not the body/flesh that is important. Vital organs are similar to tree grafting. It is the metaphysical, not the soul. The soul always does stay as a whole. For example, man made body parts such as anything artificial, heart value, etc. are temporary parts. We are not animals and should not be experimented on such as in cloning. Neither is our seed to be touched and genetically modified; this is immoral territory. Robotics? Where is the soul? Our body/flesh, after death and even in ash condition, will eventually return to the original owner wherever the soul may have traveled to. This is naturally the Day of Judgment for the living and the dead. This is promised and what I believe in. For #10, heaven, the body/flesh will be cleansed of the toxins and impurities to become reunited with our souls. For purgatory, it should send a chill through us as the twilight zone becomes our holding bin for our soul until the body/flesh reunites and is decided on Judgment Day. For hell, what else needs to be said? In time, our body/flesh will join us.

Essentially, our body/flesh is a part of our environment. In Asia, we are, indeed, different from Europe, Africa, the Middle East, the Americas, the north and south Arctic. This is what makes us unique. We should not try to change this. In a way, our land/soil becomes a part of us. For example, Japan is one of my favorite countries to visit. I like to visit it but not live there. Imagine, if you will, Japan with a little Italian community? A Hebrew community? A Syrian community? A Somalian community. A Russian community, etc. It would ruin Japan. A mixture of nationalities is for large mass countries— Russia, Australia, Africa, and the Americas—that are not saturated with people already. It's not for small countries as Japan or in the EU. It would ruin the personality and character of Japan and EU countries. The very flavor of the countries would be changed.

The best things in life are mostly free. The land of our birth should be free as in the freedoms under a democratic Republic and those selected by the people to govern. We should all have the freedom of religion. If not, it is our duty to do something about it. We have proven that it can be done without bloodshed. Starting with our body/flesh and soul, what did we pay for? Nothing, *niente*, nada. All in the metaphysical earth is of ISD and should also be shared by everyone. It is similar to birds who have no boundaries. This is too much to ask from humanity. We have too many extreme views and philosophies. The gift of our free will, as mentioned, is one of the greatest free gifts of all. It, by our choices, determines who we are. The Holy Spirit of Pentecost is free. The Gospels are free for everyone. Churches, synagogues, mosques, and all temples for worship are free. Our Blessed Virgin Maria is free to call on for intercession. The angels and saints are also free to call on for various reasons. Meditate on this. All that is required for our climb up to the summit and platform of 9.0 plus are free. What else do we want?

We should all be anthropologists that study both the past and present. The majority of us focus only on today, not yesterday or yesteryear. But it is vital. Take as a perfect example the visit of the former Soviet Union Communist Party leader, Khrushchev. This was the visit to America in the late 1950s. I just happened to see a documentary of it. It was interesting because Khrushchev really wanted to see Disney Land. He was told that his safety could not be assured there (as in being assassinated). This upset him. Naturally upon meeting with President Eisenhower, nothing was agreed upon. President Eisenhower was to be invited to Moscow, but after sending a spy plane first, the invitation was canceled. After the incident, neither side trusted the other. Who could be trusted? The Christian president of the United States or the communist leader from a supposedly secular Soviet Union? President Eisenhower was one of the generals in Europe in World War II. He knew Stalin and the Soviet Union's way of dealing with people. He obviously didn't trust

Khrushchev, the Soviet Union or communism. Khrushchev didn't trust President Eisenhower or America or capitalism. So who could have been the go-between here? Study past and present similar events such as Poland and Cuba. Now we should begin to understand why Church and state need to work together for the greatest good. Notice what happens when this is not observed. Soon after, the Soviet Union attempted to put ICBMs in Cuba. President Kennedy put a blockade on Cuba, the (Bay of Pigs Invasion) event that nearly caused World War III. Again, who was a good mediator? A man of peace, Pope John!

# EPILOGUE

In finishing this book, I will attempt to sum up everything in a small diagram of all that I covered in the past twelve chapters. The last page could be your first page of starting your climb up to the summit. It's a good reminder of our first, second journeys, and, most importantly, the third journey. It is all that is required to climb up to the summit of 9.0, the platform 9.0 plus, and ultimately *tiramisu* (pull me up).

The recycling of water has always caused me to wonder about the amazing process. First of all, the process itself I know to be ISD. It most certainly has nothing (the 3Ns) to do with humanity or the evolutionary process. Think about this: we are drinking the same water as the Egyptian three thousand-plus years ago. No new water has been added as far as I know. In fact, we may have taken a little out into space.

Now consider the origin of water. We scientists know the formula. We know the ingredients. We simply do not know who, what, when, where, and why the formula came into existence. We attempt to know, but we are limiting ourselves to the metaphysical. Hence, we will never find out the true answers. For example, without knowing who you were created to be in ISD, you can never live up to your potential abilities. We cannot be "the best that we can be," period. The best example of one who did in history is *Gesu*—there is no better example. Everyone else after Him only followed His advice after understanding three words—way, truth, and light. With these three words, He summed up this entire book and all books before Him and after Him for that matter. This includes the Old and New Testaments. Study the last page of this book. *Gesu*, in three years, covered it all, the entire process. This was only possible with His free will, the climb, and in understanding ISD, intellectual spiritual design, and ESD, emotional spiritual design in light. This had nothing (3Ns) to do with evolution. After all, for dummies, what is there to evolve without creation first?

Another example is seeds, all seeds, but in particular the seed of man. A thought just came to mind. Why do women, at times even out of wedlock, want to be impregnated with the seed of a genius? What does this do for them? In better words, what does this do for their personal climb up to the summit? Is it not just their ego at work? Now notice that the Holy Spirit does not necessarily deny them. Meditate on why. Evolution has no answers (3Ns) as for how the seed of man came to exist and from what source. So again, what came first—the chick, the egg, the hen, the rooster, the seed of the rooster, or the source of the seed? Light? Creator? How, what, when, where, and why? This is a good university project. Measure the beginning and progression of the seed of man.

We atheists, faithless become hopeless and fatalistic without the 3Rs—repentance, reconciliation, and redemption. It is only a matter of time. I have often wondered why the Holy Spirit tolerates and does not shut down humanity. When I see the smile on a child's face, I am reminded why. Love occurs in humanity through the body/flesh but is manifested from our soul's heart. When not, what exactly is it? For example, there are so many brokenhearted in this world. But recall that true love is rooted in light, and since light never dies, neither does love. When it does, we need to question what it was when it ended.

Humanity in union with the Holy Spirit has and can work miracles. Without this, we become another Chin of China or Ramses of Egypt. One of the Egyptian Pharaohs did make an attempt to one *Dio*, one light, until he was tested. Failing, he reverted back to false gods. For better words, he quit. What is the moral of this little story? We all face setups that force us to make tough choices, moral or immoral. It is similar to a metaphysical high pressure bearing down on us. The heat and stress forces us to decide, right or wrong, positive or negative. It is also like having gout in our body/flesh from abusive rich foods that we have to decide and choose a healthier lifestyle.

On the last page, notice how the events take place. I have intentionally put this page at the end as a reminder of all the bits and pieces throughout this book. Of all the books that I have read, not one gave direction on a course to take from any position on our chart. I hope that this book does.

We start from the supernatural light/spirit into transformation from/in seed with spark and start conception. I have mentioned this several times in this book, but I have to mention it again in closing. Life starts at conception, as seen on the last page. It should be noted that the Chinese figure their age from conception and not necessarily at birth. For better words, we should celebrate our birth in the month of conception rather than the day that we enter this world. This is our first journey over which we have no control, 3Ns—nothing, *niente*, nada. Conception starts the metaphysical combinable body/flesh and soul. Next comes our birth, starting our second journey. This continues into childhood, adolescence, and adulthood until death. This is essentially light, truth, and way into this world by ISD and ESD.

In this world, in our second journey with our free will, we decide—the 3Cs (choices, consequences, and conditions)—which direction to go. The 3Ss (stubbornness, stupidity, and sickness), 3Fs (foolishness, fault, and failure), and 3Ds (disgrace, despair, and death) are the false direction that bring us down on our chart. The positive correct, which are the 3Gs (grace, gratitude, and graciousness) in the 3Ls (light, love, and life) through the 3Rs (repentance, reconciliation, and redemption), is the positive correct way up and into the 3Ts—*tiramisu*, transformation, and transfiguration—home. Notice that the process is in reverse but again involves way, truth, and light. This is what takes us, soul first, body/flesh later, out of death. With our free will to climb, we are tested to learn and grow up to our summit, our platform, and finally #10, to home, where we began in light.

For young readers, a tree works in a similar way. Notice that with fire, the metaphysical tree burns in a natural light, but where does the flame end up? The flame is in the reverse process returning to supernatural light. Hence, leaving this world in fire is considered a good sign for humanity. But there are many ways home. What is important is how our departure helps humanity. I have given examples of Saint Joan of Arc of France, William Wallace of Scotland, and now the last one, Judge Giovanni Falcone of Sicily, Italia. Remember this quote, "Kill a man, not his ideas." For better words, evil through humanity can and does kill the body/flesh but not his soul's heart and mind.

The greatest prophesied event was the coming of the Messiah, which has come to pass, regardless of those who believe otherwise. An even greater prophesied event is the second coming of Christ. Yet without faith, hope, and trust in the first event, we will never believe in the second. I have given the tools, the means for the climb process. It is good to review them. I have given the assistance of others, most notably our Blessed Virgin Maria, but also the saints and angels. Show me a people, a country that does not observe or respect these souls, and I will show you a people, a country that has a high degree of injustices and inequalities. The Roman Catholic Church has the tools and means for our climb. She has had for the past two thousand years. They are free for all for the asking. Recall that the process starts with our free will and within our soul's heart and tabernacle. It is up to us to chart and track ourselves.

The Holy Spirit is always willing. The question is, are we? What is pleasing in the eyes of the Holy Spirit will not be denied the good-hearted. As for myself, I basically just have three prayers: first, my updated Lord's Prayer; second, the Ave Maria adding "Our Mother"; and third, The Apostles Creed. I always keep in mind Padre Pio on his deathbed and the two words, "*Gesu*, Maria," which he kept repeating until he passed away.

I have been a little hard on pop culture, at times forgetting that I also have been guilty of pop culture myself. I have been one of the worst sinners of all. Perhaps this is why I have been able to write this book. Satan is of superior intelligence, having been an archangel.

Humanity—separated, detached, disconnected from light—alone doesn't stand a chance. So consider this for a moment—how many married couples celebrate their fiftieth, golden, marriage anniversary these days? Twenty-fifth, silver? Tenth? Why? A combined effort? I rest my case.

The marriage institution is in crisis around the world but mainly in America. This is of great concern. Pope Francisco has worked hard in facing the issues in order to help, but there are so many dimensions to humanity. The children of the world that go to bed hungry at night, those who do not have the basic essentials of life like clean drinking water, are very worrisome. *Dio* is always hiring, the demand is in the millions, but the supply is not willing. Lightning and thunder should be a reminder of the light and voice calling us, as are the real church bells. The virtues, my friends, who are we without them? They are: 1) prudence; 2) justice; 3) temperance; 4) courage; 5) faith; 6) hope; 7) charity/love. Of all these, charity/love is infectious. They help beyond measure. Notice that people around the world are arming themselves. Why? The "Our Father" prayer with the seven petitions needs to become the seven gratitudes as in the updated version.

We don't have the time? Think about those of us who suffered in the catacombs for fear of persecution. Start with three minutes per day—easy enough? Recall that before our second journey is about over, we have roughly three minutes to decide our fate before our brain loses the oxygen necessary to survive. Yes, time is of the essence, my friends. This is real time, now, this moment, not fabricated date and time. I do not trust completely scientific time. I do not trust absolutely carbon 14 dating figured out by scientists. Who knows with certainty that we originated in Africa? Science has a difficult time dating two thousand years ago without a doubt. For ten thousand, fifty thousand, one hundred thousand? I do believe in light that doesn't measure or date. Light simply is, was, and always will be.

HOME, HEAVEN.　　#10 ORB,NUCLEUS,TRINITY

1ST JOURNEY, SEED, 9.9 3RD JOURNEY UP,3T'S

SPARK,CONCEPTION 9.0 SUMMIT,WISDOM,

BIRTH,BODY&SOUL　　POS. 3C'S, 3G'S,

2ND JOURNEY　　8.9 CHILD 3L'S, CHARITY

MORAL IMPRINT,　8.0 TAB. OXYGEN

FREE WILL,TESTS ,　　CONSCIOUSNESS

CONSCIENCE,3C'S, 7.0 THE 7 VIRTUES,

3S'S, 3F'S,　　　　PRUDENCE, JUSTICE,

3D'S, ACCEPT EVILS　TEMPERANCE, FAITH

FALSE WAY, TAB.　　COURAGE , CHARITY

DOORS CLOSING　　HOPE, DESERT, 3R'S

**MEDITATION**　　**6.0 WAY ,TRUTH, LIGHT**

**SELF QUIZ**　　**5.9 GRATITUDE, PRAYER**

AMBER LIGHT　　3.0 FREE WILL, ADVICE,TOOLS

DARKNESS, **DEEP**　2.0 to 1.0 GOOD VOICES

**DARKNESS, DEATH**　.01 to 0. GESU, BVMARIA , UP,

**A RIGHTSIDE PROCESS OF OUR SOUL'S RETURN HOME**

400

# CREDITS AND GRATITUDE

I have been blessed with an abundance of good guides up to this point in my second journey. The list below contains only a few of those people, but they stand out, and I will be forever grateful to them.

All of the Notre Dame nuns of Saint Joseph primary school in Youngstown, Ohio;

Father Susko of Our Lady of Mount Carmel Church on Summit Avenue in Youngstown, Ohio;

Father Gallagher of the Immaculata Church at the University of San Diego in San Diego, California;

Thomas Merton, monk, priest and writer;

The priests of St. Basil's Church of the St. Michael's College at the University of Toronto in Ontario, Canada;

The priests of St. Stefano Church in Lastra a Signa and St. Martino of Ponte a Signa in Florence, Italia;

The priests of St. Giovanni Batista and St. Maria a Castelo Churches in Signa, Florence, Italia;

The priests of St. Francis of Assisi and St. Gervasio&Protasius, RCChurches in Rapallo, Genova, Liguria, Italia.

# GEEK QUIZ

H ere is a quiz for all of the geeks in the world. What is an estimated total amount of natural light/energy force from the
orb (nucleus of light) given to all human life and other active
metaphysical forms today? Here is the information you need to work
with to assist you:

1.  This light/energy, enough to light up a twenty-five-watt
    bulb, is within each of the approximate seven billion peo-
    ple on the face of the earth.
2.  Figure into this the light/energy of all the animal kingdom.
3.  Add to this the light/energy of all of the sea life.
4.  Add to this the light/energy of all insect life.
5.  Add to this the light/energy of all plant life.
6.  Add to this all of the light/energy required to keep the lava
    flows moving in the core of this earth.
7.  Add to this all of the light/energy required to power our
    sun.
8.  Finally, add to this all of the light/energy required to light
    up the entire cosmos. This is transformed light/energy
    from supernatural light yet still measurable with our sci-
    entific high-tech equipment.

Please let me know when you think you may have the answer.

# ABOUT THE AUTHOR

Tommaso Grieco ia an Italian-American residing in San Diego, California, USA and in Toronto, Ontario. Canada. The accounts in this book are true and mainly his own, along with those of his family and friends.

CPSIA information can be obtained
at www.ICGtesting.com
Printed in the USA
BVOW05s0941300118

506704BV00035B/473/P